MostUsedWords.com presents

Spanish Frequency Dictionary

Essential Vocabulary

2500 Most Common Spanish Words

Book 1

First Printing, 2018

MostUsedWords.com

www.MostUsedWords.com

Contents

Why This Book?

Hello, dear reader.

Thank you for purchasing this book. We hope it serves you well on your language learning journey.

Not all words are created equal. The purpose of this frequency dictionary is to list the most common Spanish words in descending order so that you can learn this language as fast and efficiently as possible.

First, we would like to illustrate the value of a frequency dictionary. For the purpose of example, we have combined frequency data from various languages (mainly Romance, Slavic, and Germanic languages) and made it into a single chart.

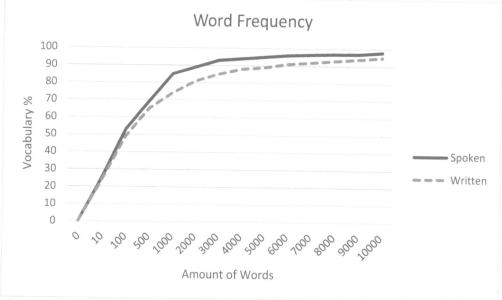

The sweet spots, according to the data, seem to be:

Amount of Words	Spoken	Written
• 100	53%	49%
• 1.000	85%	74%
• 2.500	92%	82%
• 5.000	95%	89%
• 7.500	97%	93%
• 10.000	98%	95%

Above data corresponds with Pareto´s law.

Pareto's law, also known as the 80/20 rule, states that, for many events, roughly 80% of the effects come from 20% of the causes.

In language learning, this principle seems to be on steroids. It appears that just 20% of the 20% (95/5) of the most used words in a language account for roughly all the vocabulary you need in day to day life.

To put this further in perspective: The Collins Spanish Dictionary (August 2016 edition) lists over 310.000 words in current use, while you will only need to know 1.62% (5000 words) to achieve 95% and 89% fluency in speaking and writing. Knowing the most common 10.000 words, or just 3.25%, will net you 98% fluency in spoken language and 95% fluency in written texts.

Keeping this in mind, the value of a frequency dictionary is immense. Study the most frequent words, build your vocabulary, and progress quickly. One more frequently asked question needs to be answered.

Well, how many words do you need to know for varying levels of fluency?

While it's important to note that it is impossible to pin down these numbers and statistics with 100% accuracy, these are a global average of multiple sources.

According to research, this is the amount of vocabulary needed for varying levels of fluency.

1. 250 words: the essential core of a language. Without these words, you cannot construct any meaningful sentences.
2. 750 words: are used every single day by every person who speaks the language.
3. 2500 words: should enable you to express everything you could possibly want to say, although some creativity might be required.
4. 5000 words: the active vocabulary of native speakers without higher education.
5. 10,000 words: the active vocabulary of native speakers with higher education.
6. 20,000 words: the amount you need to be able to recognize passively to read, understand, and enjoy a work of literature such as a novel by a notable author.

Caveats & Limitations.

1. **A frequency list is never "The Definite Frequency List."**

Depending on the source material analyzed, you may get different frequency lists. A corpus on spoken word differs from source texts based on a written language.

That is why we chose subtitles as our source, because, according to science, subtitles cover the best of both worlds: they correlate with both spoken and written language.

The frequency list is based on an analysis of a massive amount of Spanish subtitles.

Visualize a book with almost 16 million pages, or 80.000 books of 200 pages each, to get an idea of the amount words that have been analyzed for this book.

If you were to read the source text used for this book, it would take you around 100 years of reading 24/7. A large base text is absolutely vital in order to develop an accurate frequency list.

Since 100 years of simply reading and then trying to process the text is a bit much for one person, we have called in additional computational power to help us establish the frequency rankings.

The raw data included over 1 million entries, or different "words". The raw data has been lemmatized; words are given in their dictionary form.

2. **Creating an accurate frequency list is more complicated than it seems.**

Above mentioned method of classification does come with its own complications. Take, for example, the word

*   **poder(se)**-*vb; m* – be able; power

It is reasonable to assume that **poder** is most often used as a verb. However, you will see the word rank highly as one of the most common nouns. With our current methods, it is impossible to determine exactly how often **poder** is used as a noun as opposed to the verb.

But while we developed an accurate method of estimating the correct position of "**poder**-*m* – power" (around the 500th most common word in Spanish), we decided we don't want duplicate entries in our frequency dictionaries. Why?

Poder is a single dictionary entry, and it's choosing between either "hey, you have duplicate entries, your list sucks." and "hey, **poder** isn't the 9th most common noun, your list sucks." (actual customer feedback, paraphrased.)

Because instances like **poder** are very few and in between, we kindly ask you to use your common sense while using this dictionary. Decide for yourself on not whether you should learn a translation or not.

More difficulties arise with the conjugated verbs. Some conjugated vers can be classified as multiple parts of speech. Take, for example, **dicho**. It originally ranked somewhere around the 147th most common Spanish word.

As a conjugated verb, **dicho** is the past participle of "**decir**-*vb* – to say" and translates as "said", while as a noun, it means "saying, expression".

No way, José, that "saying, expression" is the most 147th most used Spanish word. As previously stated, our words are lemmatized, and **decir** is already listed at place 77.

We did develop a method to estimate the occurrence of **dicho** as a noun accurately. By the time of establishing the correct frequency rankings, "**dicho**-*m* – saying, expression" hovers around the 11.702th place of the most common Spanish words. It is improbable that it will enter the 10.000 most common Spanish words, and thus will be out of the scope of our frequency dictionary series.

3. Nouns

We tried our best to keep out proper nouns, such as "**James**, **Ryan**, **Alice** as well as "**Rome**, **Washington**" or "the **Louvre**". Names of countries are an exception to the rule and are included.

Some common proper nouns have multiple translations. For the ease of explanation, the following example is given in English.

"**Jack**" is a very common first name, but also a noun (a jack to lift a vehicle) and a verb (to steal something). So is the word "**can**" It is a conjugation of the verb "to be able" as well as a noun (a tin can, or a can of soft drink).

With the current technology, it is unfortunately not possible to precisely identify the correct frequency placements of the above words. We came up with a method to accurately estimate the proper placement of these words.

An example, a competitor's frequency dictionary on the English language listed the noun "**can**", like a can of coke, as the 247th most used word in the English language. Our methods would list it around the 3347th most used word. While not perfect, I *can* tell you that our method is more accurate than theirs.

4. This word doesn't belong there!

Some entries you might find odd in their respective frequency rankings. We were surprised a couple of times ourselves while creating this series. Keep in mind that the frequency list is compiled from a large amount of text, and may include words you wouldn't use yourself. But you might very well encounter them.

In our opinion, it is important that you do know these words. Store them somewhere in your passive vocabulary, instead of trying to integrate them into your active vocabulary. But in the end, it's up to you whether you think you should learn a word, or skip it.

5. This is not a Spanish word!

You might find non-Spanish loanwords in this dictionary. We decided to include them because if they´re being used in subtitle translation, it is safe to assume the word has been integrated into the Spanish general vocabulary.

6. Vulgarities

We also decided to keep out vulgarities, even though these are rather common in daily speech. We wanted to keep this book appropriate for readers of all ages. We tried to imagine what a modern-day middle American woman would take offense to, and drew the line there.

At the same time, some words absolutely needed to be clarified. On rare occasions, the usage of vocabulary items can differ severely between Spanish spoken in Latin America and Spanish spoken in Europe. It could lead to pretty awkward situations if you were not aware of these differences.

These words have been censored in a way that one can still deduce their meaning if one is already in the know. An example:

- **coger**-*vb* - to take, f*ck (LA)

7. Parallel text example sentences

Some sentences are easy; some are more difficult. Some are a direct translation; some are more loosely translated. Some mimic spoken language; some mimic written language. Some are more high-brow; some are more colloquial. In short, we tried to include a mix of different types of language, just like you would encounter in real life.

Example sentences are great because they show you Spanish word usage in context. You get to learn extra vocabulary from the sentences since they're in parallel text format. And since you'll encounter important, common words over and over again, you will ingrain those words faster into your long term memory.

8. Final thoughts

We are pretty confident our frequency ranking is as solid as it can be, keeping above pitfalls in mind. Still, this frequency list includes 25 extra words to compensate for any irregularities you might encounter. Or you might disagree with the addition of non-Spanish loanwords, or whatever it is that irks you. So instead of the 2500 most common words, you actually get the 2525 most common words. #winning.

And one more thing.

The big secret to learning language is this: build your vocabulary, learn basic grammar and go out there and speak. Make mistakes, have a laugh and then learn from your mistakes. Wash, rinse, repeat.

We hope you enjoy this frequency dictionary and that it helps you in your journey of learning Spanish.

How To Use This Dictionary

abbreviation	*abr*	prefix	*pfx*
adjective	*adj*	preposition	*prp*
adverb	*adv*	pronoun	*prn*
article	*art*	suffix	*sfx*
auxiliary verb	*av*	verb	*vb*
conjunction	*con*	verb (reflexive)	*vbr*
contraction	*contr*	singular	*sg*
interjection	*int*	plural	*pl*
noun	*f(eminine), m(asculine)*	(coll)	*colloquial language*
numeral	*num*	(se)	*reflexive verb marker*
particle	*part*	(ES)	*European Spanish*
phrase	*phr*	(LA)	*Latin America Spanish*

Verbs

Some verbs can be used reflexively. Verbs that can be used reflexively are marked by **"(se)"**. Only when the verb has a different meaning when used reflexively, we added the qualifier **"vbr"** to indicate the meaning of the reflexive verb.

Word Order

Different parts of speech are divided by "**;**".

Translations

We made the decision to give the most common translation(s) of a word, and respectively the most common part(s) of speech. It does, however, not mean that this is the only possible translations or the only part of speech the word can be used for.

International Phonetic Alphabet (IPA)

The pronunciation of foreign vocabulary can be tricky. To help you get it right, we added IPA entries for each entry. If you already have a base understanding of the pronunciation, you will find the IPA pronunciation straightforward. For more information, please visit www.internationalphoneticalphabet.org

Spanish English Frequency Dictionary

Rank	Spanish	English Translation(s)
	Part of Speech	Spanish Example Sentences
	[IPA]	-English Example Sentences

1 de
prp
[de]
of, from
¿Cuál es la capital de Finlandia?
-What's the capital city of Finland?

2 que
con; prn
['ke]
that; that
¿Es que no puedes o que no quieres?
-Is it that you can't or that you don't want to?

3 no
adv
['no]
not
Hablé con Jim durante más de una hora hasta que él dijo algo que me hizo darme cuenta de que no era un hablante nativo.
-I spoke with Jim for over an hour before he said something that made me realize he wasn't a native speaker.

4 a
prp
[a]
to, at
Me gustaría aprovechar esta oportunidad para agradecerles a todos su colaboración.
-I'd like to take this opportunity to thank you all for your cooperation.

5 el
art
[ɛl]
the
El viento es una fuente de energía limpia y barata.
-Wind is a cheap and clean source of energy.

6 y
con
[i]
and
Cuando vemos una película, jugamos a un videojuego o leemos un libro, les cogemos cariño a ciertos personajes y gradualmente llegamos a parecernos a ellos.
-When we watch a movie, play a video game, or read a book, we become emotionally attached to certain characters and gradually resemble them.

7 ser
vb; av; m
['sɛr]
be; was, were; being
Extraje bastante información fingiendo ser Norman.
-I extracted quite a lot of information pretending to be Norman.

8 en
prp
[ɛ̃n]
in, on, about
En realidad, él es un buen tipo.
-In reality, he's a good guy.

9 un
art; num
[ũn]
a, an; one
Pensé que ellos te ofrecieron un puesto de trabajo.
-I thought they offered you a job.

10 por
prp
[por]
by, for
Damos por sentado que tendrá éxito en su negocio.
-We take it for granted that he will succeed in his business.

11 qué
prn; adv
['ke]
what, which; this
Me pregunto qué país será el primero en censurar Google.
-I wonder what country will censor Google first.

12 yo
prn
['ɟjo]
I
Yo nado una vez a la semana.
-I swim once a week.

13 tú
prn
['tu]
you
Estoy listo cuando tú lo estés.
-I'm ready whenever you are.

14 saber(se)
vb
[sa.ˈβɛr]

know
¿A ti te gustaría saber cómo vas a morir?
-Would you like to know how you're going to die?

15 con
prp
[kõn]

with
Jim ha vuelto a casa con muchas manchas en la camiseta.
-Jim came home with a lot of stains on his shirt.

16 para
prp
[ˈpa.ra]

for, to
Jim le tuvo que prestar un poco de dinero a Ana para pagar el bus a casa.
-Jim had to lend Ana some money to pay the bus back home.

17 estar(se)
vb
[ɛs.ˈtar]

be
Dicha exigencia deberá estar debidamente motivada.
-Such request should be duly reasoned.

18 si
con
[si]

if
Si no te gusta, entonces no te lo comas.
-If you don't like it, then don't eat it.

19 él
prn
[ˈɛl]

he
Él sabe cómo abrir esta puerta.
-He knows how to open this door.

20 pero
con
[ˈpɛ.ro]

but
El viajero se desmayó del hambre, pero pronto recuperó la consciencia.
-The traveler fainted from hunger, but soon he regained consciousness.

21 bien
adj; adv; m
[ˈbjẽn]

well; well; good
Él se lo está pasando bien en el parque de atracciones.
-He is having a good time at the amusement park.

22 suyo
prn
[ˈsu.jo]

his, yours, theirs, hers, their
El suyo está detrás de esa puerta.
-Yours is behind that door.

23 ese
adj; prn
[ˈe.se]

that; that one
Ese era el quid de la cuestión.
-That was the crux of the matter.

24 aquí
adv
[a.ˈki]

here
Aquí han vivido muchas familias.
-A lot of families have lived here.

25 del
contr
[dɛl]

of the, for the (de+el)
El Gobierno seguiría siendo responsable del mantenimiento del orden público.
-The Government would still be responsible for the maintenance of law and order.

26 al
contr
[al]

to the, at the (a+el)
Me dijo cómo llegar al museo.
-He told me how to get to the museum.

27 como
adv; con; prp
[ˈko.mo]

as, like; since, because; as
Es rico pero vive como un mendigo.
-He is rich yet he lives like a beggar.

28 más
adj; adv; m
[ˈmas]

more; more; plus
Tienes que echar más sal o la comida sabrá sosa.
-You have to add more salt or the food will taste bland.

29 todo
adj; adv; m; prn
[ˈto.ðo]

every, each; all; whole; everything
Hoy en día, la gente sabe el precio de todo y el valor de nada.
-Nowadays, people know the price of everything and the value of nothing.

30 ya
adv
[ʝ̞ja]

already, now

Ya te dije que como suspendieras los exámenes te quedarías sin pastel.
-I already told you that if you failed the exams, you wouldn't have cake.

31 muy
adv
[mwi]

very

Muy pocos hombres gordos tienen narices largas.
-Very few fat men have long noses.

32 este
adj; prn; m
['ɛs.te]

this; this one; east

¿Qué quieres comer este fin de semana?
-What do you want to eat this weekend?

33 ir(se)
vb; vbr
['ir]

go; leave

Nunca debería ir de compras sin ti.
-I should never go shopping without you.

34 haber
av; vb
[a.ˈβɛr]

have; there is, there are

Sin aire no hay ni viento ni sonido en la luna.
-Without air there is neither wind nor sound on the moon.

35 ahora
adv
[a.ˈo.ra]

now

No, hasta ahora ella nunca se ha enamorado.
-No, until now she has never fallen in love.

36 algo
adv; prn
['al.ɣo]

something; some

A veces quiero preguntarle a Dios por qué permite que haya pobreza, hambre e injusticia en el mundo cuando él podría hacer algo al respecto, pero me preocupa que me haga exactamente la misma pregunta.
-Sometimes I want to ask God why He allows poverty, famine, and injustice in the world when He could do something about it, but I'm afraid of Him asking me exactly the same question.

37 tener
vb
[te.ˈnɛr]

have, must

No debería tener que hacer todo este trabajo yo solo.
-I shouldn't have to do all this work by myself.

38 así
adv
[a.ˈsi]

like this, like that

Nunca antes me habías hablado así.
-You had never talked to me like this before.

39 nada
adv; f
['na.ða]

nothing at all; nothing, void

Jim no le dirá nada a Ana.
-Jim will tell Ana nothing.

40 nosotros
prn
[no.ˈso.tros]

us, we

Nosotros hablamos sobre la pregunta tomando una taza de café.
-We talked about the question over a cup of coffee.

41 cuando
adv; con; prp
[ˈkwãn̪.do]

when; since, if; when

No tengas miedo de cometer errores cuando hables en inglés.
-Don't be afraid to make mistakes when you speak English.

42 ella
prn
['e.ja]

she

Él dijo que si ella no comía nada, moriría.
-He said if she doesn't eat anything, she'll die.

43 cómo
adv
['ko.mo]

how, why

Jim debería preguntarle a Ana cómo se hace.
-Jim should ask Ana how to do it.

44 solo
adv; adj
['so.lo]

only, just; alone

Solo estoy mirando, pero gracias.
-I'm just looking, but thank you.

45 o

or, either

con
[o]

¿Qué es más importante, tu carrera o tu familia?
-What is more important, your career or your family?

46 querer(se)
vb
[kɛ.ˈrɛr]

want, love

Querer protegerme de mí mismo es casi tan ingenioso como querer salvar a un pez de ahogarse.
-Wanting to protect me from myself is about as ingenious as wanting to save a fish from drowning.

47 gracias
f
[ˈgra.sjas]

thank you

Gracias a lo que has hecho por nosotros podremos seguir adelante con el proyecto de biología.
-Thanks to what you have done for us we will be able to move forward with the biology project.

48 poder(se)
vb; m
[po.ˈðɛr]

be able to, might; power

No lo vas a poder probar.
-You will not be able to try it.

49 bueno
adj; adv; int
[ˈbwe.no]

good; well, okay; enough, well

El profesor Reinhard Selten, premio nobel en economía, dijo: el esperanto es bueno para la mente.
-Professor Reinhard Selten, Nobel laureate in economics, said: Esperanto is good for the mind.

50 vez
f
[ˈbes]

time, turn

Esta vez el ganador del partido seré yo.
-This time the winner of the match will be me.

51 hacer(se)
vb; vbr
[a.ˈsɛr]

do, make; move, pretend to be

Estoy seguro de que vas a hacer un trabajo fantástico.
-I'm sure you'll do a fantastic job.

52 usted
prn
[us.ˈtɛð]

you

Como usted está cansado, sería mejor que descansara un poco.
-Since you are tired, it would be better if you had some rest.

53 señor
m; adj
[se.ˈɲor]

sir; huge

He oído que el señor Huayllacahua es carpintero.
-I've heard that Mr. Huayllacahua is a carpenter.

54 quién
prn
[ˈkjẽn]

who, whom

Jim no sabe quién pintó aquel cuadro.
-Jim doesn't know who painted that painting.

55 casa
f
[ˈka.sa]

house

Esta casa queda cerca, tiene dos dormitorios y una sala de estar, y la decoración no es mala; vale 1.500 al mes.
-This house is nearby, it has two bedrooms and a living room, and the decoration isn't bad; it's 1500 a month.

56 porque
con
[ˈpor.ke]

because

La gente se queja de otra gente porque sus puntos de vista varían.
-People complain of other people because their viewpoints vary.

57 tan
adv [ˈtãn]

so, such, as

No deberías ponerte un suéter tan feo. -You shouldn't wear such an ugly sweater.

58 por favor
m
[por fa.ˈβor]

please

Por favor, trátalo con muchísimo cuidado.
-Please, handle it with the utmost care.

59 hola

hello

	int	
	['o.la]	Estaba inscribiéndome y quería decir hola.
		-I was signing up and I wanted to say hello.
60	**dónde**	**where**
	adv	¿Todavía recuerdas dónde nos conocimos?
	['dõn̪.de]	-Do you still remember where we first met?
61	**nunca**	**never, ever**
	adv	Nunca le digas la verdad a la gente que no se lo merezca.
	['nũŋ.ka]	-Never tell the truth to people who don't deserve it.
62	**dos**	**two**
	num	Jim y Ana tienen una hija y dos hijos.
	['dos]	-Jim and Ana have one daughter and two sons.
63	**verdad**	**truth**
	f	La verdad es que quería romper con él.
	[bɛr.'ðað]	-The truth is that I wanted to break up with him.
64	**mucho**	**a lot of; many, much; a lot, lots**
	adj; prn; adv	¿Durará mucho más este espectáculo?
	['mu.ʧo]	-Will this show be much longer?
65	**entonces**	**then, so**
	adv	Sueltas una risa y entonces estas muerto.
	[ɛ̃n̪.'tõn.ses]	-You let out a little chuckle and then you die.
66	**tiempo**	**time, weather**
	m	Hace falta mucho tiempo para acostumbrarse a la vida de casado.
	['tjɛ̃m.po]	-It takes a lot of time to get used to married life.
67	**hombre**	**man**
	m	Hay un hombre en la puerta.
	['õm.bre]	-There is a man at the door.
68	**dios**	**god, deity**
	m	No todas las religiones tienen un solo dios.
	['djos]	-Not all religions have only one god.
69	**también**	**too, also**
	adv	A Jim no solo le gusta Ana sino también Alice.
	[tãm.'bjɛ̃n]	-Jim likes not only Ana but Alice too.
70	**vida**	**life**
	f	La vida es lo que hace que este planeta siga adelante.
	['bi.ða]	-Life is what makes this planet move forward.
71	**sin**	**without**
	prp	Salió de la habitación sin ni siquiera decirme adiós.
	[sĩn]	-He left the room without so much as saying goodbye to me.
72	**ver(se)**	**see, watch**
	vb	Cuando voy a ver a mi nieto, siempre le regalo algo.
	['bɛr]	-When I go to see my grandson, I always give him something.
73	**siempre**	**always, every time**
	adv	La verdad no siempre prevalece.
	['sjɛ̃m.pre]	-Truth doesn't always win.
74	**oh**	**oh**
	int	Oh, bien, tenemos un acuerdo.
	['o]	-Oh, well, we have an agreement.
75	**hasta**	**until, up to; even**

prp; adv
['as.ta]

¡Bailemos hasta que llegue el amanecer!
-Let's dance until the break of dawn!

76 **ahí**

adv
[a.'i]

there

Ahí está, el lugar en el que vimos a Jim el año pasado.
-There it is, the place where we saw Jim last year.

77 **decir(se)**

vb
[de.'sir]

say, tell, speak

No sé qué decir para hacerte sentir mejor.
-I don't know what to say to make you feel better.

78 **ni**

con
[ni]

nor, not even

Ni siquiera sé hervir agua, mucho menos asar un pavo.
-I cannot even boil water, much less roast a turkey.

79 **sobre**

prp; m
['so.βre]

on, about; envelope

Sobre aquello que me dijiste, lo he estado pensando y me gustaría ir.
-About what you told me, I have been thinking about it and I would like to go.

80 **año**

m
['a.ɲo]

year

El año que viene viviré en Sasayama.
-I will live in Sasayama next year.

81 **uno**

num
['u.no]

one

Los aviones despegaron uno tras otro.
-One plane after another took off.

82 **día**

m
['di.a]

day

Algún día te vas a dar cuenta de la importancia de ahorrar.
-One day you will realize the importance of saving.

83 **noche**

f
['no.tʃe]

night

Quiero que te quedes en casa una noche y veamos una película.
-I want you to stay home one night and watch a movie with you.

84 **cosa**

f
['ko.sa]

thing

La única cosa que le pediría a alguien como tú sería que se apartase de mi camino.
-The only thing I would ask someone like you would be to get out of my way.

85 **alguien**

prn
['al.ɣjẽn]

someone, anyone, somebody, anybody

Alguien me había empujado para adentro.
-Someone had pushed me inside.

86 **antes**

adv
['ãn̪.tes]

before, first

Sam recibió un trato injusto al ser despedido poco antes de que su trabajo se hiciera permanente.
-Sam got a raw deal when he was laid off just before his job would have become permanent.

87 **mi**

adj
[mi]

my

Mi hermana mayor se ducha todas las mañanas.
-My older sister takes a shower every morning.

88 **pocos**

adj ['po.kos]

few

Es imposible que yo termine el trabajo en unos pocos días. -I could not possibly finish the work in a few days.

89 **otro**

adj; prn
['o.tro]

other, another; other, another

¡Mañana será otro día, pero no estará aquí hasta mañana!
-Tomorrow will be another day, but it won't be here until tomorrow!

90 **nadie**

prn
['na.ðje]

nobody, no one

Jim pensó que no había nadie en casa.
-Jim thought nobody was home.

91 padre — **father**
m
[ˈpa.ðre]
El padre se lava la cara.
-The father washes his face.

92 gente — **people**
f
[ˈxɛ̃.te]
Mucha gente en el mundo está hambrienta.
-Many people in the world are hungry.

93 parecer(se) — **appear, seem; opinion**
vb; m
[pa.re.ˈsɛr]
La conclusión puede parecer trivial: el esperanto existe.
-The conclusion may seem trivial: Esperanto exists.

94 dinero — **money**
m
[di.ˈnɛ.ro]
Siendo huérfano, mi padre tuvo que comenzar a ganar dinero a los diez años.
-Being an orphan, my father had to start earning money while being ten years old.

95 hecho — **fact, incident; done, made**
m; adj
[ˈe.tʃo]
¿Alguna vez te has rascado la espalda con un rascaespaldas hecho en Japón?
-Have you ever scratched your back with a backscratcher made in Japan?

96 les — **them, to them**
prn
[ˈles]
No deberían esperar a que la ayuda les viniese de fuera, o acabarán decepcionados.
-They should not wait for help to come to them from elsewhere, or they will be disappointed.

97 mismo — **same, just**
adj
[ˈmiş.mo]
Asegúrate de no cometer el mismo error.
-Make sure that you don't make the same mistake.

98 mirar(se) — **look, watch**
vb
[mi.ˈrar]
Tienes que mirar por dónde vas o podrías provocar un accidente de coche.
-You have to look where you are going or you might cause a car accident.

99 trabajo — **work, job**
m
[tra.ˈβa.xo]
No voy a descargar el coche porque ese es el trabajo de otro.
-I won't unload the car because that's somebody else's job.

100 claro — **clear, light; of course; clearing**
adj; int; m
[ˈkla.ro]
Está claro que es culpable.
-It is clear that he is guilty.

101 mañana — **morning; future; tomorrow**
f; m; adv
[ma.ˈɲa.na]
Llámame mañana a las ocho de la mañana, por favor.
-Call me at eight tomorrow morning, please.

102 después — **after; after, later**
adv; adj
[dɛs.ˈpwes]
El presidente vetó la ley después de que el congreso la aprobara.
-The President vetoed the law after Congress passed it.

103 desde — **from, since**
prp
[ˈdɛş.ðe]
John ha estado coleccionando sellos desde que era un niño.
-John has been collecting stamps since he was a child.

104 mundo — **world**
m
[ˈmũn̯.do]
Te lo tienes muy creído, el mundo no gira alrededor tuyo.
-You are too full of yourself, the world doesn't revolve around you.

105 hablar — **talk, speak**
vb
[a.ˈβlar]
A veces no hace falta hablar la misma lengua para entenderse.
-Sometimes you don't have to speak the same language to understand each other.

106 tal — **such, that; just as**

adj; adv
['tal]

Te digo la verdad tal como es.
-I'm telling you the truth just as it is.

107 acuerdo
m
[a.ˈkwɛr.ðo]

agreement

El nuevo acuerdo incluye una disposición que se ocupa de las ramificaciones del estallido de una guerra.
-The new agreement includes a provision that deals with the ramifications of the outbreak of a war.

108 momento
m
[mo.ˈmẽn̪.to]

moment

Siempre se puede encontrar dinero cuando lo necesitamos para mandar a hombres a que los maten en la frontera, pero no queda nada cuando llega el momento de ayudarles.
-Money's always to be found when we need it to send men to be killed on the border, but there's none left when the moment to help them comes.

109 donde
adv; prp
['dõn̪.de]

where; with

Jim encontró un lugar donde podía jugar al golf gratis.
-Jim found a place where he could play golf for free.

110 hijo
m
['i.xo]

son

El hijo de Jim murió en un accidente de coche el último invierno.
-Jim's son died in a traffic accident last winter.

111 seguro
adj; m
[se.ˈɣu.ro]

safe, reliable; insurance

El sistema de tu seguro no es lo suficientemente seguro.
-Your insurance's system isn't reliable enough.

112 mujer
f
[mu.ˈxɛr]

woman

Posteriormente, él se casó con otra mujer.
-Subsequently, he married another woman.

113 amigo
m
[a.ˈmi.ɣo]

friend

Un amigo mío viene esta tarde.
-A friend of mine is coming this evening.

114 madre
f
['ma.ðre]

mother

Tendremos que hacer espacio para tu madre cuando se mude con nosotros a nuestra casa.
-We'll have to make room for your mother when she moves into our house with us.

115 allí
adv
[a.ˈʝi]

there

Él se fue allí solo.
-He went there by himself.

116 tu
adj
[tu]

your

¿Cuál es tu corte de carne favorito?
-What's your favorite cut of meat?

117 lugar
m
[lu.ˈɣar]

place

Encontré un lugar para vivir.
-I found a place to live.

118 gustar(se)
vb
[gus.ˈtar]

like

Te solía gustar salir al campo.
-You used to like to come out to the field.

119 mamá
f
[ma.ˈma]

mom

¿Cómo están mamá y papá?
-How are mom and dad?

120 mierda
f; int
['mjɛr.ða]

garbage (coll), crap (coll); shit

Me importa una mierda la comida.
-I don't give a crap about the food.

121	**papá**	**dad**
	m	Papá se aseguró de que todas las luces estuvieran apagadas antes de irse a la cama.
	[pa.ˈpa]	-Dad made sure all the lights were turned off before going to bed.
122	**esperar(se)**	**wait**
	vb	En vez de esperar un contrato, podemos tratarlo por teléfono.
	[ɛs.pɛ.ˈrar]	-Instead of waiting for a contract, we can handle it over the phone.
123	**hoy**	**today, nowadays**
	adv	Hoy hace mucho frío, ¿verdad?
	[ˈoi̯]	-It is very cold today, isn't it?
124	**estado**	**condition, government**
	m	Este microondas no está en el estado adecuado para seguir funcionando.
	[ɛs.ˈta.ðo]	-This microwave is not in the correct condition to keep operating.
125	**nuevo**	**ours**
	adj	Soy nuevo aquí, acabo de matricularme en el curso.
	[ˈnwe.βo]	-I am new here, I've just enrolled in the course.
126	**luego**	**later, then; therefore**
	adv; con	El fugitivo apareció en una pequeña ciudad a cincuenta millas de aquí, pero luego desapareció nuevamente.
	[ˈlwe.ɣo]	-The fugitive appeared in a small town fifty miles from here but then disappeared again.
127	**tres**	**three**
	num	Tenemos tres aviones en el hangar.
	[ˈtres]	-We have three airplanes in the hangar.
128	**nuestro**	**ours**
	adj	Me gustaría expresar nuestro aprecio y agradecimiento por esto.
	[ˈnwɛs.tro]	-I would like to express our appreciation and thanks for this.
129	**menos**	**fewer; less; except**
	adj; adv; prp	Cuanto menos dinero te gastes hoy en el festival, mejor.
	[ˈme.nos]	-The less money you spend today at the festival, the better.
130	**deber(se)**	**must; owe; duty**
	vb; vbr; m	Tu deber es limpiar las zonas protegidas.
	[de.ˈβɛr]	-Your duty is cleaning the protected areas.
131	**tipo**	**type; like**
	m; adj [ˈti.po]	Toda liberación conlleva el peligro de un nuevo tipo de esclavitud. -Every liberation bears within itself the danger of a new type of servitude.
132	**conmigo**	**with me**
	prn	Volverá conmigo inmediatamente a la retaguardia.
	[kõm.ˈmi.ɣo]	-You will return with me immediately to the back line.
133	**mal**	**evil; badly; bad**
	m; adv; adj	Me siento mal por ese tío.
	[ˈmal]	-I feel bad for that guy.
134	**nombre**	**name**
	m	Mi nombre completo es Ricardo Vernaut Junior.
	[ˈnõm.bre]	-My full name is Ricardo Vernaut Junior.
135	**amor**	**love**
	m	El amor es el sentimiento más intenso que pueden sentir dos personas.
	[a.ˈmor]	-Love is the most intense feeling that two persons can feel.
136	**mío**	**mine**

prn
['mi.o]

Porque esto es tan tuyo como mío.
-Because this is yours as much as it's mine.

137 eh

int

['e]

hey

¡Eh! ¿Qué te crees que estás haciendo?
-Hey! What do you think you are doing?

138 tarde

f; adv

['tar.ðe]

afternoon; late

¡Llegaré tarde a la escuela! ¡Ya me voy!
-I'm gonna be late for school! I'm leaving now!

139 importar

vb

[ĩm.por.'tar]

matter, import

Aunque no te lo creas, le importas a muchas personas.
-Even if you don't believe it, you matter to lots of persons.

140 parte

f; m

['par.te]

part; report

Una parte importante de sentirte en paz contigo mismo es no darle más vueltas a cosas que no importan.
-An important part of feeling at peace with yourself is not giving a further thought to subjects that don't matter.

141 aún

adv

[a.'ũn]

yet, still

Jim aún no se ha levantado.
-Jim didn't wake up yet.

142 tanto

adv; adj; m

['tãn.to]

so long; so much, so many; point

Si pasas tanto tiempo delante de la televisión te va a terminar doliendo la cabeza.
-If you spend so much time in front of the television you'll end up with a headache.

143 cada

adj

['ka.ða]

each, every

Cada vez que parpadeas, cierras los ojos.
-Every time you blink, you close your eyes.

144 hora

f

['o.ra]

hour, time

Es hora de cerrar el portón.
-It is time to shut the gate.

145 necesitar

vb

[ne.se.si.'tar]

need

Vas a necesitar un guardaespaldas.
-You are going to need a bodyguard.

146 quien

prn

['kjẽn]

who

Quien lucha puede perder, quien no lucha ya perdió.
-He who fights may lose, but he who doesn't has already lost.

147 demasiado

adv

[de.ma.'sja.ðo]

too much

Estás pasando demasiado tiempo en el trabajo.
-You are spending too much time at work.

148 oír(se)

vb

[o.'ir]

hear

Necesitamos oír lo que están diciendo los intérpretes.
-We need to hear what the interpreters are saying.

149 ah

int

['a]

ah

Oh, esa es difícil... ah...
-Oh, that one is complicated… ah…

150 entre

prp

['ẽn.tre]

between, among

Entre tú y yo, ¿cuál es tu película favorita de Johnny Depp?
-Between you and me, what is your favorite movie of Johnny Depp?

151 adiós

farewell; goodbye

m; int
[aˈðjos]

Los restos mortales de la actriz española Sara Montiel descansan ya en el Cementerio de San Justo de Madrid junto a su madre y su hermana tras un emotivo funeral en el que familiares, amigos y admiradores le han dado el último adiós a la actriz.
 -Spanish actress Sara Montiel's mortal remains now rest in Madrid's San Justo Graveyard beside her mother and sister, after a touching funeral in which relatives, friends, and admirers gave her a last farewell.

152 problema — **problem**

m
[proˈβle.ma]

Tenemos que tratar con el mismo problema año tras año.
 -We have to deal with the same old problem year after year.

153 cierto — **true, one; certainly**

adj; adv
[ˈsjɛr.to]

¿Es cierto que uno se recupera de un resfriado si se lo contagia a otro?
 -Is it true that you recover from colds when you give them to someone else?

154 razón — **reason**

f
[raˈsõn]

Es por esta razón que dejó la escuela.
 -It is for this reason that he left school.

155 alguno — **someone, somebody; one**

adj; prn
[alˈɣu.no]

Si te gustan estos libros, llévate alguno.
 -If you like this books, take one.

156 pues — **well, since**

con
[ˈpwes]

Sin embargo es inverosímil esperar que un gobierno proponga incentivar valores que atenten contra sus intereses, pues a ellos les conviene más mantener a la sociedad ignorante para poderla manipular con facilidad.
 -However, it's unlikely to expect that a government proposes to spread values that threaten its own interests since it's better for them to keep society ignorant in order to manipulate them with ease.

157 idea — **idea**

f
[iˈðe.a]

No tengo ni idea de como manejar este problema.
 -I have no idea how to handle this problem.

158 chico — **boy; small**

m; adj
[ˈtʃi.ko]

El chico se tropezó y cayó de rodillas.
 -The boy stumbled and fell to his knees.

159 real — **real, royal**

adj
[reˈal]

El palacio real se construyó en una colina.
 -The royal palace was built on a hill.

160 policía — **police officer; police**

m/f; f
[po.liˈsi.a]

Él ya le dijo a la policía lo que sucedió.
 -He has already told the police what happened.

161 ustedes — **you**

prn
[usˈte.ðes]

Ustedes ya pueden arrastrarse por ese agujerito.
 -You can crawl down into that little hole now.

162 quizá(s) — **maybe**

adv
[kiˈsas)]

Quizá deberías dejar de pensar en ella.
 -Maybe you should stop thinking about her.

163 serio — **serious**

adj
[ˈsɛ.rjo]

Este es un problema serio, así que deja de reírte.
 -This is a serious problem, so stop laughing.

164 cabeza — **head**

f
[kaˈβe.sa]

Su caballo le dio una coz en la cabeza.
 -She was kicked in the head by her horse.

165 hermano — **brother**

	m	
	[ɛr.ˈma.no]	

Con voz insistente, le pidió a su hermano que entregase la carta.
-In an insistent voice, he asked his brother to hand over the letter.

166 pasar(se) — **go, pass, happen (coll); go over, forget**
vb; vbr
[pa.ˈsar]

Solo estoy señalando lo peor que podría pasar.
-I'm just pointing out the worst that could happen.

167 salir(se) — **leave**
vb
[sa.ˈlir]

Voy a salir en una hora.
-I'm leaving in an hour.

168 familia — **family**
f
[fa.ˈmi.lja]

Él viajó con su familia a Hawái.
-He traveled to Hawaii with his family.

169 cariño — **affection, darling**
m
[ka.ˈri.ɲo]

Ella siente un gran cariño por sus padres.
-She has a great affection for her parents.

170 valer(se) — **cost, be good for**
vb
[ba.ˈlɛr]

Las perlas pueden valer mucho dinero.
-Pearls may cost a lot of money.

171 señora — **lady, madam**
f
[se.ˈɲo.ra]

¿No quería la señora Rodríguez ver mi redacción?
-Didn't Mrs. Rodriguez want to see my essay?

172 todavía — **yet, still**
adv
[to.ða.ˈβi.a]

Todavía estamos comprando la ropa.
-We're still buying the clothes.

173 rápido — **fast; quickly**
adj; adv
[ˈra.pi.ðo]

La hierba no crece más rápido si se tira de ella.
-Grass doesn't grow faster if you pull it.

174 viejo — **old; old man**
adj; m
[ˈbje.xo]

El viejo vive con su gato.
-The old man lives with his cat.

175 lado — **side**
m
[ˈla.ðo]

Acampamos al lado del lago.
-We camped on the side of the lake.

176 suerte — **luck**
f
[ˈswɛr.te]

Una pizca de suerte a veces lleva a eventos inesperados.
-A little bit of luck sometimes leads to unexpected events.

177 cuidado — **care; watch out**
m; int
[kwi.ˈða.ðo]

Es preciso abordarlas con sumo cuidado.
-They need to be handled with great care.

178 dar(se) — **give**
vb
[ˈdar]

¿Podrías dar más detalles de la boda?
-Could you give more details about the wedding?

179 mientras — **while; while**
con; adv
[ˈmjɛ̃n.tras]

"¿Qué te ha pasado, Ana?" preguntó Jim mientras llevaba a la pobre loca a la parte de atrás.
-"What happened to you, Ana?" asked Jim while carrying the poor crazy woman to the back.

180 miedo — **fear**
m
[ˈmje.ðo]

El miedo que sientes es muy peligroso.
-The fear you feel is very dangerous.

181 contra — **against; cons**

prp; m
['kõn.tra]
Estoy en contra de que la gente conduzca autos grandes.
 -I'm against people driving big cars.

182 puerta — **door**
f
['pwɛr.ta]
La puerta verde está abierta.
 -The green door is open.

183 pronto — **early, soon**
adv
['prõn.to]
Sin duda tendrán pronto toda esa información.
 -You will, without doubt, receive all these details as soon as possible.

184 casi — **almost**
adv
['ka.si]
Él casi siempre está en casa.
 -He is almost always at home.

185 cualquier — **any, whatever**
adj
[kwal.'kjɛr]
Cualquier parecido con personas reales, vivas o muertas, es pura coincidencia.
 -Any resemblance to real persons, living or dead, is purely coincidental.

186 agua — **water**
m
['a.ɣwa]
El agua rápidamente decreció a niveles normales dejándome en un edificio en ruinas.
 -The water rapidly subsided back to normal levels leaving me on a falling building.

187 os — **you**
prn
['os]
Sarah y Marsha, os quiero más de lo que podéis imaginar.
 -Sarah and Marsha, I love you more than you can imagine.

188 cuánto — **how many, how long**
prn
['kwãn.to]
No sé cuánto va a durar esta situación.
 -I don't know how long this situation is going to last.

189 niño — **kid**
m
['ni.ɲo]
Hace mucho tiempo, cuando Plutón aún era un planeta, había un niño llamado Jim.
 -A long time ago when Pluto was still a planet, there was a boy called Jim.

190 camino — **way**
m
[ka.'mi.no]
Perdone, ¿me podría decir el camino a la estación?
 -Excuse me, could you tell me the way to the station?

191 primer(o) — **first**
num
[pri.'mɛ.ro)]
Si alguna vez decides vender tu antigua colección de grabaciones, ¡quiero ser el primero al que se la ofrezcas!
 -If you ever decide to sell your old record collection, I want to be the first you offer them to!

192 hacia — **towards**
prp
['a.sja]
Esta casa se inclina hacia un lado.
 -This house is leaning towards one side.

193 pensar — **think**
vb
[pẽn.'sar]
No tenemos ninguna elección salvo pensar cómo queremos vivir aquí.
 -We have no choice other than thinking of how we'll live here.

194 dentro — **inside, within**
adv
['dẽn.tro]
Aparentemente, obtendremos un aumento dentro de dos meses.
 -Apparently, we'll be getting a raise within two months.

195 ciudad — **city**
f
[sju.'ðað]
Se dice que Tokio es una ciudad muy segura.
 -It is said that Tokyo is a very safe city.

196 historia — **history**

f
[is.ˈto.rja]

Hay que estudiar la historia también desde el punto de vista de los vencidos.
-One should also study history from the viewpoint of the vanquished.

197 venir(se)

vb
[be.ˈnir]

come

Ella se sentó en la playa vacía, viendo las olas venir una tras otra.
-She sat on the empty beach, watching the waves coming in one after the other.

198 dejar(se)

vb
[de.ˈxar]

leave, allow

Tienes que dejar que tu perro salga al jardín.
-You have to allow your dog to go out to the garden.

199 durante

prp
[du.ˈrãn̪.te]

during

Duermo mucho durante el día, así que me siento como si diera saltos en el tiempo.
-I sleep a lot during the day, so it feels like I'm warping through time.

200 forma

f
[ˈfor.ma]

form, way

Me gusta la forma en que canta Jim.
-I like the way Jim sings.

201 volver(se)

vb
[bol.ˈβɛr]

come back

¿Por qué el personal me echó dos veces, solo para dejarme volver ahora?
-Why did the staff toss me out twice, only to let me come back now?

202 feliz

adj
[ˈfe.lis]

happy

Me siento feliz cuando estoy contigo.
-I'm happy when I'm with you.

203 ojo

m[ˈo.xo]

eye

Jim no recuerda cómo hizo para tener el ojo morado. -Jim has no recollection of how he got his black eye.

204 guerra

f
[ˈgɛ.ra]

war

Muchos jóvenes murieron en la guerra en nombre de la democracia.
-Many young people died in the war in the name of democracy.

205 caso

m
[ˈka.so]

case

En caso de que no sobreviva, conserva mi cerebro.
-In case I don't survive, preserve my brain.

206 esposar(se)

vb
[ɛs.po.ˈsar]

handcuff

No quiero esposar a mi propio padre.
-I don't want to handcuff my own father.

207 adelante

adv; int
[a.ðe.ˈlãn̪.te]

forward, ahead; come in

Eso también sería un paso adelante decisivo.
-That, too, would be a crucial step forward.

208 cuál

prn
[ˈkwal]

what, which

Permítanme decirles cuál es nuestra principal tarea.
-Let me tell you what our main task is.

209 mano

f
[ˈma.no]

hand

Cogí de la mano a mi hermana pequeña y eché a correr.
-I grabbed my little sister's hand and started running.

210 muerte

f
[ˈmwɛr.te]

death

Jim aún te culpa por la muerte de Ana.
-Jim still blames you for Ana's death.

211 allá

adv
[a.ˈʝa]

there

Me gustaría dirigir al grupo allá.
-I'd like to lead the group over there.

212 loco

crazy; lunatic

	adj; m ['lo.ko]	Siempre está probando algo nuevo para volverlo loco. -She's always trying something new to make him crazy.
213	**por supuesto** phr [por su.'pwɛs.to]	**of course** Mientras estaba allí, intenté impresionarlo, por supuesto. -While he was there, I tried to impress him, of course.
214	**tomar(se)** vb; vbr [to.'mar]	**take; drink** Empecé queriendo tomar fotografías que solo yo podría tomar. -I started wanting to take pictures only I could take.
215	**minuto** m [mi.'nu.to]	**minute** Ya has hablado durante un minuto. -You have already spoken for one minute.
216	**entender** vb [ɛ̃n̪.tɛ̃n̪.'dɛr]	**understand** Creo que no puedes entender ese sentimiento a menos que seas de la misma generación. -I think you can't understand that feeling unless you're from the same generation.
217	**corazón** m [ko.ra.'sõn]	**heart** El recuerdo de la juventud es dulce en el corazón de los hombres mayores. -The memory of youth is sweet in the heart of old men.
218	**semana** f [se.'ma.na]	**week** Nos espera una semana ajetreada. -We have a hectic week ahead of us.
219	**jefe** m ['xe.fe]	**boss** El jefe prometió montañas de oro. -The boss promised mountains of gold.
220	**ayuda** f [a.'ʝu.ða]	**help** La ayuda legal está aquí. -The legal help is here.
221	**juntos** adj ['xũn̪.tos]	**together** Esperamos que, todos juntos, tengamos éxito. -We hope that, together, we will all succeed.
222	**suponer** vb [su.po.'nɛr]	**suppose, assume** Tenemos que suponer que hemos perdido al equipo. -We have to assume that the team's been lost.
223	**importante** adj [ĩm.por.'tãn̪.te]	**important** Ya es hora de que Japón jugara un papel importante en la comunidad internacional. -It is high time Japan played an important role in the international community.
224	**arriba** adv; int [a.'ri.βa]	**up, above; come on** El ejemplo que mostramos arriba funcionará exactamente igual. -The example we showed above will work exactly the same.
225	**persona** f [pɛr.'so.na]	**person** Jim es la clase de persona que a mucha gente simplemente no le gusta. -Jim is the kind of person lots of people just don't like.
226	**tierra** f ['tjɛ.ra]	**land, ground** Quieren quedarse en la tierra donde nacieron. -They want to remain in the land where they were born.
227	**manera** f [ma.'nɛ.ra]	**way** Está obcecado en que la única manera de solucionar el problema es la suya. -He absolutely insists that the only way to solve the problem is his way.

228 fin
m
[ˈfĩn]

end, purpose
Intenté poner fin a la discusión.
-I tried to put an end to the quarrel.

229 cara
f
[ˈka.ɾa]

face, side
Tiene un sarpullido en la cara.
-He's got a rash on his face.

230 grande
adj
[ˈgɾãn̪.de]

big
Las ramas del árbol grande cuelgan por encima del estanque.
-The boughs of the big tree overhung the pond.

231 ninguno
adj
[nĩŋ.ˈgu.no]

none
Ninguno de ellos sabe francés.
-None of them knows French.

232 cinco
num
[ˈsĩŋ.ko]

five
La biblioteca está a cinco minutos a pie.
-It is a five-minute walk to the library.

233 llamar(se)
vb; vbr
[ʎa.ˈmar]

call; name
Así puedes llamar a seguridad si alguien intenta agarrarte.
-That way you can call security in case someone tries to grab you.

234 bajo
adj; prp; m
[ˈba.xo]

low, small; under; bass
Esos medicamentos se proporcionarán a bajo coste.
-Those medications will be made available at low cost.

235 cuándo
adv
[ˈkwãn̪.do]

when
Me preocupa cuándo terminará esta conversación.
-I'm worried about when this conversation is going to end.

236 escuchar(se)
vb
[ɛs.ku.ˈtʃar]

listen
Tienes que suscribirte para escuchar esta emisora.
-You need to be a subscriber to listen to this station.

237 tío
m
[ˈti.o]

uncle, buddy (coll)
Mañana viene mi tío a visitarnos.
-My uncle is coming to see us tomorrow.

238 aunque
con
[ˈau̯ŋ.ke]

although
Está resuelto aunque no hayamos hecho nada.
-It's solved although we didn't do anything.

239 único
adj
[ˈu.ni.ko]

only, unique
Además de mí, tú eres la única persona a la que conozco que preferiría vivir en una tienda de campaña.
-You're the only person I know besides me who would prefer to live in a tent.

240 ni siquiera
phr
[ni si.ˈkjɛ.ɾa]

not even
Ni siquiera hemos intentado responder a esto.
-We did not even attempt to respond to this.

241 cerca
adv; f
[ˈsɛr.ka]

near; fence
¿Hay un campo de golf cerca de aquí?
-Is there a golf course near here?

242 pequeño
adj; m
[pe.ˈke.ɲo]

small, young; youngster
Ese riesgo se considera actualmente muy pequeño.
-The risk is now deemed to be very small.

243 seguir
vb
[se.ˈɣir]

follow
Los soldados deben seguir las órdenes.
-The soldiers must follow the orders.

244 **auto** — **car (LA)**
m
[ˈau̯.to]
¿Por qué debo pagarte por poner mi auto en mi garaje?
-Why should I pay you to put my car in my garage?

245 **cuatro** — **four**
num
[ˈkwa.tro]
Mi cuñada tuvo cuatro hijos en cinco años.
-My sister-in-law had four children in five years.

246 **igual** — **like; the same; equal**
adj; adv; m/f
[i.ˈɣwal]
Existe igual número de mujeres y hombres fumadores.
-The number of smokers among men and women is equal.

247 **listo** — **ready, smart; done**
adj; int
[ˈlis.to]
Era demasiado listo para este sitio.
-He was too smart for this place.

248 **significar** — **mean**
vb
[siɣ.ni.fi.ˈkar]
Esto puede significar muchas cosas.
-This can mean a lot of things.

249 **capitán** — **captain**
m
[ka.pi.ˈtãn]
Jim le dijo a Ana que él no era el capitán del equipo de lucha libre.
-Jim told Ana that he wasn't the captain of the wrestling team.

250 **clase** — **classroom, kind**
f
[ˈkla.se]
Un montón de niños llevan esa clase de gorro.
-A lot of kids wear that kind of hat.

251 **llegar** — **arrive, reach**
vb
[ʎe.ˈɣar]
Ya está comenzando a llegar ayuda humanitaria de distintas fuentes.
-Humanitarian aid from a variety of sources is already beginning to arrive.

252 **doctor** — **doctor**
m
[dok̚.ˈtor]
Puede que el doctor haya dicho eso.
-The doctor may have said so.

253 **suficiente** — **enough**
adj
[su.fi.ˈsjẽn̪.te]
No es suficiente hablar de supervisión y regulación.
-It is not enough to talk about supervision and regulation.

254 **vivir** — **live**
vb
[bi.ˈβir]
¿Te has acostumbrado a vivir en la residencia?
-Have you gotten used to living in the dorm?

255 **joven** — **young; young person**
adj; m/f
[ˈxo.βẽn]
En un artículo reciente acerca de actividades para mantener joven el cerebro, se menciona tanto el esperanto como el sudoku, lo cual muestra que el esperanto empieza a formar parte de la cultura popular.
-In a recent article about activities to keep your brain young, they mention Esperanto along with Sudoku, which shows that Esperanto is becoming part of popular culture.

256 **trabajar** — **work**
vb
[tra.βa.ˈxar]
Jim y Ana no pueden trabajar mañana.
-Jim and Ana can't work tomorrow.

257 **abajo** — **below, down**
adv
[a.ˈβa.xo]
Nos dimos cuenta de que no podíamos conducir colina abajo.
-We realized we couldn't drive down the hill.

258 **genial** — **great; wonderful**
adj; adv
[xe.ˈnjal]
Es genial que consiguieras el ascenso.
-It's great that you got the promotion.

259 **justo** — **fair, exact; just**

adj; adv
['xus.to]

Hay una librería justo en la esquina.
-There is a bookstore just around the corner.

260 **comer(se)**

vb
[ko.'mɛr]

eat

Jim conoce a una mujer a la que no le gusta comer chocolate.
-Jim knows a woman who doesn't like to eat chocolate.

261 **conocer(se)**

vb
[ko.no.'sɛr]

know, meet

¿Quieres conocer mi secreto? Es muy simple…
-Do you want to know my secret? It's very simple...

262 **entrar**

vb
[ẽṇ.'trar]

get in

Hay un código secreto para entrar a esa habitación.
-There's a secret code to get in that room.

263 **fuerte**

adj; m
['fwɛr.te]

strong; fort

Requerimos una organización fuerte, eficaz y eficiente.
-We require an organization that is strong, effective and efficient.

264 **número**

m
['nu.mɛ.ro]

number

Sazae siempre se olvida de su propio número de teléfono.
-Sazae is always forgetting her own phone number.

265 **morir(se)**

vb
[mo.'rir]

die

No quiero sentarme y morir.
-I just don't want to sit and die.

266 **basto**

adj
['bas.to]

coarse, rude

Esa camiseta está hecha de tejido basto.
-This shirt is made of coarse fabric.

267 **bastante**

adv; adj
[bas.'tãṇ.te]

quite a bit; enough

Hay bastante para mantenernos vivos durante varios días.
-There's enough to keep us all alive for a few more days.

268 **amar(se)**

vb
[a.'mar]

love

Nunca tuve la oportunidad de amar.
-I've never had the chance to love.

269 **atrás**

adv; int
[a.'tras]

behind; get back

Estamos dejando atrás otro año.
-We are leaving behind another year.

270 **difícil**

adj
[di.'fi.sil]

difficult

A veces es difícil distinguir a los gemelos.
-It is sometimes difficult to tell twins apart.

271 **punto**

m
['pũṇ.to]

spot, point

En este punto, mencionaré tres cuestiones concretas.
-On this point, I shall mention three specific issues.

272 **final**

adj; m
[fi.'nal]

last; end

Estos comentarios figuran al final del informe.
-These comments can be found at the end of the report.

273 **escuela**

f
[ɛs.'kwe.la]

school

Toda la escuela estuvo de acuerdo con la propuesta.
-The whole school agreed to the proposal.

274 **pueblo**

m
['pwe.βlo]

village, town

Todos en el pueblo lo admiran.
-Everybody in the village looks up to him.

275 **sangre**

blood

f
['sãŋ.gre]

El análisis de salpicaduras de sangre juega un papel importante en la determinación de lo que ha sucedido en la escena del crimen.
-Blood spatter analysis plays an important role in determining what has happened at a crime scene.

276 mes — **month**

m
['mes]

El mes pasado, nuestra hija de veinte años dio a luz una niña.
-Last month our twenty-year-old daughter gave birth to a baby girl.

277 coche — **car (ES)**

m
['ko.tʃe]

El ataque fue lanzado por un coche bomba suicida.
-The attack was launched by a suicide car bomb.

278 juego — **game**

m
['xwe.ɣo]

¿A qué juego estás jugando?
-What game are you playing?

279 encontrar(se) — **find**

vb
[ɛ̃ŋ.kõn̪.ˈtrar]

Necesitaremos una agencia caza talentos para encontrar al hombre adecuado para este puesto ejecutivo.
-We'll need a headhunting agency to find the right man for this executive position.

280 realidad — **reality**

f
[re.a.li.ˈðað]

Sería irresponsable dejar de reconocer esa realidad.
-It would be irresponsible not to acknowledge that reality.

281 cuerpo — **body**

m
['kwɛr.po]

Una habitación sin libros es como un cuerpo sin alma.
-A room without books is like a body without a soul.

282 último — **last; latest**

adj; m
['ul̪.ti.mo]

Quisiera hacer un último comentario.
-I would just like to make one last point.

283 quedar(se) — **be left; stay**

vb; vbr
[ke.ˈðar]

Tú te debes quedar aquí hasta que ellos regresen.
-You are to stay here until they return.

284 paz — **peace**

f
['pas]

En mi opinión, una paz permanente no es más que una ilusión.
-In my opinion, permanent peace is nothing but an illusion.

285 vuelta — **return, stroll**

f
['bwɛl̪.ta]

Podríais cerrar el castillo hasta su vuelta.
-You could close down the castle until they return.

286 culpar(se) — **blame**

vb
[kul.ˈpar]

Está intentando culpar a esta pobre criada.
-He is trying to blame this poor servant girl.

287 malo — **bad; villain**

adj; m
['ma.lo]

Quiere que haga algo muy malo.
-He wants me to do something really bad.

288 dólar — **dollar**

m
['do.lar]

Me pagan un dólar la hora.
-I get a dollar an hour.

289 fácil — **easy**

adj
['fa.sil]

No va a ser fácil encontrar a Jim.
-Finding Jim isn't going to be easy.

290 alto — **tall; high; stop**

adj; adv; int
['al̪.to]

El hombre alto miró a Jim y sonrió.
-The tall man looked at Jim and smiled.

291 posible

adj
[po.ˈsi.βle]

possible

Nos preocupa una posible continuación de esta tendencia.
-We are concerned about a possible continuation of this trend.

292 maldito

adj
[mal̪.ˈdi.to]

damn, cursed

No puedo encontrar el maldito teléfono.
-I can't find the darn phone.

293 dormir(se)

vb
[dor.ˈmir]

sleep

Puedes dormir aquí un rato si quieres.
-You can sleep here for a while if you want to.

294 pregunta

f
[pre.ˈɣũn̪.ta]

question

Esa es una pregunta muy complicada.
-That's a very complicated question.

295 incluso

adv; adj
[ĩŋ.ˈklu.so]

including; even

Podría decir incluso que es literal.
-I could even say that it is verbatim.

296 fiesta

f
[ˈfjɛs.ta]

party, holiday

Él fue tan gracioso en la fiesta que simplemente no pude contener la risa.
-He was so funny at the party that I simply couldn't restrain my laughter.

297 tampoco

con
[tãm.ˈpo.ko]

neither, either

Eso tampoco es una naranja.
-That is not an orange, either.

298 cama

f
[ˈka.ma]

bed

Jim suele irse a la cama antes de medianoche.
-Jim usually goes to bed before midnight.

299 lejos

adv
[ˈle.xos]

far away

Depende de lo lejos que quieras llegar.
-It depends on how far you want to go.

300 medio

m; adj; adv
[ˈme.ðjo]

middle, means; half; halfway

Todo el medio de la sección es inestable.
-The whole middle section is unstable.

301 querido

adj; m
[kɛ.ˈri.ðo]

loved, dear; lover

Todos tenemos nuestras propias opiniones, querido hermano.
-We all have our own opinions, dear brother.

302 preocupar(se)

vb
[pre.o.ku.ˈpar]

worry

No quisiera preocupar a Lady Grantham.
-I wouldn't want to worry Lady Grantham.

303 ay

int
[ˈai̯]

ouch, oh dear

Piensa que los cactus se llaman "ay".
-She thinks the word for cactus is "ouch."

304 teléfono

m
[te.ˈle.fo.no]

phone

Por favor, tráete mi teléfono contigo.
-Please, bring my phone with you.

305 tratar

vb
[tra.ˈtar]

treat, address

Los antibióticos se utilizan para tratar enfermedades infecciosas bacterianas.
-Antibiotics are used to treat infectious diseases caused by bacteria.

306 equipo

team, gear

	m [e.ˈki.po]	Jim acertó cuando dijo que nuestro equipo carece de entusiasmo y motivación. -Jim hit the nail on the head when he said our team lacks enthusiasm and motivation.
307	**palabra** f [pa.ˈla.βra]	**word** Te doy mi gran palabra de honor. -I give you my supreme word of honor.
308	**cuanto** prn [ˈkwãn̪.to]	**the more, whatever** Sabéis que haré cuanto me pidáis. -You know I'll do whatever you ask me.
309	**idiota** m/f; adj [i.ˈðjo.ta]	**idiot; idiotic** Pareceré un idiota brincando yo solo. -I'll look like an idiot pogo-sticking alone.
310	**luz** f [ˈlus]	**light** Esto adquiere importancia a la luz del creciente cambio climático. -This becomes even more significant in the light of advancing climate change.
311	**país** m [pa.ˈis]	**country** Al preguntarle de qué país venía, él respondió, "soy un ciudadano del mundo". -Asked from what country he came, he replied, "I am a citizen of the world."
312	**segundo** num [se.ˈɣũn̪.do]	**second** El baño de hombres está en el segundo piso. -The men's room is on the second floor.
313	**diablo** m [ˈdja.βlo]	**devil** ¿Le vendiste tu alma al diablo y no recibiste nada a cambio? ¿¡Qué pasa contigo!? -You sold your soul to the devil and didn't get anything in return? What's wrong with you!?
314	**oportunidad** f [o.por.tu.ni.ˈðað]	**opportunity** Debería haber aprendido alemán cuando tuve la oportunidad de hacerlo hace quince años. -I should have learned German when I had the opportunity to do it fifteen years ago.
315	**matar** vb [ma.ˈtar]	**kill** Ningún niño nace deseando odiar o matar. -No child is born wanting to hate or kill.
316	**seis** num [ˈsej̯s]	**six** Durante esos días tuvieron lugar seis reuniones diferentes. -On those days, a total of six different meetings were held.
317	**cuarto** num; m [ˈkwar.to]	**fourth; room** Puedes almorzar aquí en este cuarto. -You can eat lunch here in this room.
318	**cielo** m [ˈsje.lo]	**sky** No intentes cubrir todo el cielo con la palma de tu mano. -Don't try to cover the whole sky with the palm of your hand.
319	**vivo** adj; m [ˈbi.βo]	**alive; alive** No basta simplemente con mantener vivo al animal. -It is not enough simply to keep the animal alive.
320	**perdón** m; int [pɛr.ˈðõn]	**forgiveness; sorry** Debería haberlo tratado antes, perdón. -I should have brought it up sooner, sorry.
321	**falta**	**offense, shortage**

	f	Hay una falta drástica de donantes de órganos.
	['faḻ.ta]	-There is a drastic shortage of organ donors.
322	**creer(se)**	**believe, think**
	vb	No me puedo creer que no me hayan invitado.
	[kre.'ɛr]	-I can't believe I didn't get invited.
323	**película**	**movie**
	f	La primera película que vio fue E.T.
	[pe.'li.ku.la]	-The first movie she ever saw was E.T.
324	**además**	**besides**
	adv	Además, en la actualidad hay muchos países que experimentan graves problemas de derechos humanos.
	[a.ðe.'mas]	-Besides, there are currently many countries suffering from severe human rights problems.
325	**perro**	**dog**
	m	Un perro tiene cuatro patas.
	['pɛ.ro]	-A dog has four legs.
326	**general**	**common; general**
	adj; m/f	Quiero empezar con un comentario general.
	[xe.nɛ.'ral]	-I want to begin with a general comment.
327	**calle**	**street**
	f	Jim se resbaló en la calle congelada y se lastimó.
	['ka.ʝe]	-Jim slipped on the icy street and hurt himself.
328	**exacto**	**identical, exact; exactly**
	adj; adv	No comprendo el significado exacto de esta oración.
	[ɛk.'sak̚.to]	-I do not understand the exact meaning of this sentence.
329	**rey**	**king**
	m	El rey anuló la sentencia de muerte de una mujer condenada por conducir.
	['reɪ̯]	-The king overturned the death sentence of a woman condemned for driving.
330	**habitación**	**room**
	f	Tenemos una magnífica vista al mar desde nuestra habitación de hotel.
	[a.βi.ta.'sjõn]	-We have a magnificent view of the ocean from our hotel room.
331	**par**	**pair, couple; even, paired**
	m; adj	He escrito un par de canciones navideñas.
	['par]	-I've written a couple of Christmas songs.
332	**fuego**	**fire**
	m	Un pequeño fuego en un bosque puede propagarse con facilidad y rápidamente convertirse en un gran incendio.
	['fwe.ɣo]	-A small forest fire can easily spread and quickly become a great conflagration.
333	**música**	**music**
	f	Si fuera más creativa, intentaría escribir música.
	['mu.si.ka]	-If I were more creative, I would try to write music.
334	**sentido**	**sense, meaning**
	m	Jim no tiene sentido de orientación.
	[sẽn̪.'ti.ðo]	-Jim has no sense of direction.
335	**afuera**	**outside**
	adv	Una persona joven está esperándote afuera.
	[a.'fwɛ.ra]	-A young person is waiting for you outside.
336	**café**	**coffee, coffee shop**
	m	Hay un café por allí.
	[ka.'fe]	-There is a coffee shop over there.

337 llevar(se)   **take, wear**
vb
[ʎe.ˈβar]
Debes llevar tu pasaporte al banco.
 -You must take your passport to the bank.

338 sitio   **place**
m
[ˈsi.tjo]
Este me parece un buen sitio para empezar.
 -I think this is a good place to start.

339 libro   **book**
m
[ˈli.βro]
Llevaba un libro en la mano.
 -He had a book in his hand.

340 buscar   **search for**
vb
[bus.ˈkar]
Es fundamental buscar nuevas fuentes de recursos.
 -It is essential to seek out new sources of funds.

341 bebé   **baby**
m
[be.ˈβe]
Ella le mostró su bebé al visitante.
 -She showed the visitor her baby.

342 callar(se)   **hush**
vb
[ka.ˈʝar]
Estoy cansado de que me manden callar.
 -I'm tired of people telling me to shut up.

343 jamás   **never**
adv
[xa.ˈmas]
La prensa jamás nos dejaría solos.
 -The press would never leave us alone.

344 armar(se)   **assemble, supply with arms**
vb
[ar.ˈmar]
El material encontrado es suficiente para armar unas 500 minas terrestres.
 -That's enough material to arm about 500 landmines.

345 viaje   **trip**
m
[ˈbja.xe]
Se fueron de viaje hace unos días.
 -They went on a trip a few days ago.

346 muchacho   **lad**
m
[mu.ˈtʃa.tʃo]
Estás volviendo a pasar mucho tiempo con el muchacho.
 -You're spending too much time with the lad again.

347 perder(se)   **lose**
vb
[pɛr.ˈðɛr]
Es fácil perder la noción del tiempo cuando estás en Las Vegas.
 -It's easy to lose track of time when you are in Las Vegas.

348 jugar   **play**
vb
[xu.ˈɣar]
Mamá estaba de mal humor porque no pudo jugar al golf a causa del mal tiempo.
 -Mother was in a bad mood since she could not play golf because of bad weather.

349 diez   **ten**
num
[ˈdjes]
Apuesto diez dólares a ese caballo.
 -I bet ten dollars on that horse.

350 mil   **thousand**
num
[ˈmil]
Edu tiene más o menos mil amigos.
 -Edu has more or less a thousand friends.

351 demás   **the rest**
adj
[de.ˈmas]
Los demás también tienen derecho a participar.
 -Others, too, have a right to participation.

352 orden   **order; command**
m; f
[ˈor.ðẽn]
Debe modificarse el orden de los factores determinantes.
 -The order of the determining factors must be changed.

353	**cambio** m [ˈkãm.bjo]	**change** ¿Podría darme cambio de un billete de cien dólares? -Could you give me change out of a hundred-dollar bill?
354	**extraño** adj; m [ɛks.ˈtra.ɲo]	**strange; stranger** Me pareció extraño que no apareciera. -I thought it strange that he didn't turn up.
355	**pobre** adj; m/f [ˈpo.βre]	**poor; poor** Este condado es pobre en recursos naturales. -This county is poor in natural resources.
356	**ropa** f [ˈro.pa]	**clothes** Él proporcionó comida y ropa a su familia. -He provided food and clothes for his family.
357	**oficina** f [o.fi.ˈsi.na]	**office** Mi oficina está localizada en el centro. -My office is located downtown.
358	**sino** prp; m [ˈsi.no]	**but; fate** No deberían limitar el movimiento, sino fomentarlo. -You should not be restricting movement, but encouraging it.
359	**modo** m [ˈmo.ðo]	**mode** Debo procurar comportarme de modo responsable. -I have to be careful to behave in a responsible way.
360	**ocurrir** vb [o.ku.ˈrir]	**happen** Rogamos nos disculpen por el error y prometemos que no volverá a ocurrir de nuevo. -We apologize for the mistake and promise that it won't happen again.
361	**libre** adj [ˈli.βre]	**free** Podemos imaginarnos todo un hemisferio libre de armas nucleares. -We can imagine a whole hemisphere free of nuclear weapons.
362	**presidente** m [pre.si.ˈðɛ̃n.te]	**president** Barack Obama es el presidente de los Estados Unidos. -Barack Obama is the president of the United States.
363	**especial** adj [ɛs.pe.ˈsjal]	**special** Tengo una relación especial con mi tía. -I have a special relationship with my aunt.
364	**anoche** adv [a.ˈno.tʃe]	**last night** Anoche hubo un descenso repentino de temperatura. -There was a sudden drop in the temperature last night.
365	**millón** num [mi.ˈjõn]	**million** Ambos regímenes adoptaron medidas que costaron millones de vidas. -Both of these regimes adopted measures that cost millions of lives.
366	**acercar(se)** vb [a.sɛr.ˈkar]	**move closer** Nuestro objetivo es acercar la Unión y sus instituciones a los ciudadanos. -Our goal is to bring the Union and its institutions closer to its citizens.
367	**derecho** adj; adv; m [dɛ.ˈre.tʃo]	**right; straight; law** El consumidor tiene derecho a saber esto. -The consumer has a right to know this.
368	**negro** adj [ˈne.ɣro]	**black** Verás un coche negro estacionado enfrente. -You'll see a black car parked opposite.

369	**acá**		**here (LA)**
	adv		Estaba acá cuando Magnus estaba acá.
	[a.ˈka]		-I was here when Magnus was here.
370	**caballero**		**gentleman, knight**
	m		Jim es un caballero amoroso y atento.
	[ka.βa.ˈʝɛ.ro]		-Jim is a loving and caring gentleman.
371	**correcto**		**correct; right**
	adj; int		Asegúrese de que utiliza el formulario correcto.
	[ko.ˈrek̚.to]		-Please make sure that you are using the correct application form.
372	**frente**		**front, forehead**
	f		Hay un lago en frente de mi casa.
	[ˈfrɛ̃n.te]		-There is a lake in front of my house.
373	**detrás**		**behind**
	adv		Caminamos detrás de dromedarios en el desierto alrededor de Zagora.
	[dɛ.ˈtras]		-We walk behind the camels in the desert around Zagora.
374	**poner(se)**		**put; put on**
	vb; vbr		Es necesario poner este número en contexto.
	[po.ˈnɛr]		-It is necessary to put this number in context.
375	**asunto**		**matter**
	m		La señora González también planteó un asunto muy importante.
	[a.ˈsũn.to]		-Mrs. Gonzalez also raised a very important matter.
376	**duro**		**hard; hard**
	adj; adv		Al principio será duro, pero todo es duro al principio.
	[ˈdu.ro]		-In the beginning it'll be hard, but everything's hard at the beginning.
377	**suceder**		**happen, follow**
	vb		Han tenido que pasar muchas cosas para que eso suceda.
	[su.se.ˈðɛr]		-A great deal must have taken place for that to happen.
378	**disculpar(se)**		**forgive; apologize**
	vb; vbr		Jim piensa que Ana se debería disculpar con John.
	[dis.kul.ˈpar]		-Jim thinks Ana should apologize to John.
379	**boca**		**mouth**
	f		Tu boca no se mueve cuando hablas.
	[ˈbo.ka]		-Your mouth doesn't move when you talk.
380	**atención**		**attention**
	f		Se puso poca atención en la comodidad de los pasajeros.
	[a.tɛ̃n.ˈsjõn]		-Little attention was paid to the comfort of the passengers.
381	**encima**		**on top of, not only that**
	adv		Podría estar encima del microondas.
	[ɛ̃n.ˈsi.ma]		-It might be on top of the microwave.
382	**demonio**		**demon**
	m		Recemos para deshacernos de este demonio.
	[de.ˈmo.njo]		-Let us pray to get rid of this demon.
383	**cual**		**whom; as**
	prn; adv		Un hombre del cual podrías enamorarte.
	[ˈkwal]		-A man with whom you could fall in love.
384	**odiar**		**hate**
	vb		Dios, solía odiar ese vestido.
	[o.ˈðjar]		-God, I used to hate that nightgown.
385	**hospital**		**hospital**

m
[os.pi.ˈtal]

Jim fue al hospital porque estaba enfermo.
-Jim went to the hospital because he was sick.

386 sueño — **dream**

m
[ˈswe.ɲo]

Nuestra segunda motivación es proteger un sueño.
-Our second motivation is that of protecting a dream.

387 resto — **remainder**

m
[ˈrɛs.to]

Jim se comió parte del jamón y luego dejó el resto en el refrigerador.
-Jim ate part of the ham, and then put the rest into the refrigerator.

388 perfecto — **perfect**

adj
[pɛr.ˈfek̚.to]

Es un ejemplo perfecto de un destino cruel.
-It's a perfect example of cruel fate.

389 tranquilo — **quiet, peaceful**

adj
[trãŋ.ˈki.lo]

Está tan tranquilo que uno puede oír el tictac del reloj detrás de la pared.
-It is so quiet one can hear the clock tick behind the wall.

390 seguridad — **certainty, safety**

f
[se.ɣu.ri.ˈðað]

Soy responsable de la seguridad de Jim.
-I'm responsible for Jim's safety.

391 ayudar — **help**

vb
[a.ju.ˈðar]

Tienes que ayudar a tu madre.
-You have to help your mother.

392 largo — **long; get out (coll)**

adj; int
[ˈlar.ɣo]

Escribió cartas largas jurando no volver a hacerlo.
-You wrote long letters vowing never to do it again.

393 dar(se) pena — **feel sorry**

phr
[ˈdar ˈpe.na]

No debería darme pena a mí mismo.
-I shouldn't feel bad for myself.

394 ayer — **yesterday; past**

adv; m
[a.ˈjɛr]

Supongo que querrás preguntarme qué estuve haciendo ayer.
-I suppose you want to ask me what I was doing yesterday.

395 probar(se) — **try, prove; try on**

vb; vbr
[pro.ˈβar]

¡Intenta probar que tienes razón!
-Try to prove that you are right!

396 bonito — **pretty; tuna**

adj; m
[bo.ˈni.to]

Necesitarás algo bonito para llevar con Milly.
-You'll need something nice to wear around Milly.

397 increíble — **incredible**

adj
[ĩŋ.ˈkre.i.βle]

¡Es increíble que tu madre hable seis idiomas!
-It's incredible that your mother speaks six languages!

398 tonto — **stupid; fool**

adj; m
[ˈtõn̪.to]

Él tiene que ser tonto para hacer eso.
-He must be a fool to do so.

399 simple — **simple**

adj
[ˈsĩm.ple]

Toda persona que utilice el esperanto o trabaje con él es un esperantista, y cada esperantista tiene el justo derecho de considerar la lengua como un simple medio de comprensión internacional.
-Anyone who uses or works with Esperanto is an Esperantist, and every Esperantist has the right to consider their language a simple medium for international comprehension.

400 aire — **air**

m[ˈai̯.re]   Me gustaría abrir la ventana: necesito algo de aire. -I'd like to open the window: I need some air.

401 fuerza — **strength**
f
[ˈfwɛr.sa]
No tengo la fuerza de seguir intentándolo.
-I don't have the strength to keep trying.

402 carta — **letter**
f
[ˈkar.ta]
Esta carta no tiene firma.
-This letter has no signature.

403 trato — **agreement, behavior**
m
[ˈtra.to]
Jim, pensé que teníamos un trato.
-Jim, I thought we had an agreement.

404 plan — **plan**
m
[ˈplã]
El plan era una obra maestra del fraude.
-The plan was a masterpiece of fraud.

405 hambre — **hunger**
m
[ˈãm.bre]
La persistencia del hambre ensombrece moralmente nuestra era.
-The persistence of hunger casts an appalling moral shadow on our age.

406 empezar — **begin**
vb
[ẽm.pe.ˈsar]
Permítanme empezar agradeciéndoles su invitación de esta noche.
-Let me begin by thanking you for this invitation this evening.

407 campo — **field, countryside**
m
[ˈkãm.po]
El campo está lleno de flores silvestres.
-The field is full of wild flowers.

408 acabar — **finish**
vb
[a.ka.ˈβar]
Él puede acabar con diez cajas de cereales de maíz de un tirón.
-He can finish ten boxes of corn flakes in one sitting.

409 barco — **ship**
m
[ˈbar.ko]
Probablemente vieron a nuestro barco entrando al puerto.
-They probably saw our ship come into port.

410 hotel — **hotel**
m
[o.ˈtɛl]
Este hotel es un paraíso para los que disfrutan de una fina gastronomía, hospitalidad cordial y alojamiento confortable.
-This hotel is a haven for those who enjoy fine food, friendly hospitality, and comfortable accommodation.

411 grupo — **group**
m
[ˈgru.po]
El grupo terrorista fue responsable de la explosión de bomba en el exterior de la embajada.
-The terrorist group was responsible for the bomb explosion outside the embassy.

412 sol — **sun**
m
[ˈsol]
El sol siempre sale por el este.
-The sun always rises in the east.

413 tuyo — **yours**
prn
[ˈtu.jo]
Quieres tener algo que sea solo tuyo.
-You want to have something that's just yours.

414 voz — **voice**
f
[ˈbos]
La voz no es suficiente; también queremos ver tu expresión facial y tu lenguaje corporal.
-The voice is not enough; we also want to see your facial expression and body language.

415 baño — **bathroom**

	m [ˈba.ɲo]	En el baño hay un lavabo, un bidé, un inodoro y una ducha. Antes había una bañera. -In the bathroom there's a sink, a bidet, a toilet, and a shower. There used to be a bath.
416	**usar** vb [u.ˈsar]	**use** Está prohibido usar comercialmente esta información. -It's forbidden to use this information commercially.
417	**conseguir** vb [kõn.se.ˈɣir]	**get, achieve** Esperamos conseguir más resultados positivos en los años venideros. -We hope to achieve further positive results in the years to come.
418	**placer** m [pla.ˈsɛr]	**pleasure** No me gusta mezclar trabajo con placer. -I don't like to mix business with pleasure.
419	**profesor** m [pro.fe.ˈsor]	**teacher** Él es nuestro profesor de inglés. -He's our English teacher.
420	**lamentar(se)** vb; vbr [la.mẽn̯.ˈtar]	**regret; feel sorry for yourself** Le advertí que podría lamentar esta acción. -I warned you that you might regret this action.
421	**blanco** adj; m [ˈblãŋ.ko]	**white; target** Ha explicado que utilizó fósforo blanco de dos maneras. -He has explained that he used white phosphorous in two forms.
422	**pie** m [ˈpje]	**foot** No debería dispararse en el pie. -She should not shoot herself in the foot.
423	**andar(se)** vb; vbr [ãn̯.ˈdar]	**walk; behave** Solía verla andar por la tienda. -I used to see her walk by the store.
424	**edad** f [e.ˈðað]	**age** Por favor, indique su edad en el formulario. -Please put your age on the form.
425	**secreto** adj; m [se.ˈkrɛ.to]	**secret; secret** Tu secreto está a salvo conmigo. -Your secret is safe with me.
426	**compañía** f [kõm.pa.ˈɲi.a]	**company, firm** La compañía tiene un capital de un millón de dólares. -The company has a capital of one million dollars.
427	**tren** m [ˈtrẽn]	**train** Este tren se dirige a Nueva York. -This train is bound for New York.
428	**tras** prp [ˈtras]	**after, behind** Una palabra que anima durante un fracaso vale más que una hora de elogios tras un éxito. -A word of encouragement during a failure is worth more than an hour of praise after success.
429	**sentar(se)** vb [sẽn̯.ˈtar]	**sit** Desearía me dejara sentar al frente. -I wish you'd let me sit in the front.
430	**prisa**	**hurry**

f
['pri.sa]
Vale, tienen prisa, permítanme concluir muy brevemente.
-Right, you are in a hurry, let us conclude very briefly.

431 vista — **view**
f
['bis.ta]
En vista de ello, Filipinas quisiera resaltar algunas cuestiones.
-In view of this, the Philippines would like to stress a number of points.

432 hermoso — **beautiful**
adj
[ɛr.'mo.so]
Este hermoso vestido está hecho de seda.
-This beautiful dress is made of silk.

433 negocio — **shop, business**
m
[ne.'ɣo.sjo]
No mezcles el negocio con el placer.
-Don't mix business with pleasure.

434 pagar — **pay**
vb
[pa.'ɣar]
Quisiera pagar en efectivo. ¿El precio incluye el desayuno?
-I would like to pay with cash. Is breakfast included in the price?

435 futuro — **future; future**
adj; m
[fu.'tu.ro]
Las perspectivas de un futuro estable parecen cada vez más sombrías.
-The prospects of a stable future look increasingly dim.

436 silencio — **silence**
m
[si.'lɛ̃n.sjo]
Por unos momentos, hubo un silencio absoluto.
-For a few moments, there was complete silence.

437 médico — **doctor; medical**
m; adj
['me.ði.ko]
No me siento bien. ¿Dónde está el consultorio médico más cercano?
-I don't feel good. Where is the nearest medical center?

438 maestro — **teacher, master**
m
[ma.'ɛs.tro]
Nuestro nuevo maestro quiere que te deje con vida.
-Our new master wants me to let you live.

439 cambiar(se) — **swap, change**
vb
[kãm.'bjar]
Sería una error cambiar de dirección ahora.
-It would be a mistake to change direction now.

440 control — **control**
m
[kõn.'trol]
Toma el control del puesto de mando.
-Take control of the command post.

441 raro — **rare**
adj
['ra.ro]
Porque sería raro si un hámster hablara.
-Because it would be weird if a hamster talked.

442 novio — **boyfriend, fiancé**
m
['no.βjo]
Y ahora tienes un novio irlandés.
-And you've got yourself an Irish boyfriend.

443 diferente — **different**
adj
[di.fɛ.'rɛ̃n.te]
Pero esta vez la realidad resultó ser agradablemente diferente.
-But the reality this time turned out to be pleasantly different.

444 imposible — **impossible**
adj
[ĩm.po.'si.βle]
Es imposible predecir cuándo estarán disponibles todos los métodos alternativos necesarios.
-It is impossible to predict when all the necessary alternative methods might be available.

445 enseguida — **immediately**
adv
[ɛ̃n.se.'ɣi.ða]
Si alguien muestra interés llámeme enseguida.
-If somebody shows an interest you should call me right away.

446 llamada — **signal, call**

	f	Jim necesita hacer una llamada urgente.
	[ɟ̞ja.ˈma.ða]	-Jim needs to make an urgent telephone call.

447 avión — **plane**
m
[a.ˈβjõn]
Me pregunto si el avión llegará a tiempo.
-I wonder if the plane will arrive on time.

448 pelo — **hair**
m
[ˈpe.lo]
¿Te has secado alguna vez el pelo con un secador de pelo?
-Have you ever dried your hair with a hairdryer?

449 error — **mistake**
m
[ɛ.ˈror]
Nunca puedes cometer el mismo error dos veces, porque la segunda vez que lo hagas no es un error, es una elección.
-You can never make the same mistake twice because the second time you make it, it's no longer a mistake, it's a choice.

450 propio — **your own, typical**
adj
[ˈpro.pjo]
El resultado solo depende de tu propio esfuerzo.
-The outcome depends entirely on your own efforts.

451 siguiente — **following; next**
adj; m/f
[si.ˈɣjẽn̪.te]
Queremos y necesitamos la ampliación como siguiente paso importante.
-We want and need enlargement as our next great step forward.

452 ganar — **win**
vb
[ga.ˈnar]
Su pierna mala le impidió ganar la carrera.
-His bad leg prevented him from winning the race.

453 ley — **law**
f
[ˈlei̯]
Esto es la ley de la selva.
-This is the law of the jungle.

454 dolor — **pain**
m
[do.ˈlor]
Las guerras no traen paz; al contrario, traen dolor y tristeza a ambos bandos.
-War doesn't bring on peace; on the contrary, it brings pains and grief on both sides.

455 oro — **gold**
m
[ˈo.ro]
Te mostraré cómo separar el oro de la arena.
-I'll show you how to separate gold from sand.

456 maldición — **curse; damn**
f; int
[mal̪.di.ˈsjõn]
Los niños son considerados una maldición para su familia.
-The children are considered to be a curse on their family.

457 oficial — **official; officer**
adj; m/f
[o.fi.ˈsjal]
El oficial informó a Jim de que su solicitud de un permiso de estacionamiento había sido rechazada.
-The official informed Jim that his request for a parking permit had been rejected.

458 situación — **situation**
f
[si.twa.ˈsjõn]
La situación actual nos preocupa sobremanera.
-We are deeply concerned by the present situation.

459 daño — **damage**
m
[ˈda.ɲo]
La tormenta le causó un gran daño a su propiedad.
-The storm did great damage to her property.

460 deseo — **wish**
m
[de.ˈse.o]
Si una persona enferma hace mil grullas de papel, su deseo se cumplirá.
-If a sick person folds one thousand paper cranes, her wish will come true.

461 mente — **mind**

f
['mɛ̃n̪.te]
Lo siento, pero mi mente estaba en otra parte.
-Sorry, my mind was elsewhere.

462 ejército — **army**
m
[e.ˈxɛr.si.to]
El ejército continúa con su operación antiterrorismo.
-The army continues its anti-terrorism operation.

463 comprar(se) — **buy**
vb
[kõm.ˈprar]
¿Dónde puedo comprar café?
-Where can I buy coffee?

464 estúpido — **stupid; idiot, jerk**
adj; m
[ɛs.ˈtu.pi.ðo]
Las personas estúpidas siempre encuentran a alguien más estúpido que las admire.
-Stupid people can always find someone stupider than themselves who will admire them.

465 sonar — **sonar; sound**
m; vb
[so.ˈnar]
Comprendo que esto puede sonar loco, pero creo que me he enamorado de tu hermana menor.
-I realize that this may sound crazy, but I think I've fallen in love with your younger sister.

466 mitad — **half**
f
[mi.ˈtað]
El pájaro era de la mitad de grande que un águila.
-The bird was half as large as an eagle.

467 caballo — **horse**
m
[ka.ˈβa.ʝo]
Una yegua es un caballo hembra.
-A mare is a female horse.

468 asesino — **murderer**
m
[a.se.ˈsi.no]
Pero tu asesino tenía un conocimiento extenso de la anatomía humana.
-But your killer has an intimate knowledge of the human anatomy.

469 permiso — **permission, license**
m
[pɛr.ˈmi.so]
Tu permiso de conducir ha caducado.
-Your driver's license has expired.

470 maravilloso — **wonderful**
adj
[ma.ra.βi.ˈʝo.so]
Es maravilloso poder conocer personas de todo el mundo.
-It is wonderful to get to know people from around the globe.

471 mesa — **table**
f
[ˈme.sa]
Y tienes que esperar horas para una mesa.
-And you have to wait hours for a table.

472 divertido — **funny**
adj
[di.βɛr.ˈti.ðo]
Es divertido vivir en este mundo.
-It's funny to live in this world.

473 próximo — **next**
adj
[ˈprok.si.mo]
El próximo lunes y martes son días festivos consecutivos.
-Next Monday and Tuesday are consecutive holidays.

474 mar — **sea**
m
[ˈmar]
La mayoría de las criaturas del mar son afectadas por la contaminación.
-Most living creatures in the sea are affected by pollution.

475 siete — **seven**
num
[ˈsjɛ.te]
Todos los mamíferos tienen siete vértebras cervicales.
-All mammals have seven cervical vertebrae.

476 sexo — **sex, gender**

	m	Necesitamos igualdad de sexo para variar.
	['sɛk.so]	-We need some gender equality for a change.

477 encantar — **love, bewitch**

vb
[ẽŋ.kãn.'tar]

A tu mamá le debe encantar este lugar.
-Your mum must love this place.

478 amable — **kind**

adj
[a.'ma.βle]

Ella expresó su gratitud al Gobierno chino por su amable hospitalidad.
-He expressed gratitude to the Chinese Government for its kind hospitality.

479 mensaje — **message**

m
[mẽn.'sa.xe]

Cuando una persona normal manda un mensaje en una botella, es solo una fantasía infantil.
-When an average person sends a message in a bottle, it's just a childish fantasy.

480 información — **information**

f
[ĩm.for.ma.'sjõn]

Puedo darte algo de información útil.
-I can give you some useful information.

481 traer(se) — **bring**

vb
[tra.'ɛr]

Comida, bebida, cualquier cosa está bien. Por favor, trae una cosa.
-Food, drink, and whatever is OK. Please bring one item.

482 alma — **soul**

f
['al.ma]

Solo un cuadro puede revelar el alma; eso es lo que solía decir Jim.
-Only a painting can reveal the soul; that's what Jim used to say.

483 coronel — **colonel**

m/f
[ko.ro.'nɛl]

Fue ascendido a coronel hace dos años.
-He was promoted to colonel two years ago.

484 cena — **dinner**

f
['se.na]

Cuando la larga y copiosa cena terminó, los invitados comenzaron a bailar y cantar.
-When the long, hearty dinner was over, the guests began dancing and singing.

485 culo — **butt**

m
['ku.lo]

Levanta el culo del sofá y haz algo productivo.
-Get your butt off that couch and do something productive.

486 adentro — **inside**

adv
[a.'ðẽn.tro]

Vayamos adentro y aclaremos esto como seres humanos civilizados.
-Let's go inside and straighten this out like civil human beings.

487 canción — **song**

f
[kãn.'sjõn]

Ella tocó esa canción en su piano de cola.
-She played that song on her grand piano.

488 gobierno — **government**

m
[go.'βjɛr.no]

No creo que siempre sea correcto que los gobiernos locales se sometan al gobierno central.
-I don't think it's always right for local governments to submit to the central government.

489 temer(se) — **fear**

vb
[te.'mɛr]

No podemos ignorar ni temer esas realidades.
-We cannot ignore nor can we fear these realities.

490 abrir — **open**

vb
[a.'βrir]

Quiero abrir este debate cuanto antes.
-I want to open this discussion as soon as possible.

491 vosotros — **you**

	prn	Para vosotros es un enemigo declarado.
	[bo.ˈso.tros]	-He is an open enemy for you.
492	**freír**	**fry**
	vb	No puedo freír nada sin extractor.
	[fre.ˈir]	-I can't fry anything without a ventilator.
493	**foto**	**photo**
	f	Estoy colgando una foto de mi abuela.
	[ˈfo.to]	-I am hanging up a photo of my grandmother.
494	**accidente**	**accident**
	m	Él le reportó su accidente a la policía.
	[ak.si.ˈðɛ̃n.te]	-He reported his accident to the police.
495	**funcionar**	**work, operate**
	vb	Funciona bien, pero podría funcionar mejor.
	[fũn.sjo.ˈnar]	-It is working well, but it could work better.
496	**centro**	**center**
	m	Nuestra escuela está en el centro de la ciudad.
	[ˈsɛ̃n.tro]	-Our school is in the center of the town.
497	**necesario**	**necessary**
	adj	La rotación de los cultivos es necesaria para mantener la fertilidad del suelo.
	[ne.se.ˈsa.rjo]	-Crop rotation is necessary to preserve soil fertility.
498	**ante**	**facing, before**
	prp	El imputado podía declarar solo ante un juez.
	[ˈãn.te]	-The accused could make a statement only before a judge.
499	**terrible**	**terrible**
	adj	Le esperaba un terrible destino.
	[tɛ.ˈri.βle]	-A terrible fate awaited him.
500	**teniente**	**lieutenant**
	m/f	Lucha una guerra cara, teniente de aviación.
	[te.ˈnjɛ̃n.te]	-You fight an expensive war, flight lieutenant.
501	**luna**	**moon**
	f	Esta noche habrá luna llena.
	[ˈlu.na]	-There will be a full moon tonight.
502	**izquierdo**	**left**
	adj	Ahora probemos con tu ojo izquierdo.
	[is.ˈkjɛr.ðo]	-Now let's try it with your left eye.
503	**servicio**	**service**
	m	Cerraron el servicio de ferry porque ya no era económico.
	[sɛr.ˈβi.sjo]	-They closed down the ferry service since it was no longer economical.
504	**normal**	**normal**
	adj	A mí no me parece nada normal separar a los hijos de sus madres.
	[nor.ˈmal]	-To me, it doesn't seem at all normal to separate the children from their mothers.
505	**tienda**	**shop**
	f	La tienda no vende verduras.
	[ˈtjɛ̃n.da]	-The shop doesn't sell vegetables.
506	**Navidad**	**Christmas**
	f	¡Buenos días, señor! ¡Una feliz Navidad a usted!
	[na.βi.ˈðað]	-Good morning, sir! A merry Christmas to you!
507	**dirección**	**direction, management**

f
[di.rɛk.ˈsjõn]

Necesito tu dirección para mandarte un obsequio.
-I need your address in order to send you a present.

508 abuelo

grandfather

m
[a.ˈβwe.lo]

Mi abuelo nunca ha ido a un doctor en su vida.
-My grandfather has never consulted a doctor in his life.

509 alrededor

around

adv
[al.re.ðe.ˈðor]

Caminé alrededor de una milla.
-I walked about a mile.

510 libertad

freedom

f
[li.βɛr.ˈtað]

Tenemos que tener más libertad de elección y de movimiento.
-We must have more freedom of choice and of movement.

511 salar

salt

vb
[sa.ˈlar]

Podemos salar y secar la carne, y podremos conservarla durante mucho tiempo.
-We can salt and cure the meat, and we can keep it for a long time.

512 línea

line

f
[ˈli.ne.a]

Dibuja una línea en el folio.
-Draw a line on the paper.

513 abogar

plead

vb
[a.βo.ˈɣar]

Me gustaría abogar a favor de esta última opción.
-I would like to plead in favor of the latter option.

514 honor

honor

m
[o.ˈnor]

En la ceremonia de inauguración se descubrió una placa en honor al fundador.
-At the inauguration ceremony, a plaque was unveiled in honor of the founder.

515 regresar

return

vb
[re.ɣre.ˈsar]

Es esencial para los refugiados que desean regresar.
-It is key for the refugees who want to return.

516 papel

paper, role

m
[pa.ˈpɛl]

Los ordenadores parecen desempeñar el papel del cerebro humano, por lo que frecuentemente son llamados "cerebros eléctricos".
-Computers seem to play the role of the human brain, so they're often called "electric brains".

517 terminar

finish

vb
[tɛr.mi.ˈnar]

Creo que va a llevar más de un año terminar de construir nuestra casa.
-I think it'll take more than a year to finish building our house.

518 jurar

swear, pledge

vb
[xu.ˈrar]

Debes jurar con la mano en la Biblia.
-You must swear with your hand on the Bible.

519 dulce

sweet; candy

adj; m
[ˈdul.se]

Que mujer tan dulce y considerada eres.
-What a sweet, considerate woman you are.

520 sentir

feel

vb
[sẽn̪.ˈtir]

Jim podía sentir que Ana estaba tratando de impresionarle.
-Jim could feel that Ana was trying to impress him.

521 principio

start, principle

m
[prĩn.ˈsi.pjo]

Lo considero un excelente principio rector.
-I consider this to be an excellent guiding principle.

522 interesante

interesting

adj
[ĩn̪.tɛ.re.ˈsãn̪.te]

Yo pienso que una película es más interesante que cualquier libro.
-I think a movie is more interesting than any book.

523	**caja**	**box**
	f	Abrí la caja y miré dentro.
	[ˈka.xa]	-I opened the box and looked inside.
524	**ocho**	**eight**
	num	Mercurio es el más pequeño de los ocho planetas de nuestro sistema solar.
	[ˈo.ʧo]	-Mercury is the smallest of the eight planets in the solar system.
525	**horrible**	**horrible**
	adj	Ojalá pudiéramos irnos de este horrible lugar.
	[o.ˈri.βle]	-I just wish we could leave this horrible place.
526	**respuesta**	**answer**
	f	Me resulta difícil dar una respuesta.
	[rɛs.ˈpwɛs.ta]	-It is difficult for me to give an answer.
527	**gracioso**	**amusing; clown**
	adj; m	Debes admitir que es bastante gracioso.
	[gra.ˈsjo.so]	-You have to admit it's quite funny.
528	**personal**	**staff; personal**
	m; adj	El resto del personal fue despedido sin previo aviso.
	[pɛr.so.ˈnal]	-The rest of the staff were fired without notice.
529	**completo**	**full**
	adj	Quiero un análisis completo del evento.
	[kõm.ˈplɛ.to]	-I want a full analysis of the event.
530	**cárcel**	**prison**
	f	Mantener a un criminal en la cárcel es muy caro.
	[ˈkar.sɛl]	-Maintaining a criminal in the jail is very expensive.
531	**sistema**	**system**
	m	Jim le explicó el sistema a Ana.
	[sis.ˈte.ma]	-Jim explained the system to Ana.
532	**lindo**	**cute (LA)**
	adj	Miren ese lindo sombrerito de conejito.
	[ˈlĩn̪.do]	-Look at that cute little bunny hat.
533	**salud**	**health**
	f	Él está muy preocupado por la salud de su anciano padre.
	[sa.ˈluð]	-He is very concerned about his elderly parent's health.
534	**paso**	**step**
	m	No se puede dominar un idioma extranjero en poco tiempo; uno tiene que estudiarlo paso por paso.
	[ˈpa.so]	-You can't master a foreign language in a short time; you have to study it step by step.
535	**pase**	**pass**
	m	Necesita un pase para salir del edificio.
	[ˈpa.se]	-You'll need a pass to get out of the building.
536	**citar**	**quote, make an appointment**
	vb	Quisiera citar dos conclusiones de dicho estudio.
	[si.ˈtar]	-I would like to quote two of the findings of this report.
537	**cámara**	**camera, vault**
	f	Mi cámara siempre está en mi mochila.
	[ˈka.ma.ra]	-My camera is always in my bag.
538	**agente**	**agent**
	m	Para que lo sepas, soy un agente del FBI.
	[a.ˈxẽn̪.te]	-Just so you know, I'm an FBI agent.

539 infierno — **hell**
m
[ĩm.ˈfjɛɾ.no]
El infierno está empedrado de buenas intenciones.
-Hell is paved with good intentions.

540 regalo — **present**
m
[re.ˈɣa.lo]
¿Cuál fue el mejor regalo que recibiste la pasada Navidad?
-What was the best present you got last Christmas?

541 río — **river**
m
[ˈri.o]
Harry consiguió atravesar el río nadando.
-Harry managed to swim across the river.

542 a través de — **through**
prp
[a tra.ˈβeʂ ðe]
Los comentarios se obtendrán a través de varias plataformas.
-The feedback will be obtained through a variety of platforms.

543 carne — **meat**
f
[ˈkar.ne]
¿Qué tipos de platos de carne sirven?
-What kinds of meat dishes do you serve?

544 piso — **apartment (ES), floor, ground (LA)**
m
[ˈpi.so]
¿En qué piso vive él?
-Which floor does he live on?

545 sargento — **sergeant**
m/f
[sar.ˈxẽn̪.to]
El padre se había encontrado con el sargento el año pasado.
-The father had met the sergeant last year.

546 ambos — **both; both**
adj; prn
[ˈãm.bos]
Creo que ambos aspectos son importantes.
-I believe both of those are important aspects.

547 beber(se) — **drink**
vb
[be.ˈβɛr]
Pregúntele a su médico cuánto debe beber.
-Ask your health care provider how much you should drink.

548 calma — **calm**
f
[ˈkal.ma]
A pesar de la aparente calma, siguió habiendo problemas de seguridad.
-Despite the apparent calm, security challenges persisted.

549 vestir(se) — **dress**
vb
[bɛs.ˈtir]
No puedes vestir así para trabajar.
-You can't dress like that to work.

550 salvo — **except; unless**
prp; adv
[ˈsal.βo]
No tengo nada a declarar salvo mi genialidad.
-I have nothing to declare except my genius.

551 verdadero — **true**
adj
[bɛr.ða.ˈðɛ.ro]
No logro entender su verdadero objetivo.
-I fail to understand his true aim.

552 basura — **garbage**
f
[ba.ˈsu.ra]
No tires la basura aquí.
-Don't throw garbage away here.

553 suelo — **ground, soil**
m
[ˈswe.lo]
Esto es importante para mejorar las características físicas del suelo.
-This will be important for improving the physical characteristics of the soil.

554 carrera — **career, race**
f
[ka.ˈrɛ.ra]
Corrí una carrera con él.
-I ran a race with him.

555 cumpleaños — **birthday**

	m	Su cumpleaños es el cinco de mayo.
	[kũm.ple.ˈa.ɲos]	-His birthday is May 5th.
556	**rato**	**a short time**
	m	Después de un rato él volvió con un diccionario bajo el brazo.
	[ˈra.to]	-After a while, he came back with a dictionary under his arm.
557	**universidad**	**university**
	f	Cuando estaba en la universidad me gustaba estudiar latín.
	[u.ni.βɛr.si.ˈðað]	-When I was at university, I liked to study Latin.
558	**bailar**	**dance**
	vb	Jim nunca ha visto bailar a Ana.
	[bai̯.ˈlar]	-Jim has never seen Ana dance.
559	**triste**	**sad**
	adj	Gracias por consolarme cuando estaba triste.
	[ˈtris.te]	-Thank you for consoling me when I was sad.
560	**iglesia**	**church**
	f	Hay una pequeña iglesia al final.
	[i.ˈɣle.sja]	-There's a small church at the end.
561	**delante**	**before, in front**
	adv	Coloca el objeto delante del texto.
	[de.ˈlãn̪.te]	-Places the object in front of the text.
562	**nene**	**baby (coll), darling**
	m	Vamos, nene, hazlo por mamá.
	[ˈne.ne]	-Come on, baby, do it for mama.
563	**banco**	**bank, bench**
	m	Él pagó al banco su deuda.
	[ˈbãŋ.ko]	-He paid his loan back to the bank.
564	**existir**	**exist**
	vb	Los hechos no dejan de existir por ser ignorados.
	[ɛk.sis.ˈtir]	-Facts do not cease to exist because they are ignored.
565	**programa**	**program, schedule**
	m	Es esencial cumplir con el programa.
	[pro.ˈɣra.ma]	-It's essential to maintain our schedule.
566	**alegrar(se)**	**cheer up, be happy**
	vb	Mi madre se va a alegrar de escuchar eso.
	[a.le.ˈɣrar]	-My mom will be happy to hear that.
567	**san(to)**	**saint; saint**
	adj; m	Todo santo tiene un pasado y todo pecador tiene un futuro.
	[ˈsãn̪.to)]	-Every saint has a past and every sinner has a future.
568	**porqué**	**reason**
	m	El porqué es una mayor demanda.
	[por.ˈke]	-The reason is greater demand.
569	**broma**	**joke**
	f	solo pensé que una buena broma se merecía otra.
	[ˈbro.ma]	-Just thought one good prank deserved another.
570	**prometer**	**promise**
	vb	Tuve que prometer no donar mis riñones.
	[pro.mɛ.ˈtɛr]	-I had to promise not to donate my kidneys.
571	**partido**	**match**

	m [par.ˈti.ðo]	El entrenador suspendió el partido porque muchos de los jugadores estaban de baja con la gripe. -The coach called off the game because many of the players were down with the flu.
572	**preguntar** vb [pre.ɣũn̪.ˈtar]	**ask** No he tenido oportunidad de preguntar. -I haven't had a chance to ask.
573	**radio** f [ˈra.ðjo]	**radio** El locutor de la radio tenía una voz masculina. -The radio announcer had a masculine voice.
574	**cenar** vb [se.ˈnar]	**have dinner** Ella aceptó mi invitación de cenar conmigo. -She accepted my invitation to have dinner with me.
575	**correr** vb [ko.ˈrɛr]	**run** No puede correr, apenas puede caminar. -He can't run, he can hardly walk.
576	**disculpa** f [dis.ˈkul.pa]	**apology** Debo ofrecerle una disculpa por llegar tarde. -I must offer you an apology for coming late.
577	**cerveza** f [sɛr.ˈβe.sa]	**beer** He comprado una botella de cerveza en la licorería. -I bought a bottle of beer at the liquor store.
578	**destino** m [dɛs.ˈti.no]	**destination, fate** Llegaremos a nuestro destino cuando el sol se ponga. -By the time the sun sets, we will arrive at the destination.
579	**matrimonio** m [ma.tri.ˈmo.njo]	**marriage** Dicha capacidad se mantiene aunque se disuelva el matrimonio. -Such capacity is fully maintained even if the marriage is dissolved.
580	**norte** m [ˈnor.te]	**north** Hokkaido queda al norte de Honshu. -Hokkaido is to the north of Honshu.
581	**sala** f [ˈsa.la]	**room** No hables en la sala de lectura. -Don't talk in the reading room.
582	**según** prp; con [se.ˈɣũn]	**according to; depending on** Era fundamental que todo saliera según el plan. -So it was imperative that everything went according to the plan.
583	**ataque** m [a.ˈta.ke]	**attack** Tuve un ataque de asma. -I had an asthma attack.
584	**parir** vb [pa.ˈrir]	**give birth** Es evidente que solo las mujeres pueden quedarse embarazadas y parir. -Obviously, only women can get pregnant and give birth.
585	**ejemplo** m [e.ˈxẽm.plo]	**example** Nadie ha podido dar un ejemplo. -Nobody has been able to give an example.
586	**sorpresa** f [sor.ˈpre.sa]	**surprise** Su ensayo hacía solo un análisis superficial del problema, así que fue una gran sorpresa para él conseguir la nota más alta de la clase.

48

-His essay gave only a superficial analysis of the problem, so it was a real surprise to him when he got the highest grade in the class.

587 té — tea
m
['te]
Ponme un poco de brandy en el té.
-Put a dash of brandy in my tea.

588 club — club
m
['kluβ]
Fui miembro del club de fútbol cuando estaba en secundaria.
-I was a member of the soccer club when I was in junior high.

589 temprano — early; early
adj; adv
[tẽm.'pra.no]
A algunas personas no les gusta levantarse temprano por la mañana.
-Some people do not like to wake up early in the morning.

590 público — public; audience
adj; m
['pu.βli.ko]
El público llenó el auditorio.
-The audience filled the hall.

591 ventana — window
f
[bẽn̪.'ta.na]
Apenas podía distinguir las paredes opacas de su habitación de la ventana transparente.
-He could scarcely distinguish the transparent window from the opaque walls of his chamber.

592 duda — doubt
f
['du.ða]
Estaba asustada, no había duda.
-She was frightened, there was no doubt.

593 boda — wedding
f
['bo.ða]
Jim no llevaba anillo de boda, pero Ana se percató de una marca blanca alrededor de su dedo anular.
-Jim wasn't wearing a wedding ring, but Ana noticed a white circle on his ring finger.

594 peligro — danger
m
[pe.'li.ɣro]
Existe además el peligro de ser selectivo.
-And there is also the danger of being selective.

595 caliente — hot
adj
[ka.'ljẽn̪.te]
No querrás que se caliente demasiado.
-You don't want it to get too hot.

596 escribir — write
vb
[ɛs.kri.'βir]
Algún día me gustaría escribir su biografía.
-I would like to write his biography one day.

597 reina — queen
f
['rei̯.na]
Hércules, un antiguo héroe griego famoso por su fuerza sobrehumana, fue perseguido durante toda su vida por el odio de Juno, la diosa del nacimiento, del matrimonio y del cuidado, adorada como reina de los dioses por los romanos.
-Hercules, an ancient Greek hero celebrated for his superhuman strength, was pursued throughout his life by the hatred of Juno, the goddess of birth, matrimony, and care, worshipped as queen of gods by the Romans.

598 sin embargo — nevertheless
con
[sin ẽm.'bar.ɣo]
Debemos, sin embargo, tener en cuenta dos aspectos.
-Nevertheless, we must take two things into account.

599 sur — south
m
['sur]
En el sur de China, la situación es diferente.
-In the south of China, the situation is different.

600 enfermo — ill; sick person

adj; m
[ɛ̃ɱ.ˈfɛr.mo]

Fingí estar enfermo para quedarme en casa.
-I pretended to be unwell in order to stay at home.

601 excelente

adj; int
[ɛk.se.ˈlɛ̃n̪.te]

excellent; great

El dinero es un amo terrible pero un excelente siervo.
-Money is a terrible master but an excellent servant.

602 escena

f
[ɛs.ˈse.na]

scene

Fue Jim quien descubrió la escena del crimen.
-It was Jim who discovered the crime scene.

603 encuentro

m
[ɛ̃ŋ.ˈkwɛ̃n̪.tro]

meeting, match

Genial, porque esperamos preparar un encuentro.
-Great, because we're looking to set up a meeting.

604 asesinato

m
[a.se.si.ˈna.to]

murder

Estás bajo arresto por el asesinato de Jim Jackson.
-You're under arrest for the murder of Jim Jackson.

605 obra

f
[ˈo.βra]

work, play

Una obra de arte es el resultado único de un temperamento único.
-A work of art is the unique result of a unique temperament.

606 aquel

adj; prn
[a.ˈkɛl]

that; that one

Este perro y ese pez son míos, pero aquel pájaro no.
-This dog and that fish are mine, but that bird isn't.

607 prueba

f
[ˈprwe.βa]

test, evidence

¿Hay alguna prueba de la credibilidad del autor?
-Is there any evidence as to the credibility of the author?

608 vos

prn
[ˈbos]

you (LA)

Yo me sentía muy sola, vos solo pensás en vos.
-I felt so lonely, you're always thinking of yourself.

609 crear

vb
[kre.ˈar]

create

Fue una buena idea crear Google.
-It was a good idea to create Google.

610 apenar(se)

vb
[a.pe.ˈnar]

sadden

Has apenado mucho a tu padre.
-You've really saddened your dad.

611 llave

f
[ˈʎ̞ja.βe]

key

Agarraste la llave que no era.
-You took the wrong key.

612 regreso

m
[re.ˈɣre.so]

comeback

Siempre has estado ahí esperando su regreso.
-You have always been there waiting for her to return.

613 trasero

adj; m
[tra.ˈsɛ.ro]

rear; butt (coll)

Solo estaba diciendo que quiero patearles el trasero.
-I was just saying I want to kick them in the ass.

614 ojalá

int
[o.xa.ˈla]

hopefully

Bueno, obviamente, ojalá que eso no pase.
-Well, obviously, I hope that wouldn't be the case.

615 leer

vb
[le.ˈɛr]

read

Debiste saber que no podría leer tal carta.
-You must have known I couldn't read such a letter.

616 imbécil

imbecile; moron

m/f; adj
[ĭm.ˈbe.sil]

Ven aquí y consuélala, imbécil.
  -Get over here and comfort her, jerk.

617 **opinión**

opinion

f
[o.pi.ˈnjõn]

Todos somos seres humanos, por lo que en mi opinión, la cultura de cada país es un 90% igual.
  -We're all human beings, so in my opinion, each country's culture is 90% the same.

618 **señal**

signal, mark

f
[se.ˈɲal]

Estaban esperando la señal para empezar.
  -They were waiting for the signal to start.

619 **agradable**

pleasant

adj
[a.ɣra.ˈða.βle]

¡Qué viaje tan agradable tuvimos!
  -What a pleasant journey we had!

620 **cocina**

kitchen

f
[ko.ˈsi.na]

En la cocina del restaurante indio, Calcutta.
  -In the kitchen of the Indian restaurant, Calcutta.

621 **relación**

relationship, link

f
[re.la.ˈsjõn]

Jim tuvo que mantener su relación con Ana en secreto.
  -Jim had to keep his relationship with Ana a secret.

622 **cortar(se)**

cut

vb
[kor.ˈtar]

El cuchillo de cocina no estaba lo suficientemente afilado para cortar la carne, así que me serví de mi navaja de bolsillo.
  -The kitchen knife wasn't sharp enough to cut the meat, so I used my pocket knife.

623 **cerebro**

brain

m
[sɛ.ˈre.βro]

Te lo explicaría, pero te explotaría el cerebro.
  -I'd explain it to you, but your brain would explode.

624 **locura**

madness

f
[lo.ˈku.ra]

Aquél que vive sin locura no es tan sabio como cree.
  -He who lives without madness is not as wise as he thinks.

625 **peligroso**

dangerous

adj
[pe.li.ˈɣro.so]

Digámosla que es demasiado peligroso.
  -Let's tell her it's too risky.

626 **cine**

cinema

m
[ˈsi.ne]

Estamos viviendo los grandes momentos del cine.
  -We are watching the great moments of cinema.

627 **reunión**

meeting

f
[reu̯.ˈnjõn]

Dijo que cada reunión debería empezar con una oración.
  -He said each meeting should begin with a prayer.

628 **tocar**

touch

vb
[to.ˈkar]

No es respetuoso tocarte la cara.
  -It's not respectful to touch your face.

629 **causa**

cause

f
[ˈkau̯.sa]

¿Cuál fue la causa de la explosión?
  -What was the cause of the explosion?

630 **pelea**

fight

f
[pe.ˈle.a]

Tuvieron una pelea de almohadas.
  -They had a pillow fight.

631 **prisión**

prison

f
[pri.ˈsjõn]
Están encarcelados en una prisión civil en condiciones escandalosas.
-They are being detained in a civilian prison in disgraceful conditions.

632 **mayoría**   **most**
f
[ma.ʝo.ˈri.a]
La mayoría de la gente cree que estoy loco.
-Most people think I'm crazy.

633 **fondo**   **bottom**
m
[ˈfõn̪.do]
Jim encontró el tesoro en el fondo del lago.
-Jim found the treasure at the bottom of the lake.

634 **acaso**   **perhaps**
adv
[a.ˈka.so]
Quería hacerle una pregunta y si acaso ofrecerle una pequeña sugerencia.
-I wish to ask you a question and perhaps make a small suggestion.

635 **montón**   **pile, bunch**
m
[mõn̪.ˈtõn]
El hombre entró corriendo en el cuarto con una bota sobre su cabeza, gritó un montón de incoherencias, y salió inmediatamente.
-The man ran into the room wearing a boot on his head, shouted a bunch of gibberish, and promptly exited.

636 **comandante**   **major**
m/f
[ko.mãn̪.ˈdãn̪.te]
Jim será el comandante de todas las tropas.
-Jim will be the commander of all the troops.

637 **misión**   **mission**
f
[mi.ˈsjõn]
Esta va a ser una misión muy peligrosa.
-This will be a very dangerous mission.

638 **decisión**   **decision**
f
[de.si.ˈsjõn]
La decisión final será tomada por el presidente.
-The final decision shall be taken by the president.

639 **hogar**   **home**
m
[o.ˈɣar]
Envidio la estructura de tu hogar.
-I envy the structure of your household.

640 **rico**   **rich person; wealthy, tasty**
m; adj
[ˈri.ko]
Nunca afectará a una persona rica.
-It will never affect a rich person.

641 **tragar(se)**   **swallow**
vb
[tra.ˈɣar]
No puedo tragar estas pastillas sin un vaso de agua.
-I can't swallow these tablets without a glass of water.

642 **capaz**   **capable**
adj
[ˈka.pas]
Ana era capaz de cruzar el río a nado.
-Ana was able to swim across the river.

643 **cargo**   **position, charge**
m
[ˈkar.ɣo]
Un capitán está a cargo de su barco y de su tripulación.
-A captain is in charge of his ship and its crew.

644 **unir**   **join, unite**
vb
[u.ˈnir]
Debemos tratar de unir al mundo en lugar de dividirlo.
-We should try to unite the world, not drive it apart.

645 **lleno**   **full**
adj
[ˈʎje.no]
El estacionamiento en frente del banco estaba completamente lleno.
-The parking lot in front of the bank was completely full.

646 **bar**   **bar**
m
[ˈbar]
Estaba en el bar recolectando chismes.
-I was in the pub picking up gossip.

647 **estrella**   **star**

	f	Ana es una famosa estrella de pop.
	[ɛs.ˈtre.ja]	-Ana is a famous pop star.
648	**posición**	**position**
	f	Me niego a respaldar una posición tan hipócrita.
	[po.si.ˈsjõn]	-I refuse to go along with such a hypocritical position.
649	**estación**	**station, season**
	f	Te avisaré cuando lleguemos a la estación.
	[ɛs.ta.ˈsjõn]	-I'll let you know when we come to the station.
650	**interesar(se)**	**interest**
	vb	Pensé que le podría interesar recuperar el cuchillo.
	[ĩn̪.tɛ.re.ˈsar]	-I thought you might be interested in recovering the knife.
651	**edificio**	**building**
	m	Las dos salas de conferencias estarían ubicadas en el primer piso del edificio.
	[e.ði.ˈfi.sjo]	-Both conference rooms would be located on the first floor of the building.
652	**consejo**	**advice, council**
	m	El consejo se ha reunido para analizar la reprogramación.
	[kõn.ˈse.xo]	-The council held a meeting to analyze the rescheduling.
653	**pistola**	**gun**
	f	Una pistola no te servirá de mucho si no estás dispuesto a dispararla.
	[pis.ˈto.la]	-A gun won't do you much good if you're not willing to shoot it.
654	**humano**	**humane; human**
	adj; m	El cráneo humano tiene 23 huesos.
	[u.ˈma.no]	-The human skull consists of 23 bones.
655	**fantástico**	**fantastic**
	adj	Sería fantástico si alguien pudiera llevarnos.
	[fãn̪.ˈtas.ti.ko]	-It would be amazing if someone could take us.
656	**zapato**	**shoe**
	m	Él ató el zapato a su hijo con un nudo doble y dijo "ya está, eso debería funcionar".
	[sa.ˈpa.to]	-He tied his son's shoe with a double knot and said, "There, that should do the trick."
657	**flor**	**flower**
	f	Esa flor trató de atacarme.
	[ˈflor]	-That flower tried to attack me.
658	**ocupar(se)**	**occupy; take responsibility for**
	vb; vbr	Tratamos de ocupar nuestra mente, llenarla de información constantemente.
	[o.ku.ˈpar]	-We constantly try to occupy our mind, fill it with information.
659	**bienvenido**	**welcome; welcome**
	adj; int	Bienvenido al glamuroso mundo de la vigilancia.
	[bjẽm.be.ˈni.ðo]	-Welcome to the glamorous world of surveillance.
660	**zona**	**zone**
	f	Tenemos dos casas situadas en una zona residencial muy tranquila.
	[ˈso.na]	-We have two houses placed in a very calm residential area.
661	**contacto**	**contact**
	m	Intenté ponerme en contacto con la policía.
	[kõn̪.ˈtak.to]	-I tried to get in touch with the police.
662	**sacar**	**take out**
	vb	Creemos que ya podemos sacar algunas conclusiones.
	[sa.ˈkar]	-We believe that we can already draw some conclusions.
663	**tema**	**topic**

m
['te.ma]
Las respuestas están agrupadas por tema.
-The answers are grouped according to topic.

664 pedir — request
vb
[pe.'ðir]
Me gustaría pedir un pequeño receso.
-I would like to request a short recess.

665 cerrar — close
vb
[sɛ.'rar]
Gracias por cerrar la puerta.
-Thank you for closing the door.

666 intento — attempt
m
[ĩn̯.'tẽn̯.to]
No vamos a hacer ningún intento.
-We're not going to give it a try.

667 calor — heat
m
[ka.'lor]
Hace calor esta mañana, ¿no?
-Warm this morning, isn't it?

668 equivocar(se) — confuse; be mistaken
vb; vbr
[e.ki.βo.'kar]
Nunca te puedes equivocar con joyas.
-One can never go wrong with jewelry.

669 animal — animal; animal
adj; m
[a.ni.'mal]
No basta simplemente con mantener vivo al animal.
-It is not enough simply to keep the animal alive.

670 departamento — department, apartment (LA)
m
[de.par.ta.'mẽn̯.to]
Él está a cargo del departamento de ventas.
-He's in charge of the sales department.

671 enemigo — enemy
m
[e.ne.'mi.ɣo]
La falta de inspiración es el peor enemigo de la creatividad.
-Lack of inspiration is the worst enemy of creativity.

672 color — color
m
[ko.'lor]
Un conejo color ceniza apareció y en cuanto me acerqué, saltó y corrió hacia el bosque de nuevo.
-An ash-colored rabbit appeared and as soon as I drew near, it hopped and ran into the woods again.

673 valor — value, courage
m
[ba.'lor]
Estoy convencido de que unas semanas en un campamento de verano bien organizado pueden poseer un valor educativo mucho mayor que un año entero consagrado al trabajo escolar tradicional.
-I have the conviction that a few weeks in a well-organized summer camp may be of more value educationally than a whole year of formal school work.

674 cien(to) — hundred
num
['sjẽn̯.to)]
Están a cien metros del transporte.
-You're a hundred meters from the transport.

675 azul — blue
adj
[a.'sul]
Me gustaría probarme la falda azul rayada.
-I would like to try the blue striped skirt.

676 espacio — space
m
[ɛs.'pa.sjo]
El espacio está lleno de misterios.
-Space is full of mystery.

677 mantener(se) — keep
vb
[mãn̯.te.'nɛr]
Tiene derecho a mantenerse en silencio.
-You have the right to remain silent.

678 aprender(se) — learn

	vb	Me gusta aprender cosas nuevas.
	[a.prẽn.'dɛr]	-I like to learn new things.
679	**inteligente**	**intelligent**
	adj	Guapo, inteligente y sexy – esto describe lo que él no es.
	[ĩn.te.li.'xẽn.te]	-Beautiful, intelligent and hot - this describes what he is not.
680	**arte**	**art**
	m	Somos el portal de arte donde coexisten escritores, ilustradores, poetas y músicos.
	['ar.te]	-We are an art portal where writers, illustrators, poets, and musicians coexist.
681	**respeto**	**respect**
	m	Jim se ganó el respeto y la lealtad de sus empleados.
	[rɛs.'pɛ.to]	-Jim gained the respect and loyalty of his employees.
682	**juez**	**judge**
	m	El juez lo sentenció a un año de prisión.
	['xwes]	-The judge sentenced him to one year in prison.
683	**inglés**	**English; Englishman**
	adj; m	Jim tocó una canción popular española con su corno inglés en un restaurante chino de Francia.
	[ĩŋ.'gles]	-Jim played a Spanish folk tune on his English horn at a Chinese restaurant in France.
684	**precio**	**price**
	m	El precio depende del tamaño.
	['pre.sjo]	-The price depends on the size.
685	**rojo**	**red**
	adj	Pinta un extremo de la vara rojo y el otro azul.
	['ro.xo]	-Paint one end of the rod red and the other end blue.
686	**verano**	**summer**
	m	Este verano voy a nadar mucho.
	[bɛ.'ra.no]	-I am going to swim a lot this summer.
687	**pierna**	**leg**
	f	El soldado estaba herido en la pierna y no podía moverse.
	['pjɛr.na]	-The soldier had a leg injury and couldn't move.
688	**isla**	**island**
	f	Lanzarote es una isla que te invita a descubrirla.
	['iʂ.la]	-Lanzarote is an island that invites you to discover her.
689	**dama**	**lady**
	f	Busco información de esta encantadora dama.
	['da.ma]	-I am looking for information on this charming lady.
690	**guardia**	**police officer; police department**
	m/f; f	Sam atacó a un guardia y escapó.
	['gwar.ðja]	-Sam assaulted a police officer and escaped.
691	**espalda**	**back**
	f	Es como si tuviera un cohete atado a la espalda.
	[ɛs.'pal̪.da]	-It's like he had a rocket strapped to his back.
692	**parar**	**stop**
	vb	Esto tiene que parar y para pararlo también necesitamos recursos financieros.
	[pa.'rar]	-This must stop, and to stop it we also need financial resources.
693	**banda**	**band**
	f	Son considerados la mejor banda de rock de la historia.
	['bãn̪.da]	-They are considered the greatest rock band in history.

694 marcha
f
['mar.tʃa]

march
Planean una marcha por el centro de Helsinki.
-They are planning a march through the center of Helsinki.

695 crimen
m
['kri.mɛ̃n]

crime
La tolerancia se convierte en crimen cuando se aplica al mal.
-Tolerance becomes a crime when applied to evil.

696 diferencia
f
[di.fɛ.'rɛ̃n.sja]

difference
No puedo explicar la diferencia entre esos dos.
-I can't explain the difference between those two.

697 debajo
adv
[de.'βa.xo]

under
No quiero saber qué hay aquí debajo.
-I don't want to know what's under here.

698 compañero
m
[kõm.pa.'ɲɛ.ro]

partner
Este es el mejor compañero para una buena conversación.
-This is the best partner for a great conversation.

699 molesto
adj
[mo.'lɛs.to]

annoying
Para mí es molesto escuchar música fuerte.
-For me, listening to loud music is annoying.

700 contar
vb
[kõn̪.'tar]

count, tell
Algunas historias son demasiado peligrosas para contarlas.
-Some stories are just too dangerous to tell.

701 cansar(se)
vb
[kãn.'sar]

tire, bother
Nunca me voy a cansar de esto.
-I'll never get tired of that.

702 juicio
m
['xwi.sjo]

judgment, wisdom
Llevaba detenido ocho meses sin juicio.
-He had been detained for eight months without a trial.

703 estilo
m
[ɛs.'ti.lo]

style
El estilo me gusta, pero ¿lo tienes en otro color?
-The style is nice, but do you have it in a different color?

704 salida
f
[sa.'li.ða]

exit
¿No ven el cartel de salida de ahí?
-Don't you see the exit sign over there?

705 despierto
adj
[dɛs.'pjɛr.to]

awake
Pero sería mejor si estuviera despierto ya.
-But it would be better if he were awake by now.

706 estupendo
adj
[ɛs.tu.'pɛ̃n̪.do]

wonderful
Hoy pienso tener un día estupendo.
-Today I choose to have a great day.

707 nave
f
['na.βe]

ship, plane
La nave espacial hizo un aterrizaje perfecto.
-The spaceship made a perfect landing.

708 base
f
['ba.se]

base
Las columnas confieren una base sólida.
-Columns provide a solid foundation.

709 subir
vb
[su.'βir]

go up
Pensé haberla visto subir la escalera.
-I thought I saw her go up the stairs.

710 vuelo

flight

	m	Al final decidieron cancelar el vuelo.
	[ˈbwe.lo]	-In the end, they decided to cancel the flight.
711	**excepto**	**except**
	prp	No quiero hacer nada excepto irme de aquí.
	[ɛkˈsep̚.to]	-I don't want to do anything except get out of here.
712	**golpe**	**hit**
	m	Jim, has sufrido un golpe terrible.
	[ˈgol.pe]	-Jim, you've suffered a terrible blow.
713	**viento**	**wind**
	m	El viento sopla del este.
	[ˈbjẽn̪.to]	-The wind is blowing from the east.
714	**acción**	**action, share**
	f	Jim quiere acercarse a la acción.
	[akˈsjõn]	-Jim wants to get close to the action.
715	**tontería**	**nonsense**
	f	Creo que sería una tontería no aceptar.
	[tõn̪ˈtɛ.ri.a]	-I believe that it would be a foolishness not to accept.
716	**respecto**	**regarding**
	m	Quisiera expresar nuestro reconocimiento por sus esfuerzos respecto a esto.
	[rɛsˈpek̚.to]	-We would like to express our appreciation for their efforts in this regard.
717	**desear**	**wish**
	vb	Finalmente, quisiera desearos a todos una feliz Navidad.
	[de.seˈar]	-Finally, I would like to wish you all a happy Christmas.
718	**beso**	**kiss**
	m	No le has dado el beso especial a papá.
	[ˈbe.so]	-You have not given the special kiss to dad.
719	**cuestión**	**matter**
	f	El acuerdo es cuestión de tiempo.
	[kwɛsˈtjõn]	-The settlement is a matter of time.
720	**regla**	**rule**
	f	Como regla general, es fácil criticar pero difícil ofrecer sugerencias alternativas.
	[ˈre.ɣla]	-As a general rule, it's simple to criticize, but difficult to produce alternative suggestions.
721	**ruido**	**noise**
	m	Fui despertado bruscamente por un ruido fuerte.
	[ˈrwi.ðo]	-I was suddenly awakened by a loud noise.
722	**olvidar(se)**	**forget**
	vb	No debemos olvidar que han surgido innumerables problemas.
	[ol.βiˈðar.se)]	-We must not forget that an incredible number of problems have arisen.
723	**mentira**	**lie**
	f	Una buena mentira es más fácil de creer que la verdad.
	[mẽn̪ˈti.ra]	-A good lie is easier to believe than the truth.
724	**brazo**	**arm**
	m	El codo es la articulación entre el brazo y el antebrazo.
	[ˈbra.so]	-The elbow is the joint between the arm and forearm.
725	**calmar(se)**	**calm**
	vb	Le he dado algo para calmar sus nervios.
	[kalˈmar.se)]	-I've given her something to calm her nerves.
726	**experiencia**	**experience**

f
[ɛks.pɛ.ˈrjɛ̃n.sja]

Esa podría ser la experiencia más dolorosa de mi vida.
-That might be the most painful experience in my life.

727 esperanza

f
[ɛs.pɛ.ˈrãn.sa]

hope

La gente confunde el optimismo con la esperanza, y hay una diferencia.
-People confuse optimism and hope, and there is a difference.

728 casar

vb
[ka.ˈsar]

marry

Jim no se va a casar contigo.
-Jim isn't going to marry you.

729 drogar(se)

vb
[dro.ˈɣar.se)]

drug

Los servicios de emergencia tuvieron que drogar al gato para soltarlo.
-E.M.T.s had to drug the cat to get him to let go.

730 espíritu

m
[ɛs.ˈpi.ri.tu]

spirit

Ojalá fuera más un espíritu libre como tú.
-I wish I was more of a free spirit like you.

731 vacaciones

fpl
[ba.ka.ˈsjo.nes]

vacation

Deberías tomarte unas vacaciones cuando todo esto termine.
-You should take a vacation when all this is finished.

732 copa

f
[ˈko.pa]

cup

Llevan ganando la copa cuatro años consecutivos.
-They have been winning the cup for four consecutive years.

733 investigación

f
[ĩm.bɛs.ti.ɣa.ˈsjõn]

research

Él ha descuidado su investigación últimamente.
-He is neglecting his research these days.

734 preferir

vb
[pre.fɛ.ˈrir]

prefer

No sé cómo alguien podría preferir Nueva York.
-I don't know how anyone could prefer New York City.

735 soler

vb
[so.ˈlɛr]

used to

Solía soñar con ser millonario.
-I used to dream about being a millionaire.

736 a menudo

adv
[a me.ˈnu.ðo]

often

Un lapsus a menudo ocasiona resultados inesperados.
-A slip of the tongue often brings about unexpected results.

737 partir(se)

vb; vbr
[par.ˈtir.se)]

depart; break

La bruja vio que no había ayuda que pudiera obtener de sus viejas criadas, y que lo mejor que podía hacer era montar en su escoba y partir.
-The witch saw there was no help to be got from her old servants, and that the best thing she could do was to mount on her broom and set off.

738 visita

f
[bi.ˈsi.ta]

visit, guest

La visita al circo fue muy emocionante para los niños.
-The visit to the circus was a big thrill for the children.

739 nueve

num
[ˈnwe.βe]

nine

Trabaja de nueve a cinco y media.
-He works from nine to five-thirty.

740 bomba

f
[ˈbõm.ba]

bomb, pump

Usaron una bomba para sacar el agua.
-They used a pump to take out the water.

741 energía

f
[e.nɛr.ˈxi.a]

energy

Soy una persona feliz y saludable que está llena de energía con una actitud positiva y visión de la vida.

-I'm a happy and healthy person, who is full of energy, with a positive attitude and outlook on life.

742	**bolsa**	**bag**
	f	Comprobaré esta bolsa por usted.
	[ˈbol.sa]	-I'll check this bag for you.
743	**pan**	**bread**
	m	Compré una hogaza de pan para el desayuno.
	[ˈpãn]	-I bought a loaf of bread for breakfast.
744	**piel**	**skin**
	f	Su piel comenzó a curarse ahí mismo, delante de nosotros.
	[ˈpjɛl]	-His skin was starting to heal right there, in front of us.
745	**metro**	**metro**
	m	El metro estaba tan lleno que había unas cinco personas por metro cuadrado.
	[ˈmɛ.tro]	-The subway was so full that there were around five people per square meter.
746	**perdonar**	**forgive**
	vb	Mi trabajo era escuchar y perdonar.
	[pɛr.ðo.ˈnar]	-My job was to listen and to forgive.
747	**cuello**	**neck**
	m	Estiró el cuello un poco esperando oír lo que estaban susurrando.
	[ˈkwe.jo]	-He craned his neck a bit in hopes of hearing what they were whispering.
748	**escapar(se)**	**escape**
	vb	Los niños lograron escapar por una ventana.
	[ɛs.ka.ˈpar.se)]	-The children were able to escape through a window.
749	**salvar(se)**	**save**
	vb	Solo una operación urgente puede salvar la vida del paciente.
	[sal.ˈβar.se)]	-Only an immediate operation can save the patient's life.
750	**servir**	**serve**
	vb	Cariño, están empezando a servir las ensaladas.
	[sɛr.ˈβir]	-Dear, they're starting to serve the salads.
751	**especie**	**species, kind**
	f	No sabemos nada de esta especie.
	[ɛs.ˈpe.sje]	-We don't know anything about this species.
752	**fe**	**faith**
	f	Tenía mucha fe en ese muchacho.
	[ˈfe]	-I had a lot of faith in that boy.
753	**doble**	**double; double**
	adj; adv	La justicia en este país tiene un poco de doble rasero: está la justicia del pobre y la justicia del rico.
	[ˈdo.βle]	-Justice in this country is a bit of a double standard: there is the justice of the poor and the justice of the rich.
754	**culpable**	**guilty; culprit**
	adj; m/f	Su conciencia culpable no le dejará descansar hasta que confiese lo que ha hecho.
	[kul.ˈpa.βle]	-He'll have no rest from his guilty conscience until he confesses what he's done.
755	**bosque**	**forest**
	m	Asegúrate de cubrir cada pulgada del bosque.
	[ˈbos.ke]	-Make sure you cover every inch of the forest.
756	**taxi**	**taxi**

m

['tak.si]

¿Qué es más rápido, un taxi o el metro?

-Which is quicker, a taxi or the subway?

757 volar — **fly**

vb

[bo.'lar]

El canto le es tan natural como el volar para los pájaros.

-Singing comes as naturally to her as flying does to birds.

758 de repente — **suddenly**

adv

[de re.'pɛn̪.te]

Ella de repente se sintió pequeña, despreciable y miserable.

-Suddenly she felt tiny, worthless and miserable.

759 bromear — **joke**

vb

[bro.me.'ar]

No deberías ni bromear con algo así.

-You should not even joke about stuff like that.

760 planeta — **planet**

m

[pla.'nɛ.ta]

Júpiter es el planeta más grande del sistema solar.

-Jupiter is the most massive planet in the solar system.

761 leche — **milk**

f

['le.tʃe]

Uganda produce mucha leche de vaca.

-Uganda produces a lot of milk from cows.

762 depender — **depend**

vb

[de.pɛn̪.'dɛr]

No dependas del número de personas.

-Do not depend on the number of persons.

763 común — **common; majority**

adj; m

[ko.'mũn]

Es común decir que representamos el futuro.

-It is common to say that we represent the future.

764 informe — **report**

m

[ĩm̩.'for.me]

Él podrá entregar su informe mañana.

-He will be able to hand in his report tomorrow.

765 máquina — **machine**

f

['ma.ki.na]

Me explicó cómo operar la máquina.

-He explained to me how to use the machine.

766 principal — **main**

adj

[prĩn.si.'pal]

La válvula principal está cerrada.

-The main valve is turned off.

767 ridículo — **ridiculous; embarrassment**

adj; m

[ri.'ði.ku.lo]

Permítanme decir que es ridículo sostener esto.

-May I say that it is ridiculous to uphold this.

768 entrada — **entry**

f

[ɛn̪.'tra.ða]

Quiero que vayáis hacia esa entrada.

-I want you to head toward that entrance.

769 príncipe — **prince**

m

['prĩn.si.pe]

Tendré que escucharlo del propio príncipe.

-I will have to hear that from the prince himself.

770 preparar(se) — **prepare**

vb

[pre.pa.'rar.se)]

Es una buena idea preparar diferentes opciones para elegir.

-It is a good idea to prepare several different options to choose from.

771 propósito — **purpose**

m

[pro.'po.si.to]

Tim no parecía comprender el propósito del proyecto.

-Tim didn't seem to understand the purpose of the project.

772 cliente — **customer, client**

	m/f	
	['kljɛ̃n.te]	Mi cliente no va a decir una palabra más. -My client isn't saying another word.
773	**árbol**	**tree**
	m	
	['ar.βol]	Es placentero dormir bajo el árbol. -It is pleasant to sleep under the tree.
774	**absoluto**	**absolute**
	adj	
	[aβ.so.'lu.to]	Es un privilegio absoluto estar aquí. -It's an absolute privilege to be here.
775	**belleza**	**beauty**
	f	
	[be.'je.sa]	En Japón, estás rodeado de belleza. -In Japan, you are surrounded by beauty.
776	**intentar**	**try**
	vb	
	[ĩn.tẽn.'tar]	Estuve a punto de ahogarme al intentar rescatar a un chico. -I came near being drowned, trying to rescue a boy.
777	**vuestro**	**your; yours**
	adj; prn	
	['bwɛs.tro]	¿Hay algún plato vegano en vuestro menú? -Is there a vegan dish on your menu?
778	**oeste**	**west**
	m	
	[o.'ɛs.te]	Numerosos hombres partieron hacia el oeste en busca de oro. -Many men set out for the west in search of gold.
779	**Francia**	**France**
	f	
	['frãn.sja]	Este problema no afecta únicamente a Francia. -This issue is not only a concern in France.
780	**deprisa**	**quickly; hurry**
	adv; int	
	[de.'pri.sa]	Los países en desarrollo se recuperaron deprisa de la crisis. -Developing countries recovered quickly from the crisis.
781	**tiro**	**shot**
	m	
	['ti.ro]	Esta parece una herida de tiro a quemarropa. -This looks like a close-range gunshot wound.
782	**cerdo**	**pig**
	m	
	['sɛr.ðo]	El hechizo se rompió y el cerdo se transformó en un hombre. -The spell was broken and the pig turned into a man.
783	**gato**	**cat**
	m	
	['ga.to]	Ella tiene un gato. El gato es blanco. -She has a cat. The cat is white.
784	**vistazo**	**glance**
	m	
	[bis.'ta.so]	Queríamos echarle un vistazo en persona. -We wanted to get a glimpse of her in person.
785	**defensa**	**defense**
	f	
	[de.'fẽn.sa]	Jim asegura que disparó a Ana en defensa propia. -Jim claims he shot Ana in self-defense.
786	**reloj**	**clock**
	m	
	[re.'lox]	Nos encantaría regalarte este encantador reloj como regalo. -We'd love to give you this lovely watch as a gift.
787	**batalla**	**battle**
	f	
	[ba.'ta.ja]	Dieciocho minutos después, la batalla había terminado. -Eighteen minutes later, the battle was over.
788	**caminar**	**walk**

vb
[ka.mi.ˈnar]
Jim le dijo a Ana que no debería caminar sola al anochecer.
-Jim told Ana that she shouldn't walk alone after dark.

789 **interior**
adj; m
[ĩn̪.tɛ.ˈrjor]
interior; the inside
El interior está decorado con elegancia.
-The interior is elegantly decorated.

790 **bello**
adj
[ˈbe.ʝo]
beautiful
El duraznero es bello cuando florece.
-The peach tree is beautiful when in flower.

791 **apartamento**
m
[a.par.ta.ˈmẽn̪.to]
apartment
Podrías meter todo el apartamento aquí.
-You could fit in the whole flat in here.

792 **teatro**
m
[te.ˈa.tro]
theater
Ese teatro realiza un festival de películas extranjeras cada dos meses.
-That theater has a foreign film festival every other month.

793 **confiar**
vb
[kõɱ.ˈfjar]
trust
¿Por qué deberíamos confiar en ti?
-Why should we trust you?

794 **hielo**
m
[ˈɟʝe.lo]
ice
Las estelas de condensación son nubes largas y estrechas de cristales de hielo que se forman tras los aviones a propulsión a gran altitud a temperaturas bajo cero.
-Contrails are long, narrow, ice-crystal clouds that form behind jet planes flying at high altitudes in below-freezing temperatures.

795 **detective**
m
[dɛ.tek̚.ˈti.βe]
detective
Ella contrató a un detective privado.
-She hired a private investigator.

796 **cantar**
vb
[kãn̪.ˈtar]
sing
Empezó a cantar profesionalmente cuando tenía 16 años.
-He started to sing seriously when he was 16 years old.

797 **bajar(se)**
vb
[ba.ˈxar.se)]
lower
Tenemos que bajar su temperatura interna.
-We've got to lower her core temperature.

798 **pelear(se)**
vb
[pe.le.ˈar.se)]
fight
Solo quiere otra excusa para pelear.
-You just want another excuse to fight.

799 **lucha**
f
[ˈlu.ʧa]
fight
Los médicos han hecho grandes avances en su lucha contra el cáncer.
-Doctors have made great strides in their fight against cancer.

800 **borracho**
adj; m
[bo.ˈra.ʧo]
drunk; drunk
Jim vio a un borracho tirado en la calle.
-Jim noticed a drunkard lying in the street.

801 **héroe**
m
[ˈɛ.ro.e]
hero
Todos mis personajes tienen algo del arquetipo de héroe en ellos, que son tremendamente despojados de contexto.
-My characters all have something of the hero archetype about them, in that they are largely stripped of context.

802 **camión**
m
[ka.ˈmjõn]
truck
Este camión transporta alimentos frescos de Aomori a Tokio.
-This truck transports fresh food from Aomori to Tokyo.

803 **cabo**
ending, corporal

m
['ka.βo]
Voy a ascenderle a cabo de este regimiento.
-I'm going to appoint him a corporal in this regiment.

804 diente — **tooth**

m
['djẽn̪.te]
Ella ni siquiera tiene su primer diente.
-She hasn't even got her first tooth.

805 verde — **green**

adj
['bɛr.ðe]
Opté por verde para las cortinas.
-I have settled on green for the curtains.

806 despacio — **slowly**

adv
[dɛs.'pa.sjo]
Prometo hablar despacio y pausadamente.
-I promise to speak slowly and unhurriedly.

807 decidir(se) — **decide**

vb
[de.si.'ðir.se)]
Jim no podía decidir por quién debería votar.
-Jim was unable to decide who he should vote for.

808 sociedad — **society**

f
[so.sje.'ðað]
Me interesa la página de sociedad de ese periódico.
-I'm interested in the society page of that newspaper.

809 pareja — **couple**

f
[pa.'re.xa]
Esta pareja tiene un humor tan seco que dicen montones de chistes seguidos sin dejar salir la más mínima risa.
-This couple approaches humor so dryly that enormous chains of jokes will blossom without an iota of laughter.

810 nariz — **nose**

f
['na.ris]
La nariz del niño está sangrando.
-The child's nose is bleeding.

811 vergüenza — **shame**

f
[bɛr.'ɣwẽn.sa]
E incluso sentí vergüenza por eso.
-And I even felt a sense of shame because of that.

812 caer(se) — **fall**

vb
[ka.'ɛr.se)]
Las hojas amarillas como esta normalmente se caen antes de la cosecha.
-Yellow leaves like this usually fall off before harvest.

813 herir(se) — **hurt**

vb
[ɛ.'rir.se)]
No fue mi intención herir tus sentimientos.
-It was not my intention to hurt your feelings.

814 pista — **clue, track**

f
['pis.ta]
Para el astuto, una pista es suficiente.
-For the intelligent, a hint is sufficient.

815 sonido — **sound**

m
[so.'ni.ðo]
Esto es útil para sistemas en los que el sonido cause problemas.
-This is useful for systems where sound support causes problems.

816 sombrero — **hat**

m
[sõm.'bre.ro]
Él sacó un conejo de su sombrero con magia.
-He produced a rabbit out of his hat by magic.

817 evitar — **avoid**

vb
[e.βi.'tar]
No puedo evitar sospechar que está mintiendo.
-I can't help suspecting that he is lying.

818 memoria — **memory**

f
[me.'mo.rja]
La dama tiene mejor memoria que usted.
-The lady has a better memory than you have.

819 llorar — **cry**

| | vb | El niño puede llorar o gemir. |
| | [ʎo.ˈrar] | -The child may cry or moan. |

820 **nervioso** — **nervous**
adj
[nɛr.ˈβjo.so]
Estaba muy nervioso cuando despegó el avión.
-I was very nervous as the plane took off.

821 **lástima** — **shame, pity**
f
[ˈlas.ti.ma]
Jim no quiere la lástima de Ana.
-Jim doesn't want Ana's pity.

822 **época** — **era, time**
f
[ˈe.po.ka]
El clima es incierto en esta época del año.
-The weather is uncertain at this time of year.

823 **naturaleza** — **nature**
f
[na.tu.ra.ˈle.sa]
La matemática ciertamente no existiría si desde el principio se supiera que en la naturaleza no hay recta exacta, círculo perfecto o magnitud absoluta.
-Mathematics would certainly not have come into existence if one had known from the beginning that there was in nature no exactly straight line, no actual circle, no absolute magnitude.

824 **vender** — **sell**
vb
[bẽn̪.ˈdɛr]
Lo recuerdo porque va contra la ley vender género embotellado.
-I remember that because it's against the law to sell bottled goods.

825 **política** — **policy, politics**
f
[po.ˈli.ti.ka]
La política del Gobierno fue criticada por la oposición.
-The policy of the government was criticized by the opposition party.

826 **levantar(se)** — **lift; wake up**
vb; vbr
[le.βãn̪.ˈtar.se)]
Contratamos una grúa para levantar el nuevo aire acondicionado y ponerlo en el tejado.
-We hired a crane to lift the new air conditioner and place it on the roof.

827 **brillante** — **shiny, bright**
adj
[bri.ˈjãn̪.te]
Con una noche tan apaciguada y brillante como esta, siempre me dan ganas de dar un paseo a medianoche.
-With a mild, bright night like today, I always feel like going for a stroll at midnight.

828 **nivel** — **level**
m
[ni.ˈβɛl]
El agua hierve a los 100 grados Celsius a nivel del mar.
-Water boils at 100 degrees Celsius at sea level.

829 **permitir(se)** — **allow; afford**
vb; vbr
[pɛr.mi.ˈtir.se)]
No deberías permitir que tu hijo se comporte como un mocoso engreído.
-You shouldn't allow your son to act like a selfish brat.

830 **justicia** — **justice**
f
[xus.ˈti.sja]
Sin justicia no habrá paz.
-Without justice, there will be no peace.

831 **enorme** — **huge**
adj
[e.ˈnor.me]
Visto desde el cielo, el río parecía una enorme serpiente.
-Seen from the sky, the river looked like a huge snake.

832 **charlar** — **chat**
vb
[tʃar.ˈlar]
Me gustaría charlar contigo por e-mail.
-I would like to chat with you by e-mail.

833 **inocente** — **naive; innocent**
adj; m/f
[i.no.ˈsẽn̪.te]
Es muy inocente esperar algo diferente.
-It's a little naive to expect anything different.

834	**pantalón**	**pants**
	m	Se está apretando el cinturón del pantalón.
	[pãn̪.ˈta.lõn]	-He is tightening his trouser belt.

835	**ministro**	**minister**
	m	El primer ministro dará una conferencia de prensa mañana.
	[mi.ˈnis.tro]	-The prime minister will hold a press conference tomorrow.

836	**referir(se)**	**refer**
	vb	O te puedo referir a un especialista.
	[re.fɛ.ˈrir.se)]	-Or I can refer you to a specialist.

837	**mando**	**authority, control**
	m	Estuvo seis años bajo tu mando.
	[ˈmãn̪.do]	-He was under your command for six years.

838	**precioso**	**beautiful**
	adj	Erica, yo… creo que es precioso.
	[pre.ˈsjo.so]	-Erica I... I think that's beautiful.

839	**pesar(se)**	**weigh**
	vb	El paquete no deberá pesar más de 75 kg.
	[pe.ˈsar.se)]	-The package shall not weigh more than 75 kg.

840	**pesar**	**regret**
	m	Esto es motivo tanto de pesar como de frustración.
	[pe.ˈsar]	-This is a matter of both regret and frustration.

841	**a pesar de**	**despite**
	prp	Estos accidentes se han producido a pesar de la legislación en vigor.
	[a pe.ˈsar ðe]	-These accidents have taken place in spite of the legislation currently in force.

842	**extrañar(se)**	**surprise, miss**
	vb	No puedo evitar extrañar cosas.
	[ɛks.tra.ˈɲar.se)]	-I can't help but miss things.

843	**enamorar(se)**	**make someone fall in love**
	vb	Jeff piensa que nunca se va a enamorar.
	[e.na.mo.ˈrar.se)]	-Jeff thinks he will never fall in love.

844	**autobús**	**bus**
	m	El Parlamento Europeo está a punto de diseñar el autobús perfecto.
	[au̯.to.ˈβus]	-The European Parliament is about to design the perfect bus.

845	**recordar**	**remember**
	vb	Estoy intentando recordar todos los aniversarios.
	[re.kor.ˈðar]	-I'm making it a point to remember all the anniversaries.

846	**luchar**	**fight**
	vb	Estamos decididos a luchar por estos compromisos.
	[lu.ˈʧar]	-For those commitments, we are determined to fight.

847	**datar**	**date back to**
	vb	Es conveniente datar los artículos al almacenarlos en el congelador.
	[da.ˈtar]	-It is convenient to date the items upon storing in the freezer.

848	**contrario**	**contrary; foe**
	adj; m/f	Dejad que os de un ejemplo del caso contrario.
	[kõn̪.ˈtra.rjo]	-Let me give you an example of the opposite.

849	**movimiento**	**movement**
	m	No deberían limitar el movimiento, sino fomentarlo.
	[mo.βi.ˈmjẽn̪.to]	-You should not be restricting movement, but encouraging it.

850	**sentado**	**sitting**

adj
[sẽɲˈta.ðo]

Me quedaré aquí sentado mientras él canta.
-I'll be sitting here while he's singing.

851 motivo

m; adj
[mo.ˈti.βo]

reason; motive

No tiene motivo para quedarse más aquí.
-There's no reason for you to stay any longer.

852 puente

m
[ˈpwẽɲ.te]

bridge

Este es un puente que, insisto, no deberíamos quemar.
-This is a bridge which, I urge you, we must not burn.

853 comprender

vb
[kõm.prẽɲˈdɛr]

understand

Todos estamos intentando comprender las aspiraciones de nuestros jóvenes.
-We are all trying to understand the aspirations of our young people.

854 huevo

m
[ˈwe.βo]

egg

Ahora devolvamos ese huevo y salgamos de aquí.
-Now let's put this egg back and get out of here.

855 botella

f
[bo.ˈte.ja]

bottle

Celebraron su éxito abriendo una botella de vino.
-They celebrated his success by opening a bottle of wine.

856 costar

vb
[kos.ˈtar]

cost

Debe costar una fortuna mantenerlo.
-Must cost a fortune to keep it up.

857 confianza

f
[kõɱ.ˈfjãn.sa]

confidence, trust

Ahora es muy urgente recuperar la confianza.
-Now there is an urgent need for rebuilding confidence.

858 felicidad

f
[fe.li.si.ˈðað]

happiness

La felicidad no consiste en cuánto posees.
-Happiness does not consist of how much you possess.

859 espada

f
[ɛs.ˈpa.ða]

sword

Podrías cortar la tensión con una espada.
-You could cut the tension with a sword.

860 silla

f
[ˈsi.ja]

chair

Tienes que quitar esa silla del edificio.
-You need to remove that chair from the building.

861 noticia

f
[no.ˈti.sja]

news

Permítaseme transmitir también una noticia muy triste esta noche.
-May I also convey some very sad news this evening.

862 televisión

f
[te.le.βi.ˈsjõn]

television

No tuvimos la oportunidad de ver la televisión danesa.
-We did not have the opportunity to watch Danish television.

863 acordar(se)

vb; vbr
[a.kor.ˈðar.se)]

agree to; remember

Necesitamos acordar el lugar para la foto.
-We need to agree on the place of the photo shot.

864 pared

f
[pa.ˈrɛð]

wall

También puede instalarse en una pared.
-It can also be mounted on a wall.

865 prensa

f
[ˈprẽn.sa]

press

No quiero más artículos de prensa.
-I don't want any more newspaper articles.

866 trampa

trap

f
['trãm.pa]

Está desesperado por ponerte una trampa.
-He's desperate to set a trap for you.

867 **presente**

present; current

adj; m
[pre.ˈsɛ̃n̪.te]

Tuvimos que esperar a que estuviera presente.
-We had to wait for him to be present.

868 **jardín**

garden

m
[xar.ˈðĩn]

Hay muchos manzanos en el jardín.
-There are many apple trees in the garden.

869 **cabello**

hair

m
[ka.ˈβe.ʝo]

Estoy pensando en dejarme crecer el cabello.
-I'm thinking about letting my hair grow.

870 **espectáculo**

show

m
[ɛs.pekˈ.ta.ku.lo]

El espectáculo resultó ser tan decepcionante como decían.
-The show turned out to be just as disappointing as they said.

871 **grave**

grave

adj
[ˈgra.βe]

Tenemos un problema financiero muy grave.
-We have a serious financial problem.

872 **periódico**

newspaper; periodical

m; adj
[pɛˈrjo.ði.ko]

Llevo 4 años trabajando para este periódico.
-I have been working for this newspaper for 4 years.

873 **anillo**

ring

m
[a.ˈni.ʝo]

Tiene un anillo de valor incalculable.
-She has a ring whose value is beyond belief.

874 **monstruo**

monster

m
[ˈmõns.trwo]

No debemos alimentar al monstruo que nos amenaza con la destrucción.
-We must not feed the monster which threatens us with destruction.

875 **total**

complete; whole; in the end (coll)

adj; m; adv
[to.ˈtal]

Todavía tengo control total de la operación.
-I'm still in complete control of the operation.

876 **piedra**

stone

f
[ˈpje.ðra]

Era importante recordar que nada estaba escrito en piedra.
-It was important to remember that nothing was written in stone.

877 **contento**

happy; happiness

adj; m
[kõn̪.ˈtɛ̃n̪.to]

Estaré muy contento de aceptar tu invitación.
-I will be very happy to accept your invitation.

878 **contrato**

contract

m
[kõn̪.ˈtra.to]

El contrato indica cuánto tenemos que pagar.
-The contract states how much we have to pay.

879 **playa**

beach

f
[ˈpla.ʝa]

No sabía dónde estaba la playa.
-I did not know where the beach was.

880 **costa**

coast

f
[ˈkos.ta]

Liberia tiene 579 km de costa.
-Liberia has a coast line of 579 kilometers.

881 **asiento**

seat

m
[a.ˈsjɛ̃n̪.to]

No quieres renunciar al asiento del conductor.
-You don't want to give up the driver's seat.

882 **tarjeta**

card

	f	
	[tar.ˈxɛ.ta]	

Tienes que asegurarte de que se les muestra la tarjeta roja.
-You have to ensure that they are shown the red card.

883 restaurante — restaurant

m

[rɛs.tau̯.ˈrãn̪.te]

Siempre que tenemos invitados los llevamos a este restaurante.
-When we have guests, we always take them to this restaurant.

884 paseo — walk

m

[pa.ˈse.o]

Me prometiste que íbamos a dar un paseo.
-You promised me we were going for a ride.

885 domingo — Sunday

m

[do.ˈmĩŋ.go]

Cada domingo cuenta la misma historia.
-Every Sunday, she tells the same story.

886 velocidad — speed

f

[be.lo.si.ˈðað]

Jim, voy a subir un poco la velocidad.
-Jim, I'm increasing the speed a little.

887 proyecto — project

m

[pro.ˈjek̚.to]

Espero que este proyecto tenga éxito.
-I hope that this project will be a success.

888 operación — operation

f

[o.pɛ.ra.ˈsjõn]

Esperamos que dicha operación se pueda repetir.
-We hope that such an operation can be repeated.

889 imagen — image

f

[i.ˈma.xẽn]

Esperaba que pudiesen restaurar la imagen.
-I'd hoped that you'd be able to restore the image.

890 responsable — responsible; person responsible

adj; m/f

[rɛs.põn.ˈsa.βle]

Tengo que tener cuidado y comportarme de forma responsable.
-I have to be careful to behave in a responsible way.

891 aspecto — aspect

m

[as.ˈpek̚.to]

Éste es el primer aspecto que deseaba destacar.
-This is the first point that I wanted to emphasize.

892 sentimiento — feeling

m

[sẽn̪.ti.ˈmjẽn̪.to]

Queremos explicar brevemente las razones de este sentimiento.
-We wish to explain briefly the reasons for this feeling.

893 objetivo — impartial; objective

adj; m

[oβ.xɛ.ˈti.βo]

Esperamos que las autoridades logren ese objetivo.
-We look to the authorities to achieve that objective.

894 dormido — asleep

adj

[dor.ˈmi.ðo]

Él estaba profundamente dormido cuando estalló el fuego.
-When the fire broke out, he was sound asleep.

895 historial — history

m

[is.to.ˈrjal]

Su historial ha sido impecable hasta ahora.
-Your record has been impeccable until now.

896 arreglar(se) — repair; get ready

vb; vbr

[a.re.ˈɣlar.se)]

Ayer pasé dos horas intentando arreglar esa radio rota.
-I spent two hours yesterday trying to fix that broken radio.

897 turno — turn

m

[ˈtur.no]

Ahora es nuestro turno para empezar a crear.
-Now it's our turn to start creating.

898 montaña — mountain

	f	Es peligroso escalar una montaña con mal tiempo.
	[mõn̪.ˈta.ɲa]	-It's dangerous to climb a mountain in bad weather.
899	**enfermedad**	**disease**
	f	Primero debemos determinar cuánto se ha extendido su enfermedad.
	[ẽɱ.fɛr.me.ˈðað]	-First, we have to determine how far her sickness has spread.
900	**dedo**	**finger**
	m	Ella gira la pelota en su dedo.
	[ˈde.ðo]	-She spins the ball on her finger.
901	**guapo**	**good-looking**
	adj	Podría ser muy guapo si él quisiera.
	[ˈgwa.po]	-He could be quite good-looking if he wanted to.
902	**viernes**	**Friday**
	m	El viernes recibimos la trágica noticia.
	[ˈbjɛr.nes]	-On Friday we received the very tragic news.
903	**preocupado**	**worried**
	adj	Estoy algo preocupado por este desnivel.
	[pre.o.ku.ˈpa.ðo]	-I'm concerned with the bump here.
904	**rayo**	**ray**
	m	Se supone que estás construyendo un rayo congelador.
	[ˈra.ɟo]	-You're supposed to be building a freeze ray.
905	**Majestad**	**Majesty**
	m/f	Estamos cuidando de él, Majestad.
	[ma.xɛs.ˈtað]	-We are taking care of him, Majesty.
906	**inútil**	**useless; good-for-nothing**
	adj; m/f	Es inútil que actuemos únicamente en Europa.
	[i.ˈnu.til]	-It is useless to take action only in Europe.
907	**abierto**	**open**
	adj	Mi vida es un libro abierto. Nunca he hecho nada malo.
	[a.ˈβjɛr.to]	-My life is an open book. I've never done anything wrong.
908	**oscuridad**	**darkness**
	f	Siempre hay más batallas que luchar contra la oscuridad.
	[os.ku.ri.ˈðað]	-There are always new battles to be fought against the darkness.
909	**americano**	**American; American person**
	adj; m	Recuerdo ir con mi padre al consulado americano.
	[a.mɛ.ri.ˈka.no]	-I remember going with my father to the American consulate.
910	**primo**	**cousin; prime**
	m; adj	El dos es el único número primo cuyo sucesor es primo.
	[ˈpri.mo]	-Two is the only prime whose successor is prime.
911	**nacional**	**national**
	adj	Me pregunto cómo podría un gobierno medir la felicidad nacional bruta.
	[na.sjo.ˈnal]	-I wonder how a government would go about measuring gross national happiness.
912	**colegio**	**school**
	m	Nuestro colegio nos prohíbe ir al cine solos.
	[ko.ˈle.xjo]	-Our school prohibits us from going to the movies alone.
913	**cuchillo**	**knife**
	m	Jim siguió a Ana hasta la cocina, tomó un cuchillo y la amenazó con él.
	[ku.ˈʧi.jo]	-Jim followed Ana into the kitchen, picked up a knife and threatened her with it.
914	**diario**	**daily; diary, newspaper**

adj; m
['dja.rjo]

Alimente al perro a diario, por favor.
-Please, feed the dog every day.

915 francés

adj; m
[frãn.'ses]

French; French person

¿Cómo has aprendido a hablar francés tan bien?
-How did you learn to speak French so well?

916 orgulloso

adj
[or.ɣu.'jo.so]

proud

Está orgulloso de ser un médico.
-He is proud of being a doctor.

917 ladrón

m
[la.'ðrõn]

thief

Una pequeña mujer mayor frustró el atraco al aporrear al ladrón en la cabeza con su bastón.
-A little, old woman foiled the robbery by whacking the thief on the head with her cane.

918 central

adj; f
[sẽn.'tral]

central; headquarters

El tema central de la conferencia es la innovación.
-The central topic of the conference is innovation.

919 voluntad

f
[bo.lũn.'tað]

will

Es cuestión de deseo y voluntad.
-It's a question of desire and will.

920 militar

adj; m/f
[mi.li.'tar]

military; soldier

¿Conoces el nombre del militar más exitoso de esta región?
-Do you know the name of the most successful military man from this area?

921 agradecer

vb
[a.ɣra.ðe.'sɛr]

thank

Quisiera agradecer las contribuciones de todos esta mañana.
-I would like to thank all of you for your contributions this morning.

922 lluvia

f
['ʝu.βja]

rain

El deterioro del templo se debe, en parte, a la lluvia ácida.
-The decay of the shrine is due, in part, to acid rain.

923 natural

adj
[na.tu.'ral]

natural

El arte de enseñar no es más que el arte de despertar la curiosidad natural en las mentes jóvenes para más tarde satisfacerla.
-The art of teaching is only the art of awakening the natural curiosity of young minds to satisfy it afterward.

924 gusto

m
['gus.to]

taste

Tienes el mejor gusto en zapatos.
-You have got the greatest taste in shoes.

925 lengua

f
['lẽŋ.gwa]

language, tongue

Los perros controlan su temperatura jadeando con la lengua fuera.
-A dog controls its temperature by panting with its tongue out.

926 chino

adj; m
['tʃi.no]

Chinese; Chinese person

Es difícil encontrar a alguien que escriba en chino tan bonito como él.
-It's hard to find someone who writes Chinese as beautifully as he.

927 testigo

m/f
[tɛs.'ti.ɣo]

witness

Nadie estaba dispuesto a comparecer como testigo del incidente.
-Nobody was willing to appear as a witness to the incident.

928 cansado

adj
[kãn.'sa.ðo]

tired

Estoy cansado de ver la televisión.
-I'm tired of watching television.

929 alemán

German; German person

	adj; m	El alemán es llamado a veces la lengua de Goethe.
	[a.le.ˈmãn]	-German is sometimes called Goethe's language.
930	**pago**	**payment**
	m	Siempre pago mis deudas, tengo principios.
	[ˈpa.ɣo]	-I always pay my debts, I have principles.
931	**mirada**	**look**
	f	Por favor, déjame echar una mirada al menú.
	[mi.ˈra.ða]	-Please let me take a look at the menu.
932	**quieto**	**still**
	adj	Ana, vamos a comenzar, intenta estarte quieta.
	[ˈkjɛ.to]	-Ana, we're going to get started, so try to lie still.
933	**descansar**	**rest**
	vb	Mary espera descansar mucho durante sus vacaciones.
	[dɛs.kãn.ˈsar]	-Mary hopes to rest a lot during her vacation.
934	**mercado**	**market**
	m	Cultivan alimentos para el mercado donde venden sus excedentes.
	[mɛr.ˈka.ðo]	-They grow food crops for the market where they sell their surplus produce.
935	**humor**	**mood, humor**
	m	Jim está de mal humor hoy.
	[u.ˈmor]	-Jim is in a foul mood today.
936	**entero**	**entire**
	adj	La esperanza es una vocecita que susurra "tal vez" cuando parece que el
	[ɛ̃n̪.ˈtɛ.ro]	mundo entero está gritando "¡no!"
		-Hope is a little voice whispering "maybe" when it seems the entire world is shouting "no"!
937	**dueño**	**owner**
	m	Él es el dueño de la compañía.
	[ˈdwe.ɲo]	-He's the owner of the company.
938	**echar(se)**	**kick, pour; lie down**
	vb; vbr	Creo que nos van a echar de aquí pronto.
	[e.ˈtʃar.se]]	-I think they're going to kick us out soon.
939	**emergencia**	**emergency**
	f	Damas y caballeros, tenemos una emergencia.
	[e.mɛr.ˈxɛ̃n.sja]	-Ladies and gentlemen, we have an emergency.
940	**romper(se)**	**break**
	vb	Debemos romper el ciclo de violencia.
	[rõm.ˈpɛr.se]]	-We need to break the cycle of violence.
941	**actuar**	**act**
	vb	Para hacer eso, debemos actuar juntos.
	[ak̚.ˈtwar]	-To do that, we have to act together.
942	**inmediato**	**immediate**
	adj	Usted debe desterrar de inmediato todos los sentimientos de culpa.
	[ĩm.me.ˈðja.to]	-You must immediately banish all feelings of guilt.
943	**paciente**	**patient; patient**
	adj; m/f	El paciente no tiene pulso.
	[pa.ˈsjɛ̃n̪.te]	-The patient has no pulse.
944	**varios**	**several**
	adj	Una persona puede tener varios lugares de residencia.
	[ˈba.rjos]	-A person may have several places of residence.
945	**polvo**	**dust, powder**

m
['pol.βo]

Para hacer este pastel se necesita polvo de hornear y mantequilla sin sal.
-In order to make this cake, you need baking powder and unsalted butter.

946 coger

vb

[ko.ˈxɛr]

take, f*ck (LA)

Esperaba coger el tren del mediodía.
-I was expecting to catch the noon train.

947 distancia

f

[dis.ˈtãn.sja]

distance

¿Alguna vez has estado en una relación de larga distancia?
-Have you ever been in a long distance relationship?

948 bravo

int

[ˈbra.βo]

bravo

A quien se le haya ocurrido el juego de palabras, bravo.
-Whoever's in charge of the wordplay, bravo.

949 Europa

f

[eu̯.ˈro.pa]

Europe

Alemania está en Europa Central.
-Germany is in Central Europe.

950 recuerdo

m

[re.ˈkwɛr.ðo]

memory, souvenir

No cambiaría ese recuerdo por nada.
-I wouldn't trade that memory for anything.

951 toque

m

[ˈto.ke]

touch

Es agradable tener ese pequeño toque diferente.
-It's nice to have that little different touch.

952 ángel

m

[ˈãŋ.xɛl]

angel

Soñé que un ángel bajaba del cielo.
-I dreamed that an angel was coming down from the sky.

953 amamantar

vb

[a.ma.mãn̪.ˈtar]

breastfeed

Tengo que comer algo antes de amamantar al bebé.
-I should eat something before I nurse the baby.

954 carga

f

[ˈkar.ɣa]

load, burden

Muy pocos países hubieran aceptado tal carga.
-Very few countries would have accepted such a burden.

955 acto

m

[ˈak̚.to]

act

El suicidio es un acto de desesperación.
-Suicide is a desperate act.

956 robar

vb

[ro.ˈβar]

rob

A lo mejor estaba ayudando a radicales a robar un casino.
-Maybe she was helping radicals rob a casino.

957 desastre

m

[de.ˈsas.tre]

disaster

La inundación ocasionó un desastre en su comunidad.
-The flood caused a disaster in their community.

958 bote

m

[ˈbo.te]

boat, pot

Tenemos que subirte a un bote.
-We have got to get you into a boat.

959 oler(se)

vb

[o.ˈlɛr.se]]

smell

Las flores bonitas no tienen que oler necesariamente bien.
-Pretty flowers do not necessarily smell sweet.

960 embarazar

vb

[ẽm.ba.ra.ˈsar]

get pregnant

Todavía podría quedarme embarazada.
-I could still get pregnant.

961 mostrar(se)

show

	vb	
	[mos.ˈtrar.se)]	Deberían mostrar que están dispuestos a aprender. -They should show that they are willing to learn.
962	**gracia**	**grace**
	f	
	[ˈɡra.sja]	Quiero morir en estado de gracia. -I want to die in a state of grace.
963	**gordo**	**fat**
	adj	
	[ˈɡor.ðo]	No estaba gordo cuando nos casamos. -He wasn't fat when we got married.
964	**valiente**	**courageous; brave person**
	adj; m/f	
	[ba.ˈljẽn̪.te]	Este ha sido un valiente paso adelante. -This was a courageous step forward.
965	**gloria**	**glory**
	f	
	[ˈɡlo.rja]	Pero no pasaron mucho tiempo reviviendo sus días de gloria. -But they didn't spend a lot of time reliving the glory days.
966	**aceptar(se)**	**accept**
	vb	
	[a.sep̚.ˈtar.se)]	Cuando era pequeño, pensaba que si moría el mundo simplemente desaparecería. ¡Qué ilusión infantil! Es solo que no podía aceptar que el mundo pudiera seguir existiendo sin mí. -When I was a kid, I thought that if I died the world would just disappear. What a childish delusion! I just couldn't accept that the world could continue to exist without me.
967	**oscuro**	**dark**
	adj	
	[os.ˈku.ro]	Me levanté cuando todavía estaba oscuro. -I got up while it was still dark.
968	**cuidar(se)**	**look after**
	vb	
	[kwi.ˈðar.se)]	Hay gente capacitada para cuidar de estos chicos. -There are people trained to look after those kids.
969	**rogar**	**beg**
	vb	
	[ro.ˈɣar]	No quiero rogar, pero te lo pido como amigo. -I don't want to beg, but I'm asking you as a friend.
970	**tumba**	**tomb**
	f	
	[ˈtũm.ba]	Jim colocó las flores en la tumba de Ana. -Jim placed the flowers on Ana's grave.
971	**resultar**	**result**
	vb	
	[re.sul̪.ˈtar]	Podría resultar interesante rastrear esas apuestas. -It might prove interesting to trace those bets.
972	**comenzar**	**start**
	vb	
	[ko.mẽn.ˈsar]	Un error que cometen a menudo los jóvenes es el de comenzar a aprender demasiadas lenguas al mismo tiempo, porque subestiman sus dificultades y sobrestiman sus propias capacidades para aprenderlas. -A mistake young people often make is to start learning too many languages at the same time, as they underestimate the difficulties and overestimate their own ability to learn them.
973	**director**	**director**
	m	
	[di.rek̚.ˈtor]	Nuestro director está gestionando una autorización. -Our director is working on a clearance.
974	**área**	**area**
	m	
	[ˈa.re.a]	En este área está prohibido cazar. -Hunting is prohibited in this area.
975	**metido**	**inside, nosy (LA); meddler (LA)**

adj; m
[mɛ.ˈti.ðo]

Hay un tipo aquí metido.
-There's a guy inside here.

976 limpio

adj
[ˈlĩm.pjo]

clean

Tengo algo para limpiar las paredes.
-I have something to clean the walls.

977 descanso

m
[dɛs.ˈkãn.so]

rest

Además de a un descanso semanal, los trabajadores tienen derecho a vacaciones pagadas.
-In addition to a weekly rest, an employed person is entitled to a paid vacation.

978 posibilidad

f
[po.si.βi.li.ˈðað]

possibility

No podemos descartar la posibilidad de un accidente.
-We cannot rule out the possibility of an accident.

979 uso

m
[ˈu.so]

use

No uso palabras duras sin motivo.
-I don't use harsh words without reason.

980 talento

m
[ta.ˈlẽn.to]

talent

El autor revela un gran talento en la creación de sus personajes.
-The author shows a great talent in the creation of his characters.

981 continuar

vb
[kõn.ti.ˈnwar]

continue

No tiene sentido continuar con las negociaciones.
-It is meaningless to continue with the negotiations.

982 código

m
[ˈko.ði.ɣo]

code

Cada código pertenece a una sola categoría.
-Each code belongs to one and only one category.

983 definitivo

adj
[de.fi.ni.ˈti.βo]

definitive

Nada definitivo en la causa de la muerte.
-Nothing definitive on the cause of death.

984 directo

adj
[di.ˈrek̚.to]

direct

Pensé que irías directo al trabajo.
-I thought you were going straight to work.

985 parque

m
[ˈpar.ke]

park

Hay muchos animales en el parque.
-There are lots of animals in the park.

986 cinta

f
[ˈsĩn.ta]

ribbon, tape

Hicimos esta billetera juntos con cinta aislante.
-We made this wallet together out of duct tape.

987 mover(se)

vb
[mo.ˈβɛr.se]]

move

Jim y Ana no podían mover el pesado tronco.
-Jim and Ana couldn't move the heavy trunk.

988 disparar(se)

vb
[dis.pa.ˈrar.se]]

shoot

Esto te permitirá disparar muchas flechas sin cansarte.
-This will enable you to shoot lots of arrows without growing tired.

989 ja

int
[ˈxa]

ha

Estoy aquí porque tú me has invitado, ja.
-I'm here because you invited me, ha.

990 empresa

f
[ẽm.ˈpre.sa]

company

Éramos muy jóvenes cuando montamos esta empresa.
-We were very young when we started this company.

991 intención

intention

	f		No fue mi intención herir tus sentimientos.
	[ĩn̪.tẽn.ˈsjõn]		-It was not my intention to hurt your feelings.
992	**recibir**	**receive**	
	vb		Él es apto para recibir el premio.
	[re.si.ˈβir]		-He is entitled to receive the reward.
993	**abrigo**	**coat, shelter**	
	m		Por favor cuelga tu abrigo en la antesala.
	[a.ˈβri.ɣo]		-Please hang your coat in the anteroom.
994	**dar**	**give**	
	vb		Deberías darle esta tarea a alguna otra persona.
	[ˈdar]		-You should give this task to some other person.
995	**cerrado**	**closed**	
	adj		No es casualidad que todas las tiendas hayan cerrado temprano hoy.
	[sɛ.ˈra.ðo]		-Is not a coincidence that all the stores closed earlier today.
996	**imaginar(se)**	**imagine**	
	vb		No veo razón para imaginar ese resultado.
	[i.ma.xi.ˈnar.se)]		-I see no reason to imagine such an outcome.
997	**genio**	**genius, temper**	
	m		Resulta que soy un genio en ingeniería mecánica.
	[ˈxe.njo]		-I turned out to be a genius at mechanical engineering.
998	**profesional**	**professional; professional**	
	adj; m/f		Pagaría a un profesional para hacerlo.
	[pro.fe.sjo.ˈnal]		-I'd pay a professional to do it.
999	**opción**	**option**	
	f		Era importante elegir la opción correcta.
	[op.ˈsjõn]		-It was important to make the right choice.
1000	**tribunal**	**tribunal**	
	m		Al día siguiente fue llevado ante un tribunal.
	[tri.βu.ˈnal]		-The next day he was brought before a Court.
1001	**lago**	**lake**	
	m		En el lago se pueden practicar varias actividades acuáticas.
	[ˈla.ɣo]		-At the lake, you can practice a variety of water activities.
1002	**unidad**	**unit**	
	f		Tengo que regresar a mi unidad.
	[u.ni.ˈðað]		-I've got to get back to my unit.
1003	**efecto**	**effect**	
	m		El remedio tuvo un efecto inmediato.
	[e.ˈfek̚.to]		-The medicine had an immediate effect.
1004	**presión**	**pressure**	
	f		El pulso y la presión arterial del paciente están normales.
	[pre.ˈsjõn]		-The patient's pulse and blood pressure are normal.
1005	**robo**	**theft**	
	m		Supongo que intentó hacer que pareciera un robo.
	[ˈro.βo]		-I suppose he just tried to make it look like a robbery.
1006	**alcalde**	**mayor**	
	m		¿Sabes quién es el alcalde de Boston?
	[al.ˈkal̪.de]		-Do you know who the mayor of Boston is?
1007	**empleo**	**employment**	

m
[ẽm.ˈple.o]

Mi empleo no es estable, solamente trabajo por temporadas.
-My employment is not steady, only seasonal work.

1008 pollo

chicken

m
[ˈpo.ʝo]

Felicidades por esa franquicia de pollo que siempre quisiste.
-Congratulations on that chicken franchise you always wanted.

1009 wiski

whiskey

m
[ˈwis.ki]

¿Quiere wiski puro o lo mezclo con agua?
-Do you want your whiskey straight or should I mix it with water?

1010 carretera

road

f
[ka.rɛ.ˈtɛ.ra]

Estamos aquí para inspeccionar la carretera.
-We're here to inspect the road.

1011 sábado

Saturday

m
[ˈsa.βa.ðo]

Una semana esta dividida en siete días: lunes, martes, miércoles, jueves, viernes, sábado y domingo.
-A week is divided into seven days: Monday, Tuesday, Wednesday, Thursday, Friday, Saturday, and Sunday.

1012 aeropuerto

airport

m
[a.ɛ.ro.ˈpwɛr.to]

El avión ya había despegado cuando llegué al aeropuerto.
-The plane had already taken off when I reached the airport.

1013 medicina

medicine

f
[me.ði.ˈsi.na]

Agite la botella de medicina antes de utilizarla.
-Shake the medicine bottle before use.

1014 gratis

free; free

adj; adv
[ˈɡra.tis]

Los estudiantes reciben alojamiento y comida gratis.
-The students are provided with free board and lodging.

1015 fortuna

fortune

f
[for.ˈtu.na]

Él entregó toda su fortuna a la hija de un viejo amigo y no esperó nada a cambio.
-He gave away his entire fortune to an old friend's daughter and expected nothing in return.

1016 nieve

snow

f
[ˈnje.βe]

Hay mucha nieve durante el invierno.
-There is plenty of snow during the winter.

1017 riesgo

risk

m
[ˈrjɛʂ.ɣo]

Somos conscientes del riesgo, Jim.
-We're aware of the risk, Jim.

1018 sucio

dirty

adj
[ˈsu.sjo]

Tiene antecedentes de ser un luchador sucio.
-He has a history of being a dirty fighter.

1019 conversación

conversation

f
[kõm.bɛr.sa.ˈsjõn]

No pude evitar escuchar tu conversación con Jim.
-I couldn't help but overhear your conversation with Jim.

1020 comienzo

beginning

m
[ko.ˈmjẽn.so]

El comienzo oficial es el sábado.
-The official start is on Saturday.

1021 elección

choice

f
[e.lɛk.ˈsjõn]

Se trata de una elección personal.
-This is a matter of their personal choice.

1022 carro

car (LA), cart

	m	Venga, vámonos, te lo contaré en el carro.
	[ˈka.ro]	-Come on let's go, I'll tell you about it in the car.
1023	**rostro**	**face**
	m	Su rostro palideció de miedo.
	[ˈros.tro]	-His face went white with fear.
1024	**propiedad**	**property**
	f	El hijo mayor heredó toda la propiedad.
	[pro.pje.ˈðað]	-The eldest son succeeded to all the property.
1025	**comedor**	**dining room**
	m	Queremos saber dónde está el comedor.
	[ko.me.ˈðor]	-We would like to know where the dining room is.
1026	**familiar**	**family, familiar**
	adj	La mayoría de los humanos encuentran una imagen familiar menos estresante.
	[fa.mi.ˈljar]	-Most humans find a familiar image less stressful.
1027	**libra**	**pound**
	f	Queda una libra en la cocina.
	[ˈli.βra]	-There's a pound of it left in the kitchen.
1028	**cola**	**tail**
	f	La sirenita suspiró y miró con tristeza su cola de pez.
	[ˈko.la]	-The little mermaid sighed and looked sadly at her fish tail.
1029	**marca**	**brand, mark**
	f	¿Cuál es tu marca favorita de pintalabios?
	[ˈmar.ka]	-What's your favorite lipstick brand?
1030	**líder**	**leader**
	m/f	El líder ordenó a las tropas que retrocedieran.
	[ˈli.ðɛr]	-The leader ordered the troops to retreat.
1031	**socorro**	**help; help**
	m; int	Pensé haber escuchado a alguien pedir socorro.
	[so.ˈko.ro]	-I thought I heard somebody yell for help.
1032	**fútbol**	**football**
	m	Preferiría jugar al fútbol antes que ir a nadar.
	[ˈfut.βol]	-I'd rather play football than go swimming.
1033	**detalle**	**detail**
	m	Quisiera abordar algunos puntos en más detalle.
	[dɛ.ˈta.je]	-I would like to discuss a few points in more detail.
1034	**tesoro**	**treasure**
	m	Pensemos en el tesoro que hay adentro.
	[te.ˈso.ro]	-Let's think about the treasure that's inside.
1035	**camisa**	**shirt**
	f	Jim sacó un pequeño sobre del bolsillo de su camisa y se lo dio a Ana.
	[ka.ˈmi.sa]	-Jim took a small envelope from his shirt pocket and gave it to Ana.
1036	**conducir**	**drive, lead**
	vb	¡No seas tonto, no se puede conducir sin volante!
	[kõn̪.du.ˈsir]	-Don't be silly, you can't drive without a wheel!
1037	**alegría**	**joy**
	f	Es una gran alegría verte aquí.
	[a.le.ˈɣri.a]	-It's a great joy to see you here.
1038	**enviar**	**send**

| | vb | Quiero enviar esta carta a Japón. |
| | [ẽm.ˈbjar] | -I want to send this letter to Japan. |

1039 interés — interest

m
[ĩn̪.ˈtɛ.res]

¿Mi hijo? No parece tener interés en la música clásica. No se si será tecno o electrónica, pero siempre escucha música a un volumen muy alto.
-My son? He doesn't seem interested in classical music. I can't tell whether it's techno or electro, but he's always listening to music at a loud volume.

1040 parecido — similar; resemblance

adj; m
[pa.re.ˈsi.ðo]

Sabe muy parecido al pollo.
-It tastes a lot like chicken.

1041 pertenecer — belong

vb
[pɛr.te.ne.ˈsɛr]

Esta huella tiene que pertenecer al asesino.
-This print has got to belong to the killer.

1042 presentar(se) — introduce; appear

vb; vbr
[pre.sẽn̪.ˈtar.se)]

Me gustaría presentar al último miembro de nuestro grupo.
-I'd like to introduce the last member of our group.

1043 desayuno — breakfast

m
[de.sa.ˈʝu.no]

Tostadas con mermelada de frambuesa es mi desayuno preferido.
-Raspberry jam on toast is my favorite breakfast meal.

1044 merecer — deserve

vb
[mɛ.re.ˈsɛr]

No hice nada para merecer esto.
-I didn't do anything to deserve this.

1045 víctima — victim

f
[ˈbik̚.ti.ma]

Nadie sabe quién será la próxima víctima.
-No one knows who will be the next victim.

1046 barrio — neighborhood

m
[ˈba.rjo]

Crecí en un pequeño barrio de Madrid.
-I grew up in a small neighborhood in Madrid.

1047 oferta — offer

f
[o.ˈfɛr.ta]

Muchos de ustedes aprovecharon esa oferta.
-Many of you took advantage of that offer.

1048 desgraciado — jerk (coll), miserable; scoundrel (coll)

adj; m
[dɛs.ɣra.ˈsja.ðo]

¿Pero quién es este desgraciado?
-But who is this jerk?

1049 resultado — result

m
[re.sul̪.ˈta.ðo]

Pero podemos estar orgullosos del resultado.
-But we can be proud of the result.

1050 local — local; store

adj; m
[lo.ˈkal]

Esta noche un compositor local va a debutar con una sinfonía propia.
-Tonight, a local composer will debut a symphony of his own.

1051 responsabilidad — responsibility

f
[rɛs.põn.sa.βi.li.ˈðað]

Ella asumió toda la responsabilidad de sus actos.
-She took full responsibility for her actions.

1052 combate — combat

m
[kõm.ˈba.te]

Nunca entraría en combate con ella.
-I'd never go into combat with her.

1053 frío — cold; cold

adj; m
[ˈfri.o]

Voy a encender el calefactor porque hace mucho frío.
-I'm going to turn on the heater because it's very cold.

1054 tormenta — storm

	f	La tormenta paró el tren.
	[tor.ˈmɛ̃n̯.ta]	-The storm stopped the train.
1055	**nota**	**note, grade**
	f	Tomamos buena nota de esta contribución.
	[ˈno.ta]	-We have taken good note of that contribution.
1056	**olor**	**smell**
	m	Un olor insoportable emanaba de su persona.
	[o.ˈlor]	-There was a foul odor emanating from his person.
1057	**cantidad**	**amount**
	f	Durará solo una cierta cantidad de tiempo.
	[kã̯n̯.ti.ˈðað]	-It will only last a certain amount of time.
1058	**bala**	**bullet**
	f	No desperdiciaría una bala en usted.
	[ˈba.la]	-I wouldn't waste a bullet on you.
1059	**kilómetro**	**kilometer**
	m	Está a un kilómetro de aquí.
	[ki.ˈlo.mɛ.tro]	-It's one kilometer from here.
1060	**grandioso**	**grand**
	adj	Sería grandioso, pero no podemos.
	[grã̯n̯.ˈdjo.so]	-It would be great, but we can't.
1061	**débil**	**weak; weakling**
	adj; m/f	Estaba demasiado débil como para jugar al aire libre.
	[ˈde.βil]	-He was too frail to play games outdoors.
1062	**laboratorio**	**laboratory**
	m	La mancha de la bata de laboratorio se debe al nitrato de plata.
	[la.βo.ra.ˈto.rjo]	-The stain on the lab coat is due to silver nitrate.
1063	**fumar**	**smoke**
	vb	Fumar ha afectado a su salud.
	[fu.ˈmar]	-Smoking has affected his health.
1064	**entrenador**	**coach**
	m	Quiero presentar una denuncia contra mi entrenador.
	[ɛ̃n̯.tre.na.ˈðor]	-I want to file a case on my coach.
1065	**premio**	**prize**
	m	No le darán el premio a ella.
	[ˈpre.mjo]	-They will not give the prize to her.
1066	**a bordo**	**on board**
	adv	Había olvidado que todavía seguían a bordo.
	[a ˈβor.ðo]	-I'd forgotten you were still aboard.
1067	**agujero**	**hole**
	m	Tienes que cavar un agujero profundo.
	[a.ɣu.ˈxɛ.ro]	-You have to dig a deep hole.
1068	**asustado**	**frightened**
	adj	Estaba demasiado asustado como para pedirte salir.
	[a.sus.ˈta.ðo]	-I was too scared to ask you out.
1069	**invitado**	**invited; guest**
	adj; m	Ten en cuenta que tú aquí eres un invitado y deberías comportarte como corresponde.
	[ĩm.bi.ˈta.ðo]	-Bear in mind that you're a guest here and should behave accordingly.
1070	**mapa**	**map**

	m	¿Dónde puedo comprar un mapa de la ciudad?
	['ma.pa]	-Where can I buy a map of the city?
1071	**granja**	**farm**
	f	Él trabaja en la granja desde la mañana a la noche.
	['grãŋ.xa]	-He works on the farm from sunrise to sunset.
1072	**jurado**	**jury**
	m	La decisión del jurado será inapelable.
	[xu.'ra.ðo]	-The decision of the jury will be unappealable.
1073	**profundo**	**deep**
	adj	Sus pupilas eran tan negras y profundas como un abismo.
	[pro.'fũn̪.do]	-Her pupils were as black and deep as an abyss.
1074	**roca**	**rock**
	f	Tenemos que encontrar esa roca y quitarla.
	['ro.ka]	-We need to find that rock and remove it.
1075	**pastel**	**cake**
	m	Necesito algo de azúcar para preparar un pastel.
	[pas.'tɛl]	-I need some sugar to make a cake.
1076	**privado**	**private**
	adj	El hombre resultó ser un detective privado. -The man turned out to be a
	[pri.'βa.ðo]	private detective.
1077	**lunes**	**Monday**
	m	Mi amiga me dijo que el lunes que viene se inaugura una exposición sobre
	['lu.nes]	historia de España.
		-My friend told me that this coming Monday an exhibition about Spanish
		history is opening.
1078	**cuenta**	**bill, account**
	f	Tu cuenta ha sido bloqueada.
	['kwẽn̪.ta]	-Your account has been blocked.
1079	**socio**	**associate, member**
	m	Cuando mi socio vuelva discutiremos los detalles.
	['so.sjo]	-When my associate returns we'll discuss the details.
1080	**explicar(se)**	**explain**
	vb	No quiero explicar estas cosas.
	[ɛks.pli.'kar.se)]	-I don't want to explain these things.
1081	**necesidad**	**necessity**
	f	Es una necesidad jurídica, política y moral.
	[ne.se.si.'ðað]	-It is a legal, political, and moral necessity.
1082	**importancia**	**importance**
	f	Me gustaría convencerte de su importancia.
	[ĩm.por.'tãn.sja]	-I would like to convince you of their importance.
1083	**corriente**	**common; current, electricity**
	adj; f	Una corriente eléctrica puede generar magnetismo.
	[ko.'rjẽn̪.te]	-An electric current can generate magnetism.
1084	**desierto**	**desert; desert**
	adj; m	El desierto de China alberga a más personas que Japón.
	[de.'sjɛr.to]	-China's desert supports more people than are in Japan.
1085	**modelo**	**model, pattern**
	m	Este modelo puede combinarse con cualquier color.
	[mo.'ðe.lo]	-This model can be combined with any color.
1086	**invierno**	**winter**

	m	Probablemente no nevará mucho este invierno.
	[ĩm.ˈbjɛr.no]	-We probably won't have much snow this winter.
1087	**plata**	**silver, money (LA)**
	f	Me estás pagando mucha plata por protegerte.
	[ˈpla.ta]	-You're paying me a lot of money to protect you.
1088	**apoyo**	**support**
	m	Para lograr esto necesitamos, por encima de todo, su apoyo.
	[a.ˈpo.ʝo]	-To achieve this we need, above all, your support.
1089	**tercer(o)**	**third**
	num	No importa quién sea el tercero.
	[tɛr.ˈsɛ.ro)]	-It does not matter who is the third.
1090	**obvio**	**obvious; obviously**
	adj; int	Algunos pensarán que esto es obvio.
	[ˈoβ.βjo]	-Some people may think that this is obvious.
1091	**recién**	**newly**
	adv	Los apartamentos están recién reformados pero todavía conservan su sabor andaluz.
	[re.ˈsjẽn]	-The apartments have been recently refurbished but still conserve their Andaluz flavor.
1092	**techo**	**ceiling**
	m	También puedes cambiar el color del techo.
	[ˈte.ʧo]	-You can also change the color of the roof.
1093	**campeón**	**champion**
	m	Tiene el potencial para ser campeón del mundo.
	[kãm.ˈpe.õn]	-He has the potential to become world champion.
1094	**salón**	**lounge**
	m	Los apartamentos tienen un salón con 2 sofás cama.
	[sa.ˈlõn]	-The apartments offer a lounge with 2 sofa beds.
1095	**gas**	**gas**
	m	El petróleo y el gas se bombean en tierra o se cargan en los buques.
	[ˈgas]	-The oil and gas are pumped ashore or loaded onto ships.
1096	**cura**	**priest; cure**
	m; f	No hay cura para la estupidez.
	[ˈku.ra]	-There's no cure for stupidity.
1097	**escenario**	**stage, scene**
	m	Este podría considerarse como el peor escenario posible.
	[ɛs.se.ˈna.rjo]	-This could be regarded as the worst case scenario.
1098	**cobarde**	**cowardly; coward**
	adj; m/f	Él es demasiado cobarde para intentarlo.
	[ko.ˈβar.ðe]	-He is too much of a coward to attempt it.
1099	**asegurar(se)**	**secure; check**
	vb; vbr	El objetivo sería asegurar una transición fluida.
	[a.se.ɣu.ˈrar.se)]	-The aim would be to ensure a smooth transition.
1100	**obtener**	**obtain, acquire**
	vb	No obstante, no es necesario obtener autorización oficial.
	[oβ.te.ˈnɛr]	-It is, however, not necessary to obtain official authorization.
1101	**pecho**	**chest**
	m	Solo tengo que sacarme esto del pecho.
	[ˈpe.ʧo]	-I just have to get this off my chest.
1102	**esquina**	**corner**

	f	Solía haber una farmacia en esa esquina.
	[ɛs.ˈki.na]	-There used to be a drugstore on that corner.
1103	**sensación**	**sensation**
	f	Piensa en la sensación que quieres transmitir.
	[sẽn.sa.ˈsjõn]	-Think about the sensation that you want to transmit.
1104	**ciego**	**blind**
	adj	Tienes que estar ciego como un topo si no has podido verlo.
	[ˈsje.ɣo]	-You must be blind as a bat if you couldn't see it.
1105	**fábrica**	**factory**
	f	Tiene una fábrica de material eléctrico.
	[ˈfa.βri.ka]	-He has an electrical equipment factory.
1106	**sabido**	**known**
	adj	Hubiera sabido instantáneamente si planeábamos algo.
	[sa.ˈβi.ðo]	-He would have known instantly if we were up to something.
1107	**corto**	**short**
	adj	Esta fase puede alcanzarse a corto plazo.
	[ˈkor.to]	-This phase can be accomplished in the short term.
1108	**artista**	**artist**
	m/f	Un artista es una oveja que se separa del rebaño.
	[ar.ˈtis.ta]	-An artist is a sheep that strays from the flock.
1109	**pescado**	**fish**
	m	Ella frió pescado en aceite para ensalada.
	[pɛs.ˈka.ðo]	-She fried fish in salad oil.
1110	**desaparecer**	**disappear**
	vb	Es difícil desaparecer sin dejar rastro.
	[de.sa.pa.re.ˈsɛr]	-It's difficult to disappear without a trace.
1111	**reino**	**kingdom**
	m	Todos los hombres del reino caían bajo el hechizo de su mirada.
	[ˈrei̯.no]	-Every man in the kingdom fell under the spell of her look.
1112	**piloto**	**pilot**
	m	A medida que el avión se acercaba a las turbulencias, el piloto pidió a los pasajeros a bordo del avión que se abrochasen sus cinturones de seguridad.
	[pi.ˈlo.to]	-As the plane was approaching turbulence, the pilot asked the passengers aboard the plane to fasten their seat belts.
1113	**veinte**	**twenty**
	num	Ella deseó haber nacido veinte años antes.
	[ˈbei̯n.te]	-She wished she had been born twenty years earlier.
1114	**almuerzo**	**lunch**
	m	Tu hermana habrá preparado el almuerzo monstruoso de siempre.
	[al.ˈmwɛr.so]	-Your sister will have prepared the usual monstrous lunch.
1115	**discutir**	**argue**
	vb	No estoy intentando discutir con Tom.
	[dis.ku.ˈtir]	-I'm not trying to argue against Tom.
1116	**correo**	**mail**
	m	Parece que el correo sigue funcionando.
	[ko.ˈre.o]	-Looks like the mail's still working.
1117	**condición**	**condition**
	f	Puedes ir con la condición de que vuelvas a las cinco.
	[kõn.di.ˈsjõn]	-You may go on condition that you return by five.
1118	**violencia**	**violence**

f
[bjo.ˈlɛ̃n.sja]

Espero que no recurran a la violencia para conseguir sus objetivos.
-I hope they don't resort to violence to accomplish their goals.

1119 **presencia**

presence

f
[pre.ˈsɛ̃n.sja]

Es la primera vez que grito en presencia del gerente. ¡Vi una cucaracha enorme sobre la mesa!
-It's the first time I scream in presence of the manager. I saw a big cockroach on the table!

1120 **poco**

little; quite

adj; adv
[ˈpo.ko]

Para mí, eso sería demasiado poco.
-For me, that would be too little.

1121 **lord**

lord

m
[ˈlorð]

Este pueblo es de lord Tennyson ahora.
-This is Lord Tennyson's village now.

1122 **quitar(se)**

remove; get out of the way

vb; vbr
[ki.ˈtar.se)]

Mi mamá solía quitar los picaportes de las puertas.
-My mum used to take the door handles off.

1123 **serie**

series

f
[ˈsɛ.rje]

La vida es una serie de sensaciones conectadas a diferentes estados de conciencia.
-Life is a series of sensations connected to different states of consciousness.

1124 **labio**

lip

m
[ˈla.βjo]

Tuve que morderme el labio para evitar reírme.
-I had to bite my lip to prevent myself from laughing.

1125 **caray**

damn it, heck

int
[ka.ˈraj]

Es decir, caray, mirad esto.
-I mean, heck, look at this.

1126 **espera**

wait

f
[ɛs.ˈpɛ.ra]

Hola señor, disculpe la espera.
-Hello sir, I'm sorry for the wait.

1127 **teoría**

theory

f
[te.o.ˈri.a]

Creo que tú teoría básica es errónea.
-I think your basic theory is wrong.

1128 **actor**

actor

m
[akˈtor]

¿Quieres ser actor en una película?
-Do you want to be an actor in a movie?

1129 **enfermero**

nurse

m
[ɛ̃ɱ.fɛr.ˈmɛ.ro]

La inyección te será administrada por un médico o enfermero.
-The injection will be given to you by a doctor or a nurse.

1130 **siglo**

century

m
[ˈsi.ɣlo]

Esta es una forma excelente de comenzar el siglo.
-This is an excellent way in which to begin the century.

1131 **tamaño**

size

m
[ta.ˈma.ɲo]

El tamaño del país juega un rol importante.
-The size of the country plays an important role.

1132 **chocolate**

chocolate

m
[tʃo.ko.ˈla.te]

Mi madre preparará diez tandas de galletas de chocolate para la fiesta de mañana.
-My mom will be making ten batches of chocolate chip cookies for tomorrow's party.

1133 **virgen**

virgin; virgin

adj; m/f
['bir.xɛ̃n]

La oráculo virgen goza de visiones del futuro.
-The virgin oracle is blessed with visions of the future.

1134 manejar(se) — **manage, drive (LA); handle yourself**

vb; vbr
[ma.ne.'xar.se)]

No tiene la habilidad para manejar a ese grupo.
-He doesn't have the ability to manage that group.

1135 disco — **disk**

m
['dis.ko]

Borré mi disco duro por accidente.
-I erased my hard disk by accident.

1136 milagro — **miracle**

m
[mi.'la.ɣro]

Es un milagro que Jim siga vivo.
-It's a miracle that Jim is still alive.

1137 pelota — **ball**

f
[pe.'lo.ta]

Me pidió que le lanzara la pelota de vuelta.
-He asked me to throw the ball back.

1138 vaso — **glass**

m
['ba.so]

Tráeme un vaso de leche.
-Get me a glass of milk.

1139 universo — **universe**

m
[u.ni.'βɛr.so]

Probablemente nunca se explique el origen del universo.
-The origin of the universe will probably never be explained.

1140 gira — **tour**

f
['xi.ra]

Estoy intentando convencerla para que haga una gira.
-I'm trying to persuade her to go on a tour.

1141 salvaje — **wild, violent; savage**

adj; m/f
[sal.'βa.xe]

Quisiera informar sobre un animal salvaje peligroso.
-I'd like to report a dangerous wild animal.

1142 elegir — **choose**

vb
[e.le.'xir]

No tienes que elegir un teléfono.
-You do not need to choose a phone.

1143 curso — **course**

m
['kur.so]

Todos los estudiantes deben realizar este curso.
-All students must take this course.

1144 firma — **signature, firm**

f
['fir.ma]

Mi firma es significativa, majestuosa e inimitable.
-My signature is meaningful, majestic and inimitable.

1145 herida — **wound**

f
[ɛ.'ri.ða]

Deja que limpie la herida por ti.
-Let me clean the wound for you.

1146 queso — **cheese**

m
['ke.so]

Compraré un poco de queso y pan.
-I'll buy some cheese and bread.

1147 limpiar(se) — **clean, tidy**

vb
[lĩm.'pjar.se)]

Trabajaremos juntos para limpiar toda ese lío.
-We will work together to clean all that mess.

1148 extra — **extra; extras**

adv; mpl
['ɛks.tra]

Tendrás el dinero extra que necesitas.
-You will have the extra cash you need.

1149 parado — **standing (LA)**

adj

[pa.ˈra.ðo]

Estaba ahí parado, junto al campo.

-I was standing there, by the field.

1150 magia   **magic**

f

[ˈma.xja]

Él conoce muchos trucos de magia divertidos.

-He knows many amusing magic tricks.

1151 casado   **married; married person**

adj; m

[ka.ˈsa.ðo]

Quiero estar casada contigo, Jim.

-I want to be married to you, Jim.

1152 campamento   **campsite**

m

[kãm.pa.ˈmẽn̪.to]

Quiero montar un campamento en aquella montaña.

-I'd like to establish a camp on that mountain.

1153 mentiroso   **liar; liar**

m; adj

[mẽn̪.ti.ˈro.so]

Él era un mentiroso compulsivo.

-He was a compulsive liar.

1154 disponer(se)   **arrange, have; get ready**

vb; vbr

[dis.po.ˈnɛr.se)]

Ahora sé cómo disponer las esculturas.

-Now I know how to arrange the sculptures.

1155 firme   **firm; steady, firmly**

adj; adv

[ˈfir.me]

Tienes que ser firme en esto.

-You got to be firm on this.

1156 estómago   **stomach**

m

[ɛs.ˈto.ma.ɣo]

Estoy intentando buscar algo para aliviar mi estómago.

-I'm trying to find something to soothe my stomach.

1157 vacío   **emptiness; empty, superficial**

m; adj

[ba.ˈsi.o]

No entiendo porqué querías verme en este teatro vacío.

-I don't understand why you wanted to see me in this empty theater.

1158 tirar   **throw, waste, pull**

vb

[ti.ˈrar]

Creo que deberíamos tirar ese libro.

-I think we should throw that book away.

1159 torre   **tower**

f

[ˈto.re]

Había una torre en la cima de la montaña.

-There was a tower on the top of the mountain.

1160 destruir   **destroy**

vb

[dɛs.ˈtrwir]

La misión de los soldados era destruir el puente.

-The soldiers' mission was to destroy the bridge.

1161 frontera   **border**

f

[frõn̪.ˈtɛ.ra]

Jim vive a 10 millas de la frontera canadiense.

-Jim lives 10 miles from the Canadian border.

1162 huella   **footprint, trace**

f

[ˈwe.ja]

Esto parece una huella bastante grande.

-This looks like a pretty big footprint.

1163 antiguo   **ancient; old fashioned**

adj; m

[ãn̪.ˈti.ɣwo]

Me gustaría volver al antiguo Egipto.

-I would like to go back to ancient Egypt.

1164 material   **material; equipment**

adj; m

[ma.tɛ.ˈrjal]

Este material puede traducirse y difundirse fácilmente.

-This material can easily be translated and made available.

1165 relajar(se)   **relax**

vb

[re.la.ˈxar.se)]

Espero que ahora puedas relajarte y disfrutar del viaje.

-I hope you can relax and enjoy the journey now.

1166 judío

adj; m

[xu.ˈði.o]

Jewish; Jew

Visitaremos también los barrios judío y cristiano.

-We will also visit the districts Jewish and Christian.

1167 cadáver

m

[ka.ˈða.βɛr]

corpse

Apareció también un cadáver no identificado.

-The body of an unidentified person was found.

1168 milla

f

[ˈmi.ja]

mile

Él es capaz de correr una milla en cuatro minutos.

-He is capable of running a mile in four minutes.

1169 emperador

m

[ẽm.pɛ.ra.ˈðor]

emperor

Declaro mi derecho a hablar con el emperador.

-I claim my right of appeal to the emperor.

1170 cigarro

m

[si.ˈɣa.ro]

cigar

Estoy fumando un cigarro cubano.

-I am smoking a Cuban cigar.

1171 helado

m; adj

[e.ˈla.ðo]

ice cream; frozen

Me gusta el helado de chocolate.

-I like chocolate ice cream.

1172 miembro

m

[ˈmjẽm.bro]

member, limb

Jim ya no puede seguir siendo un miembro de nuestro comité.

-Jim can no longer be a member of our committee.

1173 social

adj

[so.ˈsjal]

social

Esos niños recibieron atención médica, social y psicológica.

-Those children were provided with medical, social and psychological care.

1174 paciencia

f

[pa.ˈsjẽn.sja]

patience

Necesitamos paciencia y perseverancia para lograr esto.

-We need patience and perseverance to achieve this.

1175 apurar(se)

vb

[a.pu.ˈrar.se)]

hurry

No se puede apurar a un olmo.

-You can't hurry an elm.

1176 superior

adj; m

[su.pɛ.ˈrjor]

greater than, upper; boss

Y tiene amoratada la parte superior de su muslo, aquí.

-And she's bruised the upper part of her thigh, here.

1177 dudar

vb

[du.ˈðar]

doubt

No quería dudar de tu entrenamiento.

-I didn't mean to doubt your training.

1178 invitar

vb

[ĩm.bi.ˈtar]

invite

Nos tiene que invitar a quedarnos.

-He's got to invite us to stick around.

1179 estudiar

vb

[ɛs.tu.ˈðjar]

study

Jim quiere estudiar en Boston.

-Jim wants to study in Boston.

1180 encantador

adj

[ẽŋ.kãn.ta.ˈðor]

charming

Parece ser muy seguro, confiable y encantador.

-He appears to be very confident, trustworthy, and charming.

1181 felicitación

congratulations

f
[fe.li.si.ta.ˈsjõn]

Quisiera expresarle mi agradecimiento y felicitación.
-I would like to congratulate and thank you.

1182 motor

m; adj
[moˈtor]

engine; motor

Este coche lleva el maletero bajo el capó. Tiene el motor detrás.
-This car has the boot under the bonnet. The engine is in the back.

1183 sobrevivir

vb
[so.βre.βiˈβir]

survive

No se puede sobrevivir sin dinero.
-One cannot survive without money.

1184 lío

m
[ˈli.o]

mess

Estoy en un pequeño lío y...
-I'm in a bit of a mess and...

1185 primavera

f
[pri.maˈβɛ.ra]

spring

No puedo esperar a que llegue la primavera para poder sentarnos bajo los árboles de cerezo.
-I can't wait for spring to come so we can sit under the cherry trees.

1186 proceso

m
[proˈse.so]

process

Creo que el proceso está equilibrado.
-I believe that the process is well balanced.

1187 sujeto

m; adj
[suˈxɛ.to]

subject; subject to

Eres sujeto de una investigación oficial.
-You're the subject of an official investigation.

1188 respirar

vb
[rɛs.piˈrar]

breathe

No quiero ni escucharte respirar.
-I don't even want to hear you breathe.

1189 gobernador

m
[go.βɛr.na.ˈðor]

governor

Un asistente del gobernador estaría presente.
-An assistant of the governor would be present.

1190 proteger(se)

vb
[pro.te.ˈxɛr.se)]

protect

Queremos proteger el mundo que tenemos.
-We want to protect this world we have.

1191 ciencia

f
[ˈsjẽn.sja]

science

La ciencia de nuestra creación es fascinante.
-The science of how we are created is fascinating.

1192 conde

m
[ˈkõn̪.de]

count

Pero el conde es perfectamente razonable.
-But the count's in his right mind.

1193 puro

adj; m
[ˈpu.ro]

pure; cigar

Era demasiado puro para este mundo.
-He was just too pure for this world.

1194 viajar

vb
[bja.ˈxar]

travel

Durante mi vida, he tenido la gran satisfacción de viajar por todo el mundo y trabajar en muchas naciones diferentes.
-Throughout my life, I've had the great pleasure of traveling all around the world and working in many diverse nations.

1195 alcohol

m
[al.ko.ˈol]

alcohol

Fumar demasiados cigarrillos y beber demasiado alcohol es peligroso.
-Smoking too many cigarettes and drinking too much alcohol is dangerous.

1196 apuesto

adj
[a.ˈpwɛs.to]

handsome

Sin mencionar que soy muy apuesto.
-Not to mention that I am very handsome.

1197	**funeral**	**funeral**
	m	El funeral de Jim es el lunes.
	[fu.nɛ.ˈral]	-Jim's funeral is on Monday.
1198	**sospechoso**	**suspicious; suspect**
	adj; m	Las cámaras registraron su comportamiento sospechoso.
	[sos.pe.ˈʧo.so]	-The cameras picked up on his suspicious behavior.
1199	**sopa**	**soup**
	f	¿Por qué me moquea la nariz cuando tomo sopa en invierno?
	[ˈso.pa]	-Why does my nose run when I eat soup in winter?
1200	**adonde**	**where; to the house of**
	adv; prp	Voy adonde me lleva mi destino.
	[a.ˈðõ̃n.de]	-I go where my destiny will take me.
1201	**orgullo**	**pride**
	m	Mi orgullo me impidió pedirle prestado dinero.
	[or.ˈɣu.jo]	-My pride prevented me from borrowing money from him.
1202	**discurso**	**speech**
	m	El discurso de despedida de Jane nos dejo muy tristes.
	[dis.ˈkur.so]	-Jane's farewell speech made us very sad.
1203	**pecar**	**sin**
	vb	Los bebés no saben qué es pecar.
	[pe.ˈkar]	-Babies don't know what sin is.
1204	**tarea**	**task, homework (LA)**
	f	La tarea es tan difícil que no puedo hacerla.
	[ta.ˈre.a]	-The task is so difficult that I cannot accomplish it.
1205	**compra**	**purchase**
	f	Tengo que saber quién realizó la compra.
	[ˈkõm.pra]	-I need to know who made the purchase.
1206	**cheque**	**check**
	m	Si funciona puedes enviarme un cheque.
	[ˈʧe.ke]	-If it works, you can send me a check.
1207	**huir**	**run away**
	vb	Y quería huir tan rápido como pudiera.
	[ˈwir]	-And I wanted to run away as fast as I could.
1208	**recoger**	**pick up, collect**
	vb	Solo necesito recoger mis listones de fútbol.
	[re.ko.ˈxɛr]	-I just need to pick up my soccer cleats.
1209	**oído**	**ear**
	m	Alguien me susurró eso al oído.
	[o.ˈi.ðo]	-Somebody whispered that in my ear.
1210	**desgracia**	**misfortune**
	f	Él tuvo la desgracia de perder a su hijo.
	[dɛs̪.ˈɣra.sja]	-He had the misfortune to lose his son.
1211	**asesinar**	**murder**
	vb	No tienes que asesinar para vivir.
	[a.se.si.ˈnar]	-You don't have to kill to survive.
1212	**averiguar**	**find out**
	vb	Ojalá pudiera averiguar cómo controlar mi apetito.
	[a.βɛ.ri.ˈɣwar]	-I wish I could figure out how to control my appetite.
1213	**palacio**	**palace**

	m	
	[pa.ˈla.sjo]	

Parece conocer el palacio muy bien.
-He seems to know the palace very well.

1214 amistad — **friendship**
f
[a.mis.ˈtað]

Tu amistad significaría mucho para mí.
-Your friendship would mean a lot to me.

1215 bola — **ball**
f
[ˈbo.la]

No importa a dónde vaya la bola.
-It doesn't matter where the ball goes.

1216 sexual — **sexual**
adj
[sɛk.ˈswal]

Nuestro cliente está siendo demandado por acoso sexual.
-Our client is being sued for sexual harassment.

1217 educación — **education**
f
[e.ðu.ka.ˈsjõn]

El rol de la educación tiene una importancia esencial.
-The role of education is of crucial importance.

1218 centavo — **penny**
m
[sɛ̃n.ˈta.βo]

Cuesta más acuñar un centavo que lo que vale el propio centavo.
-It costs more to mint a penny than the penny itself is worth.

1219 taza — **cup**
f
[ˈta.sa]

Jim me preguntó si quería una taza de café.
-Jim asked me if I wanted a cup of coffee.

1220 efectivo — **cash; effective**
m; adj
[e.fek̚.ˈti.βo]

Llevaba mucho efectivo y necesitaba un arma como protección.
-He carried a lot of cash and he needed a gun for protection.

1221 construir — **build**
vb
[kõns.ˈtrwir]

Es casi tan absurdo como construir un reactor nuclear dentro de un castillo.
-It's almost as absurd as building a nuclear reactor inside a castle.

1222 madera — **wood**
f
[ma.ˈðɛ.ra]

Venga, nos llevaremos esta madera de vuelta al camión.
-Come on, we'll take this wood back to the truck.

1223 amenaza — **threat**
f
[a.me.ˈna.sa]

Quien mucho amenaza no es peligroso.
-He who makes many threats is not dangerous.

1224 mono — **monkey; cute**
m; adj
[ˈmo.no]

Ha habido algunas quejas... Acerca del mono.
-There have been some complaints... About the monkey.

1225 false — **false, fake**
adj
[ˈfal.se]

Creía haberte dado un número falso.
-I thought I gave you a fake number.

1226 detener(se) — **stop**
vb
[dɛ.te.ˈnɛr.se)]

Nadie puede detener el transcurso del tiempo.
-No one can stop the time from passing.

1227 ocasión — **chance, occasion**
f
[o.ka.ˈsjõn]

En nuestras vidas tenemos tres o cuatro ocasiones de mostrar valentía, pero todos los días tenemos la ocasión de mostrar la falta de cobardía.
-In our lives, we have three or four occasions of showing bravery, but every day, we have the occasion to show a lack of cowardice.

1228 criminal — **criminal; criminal**
adj; m/f
[kri.mi.ˈnal]

La policía pudo encontrar al criminal.
-The police were able to find the criminal.

1229 bebida — **drink**

f
[be.ˈβi.ða]
Probablemente también pagaría por la bebida.
-She'd probably pay for the drink, too.

1230 fuente
f
[ˈfwẽn̪.te]
source, fountain
La espinaca es una fuente rica en fierro y calcio.
-Spinach is a rich source of iron and calcium.

1231 estudiante
m/f
[ɛs.tu.ˈðjãn̪.te]
student
Quiero alquilarle esta habitación a un estudiante.
-I want to rent this room to a student.

1232 consigo
prn
[kõn.ˈsi.ɣo]
with her, with him
Esta era la foto que siempre llevaba consigo.
-This was the photo he always carried with him.

1233 pájaro
m
[ˈpa.xa.ro]
bird
Echémosle un buen vistazo a este pájaro.
-Let's have a good look at this bird.

1234 sencillo
adj
[sẽn.ˈsi.ʝo]
simple
El proceso era sencillo y completamente gratuito.
-The process was simple and entirely free of charge.

1235 lección
f
[lɛk.ˈsjõn]
lesson
Este será el tema de nuestra próxima lección.
-This will be the subject of our next lesson.

1236 examen
m
[ɛk.ˈsa.mẽn]
exam
¿Conseguiré aprenderme todos los temas de gramática a tiempo para mi examen de alemán de mañana?
-Will I manage to learn all the grammar topics in time for my German exam tomorrow?

1237 indio
adj; m
[ˈĩn̪.djo]
Native Indian; Indian
Te mostraré un viejo truco indio.
-I'll show you an old Indian trick.

1238 sonrisa
f
[sõn.ˈri.sa]
smile
La sonrisa de Jim era muy dulce.
-Jim's smile was very sweet.

1239 uniforme
m; adj
[u.ni.ˈfor.me]
uniform; uniform
Llevaba un uniforme escolar y tenía una flauta.
-She wore a school uniform and had a flute.

1240 solución
f
[so.lu.ˈsjõn]
solution, answer
Una solución que sea práctica, simple y eficaz.
-A solution that is practical, simple, and effective.

1241 conciencia
f
[kõn.ˈsjẽn.sja]
conscience
No tengo problemas con mi conciencia.
-I have no problems with my conscience.

1242 bolsillo
m
[bol.ˈsi.ʝo]
pocket
Me robaron la cartera del bolsillo interior.
-I had my wallet stolen from my inner pocket.

1243 suave
adj
[ˈswa.βe]
soft
Jim habla con voz suave, considera sus respuestas cuidadosamente.
-Jim speaks with a soft voice, he considers his answers carefully.

1244 cero
num
[ˈsɛ.ro]
zero
Chicos, la cerveza tiene cero alcohol.
-Guys, the beer has zero alcohol in it.

1245 tropa
troop

f
['tro.pa]
La reputación de esta tropa está a punto de cambiar.
-This troop's reputation is about to change.

1246 **protección** **protection**

f
[pro.tɛk.'sjõn]
Jim pidió protección policial después que John y Ana lo amenazaran con matarlo.
-Jim asked for police protection after Ana and John threatened to kill him.

1247 **aparte** **unusual; aside**

adj; adv
[a.'par.te]
Lo dejé aparte para lavarlo después.
-I put it aside to hand wash it later.

1248 **venganza** **revenge**

f
[bẽŋ.'gãn.sa]
Es peligroso confundir la venganza con la justicia.
-It's dangerous to confuse vengeance with justice.

1249 **original** **original**

adj
[o.ri.xi.'nal]
En realidad, éramos el patrocinador original.
-As a matter of fact, we were the original sponsor.

1250 **comisario** **commissioner**

m
[ko.mi.'sa.rjo]
Eres el comisario, podrías hacer algo.
-You're the commissioner, you could do something.

1251 **saco** **bad, coat (LA)**

m
['sa.ko]
Solo he vuelto para devolverte tu saco.
-I just came back to return your jacket.

1252 **ritmo** **rhythm, pace**

m
['ri't.mo]
No puedo mantener este ritmo mucho tiempo.
-I can't keep up this rhythm long.

1253 **cruz** **cross**

f
['krus]
Usaré esta cruz contra un vampiro.
-I'm using this cross against a vampire.

1254 **lobo** **wolf**

m
['lo.βo]
Mi compañero de trabajo es un lobo vestido de oveja.
-My co-worker is a wolf in sheep's clothing.

1255 **mentir** **lie**

vb
[mẽn.'tir]
La policía puede mentir en un interrogatorio.
-The police are allowed to lie in an interrogation.

1256 **pintura** **painting, paint**

f
[pĩn.'tu.ra]
La disputa por la pintura de la cocina había llegado a su clímax.
-The kitchen paint dispute had reached a climax.

1257 **esfuerzo** **effort**

m
[ɛs.'fwɛr.so]
No escatimaremos ningún esfuerzo para que esto ocurra.
-We will not spare any effort to make this happen.

1258 **espejo** **mirror**

m
[ɛs.'pe.xo]
El espejo retrovisor se cayó.
-The rear-view mirror fell off.

1259 **bestia** **beast**

f
['bɛs.tja]
Sin duda sabe controlar a esa bestia.
-She's certainly in control of that beast.

1260 **camarada** **comrade; pal (coll)**

m/f; m/f
[ka.ma.'ra.ða]
Mi camarada saltó inmediatamente y lo golpeó.
-Immediately, my comrade leapt forward and struck him.

1261 **inteligencia** **intelligence**

f
[ĩn.te.li.ˈxẽn.sja]

Existen múltiples formas de comprobar la inteligencia del niño.
-There are many ways of testing a child's intelligence.

1262 curioso

adj
[ku.ˈrjo.so]

curious

Es curioso que él no reaccionara.
-It's curious that he didn't react.

1263 declaración

f
[de.kla.ra.ˈsjõn]

statement

Al día siguiente firmó una declaración confesando el asesinato.
-The next day he signed a statement confessing to the murder.

1264 aburrir(se)

vb; vbr
[a.βu.ˈrir.se)]

bore; be bored

En realidad se lo debo... Pero esa es otra historia y no le aburriré con ella.
-I owe it to him actually... But that's another story and I won't bore you with it.

1265 artículo

m
[ar.ˈti.ku.lo]

article, item

El artículo retrataba al acusado como culpable, a pesar de haberse probado su inocencia.
-The article painted the defendant as a guilty man, even though he had been proven innocent.

1266 cruel

adj
[ˈkrwɛl]

cruel

Es cruel burlarse de un ciego.
-It is cruel to mock a blind man.

1267 criatura

f
[krja.ˈtu.ra]

creature

Es una criatura de la mitología.
-It's a creature from the mythology.

1268 gritar

vb
[gri.ˈtar]

scream

Puedes gritar si quieres.
-You can scream if you want to.

1269 diversión

f
[di.βɛr.ˈsjõn]

fun

No quiero perderme la diversión.
-I don't want to miss any of the fun.

1270 aparecer(se)

vb
[a.pa.re.ˈsɛr.se)]

appear

Espera a que su abogado aparezca.
-He waits for his lawyer to show up.

1271 chaqueta

f
[ʧa.ˈkɛ.ta]

jacket

Me dejé la chaqueta en la clase.
-I left my jacket in the classroom.

1272 excelencia

f
[ɛk.se.ˈlẽn.sja]

excellence

Buscamos la excelencia en la enseñanza.
-We're looking for excellence in teaching.

1273 vídeo

m
[ˈbi.ðe.o]

video

Te enviaré una copia del vídeo.
-I'll send you a copy of the video.

1274 vecino

adj; m
[be.ˈsi.no]

adjacent; neighbor

Yo tengo un vecino judío.
-I have a Jewish neighbor.

1275 camioneta

f
[ka.mjo.ˈnɛ.ta]

van

Condujimos por ahí en esa camioneta.
-We drove around in that truck.

1276 azúcar

m
[a.ˈsu.kar]

sugar

Añade azúcar a este té.
-Add sugar to this tea.

1277 colega — **colleague, friend**
m/f
[ko.ˈle.ɣa]
No comparto el optimismo de mi colega.
-I do not share the optimism of my colleague.

1278 harto — **full, sick of**
adj
[ˈar.to]
Estoy harto de escuchar sus quejas.
-I'm sick of listening to his complaints.

1279 feo — **ugly**
adj
[ˈfe.o]
Creo que están encubriendo algo feo.
-I think something ugly is being covered up.

1280 cadena — **chain**
f
[ka.ˈðe.na]
Jim tenía su llave colgando en una cadena alrededor de su cuello.
-Jim had his key dangling around his neck on a chain.

1281 cuerda — **rope, cord**
f
[ˈkwɛr.ða]
Necesitamos la cuerda para volver arriba.
-We need the rope to get back up.

1282 pez — **fish**
m
[ˈpes]
Jim se sentó mirando fijamente al pez tropical que nadaba por el acuario en su habitación.
-Jim sat staring at the tropical fish swimming around in the aquarium in his bedroom.

1283 pérdida — **loss**
f
[ˈpɛr.ði.ða]
Su pérdida supone nuestra ganancia.
-Their loss is our gain.

1284 guarda — **guard**
m/f
[ˈgwar.ða]
El guarda señaló la fuente.
-The guard pointed to the fountain.

1285 recuperar(se) — **recover; get well**
vb; vbr
[re.ku.pɛ.ˈrar.se)]
Estoy intentando recuperar tanta información como sea posible.
-I'm trying to recover as much data as possible.

1286 promesa — **promise**
f
[pro.ˈme.sa]
No pudo cumplir la promesa que le hizo a su padre.
-He couldn't fulfill the promise he made to his father.

1287 amén — **amen**
m
[a.ˈmẽn]
Lo ruego en nombre de Jesús, amén.
-In Jesus' name I pray, amen.

1288 temporada — **season, time**
f
[tẽm.po.ˈra.ða]
El verano es la temporada más cálida.
-Summer is the hottest season.

1289 convertir(se) — **change, transform**
vb
[kõm.bɛr.ˈtir.se)]
Necesitamos convertir estos enormes retos en oportunidades.
-We need to convert these enormous challenges into moments of opportunity.

1290 humanidad — **humanity, mankind**
f
[u.ma.ni.ˈðað]
Su humanidad ha quedado enterrada bajo un exterior duro e insensible.
-Their humanity has been buried deep beneath a tough, unfeeling exterior.

1291 dato — **fact**
m
[ˈda.to]
No perdamos de vista este dato.
-Let us not lose sight of that fact.

1292 maravilla — **wonder**
f
[ma.ra.ˈβi.ja]
Solo una persona como ella podría hacer tanta maravilla junta.
-Only a person like her could make all that wonder together.

1293 maleta — **suitcase**
f
[ma.ˈlɛ.ta]
Ayer dejé mi maleta en la zona de equipajes, pero ahora parece haberse perdido.
-I put my suitcase in the baggage room yesterday, but now it seems to be missing.

1294 descubrir — **discover**
vb
[dɛs.ku.ˈβrir]
Quiero descubrir dónde compró Tim sus zapatos.
-I want to find out where Tim bought his shoes.

1295 arena — **sand, ring**
f
[a.ˈre.na]
No esperaba encontrarte jugando en la arena.
-I didn't expect to find you playing in the sand.

1296 legal — **legal**
adj
[le.ˈɣal]
Era necesario evitar cualquier fraude legal.
-It was necessary to avoid the legal fraud.

1297 doce — **twelve**
num
[ˈdo.se]
Tenías que llamarme doce veces.
-You had to call me twelve times.

1298 fiscal — **fiscal; district attorney**
adj; m/f
[fis.ˈkal]
El fiscal deberá notificar su decisión al tribunal.
-The public prosecutor shall notify the court of his decision.

1299 mina — **mine**
f
[ˈmi.na]
Según los expertos, había una mina por cada habitante.
-According to the experts, there was one mine for every inhabitant.

1300 honesto — **honest**
adj
[o.ˈnɛs.to]
Sería honesto reconocer que estos temores son racistas.
-It would be honest to recognize these fears as racist.

1301 oso — **bear**
m
[ˈo.so]
De pequeña quería tener a un oso pardo de mascota para asustar a mis vecinos.
-When I was little, I wanted to have a pet brown bear to scare my neighbors.

1302 miel — **honey**
f
[ˈmjɛl]
Me gusta ponerme miel en la tostada por las mañanas.
-I like to spread honey on my toast in the morning.

1303 pesadilla — **nightmare**
f
[pe.sa.ˈði.ja]
Está es la peor pesadilla de todo piloto.
-This is every pilot's worst nightmare.

1304 hueso — **bone**
m
[ˈwe.so]
El agujero del hueso es perfectamente circular.
-Sería honesto reconocer que estos temores son racistas.

1305 enojar(se) — **anger**
vb
[e.no.ˈxar.se)]
Se burlan de mí, me hacen enojar.
-They tease me, make me mad.

1306 sombra — **shadow**
f
[ˈsõm.bra]
La sombra del ratón al atardecer es más larga que la del gato al mediodía.
-The mouse's shadow at dusk is longer than the cat's shadow at noon.

1307 muñeca — **wrist, doll**
f
[mu.ˈɲe.ka]
Quiero comprar esta muñeca de juguete.
-I want to buy this toy doll.

1308 canal — **channel**
m
[ka.ˈnal]
Ana, tienes que cambiar de canal.
-Ana, you need to change the channel.

1309	**planta**	**plant**
	f	
	[ˈplãn̪.ta]	Esta planta creció poco a poco.
		-This plant grew little by little.

1310	**visión**	**vision, view**
	f	
	[bi.ˈsjõn]	Los posibles efectos secundarios incluyen visión borrosa y dificultad respiratoria.
		-Possible side effects include blurred vision and shortness of breath.

1311	**asqueroso**	**disgusting**
	adj	
	[as.ke.ˈro.so]	En toda mi vida nunca había visto algo tan asqueroso.
		-I've never seen anything so disgusting in all my life.

1312	**cumplir(se)**	**accomplish; expire**
	vb; vbr	
	[kũm.ˈplir.se)]	Nuestro deber es cumplir esos compromisos.
		-It is our duty to fulfill these commitments.

1313	**personaje**	**celebrity, character**
	m/f	
	[pɛr.so.ˈna.xe]	No queríamos crear un personaje convencional.
		-We didn't want to create a conventional character.

1314	**preciso**	**precise, essential**
	adj	
	[pre.ˈsi.so]	Tengo la costumbre de ser preciso.
		-I'm in the habit of being precise.

1315	**moda**	**fashion**
	f	
	[ˈmo.ða]	No tengo que hablar sobre moda.
		-I don't have to talk about fashion.

1316	**útil**	**useful; tool**
	adj; m	
	[ˈu.til]	Un centavo usado suele ser más útil que uno ahorrado.
		-A penny spent is often more useful than one saved.

1317	**revolución**	**revolution**
	f	
	[re.βo.lu.ˈsjõn]	Vivimos en un momento de revolución técnica.
		-We are living in a time of technical revolution.

1318	**impresión**	**impression**
	f	
	[ĩm.pre.ˈsjõn]	Uno siempre debe dar la impresión de que puede cambiar el rumbo de las cosas.
		-One should always give the impression that they can change the course of things.

1319	**compartir**	**share**
	vb	
	[kõm.par.ˈtir]	Quisiera compartir con usted mi asombro.
		-I would like to share with you my astonishment.

1320	**habla**	**speech**
	m	
	[ˈa.βla]	Es probable que se necesite terapia para mejorar el habla.
		-Therapy may be needed to improve speech.

1321	**paquete**	**package**
	m	
	[pa.ˈkɛ.te]	Hay un paquete en el correo para usted.
		-There's a package in the mail for you.

1322	**resolver**	**solve**
	vb	
	[re.sol.ˈβɛr]	Desde entonces hemos intentado resolver esta cuestión.
		-Since then, we have been trying to resolve this issue.

1323	**comunidad**	**community**
	f	
	[ko.mu.ni.ˈðað]	Esta comunidad sigue ejerciendo sus actividades en la capital.
		-La community continued to carry out its activities in the capital.

| 1324 | **nacer** | **be born** |

vb
[na.ˈsɛɾ]

Bueno, parece que el bebé no quiere nacer.
-Well, it seems that the baby just doesn't want to be born.

1325 nadar — **swim**
vb
[na.ˈðaɾ]

Tu hermana no puede nadar bien, ¿verdad?
-Your sister cannot swim well, can she?

1326 senador — **senator**
m
[se.na.ˈðoɾ]

Llamaré al senador para pedir una cita.
-I'll call the senator and make an appointment.

1327 favorito — **favorite; favorite**
adj; m
[fa.βo.ˈri.to]

Me dio su libro favorito como regalo de despedida y se mudó a Osaka.
-He gave me his favorite book as a farewell gift and moved to Osaka.

1328 humo — **smoke**
m
[ˈu.mo]

Nunca nos encontrarán entre este humo.
-They'll never find us in this smoke.

1329 sótano — **basement**
m
[ˈso.ta.no]

Seguiremos utilizando el sótano como taller.
-We'll continue to use the cellar as a workshop.

1330 julio — **July**
m
[ˈxu.ljo]

Las acciones alcanzaron su punto más alto el julio pasado.
-The stock reached its high point last July.

1331 venta — **sale**
f
[ˈbẽn̪.ta]

La venta de entradas comenzará el lunes.
-Ticket sales will begin Monday.

1332 sorprender(se) — **surprise**
vb
[sor.prẽn̪.ˈdɛr.se)]

Creo que te vas a sorprender cuando eclosione.
-I think you're going to be surprised when it hatches.

1333 fresco — **cool, fresh; shameless**
adj; m
[ˈfrɛs.ko]

Hacía fresco bajo la sombra de los árboles.
-It was cool in the shade of the trees.

1334 bolso — **purse**
m
[ˈbol.so]

Adelante. Te sujetaré el bolso.
-You go ahead. I'll hold your purse.

1335 meter(se) — **put, get into**
vb
[mɛ.ˈtɛr.se)]

"¡¿Cómo ha conseguido meter una maleta dentro de su bolsillo?!" preguntó la mujer, anonadada.
-"How did you fit a briefcase into your pocket?!" the woman asked, stunned.

1336 búsqueda — **search**
f
[ˈbus.ke.ða]

Todo esto agilizará la búsqueda de alternativas.
-All of this will accelerate the search for alternatives.

1337 rodilla — **knee**
f
[ro.ˈði.ʝa]

Jim se hirió la rodilla cuando se cayó.
-Jim hurt his knee when he fell down.

1338 licencia — **license**
f
[li.ˈsẽn.sja]

No eres lo suficientemente mayor para sacarte una licencia de conducir.
-You're not old enough to get a driver's license.

1339 magnífico — **magnificent**
adj
[maɣ.ˈni.fi.ko]

Debemos reconocer que están realizando un trabajo magnífico.
-We must recognize that you are doing a magnificent job.

1340 nación — **nation**

	f	Toda la nación quiere paz.
	[na.ˈsjõn]	-The whole nation wants peace.
1341	**caza**	**hunt**
	f	Has aprendido a cazar. Eso es mucho más emocionante.
	[ˈka.sa]	-You've learned to hunt. That's much more exciting.
1342	**plato**	**dish**
	m	Podemos poner media patata por plato.
	[ˈpla.to]	-We can put half a potato per plate.
1343	**fecha**	**date**
	f	Solo le recuerdo la fecha límite.
	[ˈfe.tʃa]	-I'm just reminding you of the deadline.
1344	**escalera**	**staircase**
	f	Hay una escalera que te llevará al tejado.
	[ɛs.ka.ˈlɛ.ra]	-There's a ladder that'll get you to the roof.
1345	**crédito**	**credit**
	m	Parece haber algún problema con nuestro crédito.
	[ˈkre.ði.to]	-There seems to be some issue with our credit.
1346	**aguantar(se)**	**put up with, tolerate**
	vb	No podría aguantar a este hombre otra noche.
	[a.ɣwãn̪.ˈtar.se]]	-There's no way I could stand this guy for another night.
1347	**responder**	**answer**
	vb	Intentaré responder brevemente a cada pregunta.
	[rɛs.põn̪.ˈdɛr]	-I will try to answer each question very briefly.
1348	**soportar**	**support, bear**
	vb	No podría soportar ver semejante escena.
	[so.por.ˈtar]	-I couldn't bear to see such a scene.
1349	**ira**	**anger**
	f	Había mucha ira en ese grupo.
	[ˈi.ra]	-There was so much anger among this group.
1350	**brujo**	**wizard**
	m	Algún día serás un brujo muy importante.
	[ˈbru.xo]	-You're going to be a very important sorcerer one day.
1351	**complicado**	**complicated**
	adj	Es más complicado que eso.
	[kõm.pli.ˈka.ðo]	-It's more complicated than that.
1352	**casualidad**	**chance**
	f	Me encontré con él de pura casualidad.
	[ka.swa.li.ˈðað]	-I met him by pure chance.
1353	**castigo**	**punishment**
	m	Este castigo cruel e inhumano sigue aplicándose.
	[kas.ˈti.ɣo]	-This cruel and inhuman punishment continues to be applied.
1354	**amanecer**	**dawn; wake up**
	m; vb	Habríamos esperado allí hasta el amanecer.
	[a.ma.ne.ˈsɛr]	-We would have been waiting there until dawn.
1355	**mandar**	**send, be in charge**
	vb	Es una cobardía mandar cartas sin firmarlas.
	[mãn̪.ˈdar]	-It's cowardly to send letters without signing them.
1356	**computadora**	**computer (LA)**

f
[kõm.pu.ta.ˈðo.ra]

Puedes ahorrar energía cambiando los ajustes de tu computadora.
-You can save energy by changing the settings on your computer.

1357 **controlar(se)**

vb
[kõn.tro.ˈlar.se)]

control

Cuando entendemos las causas, podemos controlar los efectos.
-When we understand the causes, we can control the effects.

1358 **suelto**

adj
[ˈswɛl.to]

loose

Dile que mire el canalón suelto.
-Ask him to look at that loose gutter.

1359 **título**

m
[ˈti.tu.lo]

title, degree

¿Cuál es el título de tu nuevo libro?
-What's the title of your new book?

1360 **jueves**

m
[ˈxwe.βes]

Thursday

Votaremos sobre ello el próximo jueves.
-We shall be voting on this next Thursday.

1361 **entrevistar**

vb
[ɛ̃n.tre.βis.ˈtar]

interview

Nunca aceptaría entrevistar a una persona modesta.
-I never would ever agree to interview a modest person.

1362 **piano**

m
[ˈpja.no]

piano

Él se sienta al piano y empieza a tocar.
-He sits at the piano and begins to play.

1363 **despacho**

m
[dɛs.ˈpa.ʧo]

office

Necesito que vengas a mi despacho.
-I need to see you in my office.

1364 **distinto**

adj
[dis.ˈtĩn.to]

different

Ella dijo que quería probar algo distinto.
-She said she wanted to try something different.

1365 **saltar(se)**

vb; vbr
[sal.ˈtar.se)]

jump; skip, break

Si quieres saltar, hazlo rápido.
-If you want to jump, do it quickly.

1366 **concertar**

vb
[kõn.sɛr.ˈtar]

arrange

Es muy importante concertar más acuerdos de este tipo.
-It is very important to conclude more such agreements.

1367 **prisionero**

m
[pri.sjo.ˈnɛ.ro]

prisoner

Él es un prisionero de guerra.
-He's a prisoner of war.

1368 **pieza**

f
[ˈpje.sa]

piece

No funcionará sin la última pieza.
-It won't work without the final piece.

1369 **visitar**

vb
[bi.si.ˈtar]

visit

Suelen estar juntos y van a la ópera o visitan galerías de arte.
-They are often together and they go to the opera or visit art galleries.

1370 **comité**

m
[ko.mi.ˈte]

committee

Todos los miembros del comité se odian.
-All the members of the committee hate one another.

1371 **fila**

f
[ˈfi.la]

row

Cada objeto debe mostrarse en una fila separada.
-Each item should be shown on a separate line.

1372 **medianoche**

midnight

	f	
	[me.ðja.ˈno.ʧe]	-It's midnight and I'm cleaning my room.
1373	**éxito**	**success**
	m	Espero que este proyecto sea un éxito.
	[ˈɛk.si.to]	-I hope that this project will be a success.
1374	**parada**	**stop**
	f	Tengo que hacer una pequeña parada.
	[pa.ˈra.ða]	-I just have a quick stop to make.
1375	**interesado**	**interested, selfish**
	adj	Estoy interesado en ser miembro.
	[ĩn̪.tɛ.re.ˈsa.ðo]	-I'm interested in becoming a member.
1376	**sección**	**section, division**
	f	Encontrarás ese libro en la sección de historia de la biblioteca.
	[sɛk.ˈsjõn]	-You will find that book in the historical section of the library.
1377	**altura**	**height**
	f	Su altura es una gran ventaja cuando juega al voleibol.
	[al̪.ˈtu.ra]	-His height is a great advantage when he plays volleyball.
1378	**documento**	**document**
	m	Necesito ayuda para traducir este documento al francés.
	[do.ku.ˈmẽn̪.to]	-I need help translating this document into French.
1379	**compromiso**	**commitment, dilemma**
	m	Hablamos del compromiso con el futuro.
	[kõm.pro.ˈmi.so]	-We speak of the commitment to the future.
1380	**martes**	**Tuesday**
	m	Solicitaste un pasaporte estadounidense el pasado martes.
	[ˈmar.tes]	-You applied for a US passport last Tuesday.
1381	**caro**	**expensive**
	adj	No puedo permitirme comprar un automóvil tan caro.
	[ˈka.ro]	-I can't afford to buy such an expensive car.
1382	**templo**	**temple**
	m	Este es el templo que solíamos visitar.
	[ˈtẽm.plo]	-This is the temple which we used to visit.
1383	**meta**	**goal**
	f	Nuestra meta final es establecer la paz mundial.
	[ˈmɛ.ta]	-Our ultimate goal is to establish world peace.
1384	**pasta**	**pasta**
	f	Ana hizo pasta con salchicha picante.
	[ˈpas.ta]	-Ana made pasta with spicy sausage.
1385	**liso**	**flat**
	adj	Todo el terreno de alrededor está liso pero el bosque es un problema.
	[ˈli.so]	-There's flat terrain all around, but the woods are a problem.
1386	**guion**	**script**
	m	Escucha, queremos hablar contigo sobre el guion.
	[ˈgjõn]	-Listen, we want to talk to you about the script.
1387	**pensamiento**	**thought**
	m	Un pensamiento impuro nunca ha cruzado su mente.
	[pẽn.sa.ˈmjẽn̪.to]	-Never has an impure thought crossed her mind.
1388	**treinta**	**thirty**

	num	El cruzó el Océano Pacífico en treinta días.
	[ˈtrei̯n.ta]	-He crossed the Pacific Ocean in thirty days.
1389	**hierba**	**grass**
	f	Para entonces habré cortado la hierba.
	[ˈ‡i̯ɛr.βa]	-I'll have mown thc grass by then.
1390	**impresionante**	**impressive**
	adj	Creo que va a ser impresionante.
	[ĩm.pre.sjo.ˈnãn̯.te]	-I think it's going to be awesome.
1391	**teta**	**tit**
	f	No has visto la teta de una mujer en la vida.
	[ˈtɛ.ta]	-You've never seen a woman's tit in your life.
1392	**pasión**	**passion**
	f	Si queremos pasión, necesitamos controversia.
	[pa.ˈsjõn]	-If we want passion, we need controversy.
1393	**actitud**	**attitude**
	f	Creo que muchos científicos tienen esta actitud.
	[ak̚.ti.ˈtuð]	-I think a lot of scientists have this attitude.
1394	**prometido**	**fiancé**
	m	El prometido ni siquiera tiene pasaporte.
	[pro.mɛ.ˈti.ðo]	-The fiancé doesn't even have a passport.
1395	**clave**	**key**
	f	Me gustaría destacar algunos puntos clave.
	[ˈkla.βe]	-I should like to single out a few key points.
1396	**acusar**	**accuse**
	vb	No quiero acusar injustamente a alguien.
	[a.ku.ˈsar]	-I don't want to wrongly accuse somebody.
1397	**lágrima**	**tear**
	f	Se secó una lágrima de su mejilla.
	[ˈla.ɣri.ma]	-She wiped a tear from her cheek.
1398	**suicidio**	**suicide**
	m	Hicieron que su muerte pareciera un suicidio.
	[swi.ˈsi.ðjo]	-Her death was made to look like a suicide.
1399	**gasolina**	**gasoline**
	f	El coste de la gasolina sigue subiendo.
	[ga.so.ˈli.na]	-The cost of gasoline keeps on going up.
1400	**jugador**	**player, gambler**
	m	Jim es un jugador compulsivo, ¿no?
	[xu.ɣa.ˈðor]	-Jim is a compulsive gambler, isn't he?
1401	**encargo**	**errand**
	m	Creo que hemos encontrado tu siguiente encargo.
	[ẽŋ.ˈkar.ɣo]	-I think we've found your next assignment.
1402	**puerto**	**port**
	m	He escuchado que tiene nuestros barcos en el puerto.
	[ˈpwɛr.to]	-I've heard that he's keeping our ships in the harbor.
1403	**urgente**	**urgent**
	adj	Es urgente concluir esta cuestión lo antes posible.
	[ur.ˈxẽn̯.te]	-It is urgent that we conclude this matter as soon as possible.
1404	**Rusia**	**Russia**

	f		Rusia está sufriendo una gran dificultad económica.
	[ˈru.sja]		-Russia is facing great financial difficulties.
1405	**elegante**	**elegant**	
	adj		No quiero sacrificar la comodidad para estar elegante.
	[e.le.ˈɣãn̪.te]		-I don't want to be stylish at the expense of comfort.
1406	**copia**	**copy**	
	f		No le entregaron una copia del informe.
	[ˈko.pja]		-He was not provided with a copy of the report.
1407	**aventura**	**adventure, affair**	
	f		Por favor, únete a nosotros en esta aventura épica.
	[a.βɛ̃n̪.ˈtu.ra]		-Please join us in this epic adventure.
1408	**entrenamiento**	**training**	
	m		Tengo que ir a nuestro último entrenamiento.
	[ɛ̃n̪.tre.na.ˈmjɛ̃n̪.to]		-I have to go to our last workout.
1409	**océano**	**ocean**	
	m		Estábamos planeando aterrizar en el océano.
	[o.ˈse.a.no]		-We were planning to land in the ocean.
1410	**ruta**	**route**	
	f		¿Cuál es la ruta a París?
	[ˈru.ta]		-Which is the route to Paris?
1411	**abandonar**	**abandon**	
	vb		Vas a abandonar a tus hijos.
	[a.βã̪n.do.ˈnar]		-You are going to abandon your children.
1412	**paraíso**	**paradise**	
	m		Tenemos este pequeño paraíso todo para nosotros.
	[pa.ra.ˈi.so]		-We've got this little paradise all to ourselves.
1413	**guía**	**guide; manual**	
	m/f; f		Es necesario concertar hora con un guía.
	[ˈgi.a]		-It is necessary to concert hour with a guide.
1414	**curiosidad**	**curiosity**	
	f		Me gustaría verlo, solo por curiosidad.
	[ku.rjo.si.ˈðað]		-I'd like to see it, just out of curiosity.
1415	**apetecer**	**crave**	
	vb		Me apetecería comer algo ahora.
	[a.pɛ.te.ˈsɛr]		-I would like to eat something now.
1416	**particular**	**peculiar, private**	
	adj		No necesitaba ningún motivo particular para no ser feliz.
	[par.ti.ku.ˈlar]		-She didn't need any special reason to be unhappy.
1417	**fotografía**	**photograph**	
	f		Quiero hablarte un poco sobre esta fotografía.
	[fo.to.ɣra.ˈfi.a]		-I want to tell you a little bit about this photograph.
1418	**poderoso**	**powerful**	
	adj		El mundo necesita un líder poderoso.
	[po.ðɛ.ˈro.so]		-The world needs a strong leader.
1419	**perdido**	**lost**	
	adj		Te he perdido todo el respeto.
	[pɛr.ˈði.ðo]		-I have lost all respect for you.
1420	**alertar**	**alert**	

vb
[a.lɛr.'tar]

Pero tendremos que alertar a las otras.
-But we'll need to alert the others.

1421 noble
adj
['no.βle]

noble, kind
Solo una noble podría permitirse comprarlo.
-Only a noble could afford to buy it.

1422 extranjero
adj; m
[ɛks.trãŋ.'xɛ.ro]

foreign; foreigner
Dominar un idioma extranjero requiere mucho trabajo duro.
-Mastering a foreign language requires a lot of hard work.

1423 rata
f
['ra.ta]

rat
Grité porque creí ver una rata.
-I screamed because I thought I saw a rat.

1424 instituto
m
[ĩns.ti.'tu.to]

high school
Estoy preparada para salir del instituto.
-I am ready to get out of high school.

1425 asco
m
['as.ko]

disgust
Siempre miro esta foto con asco.
-I always view this photo with disgust.

1426 popular
adj
[po.pu.'lar]

popular
Ella es la chica más popular de la clase.
-She's the most popular girl in the class.

1427 adorar
vb
[a.ðo.'rar]

worship
Solía adorar este juego cuando era pequeño.
-I used to love this game as a kid.

1428 imponer(se)
vb; vbr
[ĩm.po.'nɛr.se)]

impose; prevail
Jim siempre trata de imponer su voluntad sobre los demás.
-Jim is always trying to impose his will on others.

1429 piscina
f
[pis.'si.na]

swimming pool
También disponemos de una piscina infantil.
-A children's swimming pool is also available.

1430 sufrir
vb
[su.'frir]

suffer
Debemos sufrir las consecuencias de esto.
-We have to suffer the consequences of this.

1431 cómodo
adj
['ko.mo.ðo]

comfortable
Ponte cómodo, estaré contigo enseguida.
-Make yourself comfortable, I'll be right in.

1432 aviso
m
[a.'βi.so]

warning
Esa llamada telefónica fue un aviso.
-That phone call was a warning.

1433 ruso
adj; m
['ru.so]

Russian; Russian
Ojalá tuviera la oportunidad de aprender ruso.
-I wish I had the chance to learn Russian.

1434 ambulancia
f
[ãm.bu.'lãn.sja]

ambulance
Chocó un jeep militar y la ambulancia explotó.
-He crashed into a military jeep and the ambulance exploded.

1435 bendecir
vb
[bẽn.de.'sir]

bless
Quería bendecir el lugar donde murió Jim.
-He wanted to bless the place where Jim died.

1436 grado

degree

m
['gra.ðo]
Jim tiene un grado en biología.
-Jim has a degree in biology.

1437 **vaca** — **cow**

f
['ba.ka]
Su vaca murió después de tomarse la medicina que le diste.
-His cow died after she took the medicine you gave her.

1438 **territorio** — **territory**

m
[tε.ri.'to.rjo]
Estamos a punto de explorar territorio virgen.
-We're about to explore some uncharted territory.

1439 **conocimiento** — **knowledge**

m
[ko.no.si.'mjẽn̪.to]
El sabio de la tribu compartía su conocimiento con todos los jóvenes.
-The tribal wise man shared his knowledge with all the young.

1440 **reputación** — **reputation**

f
[re.pu.ta.'sjõn]
Muchos científicos tienen la reputación de ser excéntricos.
-Many scientists have the reputation of being eccentric.

1441 **imaginación** — **imagination**

f
[i.ma.xi.na.'sjõn]
Creo sinceramente que la imaginación humana no tiene límites.
-I strongly believe that human imagination is limitless.

1442 **excusa** — **excuse**

f
[ɛk.'su.sa]
Están esperando cualquier excusa para enviarte a prisión.
-They're waiting for an excuse to send you to prison.

1443 **campaña** — **campaign**

f
[kãm.'pa.ɲa]
La campaña fue un gran éxito.
-The campaign was a great success.

1444 **enseñar** — **teach, show**

vb
[ɛ̃n.se.'ɲar]
¿Acaso John vino a Japón a enseñar inglés?
-Did John come to Japan to teach English?

1445 **escritor** — **writer**

m
[ɛs.kri.'tor]
Jim es un escritor con talento.
-Jim is a talented writer.

1446 **página** — **page**

f
['pa.xi.na]
El contenido de esta página proviene de una fuente externa.
-The content in this page is coming from an external source.

1447 **atrapar** — **catch**

vb
[a.tra.'par]
No es fácil atrapar a una liebre con las manos desnudas.
-It is not easy to catch a hare with your bare hands.

1448 **autoridad** — **authority**

f
[au̯.to.ri.'ðað]
No tengo la autoridad para darte permiso.
-I don't have the authority to give you permission.

1449 **firmar** — **sign**

vb
[fir.'mar]
¿Podrías firmar el registro, por favor?
-Could you please sign the register?

1450 **paliza** — **beating**

f
[pa.'li.sa]
Esto no explica la paliza que recibiste.
-This doesn't explain the beating that you took.

1451 **armario** — **closet**

m
[ar.'ma.rjo]
Rápido, escondámonos en el armario.
-Quick, let's hide in the closet.

1452 **instante** — **instant**

m
[ĩns.ˈtãn̪.te]

Bueno, tráela a casa en este instante.
-Well, bring her home this instant.

1453 arroz — **rice**

m
[ˈa.ros]

¿Comes arroz en tu país?
-Do you eat rice in your country?

1454 crisis — **crisis**

f
[ˈkri.sis]

La crisis del sistema penitenciario parece seguir agravándose.
-The crisis in the prison system seems to be worsening.

1455 cruzar — **cross**

vb
[kru.ˈsar]

Ella ayudó al anciano a cruzar la calle.
-She helped the old man cross the road.

1456 piedad — **piety**

m
[pje.ˈðað]

Podría haberme matado pero en lugar de eso me mostró piedad.
-He could have killed me, but instead, he showed me mercy.

1457 kilo — **kilo**

m
[ˈki.lo]

¿Cuánto cuesta el kilo de cebollas?
-How much does the kilo of onions cost?

1458 divorcio — **divorce**

m
[di.ˈβor.sjo]

Ha estado llorando desde su divorcio.
-Ever since her divorce, she's been crying.

1459 anterior — **previous**

adj
[ãn̪.tɛ.ˈrjor]

Me gustaría repetir mi pregunta anterior.
-I would like to repeat my previous question.

1460 fiebre — **fever**

f
[ˈfje.βre]

El resfriado no suele presentar fiebre alta.
-The cold does not usually present a high fever.

1461 registro — **search, register**

m
[re.ˈxis.tro]

Fui yo quien autorizó el registro.
-I was the one who authorized the search.

1462 esposa — **wife**

f
[ɛs.ˈpo.sa]

El presidente y su esposa están manejando esto como deberían.
-The president and his wife are handling this as they should.

1463 caramba — **good grief, damn**

int
[ka.ˈrãm.ba]

Digo, caramba, míralo de esta manera.
-I mean, hell, look at it this way.

1464 moral — **moral; morals**

adj; f
[mo.ˈral]

Tenemos la obligación moral de actuar ante tal sufrimiento.
-We have a moral obligation to act in the face of such suffering.

1465 acceso — **access**

m
[ak.ˈse.so]

Tienen acceso a la biblioteca.
-They have access to the library.

1466 pasillo — **hall**

m
[pa.ˈsi.jo]

No quiero congregaciones en el pasillo.
-I don't want anybody congregating around the hallway.

1467 asistente — **assistant**

m/f
[a.sis.ˈtɛn̪.te]

Mi secretaria está escribiendo mis textos y mi asistente está hablando por teléfono.
-My secretary is typing my texts and my assistant is talking on the telephone.

1468 tráfico — **traffic**

	m	El tráfico es intenso aquí, sobre todo por las mañanas.
	['tra.fi.ko]	-The traffic is heavy here, especially in the morning.
1469	**faltar**	**lack, miss**
	vb	Pueden faltar unos días a clase.
	[faḷ.'tar]	-You can miss a few days of school.
1470	**secundario**	**secondary; side effect**
	adj; m	Hay varias escuelas privadas a nivel tanto primario como secundario.
	[se.kũn̪.'da.rjo]	-There are also a number of private schools at both the primary and secondary levels.
1471	**garganta**	**throat**
	f	Tengo dolor de garganta y moqueo.
	[gar.'ɣãn̪.ta]	-I got a sore throat and a runny nose.
1472	**asustar(se)**	**scare**
	vb	No queremos asustar innecesariamente a nadie.
	[a.sus.'tar.se)]	-We don't want to unnecessarily frighten anyone.
1473	**enfrente**	**opposite**
	adv	Verás un coche negro estacionado enfrente.
	[ẽm.'frẽn̪.te]	-You'll see a black car parked opposite.
1474	**museo**	**museum**
	m	Este museo necesita un nuevo guía.
	[mu.'se.o]	-This museum needs a new guide.
1475	**valle**	**valley**
	m	Bajamos al valle donde está el pueblo.
	['ba.ʝe]	-We went down to the valley where the village is.
1476	**misterio**	**mystery**
	m	Aún así vamos a resolver este misterio.
	[mis.'te.rjo]	-We're still going to solve this mystery.
1477	**alarma**	**alarm**
	f	Si suena la alarma, camina, no corras.
	[a.'lar.ma]	-In case the alarm rings, walk, don't run.
1478	**contestar**	**answer**
	vb	Me gustaría tratar de contestar algunas preguntas específicas.
	[kõn̪.tes.'tar]	-I would like to try and answer some specific questions.
1479	**joya**	**jewel**
	f	Encontraron la joya en un lugar inesperado.
	['xo.ʝa]	-The jewel was found in an unlikely place.
1480	**coma**	**comma; coma**
	f; m	No cambió ningún punto, coma, ni siquiera corrigió los errores ortográficos.
	['ko.ma]	-He didn't change a period, a comma, or even correct the spelling mistakes.
1481	**auxilio**	**help; help**
	m; int	Sus gritos de auxilio fueron ahogados por el rugido de las olas.
	[au̯k.'si.ljo]	-His cries for help were drowned by the roar of the waves.
1482	**zorro**	**fox**
	m	El rápido zorro marrón no saltó por encima del perro vago.
	['so.ro]	-The quick brown fox didn't jump over the lazy dog.
1483	**franco**	**honest**
	adj	Ojala pudiera ser franco con ella.
	['frãŋ.ko]	-I wish I could be frank with her.
1484	**don**	**talent**

m
['dõn]

Tienes un don increíble y te necesitamos.
-You have an incredible gift and we need you.

1485 **entrega**

f
[ẽn̪.'tre.ɣa]

delivery

Tengo una entrega para Jim.
-I have a delivery for Jim.

1486 **celda**

f
['sɛl̪.da]

cell

Dijo que estaba en una celda con otros tres prisioneros.
-He said that he was with three other prisoners in a cell.

1487 **ganador**

m
[ga.na.'ðor]

winner

Si el perdedor sonriera, el ganador perdería la emoción de la victoria.
-If the loser smiled, the winner would lose the thrill of victory.

1488 **cubrir(se)**

vb
[ku.'βrir.se)]

cover

Ese dinero es suficiente para cubrir los gastos.
-That's enough money to cover the expenses.

1489 **serpiente**

f
[sɛr.'pjẽn̪.te]

snake

Todas y cada una de las serpientes del zoo ha desaparecido.
-Every single snake at the zoo has disappeared.

1490 **Biblia**

f
['bi.βlja]

Bible

Yo preferiría usar mi propia Biblia.
-I'd prefer to use my own Bible.

1491 **terreno**

m
[tɛ.'re.no]

land

El terreno que pertenece a la propiedad está completamente vallado.
-The land belonging to the property is entirely fenced-in.

1492 **fantasma**

m
[fãn̪.'taʂ.ma]

ghost

Después de esto, nadie volvió a ver el fantasma de la anciana de nuevo en ese callejón.
-After this, nobody ever saw the ghost of the old woman again in that alley.

1493 **alegre**

adj
[a.'le.ɣre]

happy

Por ejemplo, hoy estoy muy alegre.
-For instance, today I'm very happy.

1494 **explosión**

f
[ɛks.plo.'sjõn]

explosion

La explosión que ha tenido lugar hoy aquí destruyó su hogar al completo.
-The explosion that happened here today has completely destroyed this home.

1495 **cuán**

adv
['kwãn]

how

Puede no saber cuán aterrador es o cuán peligroso es.
-It may not know how frightening it is or how dangerous it is.

1496 **circunstancia**

f
[sir.kũns.'tãn.sja]

circumstance

El uso de la fuerza en cualquier otra circunstancia es ilegal e ilegítimo.
-The use of force in any other circumstance is illegal and illegitimate.

1497 **cable**

m
['ka.βle]

cable

Necesito un nuevo cable USB.
-I need a new USB cable.

1498 **prohibir**

vb
[pro.i.'βir]

prohibit

Por consiguiente, es posible prohibir las actividades mencionadas.
-Therefore, it is possible to prohibit the activities in question.

1499 **celular**

m
[se.lu.'lar]

cell phone (LA)

Estoy cansadísimo de este viejo celular.
-I'm sick to death of this old cell phone.

1500 **puesto**

post, stand

	m	
	[ˈpwɛs.to]	Dice que puede conseguirte un puesto en su instituto. -He says he can get you a job in his school.
1501	**ambiente**	**environment**
	m	
	[ãm.ˈbjẽ̞.te]	La destrucción del medio ambiente es atroz. -The destruction of the environment is appalling.
1502	**lograr**	**achieve**
	vb	
	[lo.ˈɣrar]	Esta tecnología nos permitirá lograr nuestro objetivo. -This technology will allow us to achieve our goal.
1503	**bota**	**boot**
	f	
	[ˈbo.ta]	La huella parece ser de una bota militar corriente. -The tread looks like a standard military boot.
1504	**pene**	**penis**
	m	
	[ˈpe.ne]	Nuestros ejercicios reafirman los músculos del pene y ayudan a mantener una buena circulación sanguínea. -Our exercises develop the penis muscles and allow an optimal blood circulation.
1505	**costumbre**	**custom**
	f	
	[kos.ˈtũm.bre]	Es costumbre en Asia quitarse los zapatos antes de entrar a una casa o templo. -In Asian culture, it's customary to take one's shoes off before entering a house or temple.
1506	**cuadro**	**painting, frame**
	m	
	[ˈkwa.ðro]	El cuadro más famoso de la exposición representaba a un cielo estrellado sobrevolado por murciélagos. Era un poco siniestro. -The most famous painting in the exposition depicted a starry sky with bats flying over it. It was a little sinister.
1507	**experto**	**expert; expert**
	adj; m	
	[ɛks.ˈpɛr.to]	Únicamente un experto podría estudiarlo y entenderlo. -Only an expert could study it and understand it.
1508	**veneno**	**venom**
	m	
	[be.ˈne.no]	Escuché que podría haber sido veneno. -I heard that it could have been poison.
1509	**partida**	**departure, game**
	f	
	[par.ˈti.ða]	Estamos preocupados por su inesperada partida. -We are worried because of his unexpected departure.
1510	**bandera**	**flag**
	f	
	[bãn̪.ˈdɛ.ra]	Capitán, su bandera sigue allí arriba. -Captain, his flag's still up there.
1511	**combustible**	**fuel; combustible**
	m; adj	
	[kõm.bus.ˈti.βle]	No le grites al niño que está llorando. Solo le echas combustible al fuego. -Don't shout at the crying child. It only adds fuel to the fire.
1512	**recompensa**	**reward**
	f	
	[re.kõm.ˈpẽn.sa]	La decisión de hoy es una recompensa por nuestros esfuerzos. -Today's decision is a reward for our efforts.
1513	**organización**	**organization**
	f	
	[or.ɣa.ni.sa.ˈsjõn]	Además, su organización ayudó a la policía. -In addition, his organization helped the police.
1514	**cáncer**	**cancer**
	m	
	[ˈkãn.sɛr]	Aquel hombre murió de cáncer al pulmón hace una semana. -That man died of lung cancer a week ago.
1515	**deuda**	**debt**

f

['deu̯.ða]

Estoy profundamente en deuda con mis amigos por toda su ayuda.
-I am deeply indebted to my friends for all their help.

1516 raza   **race**

f

['ra.sa]

Hemos sido invadidos por una raza alienígena.
-We've been invaded by an alien race.

1517 juventud   **youth**

f

[xu.βẽn̯.'tuð]

Lloro por mi juventud perdida.
-I weep for my lost youth.

1518 crecer   **grow**

vb

[kre.'sɛr]

Buscamos personas que quieran crecer con nosotros.
-We are looking for people who want to grow with us.

1519 comportamiento   **behavior**

m

[kõm.por.ta.'mjẽn̯.to]

No tiene que aguantar este tipo de comportamiento.
-You don't have to put up with this kind of behavior.

1520 reír   **laugh**

vb

[re.'ir]

Podía hacerme reír más que nadie.
-She could make me laugh more than anyone.

1521 rescatar   **rescue**

vb

[rɛs.ka.'tar]

Una mujer cruzó el foso de un castillo para rescatar a un perro viejo atrapado.
-A woman crossed a castle moat to rescue a stranded old dog.

1522 repetir   **repeat**

vb

[re.pɛ.'tir]

No podemos repetir los mismos errores que ocurrieron en Copenhague.
-We cannot repeat the same errors that occurred in Copenhagen.

1523 montar   **mount**

vb

[mõn̯.'tar]

No tenemos que montar una organización gigante.
-We don't have to mount a large organization.

1524 plaza   **square**

f

['pla.sa]

Solíamos sentarnos juntos en la plaza.
-We used to sit together in the square.

1525 rumbo   **in the direction of**

m

['rũm.bo]

Seguir tal rumbo no sería útil.
-Embarking on such a course would not be helpful.

1526 pata   **leg**

f

['pa.ta]

La grulla estaba paraba en una pata.
-The crane was standing on one leg.

1527 decente   **proper**

adj

[de.'sẽn̯.te]

Es difícil encontrar a un tipo decente.
-It's difficult to find a decent guy.

1528 producción   **production**

f

[pro.ðuk.'sjõn]

Necesitamos más producción u ocurrirá un desastre.
-We need more production or there will be a disaster.

1529 nacimiento   **birth**

m

[na.si.'mjẽn̯.to]

Ana sufrió una severa depresión posparto después del nacimiento de su primer hijo.
-Ana suffered from severe postnatal depression after the birth of her first child.

1530 aldea   **village**

f

[al̯.'de.a]

La aldea parece completamente aislada del mundo exterior.
-The village seems completely cut off from the outside world.

1531 letra   **letter**

	f	Empieza con una letra del alfabeto.
	[ˈlɛ.tra]	-It starts with a letter of the alphabet.
1532	**biblioteca**	**library**
	f	Su excelente biblioteca e instalaciones merecen ser mejoradas.
	[bi.βljo.ˈte.ka]	-Its excellent library and facilities deserve to be further improved.
1533	**probable**	**likely**
	adj	Es probable que consiga la beca.
	[pro.ˈβa.βle]	-He is likely to win the scholarship.
1534	**marco**	**framework, frame**
	m	Simplificará considerablemente el marco reglamentario actual.
	[ˈmar.ko]	-It will simplify to a great extent the current regulatory framework.
1535	**explicación**	**explanation**
	f	Su explicación no es clara.
	[ɛks.pli.ka.ˈsjõn]	-His explanation is not clear.
1536	**exterior**	**exterior; external**
	m; adj	También tiene un parking exterior para 100 vehículos.
	[ɛks.tɛ.ˈrjor]	-It also has an exterior coach park for 100 vehicles.
1537	**incendio**	**fire**
	m	La causa del incendio es desconocida.
	[ĩn.ˈsẽn.djo]	-The source of the fire is unknown.
1538	**atacar**	**attack**
	vb	No pretendo atacar a los científicos.
	[a.ta.ˈkar]	-I do not intend to attack the scientists.
1539	**unión**	**union**
	f	Dice que queremos una unión económica.
	[u.ˈnjõn]	-He is saying that we want an economic union.
1540	**desagradable**	**unpleasant**
	adj	Deberías disfrutar tu vida sin hacer desagradable la vida de los otros.
	[de.sa.ɣra.ˈða.βle]	-You should enjoy your life without making others' lives unpleasant.
1541	**distrito**	**district**
	m	Ella ni siquiera vive en nuestro distrito.
	[dis.ˈtri.to]	-She doesn't even live in our district.
1542	**apellido**	**surname**
	m	Será creíble ya que comparten el mismo apellido.
	[a.pe.ˈʝi.ðo]	-It will be believable since you share the same surname.
1543	**patio**	**courtyard**
	m	Teníamos un manzano en el patio.
	[ˈpa.tjo]	-We had an apple tree in the backyard.
1544	**comercial**	**commercial**
	adj	Queréis darles la mejor formación comercial a vuestros aprendices.
	[ko.mɛr.ˈsjal]	-You want to give the best commercial formation to your trainees.
1545	**lento**	**slow; slowly**
	adj; adv	Parece estar yendo a un ritmo muy lento.
	[ˈlẽn.to]	-It seems to be going at a very slow pace.
1546	**diamante**	**diamond**
	m	Este anillo de diamante es muy extravagante para mí.
	[dja.ˈmãn.te]	-This diamond ring is too extravagant for me.
1547	**ducha**	**shower**

f
['du.tʃa]
Ellos tienen un ducha con un sistema termostático de lujo.
-They have a deluxe thermostatic shower system.

1548 fijar(se) — **set; pay attention to**
vb; vbr
[fi.ˈxar.se)]
Esto nos permitirá fijar restricciones ambiciosas pero realistas.
-This will enable us to set ambitious but realistic constraints.

1549 mayo — **May**
m
[ˈma.jo]
Entonces cerramos completamente hasta el siguiente mayo.
-Then we close down completely until the following May.

1550 ayudante — **assistant; assistant**
adj; m
[a.ju.ˈðãn̪.te]
Será su ayudante mientras esté aquí.
-She'll be your helper while you're here.

1551 italiano — **Italian; Italian**
adj; m
[i.ta.ˈlja.no]
En italiano todo se escribe como se pronuncia.
-In Italian, everything is written the way you pronounce it.

1552 saludo — **greeting**
m
[sa.ˈlu.ðo]
Se utiliza tanto como saludo que como advertencia.
-It is used both as a greeting and as a warning.

1553 pantalla — **screen**
f
[pãn̪.ˈta.ja]
Tenemos una pantalla de plasma en el autobús.
-We got a plasma screen on the tour bus.

1554 ilegal — **illegal**
adj
[i.le.ˈɣal]
Consideran que esta práctica debe declararse ilegal.
-They consider that this practice should be made illegal.

1555 colina — **hill**
f
[ko.ˈli.na]
Vimos que no podíamos conducir colina abajo.
-We realized we couldn't drive down the hill.

1556 porquería — **filth**
f
[por.kɛ.ˈri.a]
Jack, estás comiendo demasiada porquería.
-Jack, you're eating too much junk.

1557 civil — **civil; civilian**
adj; m/f
[si.ˈβil]
Están encarcelados en una prisión civil en condiciones escandalosas.
-They are being detained in a civilian prison in disgraceful conditions.

1558 cementerio — **cemetery**
m
[se.mẽn̪.ˈtɛ.rjo]
Fue enterrado en el Cementerio de la Recoleta.
-He was buried in the La Recoleta Cemetery.

1559 ala — **wing**
m
[ˈa.la]
Cerraron ambos lados de esta ala.
-They sealed off this wing at both ends.

1560 conductor — **driver**
m
[kõn̪.dukˈtor]
Jim es un conductor imprudente.
-Jim is a reckless driver.

1561 guardar(se) — **keep, retain; take precautions against**
vb; vbr
[gwar.ˈðar.se)]
No tengo suficiente espacio para guardar estas cajas.
-I don't have enough space to store these boxes.

1562 periodista — **journalist**
m/f
[pɛ.rjo.ˈðis.ta]
Él es un periodista independiente.
-He is a freelance journalist.

1563 emocionante — **exciting**

	adj [e.mo.sjo.ˈnãn̪.te]	Empiezan una parte emocionante de sus propias carreras políticas. -They start an exciting part of their own political careers.
1564	**tripulación** f [tri.pu.la.ˈsjõn]	**crew** A la tripulación le alegrará saberlo. -Our crew will be glad to know that.
1565	**afortunado** adj [a.for.tu.ˈna.ðo]	**lucky** Es afortunado de tenerte como madre. -He's lucky to have you for a mom.
1566	**estupidez** f [ɛs.tu.ˈpi.ðes]	**stupidity** Te lo suplico, perdona mi estupidez. -I beg you, forgive my foolishness.
1567	**circo** m [ˈsir.ko]	**circus** Ese chico causaría sensación en un circo. -That kid would be a sensation in a circus.
1568	**trabajador** m; adj [tra.βa.xa.ˈðor]	**worker; hard-working** El término trabajador de saneamiento es un eufemismo de basurero. -The term sanitation worker is a euphemism for a garbage man.
1569	**federal** adj [fe.ðɛ.ˈral]	**federal** La policía no hará arrestos en territorio federal. -The police will not make any arrest on federal land.
1570	**quince** num [ˈkĩn.se]	**fifteen** En aquel entonces tan solo teníamos quince años. -At the time, we were just fifteen years old.
1571	**demostrar** vb [de.mos.ˈtrar]	**prove, show** El trabajo del abogado es demostrar la inocencia de su cliente. -The lawyer's job is to prove that her client is innocent.
1572	**león** m [le.ˈõn]	**lion** Es como un león entre ovejas asustadas. -He is like a lion among a lot of frightened sheep.
1573	**aliento** m [a.ˈljẽn̪.to]	**breath** Su aliento apesta a alcohol. -His breath reeks of alcohol.
1574	**patrón** m [pa.ˈtrõn]	**pattern** El patrón de ondas es asombroso. -The wave pattern is astonishing.
1575	**ron** m [ˈrõn]	**rum** Te compré algo con ron y pasas. -I bought you something with rum and raisins.
1576	**adivinar** vb [a.ði.βi.ˈnar]	**guess** Puedo adivinar lo que algunos están pensando. -I can guess what some of you are thinking.
1577	**equipaje** m [e.ki.ˈpa.xe]	**luggage** Perdimos todo el equipaje, excepto dos maletas. -We lost all of our baggage, except for two pieces.
1578	**salsa** f [ˈsal.sa]	**sauce** No es sangre. Es salsa de tomate. -It's not blood. It's tomato sauce.
1579	**escritorio**	**desk**

m
[ɛs.kri.ˈto.rjo]
Voy a pedir un nuevo escritorio.
-I'm going to ask for a new desk.

1580 ciudadano
m; adj
[sju.ða.ˈða.no]
citizen; civic
Yo soy un ciudadano romano.
-I am a Roman citizen.

1581 traidor
m; adj
[trai̯.ˈðor]
traitor; treacherous
Hay un traidor entre nosotros, estoy seguro.
-We've got a traitor among us, I'm sure of it.

1582 alquiler
m
[al.ki.ˈlɛr]
rent
Estuvimos allí durante seis años sin pagar ningún alquiler.
-We stayed there for six years without paying any rent.

1583 instrucción
f
[ĩns.truk.ˈsjõn]
instruction
Esas escuelas seguirán usando el inglés como idioma de instrucción.
-Those schools will continue to use English as the medium of instruction.

1584 atreverse
vbr
[a.tre.ˈβɛr.se]
dare
Que nadie más se atreva a tocarlo.
-No one else dare touch it.

1585 práctica
f
[ˈprak̚.ti.ka]
practice
Lamentablemente, no podré continuar hoy esta práctica.
-Unfortunately, I will not be able to continue that practice today.

1586 España
f
[ɛs.ˈpa.ɲa]
Spain
Muchos jóvenes en España son desempleados.
-Many young people in Spain are unemployed.

1587 celebrar
vb
[se.le.ˈβrar]
celebrate
Hoy creo que podemos celebrar el cumplimiento de estos objetivos.
-Today I believe that we can celebrate the achievement of these objectives.

1588 duque
m
[ˈdu.ke]
duke
El duque tiene muchas tierras.
-The duke holds a lot of land.

1589 límite
m
[ˈli.mi.te]
limit
Pero esta opción tiene un límite.
-But there is a limit to this option.

1590 arresto
m
[a.ˈrɛs.to]
arrest
Estoy buscando información sobre un arresto que hizo en Agosto.
-I'm looking for some information on an arrest that you made back in August.

1591 permanecer
vb
[pɛr.ma.ne.ˈsɛr]
stay, remain
Usted deberá permanecer inmóvil durante el examen.
-You will need to remain still during the test.

1592 superficie
f
[su.pɛr.ˈfi.sje]
surface
Solo la superficie de las cosas revela su esencia.
-Only the surface of things reveals the essence of things.

1593 tono
m
[ˈto.no]
tone
Su tono me llevó a pensar que ya lo sabía.
-His tone lead me to think that he already knew.

1594 aparente
adj
[a.pa.ˈrẽn.te]
apparent
No hay daño aparente al hueso.
-There's no apparent damage to the bone.

1595 condado
county

m
[kõn̪.ˈda.ðo]

Podríamos haber utilizado eso para salir del condado.
-We could've used that to get out of the county.

1596 religión — religion

f
[re.li.ˈxjõn]

A veces desearía profesar otra religión diferente.
-Sometimes I wish I had a different religion.

1597 absurdo — absurd; nonsense

adj; m
[aβ.ˈsur.ðo]

Mira, sé que suena absurdo, pero soy astrofísico.
-Look, I know it sounds preposterous, but I'm an astrophysicist.

1598 miserable — miserable

adj
[mi.sɛ.ˈra.βle]

Quiero alejarte de este lugar miserable.
-I want to take you away from this wretched place.

1599 homicidio — homicide

m
[o.mi.ˈsi.ðjo]

Ellos investigaban un homicidio que no ocurrió.
-They were investigating a homicide that didn't happen.

1600 cultura — culture

f
[kul̪.ˈtu.ra]

Fomentaremos una cultura de inclusión.
-We will foster a culture of inclusion.

1601 ceremonia — ceremony

f
[sɛ.re.ˈmo.nja]

Prometió enviar un representante a esa ceremonia.
-He promised to send a representative to that ceremony.

1602 punta — tip

f
[ˈpũn̪.ta]

Esto fue solamente la punta del iceberg.
-This was just the tip of the iceberg.

1603 anuncio — advertisement, announcement

m
[a.ˈnũn.sjo]

Señor, quisiera hacer un anuncio.
-Sir, I would like to make an announcement.

1604 nube — cloud

f
[ˈnu.βe]

Mira esa nube de allá.
-Look at the cloud over there.

1605 gigante — gigantic; giant

adj; m
[xi.ˈɣã n̪.te]

Olvidó mencionar que era un gigante.
-You forgot to mention that he was a giant.

1606 sacerdote — priest

m
[sa.sɛr.ˈðo.te]

El sacerdote entró desesperado a la iglesia diciendo que tenía un mensaje de Dios.
-The priest frantically came into the church saying he had a message from God.

1607 estudio — studio, survey

m
[ɛs.ˈtu.ðjo]

Encontraba la idea del estudio muy útil.
-He found the concept of the study very useful.

1608 dirigir — lead, address

vb
[di.ri.ˈxir]

No tienes la experiencia necesaria para dirigir tal expedición.
-You do not have the experience necessary to lead such an expedition.

1609 coincidencia — coincidence

f
[koin̪.si.ˈðɛ̃n.sja]

No era una coincidencia que Jim y Ana estuvieran en la cafetería al mismo tiempo.
-It was no coincidence that both Jim and Ana were in the cafeteria at the same time.

1610 mental — mental

adj
[mẽn̪.ˈtal]

Al mismo tiempo, recibieron asistencia psicológica y mental.
-At the same time, they received psychological and mental help.

1611 **Internet**

m/f
[ĩn̪.tɛr.ˈnɛt]

Internet

Resulta especialmente alentador que los textos puedan consultarse en Internet.
-It was particularly gratifying that the texts had become available on the Internet.

1612 **carácter**

m
[ka.ˈrak̚.tɛr]

personality

Además es una gran persona, con mucho carácter.
-She is a great person as well, with a great personality.

1613 **celoso**

adj
[se.ˈlo.so]

jealous

Nunca antes me he sentido enfadado o celoso.
-I've never felt angry or jealous before.

1614 **sesión**

f
[se.ˈsjõn]

session

La sesión será interrumpida durante dos minutos.
-The sitting will be suspended for two minutes.

1615 **medir(se)**

vb
[me.ˈðir.se)]

measure

Voy a medir el edificio luego.
-I'm going to measure the building later.

1616 **sofá**

m
[so.ˈfa]

sofa

Es hora de levantarse del sofá.
-It's time to get up off the couch.

1617 **tratamiento**

m
[tra.ta.ˈmjẽn̪.to]

treatment

El tratamiento está siendo todo un éxito.
-The treatment is going successfully.

1618 **despertar(se)**

m; vb
[dɛs.pɛr.ˈtar.se)]

awakening; wake up

Cerré suavemente la puerta para no despertar al bebé.
-I closed the door quietly so I wouldn't wake the baby up.

1619 **conexión**

f
[ko.nɛk.ˈsjõn]

connection

Luego explicaré la conexión entre estos dos comportamientos.
-Then I'll draw the connection between these two behaviors.

1620 **rumor**

m
[ru.ˈmor]

rumor

Quiero averiguar el origen de este irresponsable rumor.
-I want to find out the source of this irresponsible rumor.

1621 **sincero**

adj
[sĩn.ˈsɛ.ro]

sincere

Me gustaría que fueras siempre sincero conmigo.
-I'd like it if you were always honest with me.

1622 **leyenda**

f
[le.ˈjẽn̪.da]

legend

La leyenda cuenta que él era invulnerable.
-The legend says he was invulnerable.

1623 **sugerir**

vb
[su.xɛ.ˈrir]

suggest

Me gustaría sugerir un enfoque diferente.
-I'd like to suggest a different approach.

1624 **lenguaje**

m
[lẽn.ˈgwa.xe]

language

Deberías moderar tu lenguaje cuando hables con ella.
-You should watch your language when you talk to her.

1625 **despedir(se)**

vb; vbr
[dɛs.pe.ˈðir.se)]

dismiss, lay off; say goodbye

No quería tener que despedir a nadie más nunca.
-She didn't want to have to fire anyone ever again.

1626 **clima**

climate

m
['kli.ma]
El clima de aquí se parece mucho al de Inglaterra.
-The climate here is very similar to that of England.

1627 **enfadar(se)** **irritate**
vb
[ẽɱ.fa.ˈðar.se)]
No queríamos hacer enfadar a Jim.
-We didn't want to upset Jim.

1628 **barato** **cheap**
adj
[ba.ˈra.to]
Vivo en un país donde el precio de un litro de petróleo es más barato que un litro de agua.
-I live in a country where the cost of a liter of petrol is cheaper than a liter of water.

1629 **español** **Spanish; Spaniard**
adj; m
[ɛs.pa.ˈɲol]
Obviamente, habla inglés, pero también puede hablar español.
-Obviously, he speaks English, but he can even speak Spanish.

1630 **esconder(se)** **hide**
vb
[ɛs.kõn̪.ˈdɛr.se)]
Jim, no necesitas esconder esto.
-Jim, you don't need to hide this.

1631 **condenar** **condemn**
vb
[kõn̪.de.ˈnar]
Tenemos que condenar estos incidentes.
-We must condemn these incidents.

1632 **reservar(se)** **save, book**
vb
[re.sɛr.ˈβar.se)]
Quisiera reservar un asiento en este tren.
-I'd like to reserve a seat on this train.

1633 **asombroso** **amazing**
adj
[a.sõm.ˈbro.so]
Empecé mi curso hoy y es absolutamente asombroso y maravilloso.
-I started my course today and it is absolutely amazing and wonderful.

1634 **virus** **virus**
m
[ˈbi.rus]
Hay que tomar medidas drásticas para impedir que el virus se propague más.
-Drastic measures must be taken to prevent the further spread of the virus.

1635 **pánico** **panic; panic**
adj; m
[ˈpa.ni.ko]
Los presos entraron en pánico y empezaron un motín.
-The prisoners panicked and started a riot.

1636 **acero** **steel**
m
[a.ˈsɛ.ro]
Hemos resuelto el problema del acero.
-We've solved the issue of the steel.

1637 **cocinar** **cook**
vb
[ko.si.ˈnar]
Jane me preguntó si querría cocinar.
-Jane asked me if I would like to cook.

1638 **helicóptero** **helicopter**
m
[e.li.ˈkop̚.tɛ.ro]
Los pasajeros desembarcaron y el helicóptero despegó nuevamente unos minutos después.
-Passengers disembarked, and the helicopter took off again a few minutes later.

1639 **pasaporte** **passport**
m
[pa.sa.ˈpor.te]
Debes llevar tu pasaporte al banco.
-You must take your passport to the bank.

1640 **sal** **salt**
f
[ˈsal]
Esto es lo que pasa cuando no tienes sal.
-This is what happens when you don't have salt.

1641 **bicicleta** **bicycle**

f
[bi.si.ˈklɛ.ta]
Te daré una bicicleta por tu cumpleaños.
-I will give you a bicycle for your birthday.

1642 cincuenta — **fifty**
num
[sĩŋ.ˈkwẽṇ.ta]
Cincuenta familias viven en este pequeño pueblo.
-Fifty families live in this tiny village.

1643 objeto — **object, goal**
m
[oβ.ˈxɛ.to]
Coloca el objeto delante del texto.
-Place the object in front of the text.

1644 coraje — **courage**
m
[ko.ˈra.xe]
Tardé años en encontrar el coraje.
-It took me years to find the courage.

1645 aceite — **oil**
m
[a.ˈsei̯.te]
¿Por qué se aplica aceite de oliva en sus pestañas?
-Why does she apply olive oil on her lashes?

1646 billete — **ticket, bill**
m
[bi.ˈʝɛ.te]
No sé cómo consiguió un billete.
-I don't know how you got a ticket.

1647 publicidad — **advertising**
f
[pu.βli.si.ˈðað]
Se reducirán los gastos en publicidad.
-Expenditures on advertising will be curtailed.

1648 mortal — **lethal; mortal**
adj; m/f
[mor.ˈtal]
El tratamiento sería mortal para él.
-The treatment would be fatal to him.

1649 botón — **button**
m
[bo.ˈtõn]
Jim no sabe cuál botón presionar.
-Jim doesn't know which button to push.

1650 cristal — **crystal**
m
[kris.ˈtal]
Él observó profundamente dentro de su esfera de cristal y predijo mi futuro.
-He looked deeply into his crystal ball and predicted my future.

1651 pizza — **pizza**
f
[ˈpis.sa]
El repartidor de pizza aún no ha llegado.
-The pizza delivery guy hasn't come by yet.

1652 moneda — **currency, coin**
f
[mo.ˈne.ða]
El muchacho robó la moneda de cobre.
-The boy stole the copper coin.

1653 apestar — **stink**
vb
[a.pɛs.ˈtar]
Bueno, las personas de por aquí empiezan a apestar.
-Well, people around here are starting to stink.

1654 metal — **metal**
m
[mɛ.ˈtal]
Recuperamos tres tipos diferentes de metal.
-We've recovered three different types of brass.

1655 opinar — **believe, give your opinion**
vb
[o.pi.ˈnar]
Ni siquiera tuve oportunidad de opinar.
-I never even had the chance to have an opinion.

1656 japonés — **Japanese; Japanese person**
adj; m
[xa.po.ˈnes]
Hablo japonés, inglés y francés.
-I speak Japanese, English, and French.

1657 septiembre — **September**

	m	Ya estamos a finales de septiembre.
	[sepˈtjẽm.bre]	-We are already at the end of September.
1658	**petróleo**	**oil**
	m	Tenemos que centrarnos en disminuir el petróleo.
	[pɛˈtro.le.o]	-We need to focus on reducing the oil.
1659	**archivo**	**archive, file**
	m	Necesita especificar el archivo a abrir.
	[arˈtʃi.βo]	-You need to specify the file to open.
1660	**vera**	**edge, side**
	f	Un camionero la halló caminando sola a la vera del camino.
	[ˈbɛ.ra]	-A trucker found her walking alone on the side of the road.
1661	**versión**	**version**
	f	Jim dijo que prefería la primera versión.
	[bɛrˈsjõn]	-Jim said he preferred the first version.
1662	**pozo**	**well**
	m	Sería horrible morir en un pozo.
	[ˈpo.so]	-It'll be horrible to die in a well.
1663	**ventaja**	**advantage**
	f	Una pequeña ventaja puede ser decisiva.
	[bẽn̪ˈta.xa]	-A tiny advantage can make all the difference.
1664	**dormitorio**	**bedroom**
	m	Podía oírla sollozar en su dormitorio.
	[dor.mi.ˈto.rjo]	-I could hear her sobbing in her bedroom.
1665	**cartera**	**wallet, schoolbag**
	f	Quédate aquí, voy a volver a por mi cartera.
	[karˈtɛ.ra]	-You just stay here and I'll go back and get my wallet.
1666	**mediodía**	**midday**
	m	Creía que no entrabas hasta mediodía.
	[me.ðjo.ˈði.a]	-I thought you weren't on until noon.
1667	**romántico**	**romantic**
	adj	Disfruta del ambiente romántico de una de nuestras habitaciones o
	[ro.ˈmãn̪.ti.ko]	apartamentos de invitados.
		-Enjoy the romantic atmosphere of one of the guest rooms or apartments.
1668	**alcance**	**scope, significance**
	m	También es fundamental definir claramente el alcance de cualquier evaluación.
	[alˈkãn.se]	-It is also critical to clearly define the scope of any assessment.
1669	**internacional**	**international**
	adj	La cooperación internacional desempeñó un papel decisivo.
	[ĩn̪.tɛr.na.sjo.ˈnal]	-International cooperation played an essential role.
1670	**competencia**	**competition, rival**
	f	El grado de competencia parece ser significativo.
	[kõm.pɛ.ˈtẽn.sja]	-The degree of competition appears to be significant.
1671	**esclavo**	**slave**
	m	El esclavo se convirtió en un gladiador.
	[ɛsˈkla.βo]	-The slave became a gladiator.
1672	**escándalo**	**scandal**
	m	No entiendo por qué armas tal escándalo.
	[ɛsˈkãn̪.da.lo]	-I don't know why you're making such a fuss.
1673	**tecnología**	**technology**

f
[tekˌno.lo.ˈxi.a]

La formación y el movimiento de los huracanes son caprichosos, incluso para la tecnología actual.
-The formation and movement of hurricanes are capricious, even with our present-day technology.

1674 **sobrino**

nephew

m
[so.ˈβri.no]

Mi sobrino estaba acostumbrado a quedarse despierto hasta tarde.
-My nephew was accustomed to staying up late.

1675 **rueda**

wheel

f
[ˈrwe.ða]

No tratemos de reinventar la rueda.
-Let us not attempt to reinvent the wheel.

1676 **división**

division, split

f
[di.βi.ˈsjõn]

Comenzaré a formar una división inmediatamente.
-I'll start assembling a division at once.

1677 **desconocer**

not know, not recognize

vb
[dɛs.ko.no.ˈsɛr]

No podemos desconocer los trágicos conflictos humanos que siguen asolando a diversas partes del mundo.
-We cannot ignore the tragic human conflicts that still rage on in various parts of the world.

1678 **ascensor**

elevator

m
[as.sẽn.ˈsor]

¿Puedes hacerme el favor de avisar al portero de que el ascensor no funciona?
-Could you do me the favor of telling the doorman the elevator doesn't work?

1679 **crema**

cream

f
[ˈkre.ma]

Le gustan las ensaladas con crema agria.
-He likes salads that contain sour cream.

1680 **hierro**

iron

m
[ˈɟjɛ.ro]

Solo recuerdo algo frío como el hierro.
-All I remember is something cold like iron.

1681 **pastor**

pastor, shepherd

m
[pas.ˈtor]

Un pastor tenía un perro fiel llamado Sultán, que se había hecho muy viejo y había perdido todos sus dientes.
-A shepherd had a faithful dog, called Sultan, who was grown very old and had lost all his teeth.

1682 **razonable**

reasonable

adj
[ra.so.ˈna.βle]

Me parece una solución muy razonable.
-I consider this to be a very reasonable solution.

1683 **miércoles**

Wednesday

m
[ˈmjɛr.ko.les]

Espero poder hacer esto el próximo miércoles.
-I hope to do this by next Wednesday.

1684 **hombro**

shoulder

m
[ˈõm.bro]

Jim se inclinó hacia delante y golpeó suavemente el hombro del conductor del taxi.
-Jim leaned forward and tapped the cab driver on the shoulder.

1685 **comisión**

commission

f
[ko.mi.ˈsjõn]

Una comisión gubernamental especial coordina todas estas actividades.
-All these activities are coordinated by a special government commission.

1686 **calidad**

quality

f
[ka.li.ˈðað]

También debemos evaluar la calidad de estos paquetes.
-We also need to assess the quality of these packages.

1687 **identidad**

identity

f
[i.ðẽn̪.ti.ˈðað]

Quieren integrarse, aunque manteniendo su identidad.
-They want to integrate while retaining their identity.

1688	**apagar**	**turn off**
	vb	¿Cómo puedo apagar esta luz?
	[a.pa.ˈɣar]	-How can I turn off this light?
1689	**palo**	**stick**
	m	Alguien tiene que quitarle ese palo.
	[ˈpa.lo]	-Somebody's got to get that stick away from him.
1690	**moto**	**motorcycle**
	f	Nunca había visto una moto como esta.
	[ˈmo.to]	-I've never seen a motorcycle like this.
1691	**manzana**	**apple**
	f	Una manzana podrida estropea todo el barril.
	[mãn.ˈsa.na]	-One rotten apple spoils the barrel.
1692	**capital**	**primary; capital; resources**
	adj; f; m	Ankara es la capital de Turquía.
	[ka.pi.ˈtal]	-Ankara is the capital of Turkey.
1693	**conejo**	**rabbit**
	m	Supongo que es un conejo bastante listo.
	[ko.ˈne.xo]	-I guess that's some smart rabbit.
1694	**agarrar(se)**	**grab**
	vb	Fue muy valiente al agarrar ese cuchillo.
	[a.ɣa.ˈrar.se]]	-You were really brave to grab that knife.
1695	**actuación**	**performance**
	f	No quería interrumpir tu excelente actuación.
	[ak̚.twa.ˈsjõn]	-I didn't want to interrupt your terrific acting.
1696	**nervio**	**nerve**
	m	Podría necesitar otros tratamientos si la causa del espasmo fue un nervio
	[ˈnɛr.βjo]	irritado.
		-You might need other treatments if an irritated nerve caused the spasm.
1697	**conferencia**	**conference**
	f	La conferencia terminó a las cinco.
	[kõɱ.fɛ.ˈrẽn.sja]	-The conference ended at five.
1698	**junio**	**June**
	m	Podríamos mudarnos a finales de junio, juntos.
	[ˈxu.njo]	-We could move there at the end of June, together.
1699	**grano**	**grain, pimple**
	m	El centeno fue llamado el grano de la pobreza.
	[ˈgra.no]	-Rye was called the grain of poverty.
1700	**espía**	**spy**
	m/f	Puse un espía en la resistencia.
	[ɛs.ˈpi.a]	-I've planted a spy in the resistance.
1701	**atractivo**	**attractive; attraction**
	adj; m	Ya sabes, eres muy atractivo.
	[a.trak̚.ˈti.βo]	-You know, you're really attractive.
1702	**recibo**	**invoice, receipt**
	m	Tengo aquí un recibo de un aire acondicionado.
	[re.ˈsi.βo]	-I got this invoice here for an air conditioner.
1703	**resistencia**	**resistance**
	f	Pero encontraríamos resistencia en el este.
	[re.sis.ˈtẽn.sja]	-But we'd encounter resistance in the east.

1704	**transporte**	**transport**
	m	Una inundación masiva paralizó la red de transporte local.
	[trãns.'por.te]	-A massive flood paralyzed the local transportation network.

1705	**frase**	**phrase**
	f	Pensó que la frase debería suprimirse.
	['fra.se]	-He thought that the sentence should be deleted.

1706	**delicioso**	**delicious**
	adj	Te hemos preparado un almuerzo delicioso.
	[de.li.'sjo.so]	-We've prepared a delicious brunch for you.

1707	**infeliz**	**unhappy; poor thing, fool**
	adj; m/f	Su infancia infeliz afectó a su visión de la vida.
	[ĩm.'fe.lis]	-His unhappy childhood affected his outlook on life.

1708	**cinturón**	**belt**
	m	Por favor, asegúrese de que su cinturón de seguridad está bien puesto.
	[sĩn̪.'tu.rõn]	-Please make sure that your seat belt is securely fastened.

1709	**dragón**	**dragon**
	m	Tenemos que descubrir qué clase de dragón le hizo esa cicatriz.
	[dra.'ɣõn]	-We have to find out what kind of dragon made that scar.

1710	**peor**	**worse; worse**
	adj; adv	Esto nos exige prepararnos para lo peor.
	[pe.'or]	-This requires us to prepare for the worst.

1711	**científico**	**scientific; scientist**
	adj; m/f	Ese científico es responsable de muchos descubrimientos.
	[sjẽn̪.'ti.fi.ko]	-That scientist is responsible for many discoveries.

1712	**cantante**	**singer**
	m/f	Además, no tenemos ni instrumentos ni cantante.
	[kãn̪.'tãn̪.te]	-Plus we have no instruments and no singer.

1713	**esperanza**	**hope**
	f	Ha resultado ser una esperanza vana.
	[ɛs.pɛ.'rãn.sa]	-It has proven to be a vain hope.

1714	**rosa**	**pink; rose**
	adj; f	No hay rosa sin espinas.
	['ro.sa]	-There is no rose without thorns.

1715	**pasajero**	**passenger; temporary**
	m; adj	Tenemos bastante sitio para ustedes y su pasajero.
	[pa.sa.'xɛ.ro]	-We have plenty of room for you and your passenger.

1716	**almorzar**	**have lunch**
	vb	Recuerda, nos vemos mañana para almorzar.
	[al.mor.'sar]	-So remember, we'll meet for lunch tomorrow.

1717	**adecuado**	**suitable**
	adj	Creo que hemos enviado el mensaje adecuado.
	[a.ðe.'kwa.ðo]	-I believe that we have sent out the right message.

1718	**vía**	**street, tract**
	f	Le garantizo que continuaremos por esta vía.
	['bi.a]	-I can assure you that we will continue in this way.

1719	**cometido**	**mission**
	m	Digamos que he cometido algunos errores.
	[ko.mɛ.'ti.ðo]	-Let's just say that I made some mistakes.

| 1720 | **función** | **function** |

	f	Afectó a la función principal del avión.
	[fũn.ˈsjõn]	-It's affected the airplane's primary function.
1721	**industria**	**industry**
	f	No sabía que seguías en la industria.
	[ĩn̪.ˈdus.trja]	-Didn't realize you were still in the business.
1722	**corona**	**crown**
	f	Bajo ninguno circunstancia llevaré mi corona.
	[ko.ˈro.na]	-Under no circumstances will I wear my crown.
1723	**asalto**	**assault**
	m	Estás arrestado por asalto y robo a mano armada.
	[a.ˈsal̪.to]	-You're under arrest for assault and armed robbery.
1724	**flota**	**fleet**
	f	Necesitamos reconstruir y modernizar nuestra flota.
	[ˈflo.ta]	-We need to rebuild and modernize our fleet.
1725	**político**	**political; politician**
	adj; m	El hombre es un animal político por naturaleza.
	[po.ˈli.ti.ko]	-Man is by nature a political animal.
1726	**revisar**	**inspect, examine**
	vb	Creo que todavía debemos revisar nuestras ideas.
	[re.βi.ˈsar]	-I think we still need to revise our ideas.
1727	**imperio**	**empire**
	m	Quizás conquistemos un imperio sin luchar.
	[ĩm.ˈpɛ.rjo]	-Maybe we will conquer an empire without fighting.
1728	**llegada**	**arrival**
	f	Jim está esperando la llegada del tren.
	[ʎe.ˈɣa.ða]	-Jim is waiting for the arrival of the train.
1729	**rifle**	**rifle**
	m	Siempre he querido un rifle como este.
	[ˈri.fle]	-I've always wanted a rifle like this.
1730	**solitario**	**solitary, empty**
	adj	Sabemos que es un hombre solitario.
	[so.li.ˈta.rjo]	-We know he's a lonely man.
1731	**refugio**	**refuge**
	m	Quiero crear un refugio para estos artistas.
	[re.ˈfu.xjo]	-I want to create a refuge for these artists.
1732	**ideal**	**likely, theoretical; ideal**
	adj; m	Era un día ideal para caminar.
	[i.ðe.ˈal]	-It was an ideal day for walking.
1733	**rubio**	**blond**
	adj	El color rubio es una elección fantástica para los meses de verano.
	[ˈru.βjo]	-Blonde is a great color choice for the summer months.
1734	**cabaña**	**cabin**
	f	Ni siquiera sabía que teníamos una cabaña.
	[ka.ˈβa.ɲa]	-I didn't even know that we had a cabin.
1735	**sufrimiento**	**suffering**
	m	Tenemos la obligación moral de actuar ante ese sufrimiento.
	[su.fri.ˈmjẽn̪.to]	-We have a moral obligation to act in the face of such suffering.
1736	**expresión**	**expression**

f
[ɛks.pre.'sjõn]

La moda se considera una forma de expresión personal.
-Fashion is seen as a means of personal expression.

1737 fiel
adj; m
['fjɛl]

faithful; believer
Permaneció fiel a su juramento de soldado.
-He stayed true to his oath as a soldier.

1738 secretario
m
[se.krɛ.'ta.rjo]

secretary
Mi secretario estará en contacto contigo.
-My secretary will be in touch with you.

1739 cuartel
m
[kwar.'tɛl]

headquarters
No quieren que salgamos del cuartel.
-They don't want us to leave the station.

1740 soñar
vb
[so.'ɲar]

dream
Yo solía soñar con ser millonario.
-I used to dream about being a millionaire.

1741 ejercicio
m
[e.xɛr.'si.sjo]

exercise
El ejercicio moderado estimula la circulación de la sangre.
-Moderate exercise stimulates the circulation of the blood.

1742 fabuloso
adj
[fa.βu.'lo.so]

fabulous
Espero que estéis hambrientos porque tenemos un bufé fabuloso.
-I hope you guys are hungry because we have a fabulous buffet.

1743 básico
adj
['ba.si.ko]

basic
Veo que tienes algún tipo de entrenamiento básico.
-I see you've had some kind of basic training.

1744 grito
m
['gri.to]

shout
Escuché un grito y quise ayudar.
-I heard a scream and wanted to help.

1745 picar
vb
[pi.'kar]

sting
Por aquí tenemos algunas avispas que se mueren de ganas de picar.
-We have a few wasps here who are anxious to sting.

1746 túnel
m
['tu.nɛl]

tunnel
Hay otro túnel por allá.
-There is another tunnel up there.

1747 arrestar
vb
[a.rɛs.'tar]

arrest
La práctica es arrestar primero y preguntar después.
-The practice is to arrest first, ask questions later.

1748 identificación
f
[i.ðẽn.ti.fi.ka.'sjõn]

identification
Ella no tenía ninguna identificación encima.
-She didn't have any identification on her.

1749 rastro
m
['ras.tro]

trail
Deberíamos separarnos e intentar encontrar el rastro principal.
-We should split up and try to find the main trail.

1750 invitación
f
[ĩm.bi.ta.'sjõn]

invitation
La poesía es una exploración, una revelación y una invitación al diálogo.
-Poetry is an exploration, a revelation, and an invitation for dialogue.

1751 cañón
m
[ka.'ɲõn]

cannon
Ataremos el cañón a esta plataforma.
-We'll lash the cannon to this platform.

1752 alguacil

sheriff

m/f
[al.ɣwa.ˈsil]
Creo que uno de nosotros debería ir a buscar al alguacil.
-I think one of us ought to go get the Sheriff.

1753 risa — **laughter**
f
He estado practicando mi risa siniestra.
['ri.sa]
-I've been working on my evil laugh.

1754 desnudo — **naked; nude**
adj; m
Él estaba limpiando nuestra casa desnudo.
[dɛs̺.ˈnu.ðo]
-He was cleaning our house in the nude.

1755 gasto — **spending**
m
El gasto nacional en salud varía cada año.
['gas.to]
-National health expenditure is changing from year to year.

1756 once — **eleven**
num
A las once y media del andén número uno.
['õn.se]
-At eleven thirty from platform number one.

1757 golf — **golf**
m
Quizá quiera compartir con nosotros algo de su experiencia en el golf.
['golf]
-Maybe you'd like to share with us some of your golfing expertise.

1758 monte — **hill**
m
He decidido que voy a escalar el monte Everest.
['mõn̪.te]
-I've decided I'm going to climb Mount Everest.

1759 breve — **brief**
adj
Seré muy breve en mis observaciones.
['bre.βe]
-I will be very brief in my comments.

1760 terror — **terror**
m
No podemos ser neutrales contra el terror.
[tɛ.ˈror]
-We cannot be neutral against terror.

1761 práctico — **practical**
adj
Quisiera comenzar con un aspecto práctico.
[ˈprak̚.ti.ko]
-I would like to start on a practical note.

1762 hallar(se) — **find; be**
vb; vbr
Tendremos que hallar la forma de avanzar.
[a.ˈjar.se)]
-We will have to find the means to move forward.

1763 disfrutar — **enjoy**
vb
Tienes que dejarme disfrutar de mi boda.
[dis.fru.ˈtar]
-You have to let me enjoy my wedding.

1764 tanque — **tank**
m
Has gastado medio tanque de agua.
['tãŋ.ke]
-You've wasted half a tank of water.

1765 vehículo — **vehicle**
m
Abrimos y pidieron las llaves del vehículo.
[be.ˈi.ku.lo]
-We opened and they asked for the keys of the car.

1766 capacidad — **capacity**
f
Esta prisión tiene capacidad para 312 reclusos.
[ka.pa.si.ˈðað]
-This prison has a holding capacity of 312 prisoners.

1767 alcanzar — **reach**
vb
Mi país considera que aún es posible alcanzar resultados positivos.
[al.kãn.ˈsar]
-My country believes that it is still possible to achieve positive results.

1768 viuda — **widow**

	f	La viuda sufría de cáncer de estómago.
	['bju.ða]	-The widow suffered from stomach cancer.
1769	**oreja**	**ear**
	f	Pondré este comunicador en tu oreja.
	[o.'re.xa]	-I will put this communicator in your ear.
1770	**concurso**	**contest**
	m	¿Te apuntaste al concurso de canto?
	[kõŋ.'kur.so]	-Did you enter the singing contest?
1771	**alternativo**	**alternative**
	adj	Yo apoyaría esto como un compromiso alternativo.
	[al̪.tɛr.na.'ti.βo]	-I would support this as an alternative compromise.
1772	**planear**	**plan**
	vb	Ve a planear alguna estrategia nueva.
	[pla.ne.'ar]	-You go plan some new strategy.
1773	**gallina**	**hen; coward**
	f; adj	La gallina puso cinco huevos.
	[ga.'ʝi.na]	-The hen hatched five eggs.
1774	**extraordinario**	**extraordinary**
	adj	Es un conflicto de naturaleza extraordinaria.
	[ɛks.tra.or.ði.'na.rjo]	-It is a conflict of an extraordinary nature.
1775	**depósito**	**deposit, warehouse**
	m	Pero guardaste algo en tu depósito.
	[de.'po.si.to]	-But you kept some of it in your warehouse.
1776	**egoísta**	**selfish; selfish person**
	adj; m/f	Vale, ahora estás siendo egoísta.
	[e.ɣo.'is.ta]	-All right, now you're being selfish.
1777	**vestido**	**dress**
	m	Necesito mucha tela para hacer un vestido largo.
	[bɛs.'ti.ðo]	-I need a lot of cloth to make a long dress.
1778	**tragedia**	**tragedy**
	f	Hay una gran posibilidad de una tragedia nuclear.
	[tra.'xe.ðja]	-There's a strong probability of a nuclear tragedy.
1779	**círculo**	**circle**
	m	Necesitamos romper este círculo de violencia.
	['sir.ku.lo]	-We need to break this cycle of violence.
1780	**golpear(se)**	**hit**
	vb	Buscad cualquier cosa que pueda utilizarse para golpear la pared.
	[gol.pe.'ar.se)]	-Search for anything around that can be used to hit the wall.
1781	**gafas**	**glasses**
	fpl	Jim se quitó sus gafas de seguridad.
	['ga.fas]	-Jim took off his protective glasses.
1782	**abril**	**April**
	m	Se espera que el despliegue esté terminado a finales de abril.
	[a.'βril]	-The deployment is expected to be completed by the end of April.
1783	**payaso**	**clown**
	m	Ojalá seas mejor que este payaso.
	[pa.'ʝa.so]	-I hope you're better than this clown.
1784	**emoción**	**emotion**

f
[e.mo.ˈsjõn]
Hay mucha emoción en esos ojos.
-There's so much emotion in those eyes.

1785 borde — **edge**
m
[ˈbor.ðe]
No debí haber puesto mi portátil tan cerca del borde de la mesa.
-I shouldn't have put my laptop so close to the edge of the table.

1786 sensible — **sensitive**
adj
[sẽn.ˈsi.βle]
Ella es sensible al calor.
-She is sensitive to the heat.

1787 existencia — **existence**
f
[ɛk.sis.ˈtẽn.sja]
Tres de cada cuatro americanos creen en la existencia de fenómenos paranormales.
-Three out of four Americans believe in the existence of paranormal phenomena.

1788 clínica — **clinic**
f
[ˈkli.ni.ka]
En esta clínica él revisó, operó, recetó y aplicó medicamentos al menos a nueve perros.
-In this clinic, he checked, operated, prescribed and gave medicine to at least nine dogs.

1789 escape — **escape**
m
[ɛs.ˈka.pe]
Más bien estaba pensando en nuestro osado e inminente escape.
-I was thinking more about our imminent and daring escape.

1790 barón — **baron**
m
[ba.ˈrõn]
Nunca vencerás al barón con esto.
-You'll never beat the baron with this.

1791 incidente — **incidental; incident**
adj; m
[ĩn.si.ˈðẽn̪.te]
Recuerdo el incidente bastante bien.
-I do remember the incident quite well.

1792 actual — **present**
adj
[akˈ.ˈtwal]
También necesitamos una evaluación del sistema actual.
-We also need an evaluation of the existing system.

1793 mejorar — **improve**
vb
[me.xo.ˈrar]
Me gustaría ir a China a estudiar para mejorar mi nivel de chino.
-I'd like to study in China to improve the level of my Chinese.

1794 significado — **meaning; important**
m; adj
[siɣ.ni.fi.ˈka.ðo]
No entiendo el significado de esta palabra.
-I can't understand the meaning of this word.

1795 cima — **top**
f
[ˈsi.ma]
La crisis empeoró y llegó a su cima.
-The crisis worsened and reached a peak.

1796 temperatura — **temperature**
m
[tẽm.pɛ.ra.ˈtu.ra]
Este invierno, la temperatura es más alta que el promedio.
-The temperature is above average this winter.

1797 lucir(se) — **flaunt**
vb
[lu.ˈsir.se)]
Nunca solías lucir prendas como estas.
-You never used to wear stuff like that.

1798 terrorista — **terrorist; terrorist**
adj; m/f
[tɛ.ro.ˈris.ta]
Un grupo terrorista ha reivindicado este atentado.
-A terrorist group has claimed responsibility for this attack.

1799 sagrado — **sacred**

adj
[sa.ˈɣra.ðo]

Moriría antes que traicionar ese pacto sagrado.
-I'd rather die than betray that sacred pact.

1800 físico

adj; m/f
[ˈfi.si.ko]

physical; physicist

La oxitocina te hace anhelar el contacto físico con amigos y familiares.
-Oxytocin makes you crave physical contact with your friends and family.

1801 reacción

f
[re.ak.ˈsjõn]

reaction

Espero que los ciudadanos escuchen esta reacción.
-I hope that the public will hear this reaction.

1802 revés

m
[re.ˈβes]

setback

Podremos soportar este revés, Jim.
-This is a setback we will endure, Jim.

1803 emplear(se)

vb
[ẽm.ple.ˈar.se)]

use

Podremos emplear ese tiempo para hacer unas reparaciones.
-We can use the time to make some repairs.

1804 tigre

m
[ˈti.ɣre]

tiger

No importa por qué van vestidos de tigre.
-It doesn't matter why they're dressed as a tiger.

1805 entregar

vb
[ẽn̪.tre.ˈɣar]

deliver

Bueno, aún tengo una carga por entregar.
-Well, I still got a load to deliver.

1806 aprecio

m
[a.ˈpre.sjo]

appreciation

Merecen todo nuestro aprecio y gratitud.
-They deserve all of our appreciation and gratitude.

1807 destrucción

f
[dɛs.truk.ˈsjõn]

destruction

La destrucción de la capa de ozono afecta al medio ambiente.
-The destruction of the ozone layer affects the environment.

1808 patrullar

vb
[pa.tru.ˈʝar]

patrol

Regresaré por la mañana para patrullar.
-I'll be back in the morning, for patrol.

1809 sabor

m
[sa.ˈβor]

taste

Hace el sabor algo más tolerable.
-It makes the taste a little more tolerable.

1810 perdedor

m
[pɛr.ðe.ˈðor]

loser

Déjenme contarles la historia de otro perdedor.
-Let me tell you the story of another loser.

1811 ensayo

m
[ẽn.ˈsa.jo]

rehearsal, essay

Recuérdame ver ese ensayo por la mañana.
-Remind me to see that rehearsal in the morning.

1812 sueldo

m
[ˈswɛl̪.do]

salary

Quería platicar contigo sobre mi sueldo.
-I've been meaning to speak to you about my salary.

1813 construcción

f
[kõns.truk.ˈsjõn]

construction

La construcción del edificio comenzará el próximo año.
-The construction of the building will be started next year.

1814 delito

m
[de.ˈli.to]

crime

No es delito tener una aventura.
-It's not a criminal offense to be having an affair.

1815 ofrecer

offer

	vb	
	[o.fre.ˈsɛr]	

No puedo ofrecer nada aparte de sangre, esfuerzo, sudor y lágrimas.
  -I have nothing to offer but blood, toil, tears, and sweat.

1816 máscara   **mask**

f

[ˈmas.ka.ra]

Hice una máscara aterradora en clase de arte.
  -The candle grew shorter and shorter, until at last it went out.

1817 guitarra   **guitar**

f

[gi.ˈta.ra]

Él solo sabe rasguear la guitarra.
  -He only knows how to strum the guitar.

1818 figura   **figure**

f

[fi.ˈɣu.ra]

Puedes ver la figura del artista pintado.
  -You can see the figure of the artist painting.

1819 tranquilizar(se)   **calm down**

vb

[trãŋ.ki.li.ˈsar.se)]

Solo queremos tranquilizar a la madre del bebé.
  -We just want to reassure the baby's mother.

1820 análisis   **analysis**

m

[a.ˈna.li.sis]

En realidad, estamos de acuerdo con el análisis del superintendente.
  -Actually, we agree with the superintendent's analysis.

1821 vendedor   **seller**

m

[bẽn.de.ˈðor]

Un buen vendedor debe conocer su producto.
  -A good salesman's got to know his product.

1822 admitir   **admit**

vb

[að.mi.ˈtir]

Debemos admitir que nuestras negociaciones no progresan al ritmo al que deberían.
  -We have to admit that our negotiations are not progressing as quickly as they should.

1823 consecuencia   **consequence**

f

[kõn.se.ˈkwẽn.sja]

Hay otra consecuencia directa de un presupuesto ajustado.
  -There is another direct consequence of a tight budget.

1824 cazar   **hunt**

vb

[ka.ˈsar]

Estos cazadores saldrán temprano por la mañana a cazar búfalos.
  -These hunters are going out early in the morning to shoot buffalo.

1825 personalidad   **personality**

f

[pɛr.so.na.li.ˈðað]

No tengo teléfono celular, fotos llamativas, ni una personalidad graciosa.
  -I have no cell phone, no showy photos, no funny personality.

1826 disparo   **shot**

m

[dis.ˈpa.ro]

Sospecharán algo si hay otro disparo.
  -They will suspect something if there is another gunshot.

1827 ajustado   **tight**

adj

[a.xus.ˈta.ðo]

Hay otra consecuencia directa de un presupuesto ajustado.
  -There is another direct consequence of a tight budget.

1828 traducción   **translation**

f

[tra.ðuk.ˈsjõn]

Las consecuencias de una traducción incorrecta pueden a veces ser catastróficas.
  -The consequence of a wrong translation can sometimes be catastrophic.

1829 profesión   **profession**

f

[pro.fe.ˈsjõn]

He estado más interesada en mi profesión.
  -I have been more interested in my career.

1830 pastilla   **pill**

f

[pas.ˈti.ja]

Debería haber tomado la pastilla azul.
  -I should have taken the blue pill.

1831 espacial — **spatial**
adj
[ɛs.pa.ˈsjal]
Cariño, sería la primera boda espacial.
-Honey, it would be the first space wedding.

1832 disponible — **available**
adj
[dis.po.ˈni.βle]
Reduce la cantidad de oxígeno disponible para la respiración.
-It reduces the amount of oxygen available for breathing.

1833 votar — **vote**
vb
[bo.ˈtar]
Jim y Ana están planeando votar al mismo candidato.
-Jim and Ana are planning to vote for the same candidate.

1834 habilidad — **skill**
f
[a.βi.li.ˈðað]
Ya ha conseguido un montón de cosas, con valentía y habilidad.
-He has already accomplished a great deal, with courage and skill.

1835 galleta — **cookie**
f
[ga.ˈʝɛ.ta]
Faltaba una galleta del frasco.
-There was a cookie missing from the jar.

1836 costado — **side**
m
[kos.ˈta.ðo]
Mira el costado derecho del puente.
-Check out the right side of the bridge.

1837 remedio — **remedy**
m
[re.ˈme.ðjo]
¿Hay algún remedio casero para eso?
-Is there a home remedy for that?

1838 aniversario — **anniversary**
m
[a.ni.βɛr.ˈsa.rjo]
Esta semana celebramos su cincuenta aniversario.
-This week has found us observing its fiftieth anniversary.

1839 generación — **generation**
f
[xe.nɛ.ra.ˈsjõn]
Mi confianza en la próxima generación está creciendo.
-My faith in the next generation is increasing.

1840 trozo — **piece**
m
[ˈtro.so]
Guárdame un trozo de tarta, tengo que irme.
-Put a piece of cake aside for me. I have to go.

1841 caída — **drop**
f
[ka.ˈi.ða]
Solo trataba de bloquear su caída.
-I was just trying to block your fall.

1842 adulto — **adult; adult**
adj; m
[a.ˈðul̪.to]
Puedes elegir actuar como un adulto.
-You can choose to act like an adult.

1843 encerrar(se) — **lock somebody up**
vb
[ẽn.sɛ.ˈrar.se)]
Deberíais encerrar a los delincuentes.
-You should lock up the criminals.

1844 caos — **chaos**
m
[ˈka.os]
Un proceso muy apresurado solo creará caos e inestabilidad.
-Too hasty a process will only lead to chaos and instability.

1845 apostar — **bet**
vb
[a.pos.ˈtar]
No puedo apostar en mis propiedades.
-I can't gamble on my own properties.

1846 prostituta — **prostitute**
f
[pros.ti.ˈtu.ta]
Nada impide a una prostituta tener varias relaciones.
-There is nothing precluding a prostitute from having several relationships.

1847 pescar — **fish**

	vb		Mi hermano va a pescar todos los fines de semana.
	[pɛs.ˈkar]		-My brother goes fishing every weekend.
1848	**producto**		**product**
	m		Nos gustaría distribuir su producto en Japón.
	[pro.ˈðuk.to]		-We would like to distribute your product in Japan.
1849	**auténtico**		**authentic**
	adj		Tenéis un auténtico mártir por amigo.
	[au̯.ˈtẽn̪.ti.ko]		-You boys got yourself a real martyr for a friend.
1850	**condesa**		**countess**
	f		La condesa descansó aquí el jueves por la noche.
	[kõn̪.ˈde.sa]		-The countess rested here Thursday evening.
1851	**estadounidense**		**American; American person**
	adj; m		Comprendemos el sufrimiento del pueblo estadounidense.
	[ɛs.ta.ðou̯.ni.ˈðẽn.se]		-We understand the suffering of the American people.
1852	**octubre**		**October**
	m		La piscina está climatizada de abril a octubre.
	[ok.ˈtu.βre]		-The swimming pool is heated from April to October.
1853	**poesía**		**poetry**
	f		Siempre podrías dedicarte a la poesía.
	[po.e.ˈsi.a]		-You could always write poetry for a living.
1854	**electricidad**		**electricity**
	f		La central eléctrica proporciona electricidad al distrito lejano.
	[e.lek.tri.si.ˈðað]		-The power plant supplies the remote district with electricity.
1855	**sonreír**		**smile**
	vb		Nunca he visto a Jim sonreír tanto.
	[sõn.ˈre.ir]		-I've never seen Jim smile so much.
1856	**molestar(se)**		**disturb; be offended**
	vb; vbr		Tal vez lo hizo para tratar de molestar a alguien.
	[mo.lɛs.ˈtar.se)]		-Perhaps she did it to try and annoy someone.
1857	**consciente**		**aware**
	adj		Ni siquiera sabía que estaba consciente.
	[kõns.ˈsjẽn̪.te]		-I didn't even know she was conscious.
1858	**pasear**		**walk**
	vb		Creo que ahora podremos pasear a nuestros perros.
	[pa.se.ˈar]		-I think we'll be able to walk our dogs now.
1859	**reverendo**		**reverend**
	m		Obedecerás las órdenes del reverendo.
	[re.βɛ.ˈrẽn.do]		-You will follow the reverend's orders.
1860	**sacrificio**		**sacrifice**
	m		Haréis cualquier sacrificio necesario para protegerme.
	[sa.kri.ˈfi.sjo]		-You will make any sacrifice that is required to protect me.
1861	**propuesta**		**proposal**
	f		La propuesta también contiene aspectos negativos.
	[pro.ˈpwɛs.ta]		-The proposal also has some negative aspects.
1862	**amarillo**		**yellow**
	adj		Juraría que había un submarino amarillo.
	[a.ma.ˈri.jo]		-I could have sworn there was a yellow submarine.
1863	**experimento**		**experiment**

m
[ɛks.pɛ.ɾiˈmɛ̃n.to]

Permanecerá en observación mientras dure el experimento.
-He'll remain under observation for the duration of the experiment.

1864 **hoja**

f

[ˈo.xa]

leaf, sheet

Este árbol todavía tiene una hoja.
-This tree's still got a leaf on it.

1865 **comisaría**

f

[ko.mi.saˈɾi.a]

police station

Junto con muchos otros de tu comisaría.
-Along with a lot of others in your precinct.

1866 **reconocer**

vb

[re.ko.no.ˈsɛɾ]

recognize

Hay que reconocer que todo se lo debemos a ella.
-It must be recognized that we owe it all to her.

1867 **barba**

f

[ˈbar.βa]

beard

Llevo mucho tiempo con esta barba.
-I've had this beard for a long time.

1868 **sorprendente**

adj

[sor.prẽn.ˈdẽn.te]

surprising

Considero que esto es un cambio sorprendente.
-I consider this to be an amazing change.

1869 **jersey**

m

[xɛɾ.ˈsei̯]

jersey

Los competidores deben llevar el jersey en todas las actividades.
-Competitors must wear the jersey for all activities.

1870 **toro**

m

[ˈto.ro]

bull

Estaba sudando como un toro cuando volvió.
-He was sweating like a bull when he got back.

1871 **comunicación**

f

[ko.mu.ni.ka.ˈsjõn]

communication

Abrió los canales de comunicación entre diferentes religiones.
-He opened the channels of communication between different religions.

1872 **vigilancia**

f

[bi.xi.ˈlãn.sja]

surveillance

Solo tienen que mantenerlo bajo vigilancia.
-They're to keep him under surveillance only.

1873 **arreglo**

m

[a.ˈre.ɣlo]

arrangement, repair

Esperamos que este arreglo no siente un precedente.
-We hope that this arrangement will not set a precedent.

1874 **renunciar**

vb

[re.nũn.ˈsjar]

give up

No quieres renunciar al asiento del conductor.
-You don't want to give up the driver's seat.

1875 **discusión**

f

[dis.ku.ˈsjõn]

argument, debate

Se metió en una discusión con unos tipos afuera.
-He got into an argument with some guys outside.

1876 **encargar(se)**

vb; vbr

[ɛ̃ŋ.kar.ˈɣar.se)]

order, request; take charge of

Me voy a encargar del virus.
-I'll take care of the virus.

1877 **lealtad**

f

[le.al̪.ˈtað]

loyalty

Confío en tu lealtad hacia mí.
-I'm confident in your loyalty to me.

1878 **ánimo**

m

[ˈa.ni.mo]

spirits, mood

Me preocupa tu estado de ánimo.
-I have concerns about your state of mind.

1879 **musical**

musical; musical

	adj; m	David tiene un apasionado interés por la estética - las cualidades de un cuadro, una escultura, una composición musical o un poema que la hacen agradables al ojo, al oído o a la mente.
	[mu.si.ˈkal]	-David has a keen interest in aesthetics — the qualities that make a painting, sculpture, musical composition, or poem pleasing to the eye, ear, or mind.
1880	**champán**	**champagne**
	m	Verás, querría una copa de champán.
	[tʃãm.ˈpãn]	-You see, I should like a glass of champagne.
1881	**algún**	**some, any**
	adj	Tu país se arrepentirá de esto algún día.
	[al.ˈɣũn]	-Your country will regret this someday.
1882	**convencer**	**convince**
	vb	Es importante convencer a los jefes de tu capacidad y habilidades.
	[kõm.bẽn.ˈsɛr]	-It is important to convince the employers of your competence and skills.
1883	**fatal**	**fatal**
	adj	Aceptar ese dilema sería fatal para nuestra civilización.
	[fa.ˈtal]	-To accept that dilemma would be fatal for our civilization.
1884	**salto**	**jump**
	m	Es un salto que deberías poder hacer fácilmente.
	[ˈsal̦.to]	-It's a jump you should easily be able to make.
1885	**cabina**	**cabin**
	f	Venga, déjeme demostrarle su cabina.
	[ka.ˈβi.na]	-Come, let me show you your cabin.
1886	**cercano**	**nearby**
	adj	Muy pronto aterrizaremos en un aeropuerto cercano.
	[sɛr.ˈka.no]	-We'll be landing very soon at an airport nearby.
1887	**telegrama**	**telegram**
	m	Me envió un telegrama urgente.
	[te.le.ˈɣra.ma]	-She sent me an urgent telegram.
1888	**requerir**	**require**
	vb	El último aspecto parece requerir ciertas mejoras.
	[re.kɛ.ˈrir]	-The latter appears to be in need of improvement.
1889	**fracaso**	**failure**
	m	Jim es un completo fracaso como padre.
	[fra.ˈka.so]	-Jim is a complete failure as a father.
1890	**guau**	**wow**
	int	Oh, guau, eso ha dolido.
	[ˈgwau̯]	-Ow, wow, that kinda hurt.
1891	**fallar**	**fail**
	vb	No creí que fuera posible fallar por tanto.
	[fa.ˈʝar]	-I didn't think it was possible to miss by that much.
1892	**anciano**	**elder; old**
	m; adj	Ese anciano tiene que estar loco.
	[ãn.ˈsja.no]	-That old man must be insane.
1893	**agradar**	**please**
	vb	Después de veinte años, finalmente comienzas a agradarme.
	[a.ɣra.ˈðar]	-After twenty years, I'm finally starting to like you.
1894	**corbata**	**tie**
	f	Esa corbata va bien con tu camisa.
	[kor.ˈβa.ta]	-That tie goes well with your shirt.

1895	**canto**	**singing**
	m	Odio este canto en un idioma desconocido.
	[ˈkãn̪.to]	-I hate this singing in an unknown tongue.

1896	**poema**	**poem**
	m	Es difícil traducir un poema a otro idioma.
	[po.ˈe.ma]	-It is difficult to translate a poem into another language.

1897	**sano**	**healthy**
	adj	No es sano perder mucho peso demasiado rápido.
	[ˈsa.no]	-It is not healthy to lose too much weight too quickly.

1898	**truco**	**trick**
	m	Estoy enseñándole cómo hacer el truco.
	[ˈtru.ko]	-I'm showing him how to do the trick.

1899	**fantasía**	**fantasy**
	f	Debe haberse inspirado en una nueva fantasía.
	[fãn̪.ˈta.si.a]	-He must have been inspired by a new fantasy.

1900	**vela**	**candle**
	f	La vela se hacía más y más corta, hasta que se apagó.
	[ˈbe.la]	-The candle grew shorter and shorter until at last, it went out.

1901	**tradición**	**tradition**
	f	Ellos no pudieron transmitir esa tradición a la siguiente generación.
	[tra.ði.ˈsjõn]	-They weren't able to pass on that tradition unto the next generation.

1902	**apropiado**	**appropriate**
	adj	Sería apropiado que lo hiciera.
	[a.pro.ˈpja.ðo]	-It would be appropriate for him to do so.

1903	**rezar**	**pray**
	vb	Ella solía rezar antes de acostarse.
	[re.ˈsar]	-She used to pray before going to bed.

1904	**móvil**	**mobile; cell phone**
	adj; m	Sabes la contraseña de mi móvil.
	[ˈmo.βil]	-You know the password to my cell phone.

1905	**compasión**	**sympathy**
	f	Pareces tener una fuerte compasión por Jim.
	[kõm.pa.ˈsjõn]	-You seem to have a strong sympathy for Jim.

1906	**placa**	**nameplate, badge**
	f	Quiero que despejes tu oficina y devuelvas la placa.
	[ˈpla.ka]	-I want you to clean out your office and hand in your badge.

1907	**prestado**	**borrowed**
	adj	Siento no haberte prestado toda la atención que necesitabas.
	[prɛs.ˈta.ðo]	-I'm sorry I haven't given you all the attention you need.

1908	**camarero**	**waiter**
	m	Llevo trabajando en este restaurante cuatro años como camarero.
	[ka.ma.ˈrɛ.ro]	-I've been working at this restaurant for four years as a bartender.

1909	**collar**	**necklace**
	m	Jim dice que no sabe dónde compró Ana el collar de perlas.
	[ko.ˈʝar]	-Jim says he doesn't know where Ana bought her pearl necklace.

1910	**defender(se)**	**defend**
	vb	Debemos defender nuestra libertad cueste lo que cueste.
	[de.fẽn̪.ˈdɛr.se)]	-We must defend our freedom at all cost.

1911	**plano**	**level; plan, map**

adj; m
['pla.no]

En el plano social, la tecnología nunca es neutra.
-At a social level, technology is never neutral.

1912 **lanzamiento** — **launch**
m
[lãn.sa.ˈmjẽn̪.to]

Si lo destruyo él no puede iniciar el lanzamiento.
-If I destroy it, then he can't initiate the launch.

1913 **maquillaje** — **makeup**
m
[ma.ki.ˈja.xe]

Solo estoy probando este maquillaje verde nuevo.
-I'm just trying out this new green makeup.

1914 **almirante** — **admiral**
m/f
[al.mi.ˈrãn̪.te]

Ya le ofrecí mi renuncia al almirante.
-I've already offered my resignation to the admiral.

1915 **semejante** — **similar**
adj
[se.me.ˈxãn̪.te]

Siempre es bueno poder iniciar un debate semejante.
-It is always good to be able to start such a debate.

1916 **huelga** — **strike**
f
['wɛl.ɣa]

Los sindicatos habían amenazado al gobierno con una huelga general.
-The labor unions had been threatening the government with a general strike.

1917 **caridad** — **charity**
f
[ka.ri.ˈðað]

Dejé algo para su caridad favorita.
-I have left something for your favorite charity.

1918 **productor** — **producer; producer**
m; adj
[pro.ðuk̚.ˈtor]

Estados Unidos es el productor de queso más grande del mundo.
-The United States is the largest producer of cheese in the world.

1919 **investigar** — **investigate**
vb
[ĩm.bɛs.ti.ˈɣar]

Creo que deberías investigar al primer ministro primero.
-I think you should look into the prime minister first.

1920 **colección** — **collection**
f
[ko.lɛk.ˈsjõn]

A uno le gustaría tener una colección de las últimas palabras de personas famosas.
-One would like to have a collection of last words of famous people.

1921 **fama** — **fame**
f
['fa.ma]

Gran parte de su fama póstuma vino de los resultados de su autopsia.
-Most of his posthumous fame came from his autopsy results.

1922 **maíz** — **corn**
m
[ma.ˈis]

Somos amigos desde que vigilábamos el maíz.
-We've been friends since we guarded the corn.

1923 **cumplido** — **compliment; courteous**
m; adj
[kũm.ˈpli.ðo]

No sé si tomarlo como un cumplido o un insulto.
-I do not know whether to take it as a compliment or an insult.

1924 **gris** — **gray**
adj
['gris]

Si tuviera pelo, ya estaría gris.
-If I had any hair, it'd be gray by now.

1925 **onda** — **wave**
f
['õn̪.da]

El patrón de onda es asombros.
-The wave pattern is astonishing.

1926 **molestia** — **annoyance**
f
[mo.ˈlɛs.tja]

Y ahórranos a los dos la molestia de fingir.
-And save us both the trouble of pretending.

1927 **advertir** — **warn**

vb
[að.βɛr.ˈtir]
Les podría advertir si alguien me escuchara.
-I could warn them if someone would just listen to me.

1928 seco — **dry**
adj
[ˈse.ko]
Necesitas mantener esto limpio y seco.
-You need to keep this clean and dry.

1929 congreso — **congress**
m
[kõŋ.ˈgre.so]
El partido no tiene representantes en el congreso peruano.
-The party does not have any representatives in the Peruvian congress.

1930 cuarenta — **forty**
num
[kwa.ˈrẽn.ta]
Estamos a cuarenta kilómetros de la capital.
-We are forty kilometers away from the capital city.

1931 negativo — **negative**
adj
[ne.ɣa.ˈti.βo]
Estás diciendo algo negativo, pero suena positivo.
-You're saying something negative, but it sounds positive.

1932 traición — **treason**
f
[trai̯.ˈsjõn]
Ellos no participarán en semejante traición.
-They will not be part of such treason.

1933 multitud — **crowd**
f
[mul̪.ti.ˈtuð]
Una multitud esperaba para verlo.
-A crowd waited to see him.

1934 macho — **manly; male**
adj; m
[ˈma.tʃo]
Ese macho debe ser trasladado al zoológico.
-That male is to be transferred to the zoo.

1935 frecuencia — **frequency**
f
[fre.ˈkwẽn.sja]
Necesito que bajes su frecuencia respiratoria.
-I need you to lower her respiratory rate.

1936 mago — **magician**
m
[ˈma.ɣo]
Podemos seguir al mago con tu rastreador.
-We can follow the mage with your tracking device.

1937 pariente — **relative**
m/f
[pa.ˈrjẽn.te]
Escucha, es una pariente lejana.
-Listen, she's a distant relative of mine.

1938 limpieza — **cleaning**
f
[lĩm.ˈpje.sa]
Debemos hacer una limpieza general del motor.
-We have to do an overall cleaning of the engine.

1939 influencia — **influence**
f
[ĩɱ.ˈflwẽn.sja]
Como industria tiene una influencia mundial.
-As an industry, it has a worldwide influence.

1940 lista — **list**
f
[ˈlis.ta]
Jim añadió su nombre a la lista de personas que querían asistir al baile.
-Jim added his name to the list of people who wanted to attend the dance.

1941 enhorabuena — **congratulations; congratulations**
f; int
[e.no.ra.ˈβwe.na]
Sigo esperando la enhorabuena por mi compromiso.
-I'm still waiting for the congrats on my engagement.

1942 satisfacer — **satisfy**
vb
[sa.tis.fa.ˈsɛr]
Pero solo era para satisfacer sus propias fantasías retorcidas.
-But it was only to satisfy his own twisted needs.

1943 representar — **represent**

vb
[re.pre.sɛ̃n.ˈtar]
Han sido escogidos para representar a la escuela.
-They've been picked to represent the school.

1944 **papa**
m; f
[ˈpa.pa]
pope; potato (LA)
El papa visitó Brasil y Roma.
-The pope visited Brazil and Rome.

1945 **besar**
vb
[be.ˈsar]
kiss
Puede besar a la novia.
-You may kiss the bride.

1946 **conducta**
f
[kõn.ˈduk.ta]
behavior
Quizás es porque la conducta humana es mi profesión.
-Maybe that's because human behavior is my profession.

1947 **idioma**
m
[i.ˈðjo.ma]
language
Un idioma es un dialecto con armada y navío.
-A language is a dialect with an army and navy.

1948 **cueva**
f
[ˈkwe.βa]
cave
Imaginen nuestras conversaciones cuando explorábamos la cueva.
-You can imagine our talks when we were exploring the cave.

1949 **batería**
f
[ba.tɛ.ˈri.a]
battery, drums
Sostiene su radio mientras recarga la batería.
-It holds your radio in place while recharging the battery.

1950 **técnico**
adj; m/f
[ˈtek.ni.ko]
technical; technician
Algunas personas criticaron el informe porque era demasiado técnico.
-Certain people criticised that report because it was far too technical.

1951 **explotar**
vb
[ɛks.plo.ˈtar]
explode, exploit
El objetivo de este juego es explotar todas las bombas de la pantalla.
-The aim of this game is to explode all the bombs on the screen.

1952 **barra**
f
[ˈba.ra]
bar
Son cortesía de los caballeros de la barra.
-They're courtesy of the gentlemen at the bar.

1953 **engañar**
vb
[ɛ̃ŋ.ga.ˈɲar]
deceive
Él sabe muy bien cómo engañar a la gente.
-He knows very well how to deceive people.

1954 **marchar(se)**
vb; vbr
[mar.ˈʧar.se)]
march; leave
Podemos solucionar esto, pero debe dejarla marchar.
-We can work this out, but you have to let her go.

1955 **cargar**
vb
[kar.ˈɣar]
load
Creo que olvidé cargar mi cepillo eléctrico.
-I think I forgot to charge my electric toothbrush.

1956 **cuento**
m
[ˈkwẽn.to]
story
No voy a leerte un cuento esta noche.
-I won't read you a story tonight.

1957 **sentencia**
f
[sɛ̃n.ˈtɛn.sja]
sentence
Lo delataste para reducir tu sentencia.
-You ratted him out to reduce your sentence.

1958 **mueble**
m
[ˈmwe.βle]
piece of furniture
La casa parecía no tener ningún mueble.
-The house did not seem to have any furniture.

1959 **villa**
villa

f
['bi.ja]

Tal vez los ancianos de la villa intervengan para reconciliarlos.
-Maybe the village elders will intervene to reconcile them.

1960 **horror**

m
[o.'ror]

horror

Debemos buscar soluciones viables y directas para este horror.
-We must seek feasible but direct solutions to this horror.

1961 **embajador**

m
[ẽm.ba.xa.'ðor]

ambassador

El embajador abandona Japón esta noche.
-The ambassador is leaving Japan tonight.

1962 **ministerio**

m
[mi.nis.'tɛ.rjo]

ministry

El ministerio deberá inaugurarse el próximo mes.
-The ministry is due to be inaugurated next month.

1963 **comunista**

adj; m/f
[ko.mu.'nis.ta]

communist; communist

Para los norteamericanos soy un comunista.
-To the Americans, I'm a Communist.

1964 **diciembre**

m
[di.'sjẽm.bre]

December

El asedio se intensificó en diciembre de 2013.
-The siege intensified in December 2013.

1965 **voto**

m
['bo.to]

vote

Te dije que necesitábamos un voto unánime.
-I told you we needed a unanimous vote.

1966 **actividad**

f
[ak.ti.βi.'ðað]

activity

Ahora seguimos con nuestra actividad normal.
-We will now proceed with our normal business.

1967 **fotografiar**

vb
[fo.to.ɣra.'fjar]

photograph

Fui la primera en fotografiar este lugar.
-I was the first one to shoot this location.

1968 **lavar(se)**

vb
[la.'βar.se)]

wash

Tendrás que lavar al bebé cuando nazca.
-You'll have to wash the baby when it's born.

1969 **nuclear**

adj
[nu.kle.'ar]

nuclear

El uso de una bomba nuclear tendría efectos devastadores.
-The use of a nuclear bomb would have devastating effects.

1970 **notar**

vb
[no.'tar]

notice

Jim parecía no notar ningún problema.
-Jim didn't seem to notice any problems.

1971 **trono**

m
['tro.no]

throne

El sucesor al trono ha sido asesinado.
-The successor to the throne has been assassinated.

1972 **pato**

m
['pa.to]

duck

Encontré la receta del pato online.
-I found the recipe for the duck online.

1973 **jugo**

m
['xu.ɣo]

juice (LA)

Les exprimí el jugo a las naranjas.
-I squeezed the juice out of the oranges.

1974 **rutina**

f
[ru.'ti.na]

routine

El aburrimiento, la rutina y la falta de curiosidad son los mayores enemigos de nuestro cerebro.
-The boredom, routine and lack of curiosity are the major enemies of our brain.

1975 **patria**

homeland

	f	
	['pa.trja]	No puedes deshacerte de tu patria.
		-You can't get rid of your motherland.

1976 taller — **workshop**

m

[ta.'jɛr]

Las actas del taller serán publicadas.
-The proceedings of the workshop will be published.

1977 muestra — **sample**

f

['mwɛs.tra]

Toma esto como muestra de mi afecto.
-Take this as a token of my affection.

1978 devolver — **return**

vb

[de.βol.'βɛr]

Y ahora planean devolver el favor.
-And now you plan to return the favor.

1979 desayunar — **have breakfast**

vb

[de.sa.ju.'nar]

Jim suele ducharse antes de desayunar.
-Jim usually takes a shower before eating breakfast.

1980 casino — **casino**

m

[ka.'si.no]

En nuestro casino aceptamos todo tipo de jugadores.
-In our casino, we cater to all types of players.

1981 gerente — **manager**

m/f

[xɛ.'rẽn.te]

Disculpe, estamos buscando al gerente del hotel.
-Excuse me, we're looking for the manager of the hotel.

1982 practicar — **practice**

vb

[prak.ti.'kar]

Creo que el gobierno debería permitirnos practicar nuestra religión abiertamente.
-I think the government should allow us to practice our religion openly.

1983 alumno — **student**

m

[a.'lũm.no]

He venido a presentarles un nuevo alumno.
-I came to present to you a new student.

1984 diseño — **design**

m

[di.'se.ɲo]

¿Estás sugiriendo que se trata de un defecto de diseño?
-Are you suggesting it's a design flaw?

1985 vigilar — **guard**

vb

[bi.xi.'lar]

Desde aquí podemos vigilar la carretera.
-From here, we can keep an eye on the road.

1986 reporte — **report**

m

[re.'por.te]

Recibirá el reporte cuando esté escrito.
-You'll be given the report when it is written.

1987 masa — **mass, dough**

f

['ma.sa]

Puedo oler la masa frita desde aquí.
-I can smell the fried dough over here.

1988 guerrero — **fighter; warlike**

m; adj

[gɛ.'rɛ.ro]

Tengo más ambiciones que ser solo un guerrero.
-I have bigger ambitions than just being a warrior.

1989 niebla — **fog**

f

['nje.βla]

La niebla era tan espesa que no veía por donde iba.
-The fog was so thick that I couldn't see where I was going.

1990 rondar — **wander around**

vb

[rõn.'dar]

Solía rondar por ese sitio.
-He used to hang around the place.

1991 noviembre — **November**

	m [no.ˈβjɛ̃m.bre]	Nos gustaría casarnos a finales de noviembre. -We'd like to get married at the end of November.
1992	**logro** m [ˈlo.ɣɾo]	**achievement** Este es un gran logro para mí. -This is a huge accomplishment for me.
1993	**naranja** f; adj [na.ˈɾãŋ.xa]	**orange; orange** Le dieron un vaso de zumo de naranja mezclado con vodka. -They gave him a glass of orange juice laced with vodka.
1994	**considerar(se)** vb [kõn.si.ðɛ.ˈɾar.se)]	**consider** Esta frase permite muchas interpretaciones que tuve que considerar al traducirla. -This sentence allows for multiple interpretations that I had to consider when translating.
1995	**garaje** m [ga.ˈɾa.xe]	**garage** El hotel tiene un garaje solo para bicis, no para coches. -The hotel has a garage only for bicycles, not for cars.
1996	**ingeniero** m [ĩŋ.xe.ˈnjɛ.ɾo]	**engineer** Jim está trabajando como ingeniero de software. -Jim is working as a software engineer.
1997	**generoso** adj [xe.nɛ.ˈɾo.so]	**generous** Jim es generoso con su dinero. -Jim is generous with his money.
1998	**academia** f [a.ka.ˈðe.mja]	**academy** Hay una academia militar en el castillo de Kaltenborn. -There is a military academy in Kaltenborn Castle.
1999	**cretino** adj; m [kɾɛ.ˈti.no]	**stupid; idiot** No me envíe a ese cretino nunca más. -Don't send that cretin to me anymore.
2000	**recurso** m [re.ˈkur.so]	**resource** Necesita autenticarse para acceder al recurso solicitado. -You need to authenticate to access the requested resource.
2001	**poeta** m [po.ˈɛ.ta]	**poet** Es un poeta digno de ese apelativo. -He is a poet worthy of the title.
2002	**dignidad** f [diɣ.ni.ˈðað]	**dignity** Salí con mi dignidad intacta. -I got through with my dignity intact.
2003	**testamento** m [tɛs.ta.ˈmɛ̃n̪.to]	**will** He hecho algunas modificaciones a mi testamento. -I've made a few changes in my will.
2004	**infancia** f [ĩɱ.ˈfãn.sja]	**childhood** Pasé mi infancia escuchándola hablar de estas cosas. -I spent my childhood listening to her talk about these things.
2005	**roto** adj [ˈro.to]	**broken** No puedo encenderlo porque el interruptor está roto. -I can't turn it on, because the switch is broken.
2006	**población** f [po.βla.ˈsjõn]	**population** La población de Japón es mucho mayor que la de Australia. -The population of Japan is much larger than that of Australia.
2007	**almacén**	**storehouse**

m
[al.ma.ˈsɛ̃n]
Creo que estamos buscando un almacén.
-I think we're looking for a warehouse.

2008 soledad — **loneliness**
f
[so.le.ˈðað]
No estaba seguro de si su aflicción era soledad o era locura.
-He was not certain if his affliction was loneliness or madness.

2009 medalla — **medal**
f
[me.ˈða.ja]
Gané una medalla en 2003.
-I won a medal in 2003.

2010 soltero — **single; single man**
adj; m
[sol̪.ˈtɛ.ro]
Ojalá hubieses dicho eso cuando estaba soltero.
-I wish you would have said that when I was single.

2011 suma — **sum**
f
[ˈsu.ma]
La suma de 5 con 3 es 8.
-The sum of 5 and 3 is 8.

2012 escuadrón — **squadron**
m
[ɛs.kwa.ˈðrõn]
Ni siquiera formaba parte del escuadrón.
-He wasn't even part of the squadron.

2013 abrazar — **hug**
vb
[a.βra.ˈsar]
Quizás deberías abrazar tu pasado.
-Maybe you should embrace your past.

2014 enterarse — **realize, find out**
vbr
[ɛ̃n̪.tɛ.ˈrar.se]
Prométeme que nadie se puede enterar.
-But promise me, no one can find out.

2015 colgar(se) — **hang, hang up**
vb
[kol.ˈɣar.se)]
Decidí que este año debería colgar de tu árbol.
-I've decided that this year, it should hang on your tree.

2016 típico — **typical**
adj
[ˈti.pi.ko]
No es típico para este procedimiento.
-It's not typical for this type of procedure.

2017 confundir(se) — **confuse; make a mistake**
vb; vbr
[kõɱ.fũn̪.ˈdir.se)]
No querías confundir a los jugadores.
-You didn't want to confuse the players.

2018 utilizar — **use**
vb
[u.ti.li.ˈsar]
Era más eficiente utilizar menos energía.
-It was more efficient to use less energy.

2019 tristeza — **sadness**
f
[tris.ˈte.sa]
Su rostro refleja indignación y tristeza en vez de ira.
-Her face reflects disgust and sadness, rather than anger.

2020 deporte — **sport**
m
[de.ˈpor.te]
Echan demasiado deporte en la televisión.
-There's too much sport on TV.

2021 recepción — **reception**
f
[re.sɛp.ˈsjõn]
Su nuevo libro tuvo una recepción favorable.
-His new book met with a favorable reception.

2022 festival — **festival**
m
[fɛs.ti.ˈβal]
Me enfocaré en la explicación del festival. -I will focus on the explanation of the festival.

2023 progreso — **progress**

m
[pro.ˈɣre.so]

Esto ha afectado al progreso de investigación.
-This has affected the progress of the investigation.

2024 **brindis**   **toast**

m
[ˈbrĩn̪.dis]

Hicimos un brindis por el próximo paso.
-We made a toast for the next step.

2025 **fascinante**   **fascinating**

adj
[fas.si.ˈnãn̪.te]

Es un reto fascinante que aceptaremos gustosos.
-It is a fascinating challenge which we will gladly accept.

2026 **región**   **region**

f
[re.ˈxjõn]

Es necesario promover mercados abiertos y transparentes en la región.
-It is necessary to foster open, transparent markets in the region.

2027 **arruinar(se)**   **ruin**

vb
[a.rwi.ˈnar.se)]

¿La mancha de café arruinará la alfombra?
-Will the coffee stain ruin the carpet?

2028 **terapia**   **therapy**

f
[tɛ.ˈra.pja]

La terapia está en curso.
-The therapy is in session.

2029 **hoyo**   **hole**

m
[ˈo.ʝo]

Ve al primer hoyo del campo.
-Go to the first hole in the course.

2030 **arco**   **arc**

m
[ˈar.ko]

Es un arco compuesto, probablemente.
-It's a compound bow, most likely.

2031 **pesca**   **fishing**

f
[ˈpɛs.ka]

No hay pesca suficiente, amigos.
-There is not enough fish, my friends.

2032 **acostumbrar(se)**   **get used to**

vb
[a.kos.tũm.ˈbrar.se)]

Me podría acostumbrar a un sitio como este.
-I could get used to a place like this.

2033 **ola**   **wave**

f
[ˈo.la]

Podría ser el principio de una ola de crímenes.
-It may be the beginning of a crime wave.

2034 **eterno**   **eternal**

adj
[ɛ.ˈtɛr.no]

Esto me ha hecho pensar en el eterno problema de la maldad.
-This got me thinking about the eternal problem of evil.

2035 **obligar(se)**   **force**

vb
[o.βli.ˈɣar.se)]

Y tú no me vas a obligar.
-And you're not going to force me.

2036 **formar**   **form, train**

vb
[for.ˈmar]

Era imposible formar un gobierno sin su participación.
-It was impossible to form a government without its participation.

2037 **ordenar**   **order, arrange**

vb
[or.ðe.ˈnar]

Me gustaría ordenar un escáner cerebral.
-I'd like to order a brain scan.

2038 **tabaco**   **tobacco**

m
[ta.ˈβa.ko]

Me da igual cuánto tabaco les ofrezcáis.
-I don't care how much tobacco you offer them.

2039 **capítulo**   **chapter**

	m	El capítulo terminará con una descripción general del manual.
	[ka.ˈpi.tu.lo]	-The chapter will conclude with a general overview of the handbook.

2040 selva — jungle
f
[ˈsɛl.βa]
La selva es muy delicada y nosotros debemos protegerla.
-The rainforest is very delicate and we must protect it.

2041 columna — column
f
[ko.ˈlũm.na]
Sabes que nunca me pierdo la columna de sociedad.
-You know I never miss the society column.

2042 enterrar(se) — bury
vb
[ẽn̪.tɛ.ˈrar.se)]
Le dijimos dónde enterrar el cadáver.
-We told him where to bury the corpse.

2043 cortado — shy; coffee
adj; m
[kor.ˈta.ðo]
Jim estaba un poco cortado.
-Jim was a bit shy.

2044 impacto — impact
m
[ĩm.ˈpak̚.to]
Él sobrevivió al impacto de una bomba.
-He survived the impact of a bomb.

2045 herramienta — tool
f
[ɛ.ra.ˈmjẽn̪.ta]
Si se usa bien, esta herramienta será de mucha utilidad.
-If it is used properly, this tool will be a great help.

2046 balón — ball
m
[ba.ˈlõn]
Estaba enseñándole un truco con el balón.
-I was showing him a trick with the ball.

2047 fingir — pretend
vb
[fĩŋ.ˈxir]
No puedo fingir que me gusta.
-I can't pretend to like him.

2048 confesión — confession
f
[kõɱ.fe.ˈsjõn]
La ley no permite la confesión bajo tortura.
-The law does not accept confession under torture.

2049 símbolo — symbol
m
[ˈsĩm.bo.lo]
El huevo es un símbolo universal de vida y renacimiento.
-The egg is a universal symbol of life and rebirth.

2050 expediente — record
m
[ɛks.pe.ˈðjẽn̪.te]
Según tu expediente, tienes una deficiencia crónica de hierro.
-According to your record, you have a chronic iron deficiency.

2051 petición — request
f
[pɛ.ti.ˈsjõn]
Los donantes accedieron a esta petición.
-The donors gave their consent to this request.

2052 participar — participate
vb
[par.ti.si.ˈpar]
Estamos preparados para participar en ese debate.
-We are prepared to take part in such a discussion.

2053 casco — helmet
m
[ˈkas.ko]
El casco protegió su cabeza del golpe.
-His helmet protected his head during the crash.

2054 patata — potato
f
[pa.ˈta.ta]
Podemos poner media patata por plato.
-We can put half a potato per plate.

2055 pandilla — gang

| | f | Esperaba que estuvieras en una pandilla. |
| | [pãn̪.ˈdi.ɟa] | -I was kind of hoping you were in a gang. |

2056 **preocupación** — **concern**
f
[pre.o.ku.pa.ˈsjõn]
Podemos asegurarles que compartimos su preocupación.
-We can assure them that we share their concern.

2057 **advertencia** — **warning**
f
[að.βɛr.ˈtɛ̃n.sja]
Espero que nuestra advertencia sea atendida.
-I hope that our warning will be heeded.

2058 **preso** — **prisoner**
m
[ˈpre.so]
Hasta un preso tiene derecho a respirar.
-Even a convict's got a right to breathe.

2059 **otoño** — **autumn**
m
[o.ˈto.ɲo]
Las cifras exactas estarán disponibles en otoño.
-The actual figures will be available in the autumn.

2060 **estatua** — **statue**
f
[ɛs.ˈta.twa]
Están cincelando una estatua de mármol.
-They are chiseling a statue out of marble.

2061 **perrito** — **puppy**
m
[pɛ.ˈri.to]
Es la fealdad de este perrito lo que lo hace tan simpático.
-It's the ugliness of this puppy that makes it very nice.

2062 **violación** — **violation**
f
[bjo.la.ˈsjõn]
Pero esto sería una violación de todos mis principios.
-But this would be a violation of all my principles.

2063 **corredor** — **corridor, runner**
m
[ko.re.ˈðor]
En el corredor había un borracho esposado.
-There was a drunk cuffed out in the corridor.

2064 **guante** — **glove**
m
[ˈgwãn̪.te]
Quiere ese guante especial y voy a conseguírselo.
-He wants that special glove, and I'm going to get it for him.

2065 **vaquero** — **cowboy, denim**
m
[ba.ˈkɛ.ro]
No debiste haber vuelto, vaquero.
-You shouldn't have come back, cowboy.

2066 **cita** — **appointment, date**
f
[ˈsi.ta]
Tengo una cita con él a las seis.
-I have a date with him at six.

2067 **pegar** — **hit, glue**
vb
[pe.ˈɣar]
No puedes pegarme, llevo gafas.
-You can't hit me, I've got glasses.

2068 **simpático** — **likeable**
adj
[sĩm.ˈpa.ti.ko]
Mi hermano ha sido simpático con él.
-My brother has been friendly to him.

2069 **jaula** — **cage**
f
[ˈxau̯.la]
Construí esa jaula con mis propias manos.
-I built that cage with my own two hands.

2070 **incluir** — **include**
vb
[ĩŋ.ˈklwir]
También queremos incluir nuestro patrimonio industrial.
-We also want to include our industrial heritage.

2071 **ratón** — **mouse**

	m	Para este ejercicio deberá utilizar su ratón.
	[ra.ˈtõn]	-For this exercise, you will need to use your mouse.
2072	**período**	**period**
	m	Tenemos que utilizar este período para progresar.
	[pɛ.ˈri.o.ðo]	-We need to use this period to move forward.
2073	**capa**	**layer**
	f	También removerían una capa de tinta.
	[ˈka.pa]	-They would also remove a layer of ink.
2074	**gota**	**drop**
	f	Fue duro, pero cada gota de sudor valió la pena.
	[ˈgo.ta]	-It was tough, but worth every drop of sweat.
2075	**docena**	**dozen**
	f	Quiero comprar una docena de plátanos.
	[do.ˈse.na]	-I want to buy a dozen bananas.
2076	**traje**	**suit**
	m	Mamá me hizo un traje nuevo.
	[ˈtra.xe]	-Mother made me a new suit.
2077	**vomitar**	**vomit**
	vb	Se dirige al vestuario a vomitar.
	[bo.mi.ˈtar]	-She's headed to the locker room to throw up.
2078	**testimoniar**	**testify**
	vb	¿Le pidió que viniese aquí a testimoniar a su favor?
	[tɛs.ti.mo.ˈnjar]	-Did you ask him to come here and testify on your behalf?
2079	**jugada**	**play**
	f	Nuestra próxima jugada debe ser inteligente.
	[xu.ˈɣa.ða]	-And our next move has to be smart.
2080	**evento**	**event**
	m	Este festival ha sido declarado evento de interés turístico.
	[e.ˈβẽn̪.to]	-This festival has been officially declared an event of touristic interest.
2081	**suplicar**	**supplicate**
	vb	No puedes hacer suplicar a los amigos.
	[sup.li.ˈkar]	-You can't make friends beg.
2082	**administración**	**administration**
	f	La asociación tiene un presidente, vicepresidente y administración.
	[að.mi.nis.tra.ˈsjõn]	-The association has a president, vice-president, and management.
2083	**alfombra**	**carpet**
	f	Tu alfombra es totalmente blanca.
	[al.ˈfõm.bra]	-Your carpet is completely white.
2084	**vecindario**	**neighborhood**
	m	Hay un montón de casas abandonadas en el vecindario.
	[be.sĩn̪.ˈda.rjo]	-There are a lot of abandoned houses in the neighborhood.
2085	**presentación**	**presentation**
	f	Ahora quiero comentar brevemente cada presentación.
	[pre.sẽn̪.ta.ˈsjõn]	-I would now like to comment briefly on each presentation.
2086	**reciente**	**recent**
	adj	No veo indicios de ocupación reciente. -I see no signs of any recent
	[re.ˈsjẽn̪.te]	occupation.
2087	**retraso**	**delay**

	m		Hay un retraso de veinte minutos.
	[rɛ.ˈtra.so]		-There is a twenty-minute delay.
2088	**pintar**	**paint**	
	vb		¿Estás diciendo que no quieres ayudarnos a pintar el techo?
	[pĩn̪.ˈtar]		-Are you saying you don't want to help us paint the ceiling?
2089	**plástico**	**plastic; plastic**	
	adj; m		El papel, el vidrio y el plástico son materiales reciclables.
	[ˈplas.ti.ko]		-Paper, glass, and plastic are recyclable materials.
2090	**marzo**	**March**	
	m		Nací el 23 de marzo de 1969 en Barcelona.
	[ˈmar.so]		-I was born on March, 23rd, 1969 in Barcelona.
2091	**escoger**	**choose**	
	vb		Quiere disculparse por hacerme escoger entre la firma y tú.
	[ɛs.ko.ˈxɛr]		-He wants to apologize for making me choose between you and the firm.
2092	**sector**	**sector**	
	m		El sector de la salud es uno de los problemas más grandes del país.
	[sek̚.ˈtor]		-The health sector is one of the biggest problems for the country.
2093	**sindicato**	**union**	
	m		Estuve mucho tiempo en el sindicato.
	[sĩn.di.ˈka.to]		-I was in the union for a long time.
2094	**cometer**	**commit**	
	vb		Porque le obligaron a cometer un crimen así de espantoso.
	[ko.mɛ.ˈtɛr]		-Because you made him commit that ghastly crime.
2095	**bondad**	**kindness**	
	f		Estoy muy feliz por su bondad.
	[bõn̪.ˈdað]		-I'm so happy because of your kindness.
2096	**temor**	**fear**	
	m		Además soy la última persona que suscitaría temor.
	[te.ˈmor]		-I am also the last person who would arouse fear.
2097	**cuyo**	**whose**	
	adj		La casa cuyo techo puedes ver es del Sr. Baker.
	[ˈku.jo]		-The house whose roof you can see is Mr. Baker's.
2098	**retrato**	**portrait**	
	m		Bob montó el retrato en un ostentoso marco, pero estaba del revés.
	[rɛ.ˈtra.to]		-Bob mounted the portrait in a fancy frame, but it was upside down.
2099	**ópera**	**opera**	
	f		Gracias por invitarnos a la ópera.
	[ˈo.pɛ.ra]		-Thank you for asking us to the opera.
2100	**mencionar**	**mention**	
	vb		Permitidme mencionar algunos de nuestros logros principales.
	[mɛ̃n.sjo.ˈnar]		-Allow me to mention some of our key achievements.
2101	**nieto**	**grandson**	
	m		Me gustaría hablar con usted sobre su nieto, Jim.
	[ˈnjɛ.to]		-I'd like to speak with you about your grandson, Jim.
2102	**campeonato**	**championship**	
	m		Seguro que gana el campeonato de natación.
	[kãm.pe.o.ˈna.to]		-He is sure to win the swimming championship.
2103	**retiro**	**retirement**	

m
[rɛ.ˈti.ro]

Pensé que tenía muchos planes para su retiro.
-I thought you had lots of plans for your retirement.

2104 sordo

adj; m
[ˈsor.ðo]

deaf; deaf

Jim es sordo de un oído.
-Jim is deaf in one ear.

2105 convenir

vb
[kõm.be.ˈnir]

be advisable

Todo lo que falta es convenir un precio.
-All that remains is to agree upon a price.

2106 romance

m
[ro.ˈmãn.se]

romance

Jim y Ana tuvieron un romance relámpago.
-Jim and Ana had a whirlwind romance.

2107 representante

m/f
[re.pre.sẽn̪.ˈtãn̪.te]

representative

El representante de la ciudad hizo una declaración.
-A statement was made by the representative of the city.

2108 boleto

m
[bo.ˈlɛ.to]

ticket

Me dieron un boleto de primera clase.
-They've given me a first class ticket.

2109 negar(se)

vb; vbr
[ne.ˈɣar.se)]

deny; refuse

Sería absurdo negar que está lloviendo fuera.
-It would be absurd to deny that it is raining outside.

2110 oxígeno

m
[ok.ˈsi.xe.no]

oxygen

No debemos quemar nuestro bosque porque es la fuente del oxígeno que respiramos.
-We mustn't burn our forest, because it is the source of the oxygen we breathe.

2111 liga

f
[ˈli.ɣa]

league

Seguro que la liga hará una excepción.
-I bet the league will make an exception.

2112 ceniza

f
[se.ˈni.sa]

ash

La ceniza del suelo cubre al menos 2 pulgadas.
-The ash on the ground is at least two inches thick.

2113 ave

m
[ˈa.βe]

bird

El ave canta alegremente en la jaula.
-The bird in the cage is singing happily.

2114 furioso

adj
[fu.ˈrjo.so]

furious

Estaba furioso por aquella injusticia.
-I was furious at the injustice of it.

2115 bendición

f
[bẽn̪.di.ˈsjõn]

blessing

Es una bendición que estés aquí.
-It's a godsend that you're here.

2116 pesado

adj
[pe.ˈsa.ðo]

heavy

Es pesado, no puedo sostenerlo.
-It's heavy, I can't hold it.

2117 británico

adj; m
[bri.ˈta.ni.ko]

British; Briton

Serví 30 años en el ejército británico.
-I served in the British Army for 30 years.

2118 economía

f
[e.ko.no.ˈmi.a]

economy

Hay un considerable optimismo en que la economía mejorará.
-There is considerable optimism that the economy will improve.

2119 lanzar(se)

launch

	f	
	[lãn.ˈsar.se)]	Están preparándose para lanzar los nuevos cazas.
		-They're getting ready to launch the new fighters.
2120	**ensalada**	**salad**
	f	Aunque recuerdo haber pedido mi ensalada sin aceitunas.
	[ẽn.sa.ˈla.ða]	-Although, I do recall asking for no olives in my salad.
2121	**motel**	**motel**
	m	No alquile más habitaciones en este motel.
	[mo.ˈtɛl]	-Don't rent out any more rooms in this motel.
2122	**susto**	**scare**
	m	Menudo susto nos diste esta mañana.
	[ˈsus.to]	-You gave us quite a scare this morning.
2123	**pluma**	**pen, feather**
	f	Jim, esta pluma está completamente seca.
	[ˈplu.ma]	-Jim, this pen is all dried out.
2124	**demanda**	**demand**
	f	Cualquiera de ellos podría presentar la misma demanda.
	[de.ˈmãn.da]	-Anyone of them could make the same claim.
2125	**comando**	**commando**
	m	Soy un doctor, no un comando.
	[ko.ˈmãn.do]	-I'm a doctor, not a commando.
2126	**embajada**	**embassy**
	f	Tengo derecho a contactar con mi embajada.
	[ẽm.ba.ˈxa.ða]	-I have the right to contact my embassy.
2127	**fruta**	**fruit**
	f	Hemos cogido más fruta para usted.
	[ˈfru.ta]	-We've picked some more fruit for you.
2128	**vodka**	**vodka**
	m	Cada persona recibirá una botella de vodka.
	[ˈboð.ka]	-Each person is to get a bottle of vodka.
2129	**quinto**	**fifth**
	num	Ella bajó al quinto piso.
	[ˈkĩn.to]	-She went down to the fifth floor.
2130	**coca**	**cocaine**
	f	La planta de coca es tan antigua como el hombre.
	[ˈko.ka]	-The coca plant is as old as man.
2131	**atender**	**deal with, pay attention**
	vb	Primero tengo que atender unos asuntos familiares.
	[a.tẽn.ˈdɛr]	-I've to deal with my family affairs first.
2132	**préstamo**	**loan**
	m	Podría pedir un préstamo o algo.
	[ˈprɛs.ta.mo]	-I could get a loan or something.
2133	**pañuelo**	**handkerchief**
	m	Este pañuelo está hecho de papel.
	[pa.ˈɲwe.lo]	-This handkerchief is made of paper.
2134	**ataúd**	**coffin**
	m	Él pensó que su piano sería un buen ataúd para él.
	[a.ta.ˈuð]	-He thought his piano would make a good coffin for him.
2135	**saludar**	**greet**

vb

[sa.lu.ˈðar]

Me aseguraré de decirle que pasaste a saludar.
-I'll be sure to tell him you stopped by to say hello.

2136	**sobrar**	**be left over**

vb

[so.ˈβrar]

Pero van a sobrar muchos.
-But many will be left over.

2137	**tensión**	**tension**

f

[tɛ̃n.ˈsjõn]

Ayudará a aliviar algo de tensión.
-It'll help relieve some of the stress.

2138	**robot**	**robot**

m

[ro.ˈβot]

Está usando ese robot contra los otros robots.
-It's using that drone against the other drones.

2139	**aumento**	**increase**

m

[au̯.ˈmɛ̃n̪.to]

Este es un aumento significativo y debe destacarse.
-This is a significant increase and should be noted.

2140	**extremo**	**extreme; end**

adj; m

[ɛks.ˈtre.mo]

Lamentamos haber llegado a este extremo.
-We regret that we have come to this point.

2141	**pulso**	**pulse**

m

[ˈpul.so]

Doctor, el pulso sigue disminuyendo.
-Doctor, the heart rate is still decreasing.

2142	**pensión**	**pension, hostel**

f

[pɛ̃n.ˈsjõn]

Podemos ofrecerte pensión completa y beneficios.
-We can offer you full pension and benefits.

2143	**juguete**	**toy**

m

[xu.ˈɣɛ.te]

No, definitivamente no diseño aviones de juguete.
-No, I most certainly do not design toy planes.

2144	**invisible**	**invisible**

adj

[ĩm.bi.ˈsi.βle]

Estamos conectados más estrechamente con lo invisible que con lo visible.
-We are more closely connected to the invisible than to the visible.

2145	**cirugía**	**surgery**

f

[si.ru.ˈxi.a]

Jim, vas a necesitar cirugía.
-Jim, you're going to need surgery.

2146	**eternidad**	**eternity**

f

[ɛ.tɛr.ni.ˈðað]

Quiero estar contigo para toda la eternidad.
-I want to be with you through eternity.

2147	**bailarín**	**dancer**

m

[bai̯.la.ˈrĩn]

Cada movimiento del bailarín fue perfecto.
-Each movement of the dancer was perfect.

2148	**chance**	**chance (LA)**

m/f

[ˈtʃãn.se]

Creo que tenemos una buena chance.
-I think we have a good shot.

2149	**cobrar**	**collect, charge**

vb

[ko.ˈβrar]

Podríamos cobrar 50 dólares por cabeza ahora. -We could charge 50 bucks a head now.

2150	**realizar**	**perform**

vb

[re.a.li.ˈsar]

Estoy decidido a realizar este plan.
-I am determined to carry out this plan.

2151	**infantil**	**infantile**

adj
[ĩm.fãn̯.ˈtil]

Soy profesor de primaria y educación infantil.
-I'm a primary and infant school teacher.

2152 pavo — **turkey**

m
[ˈpa.βo]

Vale, quizá debería trinchar el pavo.
-Okay, maybe I should carve the turkey.

2153 custodiar — **flank**

vb
[kus.to.ˈðjar]

Me propuse custodiar mis posesiones muy atentamente.
-I make it a point to guard my possessions very carefully.

2154 ultimar — **finalize**

vb
[ul̯.ti.ˈmar]

Me tomé el día libre para ultimar mi hipoteca.
-I took the day off to finalize my mortgage.

2155 encender — **turn on**

vb
[ẽn.sẽn̯.ˈdɛr]

Podéis encender una vela si queréis.
-You can light a candle if you like.

2156 civilización — **civilization**

f
[si.βi.li.sa.ˈsjõn]

Debemos construir una civilización digna del ser humano.
-We must build a civilization worthy of the human person.

2157 burro — **donkey**

m
[ˈbu.ro]

Oye, pequeño burro, mírame a mí.
-Listen, little donkey, take a look at me.

2158 democracia — **democracy**

f
[de.mo.ˈkra.sja]

Sabemos que sin democracia no hay verdadero desarrollo social.
-We know that without democracy there is no real social development.

2159 gimnasio — **gym**

m
[xĩm.ˈna.sjo]

Transformaremos tu habitación en un gimnasio.
-We're turning your room into a gym.

2160 patético — **pathetic**

adj
[pa.ˈtɛ.ti.ko]

Me dejaste claro que pensabas que era patético.
-You've made it clear you find me pathetic.

2161 observar — **observe**

vb
[oβ.sɛr.ˈβar]

Estamos empezando a observar los resultados de nuestros esfuerzos.
-We are beginning to see the results of our efforts.

2162 fase — **phase**

f
[ˈfa.se]

Estamos entrando en una nueva fase en la guerra.
-We are entering a new phase in the war.

2163 ilusión — **hope, thrill**

f
[i.lu.ˈsjõn]

Mi única ilusión es que seamos felices.
-My only hope is for us to be happy.

2164 debilidad — **weakness**

f
[de.βi.li.ˈðað]

No debe confundirse nuestra nobleza con debilidad.
-Our being noble must not be mistaken for weakness.

2165 psiquiatra — **psychiatrist**

m/f
[si.ˈkja.tra]

Me gustaría hablar con mi psiquiatra.
-I'd like to talk to my psychiatrist.

2166 autor — **author**

m
[au̯.ˈtor]

El autor afirma que esto perjudicó su defensa.
-The author states that this was prejudicial to his defense.

2167 condena — **conviction**

	f	Actualmente cumple condena en régimen de máxima seguridad.
	[kõn.ˈde.na]	-He is currently serving his sentence under a maximum security regime.
2168	**muelle**	**dock, spring**
	m	Estaba en el muelle cuando llegó.
	[ˈmwe.je]	-I was on the dock when you arrived.
2169	**estatal**	**state**
	adj	Se te ascendería a investigador estatal.
	[ɛs.ta.ˈtal]	-You'd be detailed as a state's investigator.
2170	**repugnante**	**disgusting**
	adj	Eres repugnante por pensarlo y me repugna oírlo.
	[re.puɣ.ˈnãn.te]	-You're disgusting to think it and I am disgusted to hear it.
2171	**aterrizar**	**land**
	vb	Estábamos planeando aterrizar en el océano.
	[a.tɛ.ri.ˈsar]	-We were planning to land in the ocean.
2172	**vencer**	**overcome**
	vb	Están luchando para vencer al sistema imperialista.
	[bɛ̃n.ˈsɛr]	-They are fighting to defeat the imperialist system.
2173	**copiar**	**copy**
	vb	La Sra. Takada acusó al muchacho de copiar la tarea de otro estudiante.
	[ko.ˈpjar]	-Ms. Takada accused the boy of copying another student's homework.
2174	**dibujo**	**drawing**
	m	Quiero mostrarte un dibujo, Olivia.
	[di.ˈβu.xo]	-I want to show you a drawing, Olivia.
2175	**causar**	**cause**
	vb	No quiero causar el pánico.
	[kau̯.ˈsar]	-I don't want to cause a panic.
2176	**mantequilla**	**butter**
	f	Hay demasiada mantequilla en esas bandejas.
	[mãn.te.ˈki.ja]	-There is too much butter on those trays.
2177	**aparato**	**device**
	m	Han desarrollado un nuevo aparato.
	[a.pa.ˈra.to]	-They've developed a new device.
2178	**pleno**	**full; plenary session**
	adj; m	Tienes pleno acceso a su oficina.
	[ˈple.no]	-You've got full access to his office.
2179	**sospechar**	**suspect**
	vb	Comenzaba a sospechar alguna clase de anomalía.
	[sos.pe.ˈʧar]	-I was beginning to suspect some kind of anomaly.
2180	**cazador**	**hunter**
	m	El cazador disparó a un zorro.
	[ka.sa.ˈðor]	-The hunter shot a fox.
2181	**hall**	**hall**
	m	Este es nuestro pequeño hall de entrada.
	[ˈaj]	-Here's a small entrance hall.
2182	**autopista**	**freeway**
	f	Llámame cuando estés en la autopista.
	[au̯.to.ˈpis.ta]	-Give me a call when you're on the motorway.
2183	**canalla**	**swine (coll); despicable**

m/f; adj

[ka.ˈna.ja]

Obviamente, el canalla no está prestando atención.
 -Obviously, the little swine is not paying attention.

2184 **informar(se)**

vb; vbr

[ĩm.for.ˈmar.se)]

inform; find out

Todos nosotros estamos de acuerdo en la necesidad de informar al ciudadano.
 -All of us agree on the need to inform the citizen.

2185 **despejar(se)**

vb; vbr

[dɛs.pe.ˈxar.se)]

clear; clear your mind

Solo quiero pasear un poco, despejar la mente.
 -I just want to walk a little, clear my head.

2186 **postre**

m

[ˈpos.tre]

dessert

Compré tres manzanas y dos racimos de uvas para el postre en el mercado.
 -I bought three apples and two bunches of grapes for dessert at the market.

2187 **concepto**

m

[kõn.ˈsep.to]

concept

La Comisión deberá aclarar este concepto.
 -The Commission will have to clarify this concept.

2188 **desarrollo**

m

[de.sa.ˈro.jo]

development

Esto es muy importante en términos de desarrollo.
 -This is very important in terms of development.

2189 **digno**

adj

[ˈdiɣ.no]

worthy

Procuraré ser un hijo digno de usted.
 -I'll try to be a worthy son to you.

2190 **juramento**

m

[xu.ra.ˈmẽn.to]

oath

Bien, no querríamos que rompiera ese juramento.
 -Well, we wouldn't want you to break that vow.

2191 **vampiro**

m

[bãm.ˈpi.ro]

vampire

Usaré esta cruz contra un vampiro.
 -I'm using this cross against a vampire.

2192 **combinación**

f

[kõm.bi.na.ˈsjõn]

combination

Debemos recurrir a una combinación de estrategias.
 -We have to resort to a combination of strategies.

2193 **término**

m

[ˈtɛr.mi.no]

term

Tenemos que negociar el término del embargo petrolero.
 -We need to negotiate the end of the oil embargo.

2194 **cartel**

m

[kar.ˈtɛl]

poster

Todos nuestros sabores están listados en ese cartel.
 -All our flavors are listed on that sign.

2195 **sangrar**

vb

[sãŋ.ˈgrar]

bleed

Quizás deberíamos dejarlo sangrar un rato.
 -Maybe we should let him bleed a while.

2196 **toalla**

f

[to.ˈa.ja]

towel

Incluso hubo momentos en los que pensamos arrojar la toalla.
 -There were even times when we'd consider throwing in the towel.

2197 **autorización**

f

[au̯.to.ri.sa.ˈsjõn]

authorization

No obstante, no es necesario obtener autorización oficial.
 -It is, however, not necessary to obtain official authorization.

2198 **bombero**

m/f

[bõm.ˈbɛ.ro]

firefighter

Quizás sea porque es bombero.
 -It might be because he is a fireman.

2199 **gravedad**

gravity

f
[gra.βe.'ðað]
Jim no tenía presente la gravedad de la situación.
-Jim wasn't aware of the gravity of the situation.

2200 **marinero**
m; adj
[ma.ri.'nɛ.ro]
sailor; naval
Bien, hijo, pareces un auténtico marinero.
-Well, my boy, you look like a true sailor.

2201 **tortura**
f
[tor.'tu.ra]
torture
Aún sufre graves secuelas físicas de la tortura.
-He still suffers from violent physical after-effects of the torture.

2202 **rehén**
m/f
[re.'ẽn]
hostage
Con ella como rehén, detendrán su ataque.
-With her as your hostage, they will call off their attack.

2203 **chaval**
m
[tʃa.'βal]
kid (ES) (coll)
Parece que es un chaval bastante independiente.
-He sounds like he's a pretty independent kid.

2204 **oveja**
f
[o.'βe.xa]
sheep
Nunca una oveja perdida tuvo tantos pastores.
-Never did a lost sheep have so many shepherds.

2205 **violento**
adj
[bjo.'lɛ̃n.to]
violent
Fuiste víctima de un crimen violento.
-You were the victim of a violent crime.

2206 **feria**
f
['fɛ.rja]
fair
Ellos quieren ver la feria.
-They want to visit the fair.

2207 **desafío**
m
[de.sa.'fi.o]
challenge
El desafío está en llegar a tiempo.
-The challenge there is getting on time.

2208 **origen**
m
[o.'ri.xẽn]
origin
Necesitamos ver el origen de la explosión.
-We need to see the origin of the blast.

2209 **constante**
adj
[kõns.'tãn.te]
constant
Hemos presenciado una evolución constante en los últimos años.
-We have seen a steady development in the last few years.

2210 **humilde**
adj
[u.'mil̪.de]
humble
Nunca le consideré del tipo humilde.
-I never thought of you as the humble type.

2211 **patada**
f
[pa.'ta.ða]
kick
La patada debe haber causado algún tipo de herida interna.
-The kick must have caused some sort of internal bruise.

2212 **ocultar(se)**
vb
[o.kul̪.'tar.se)]
hide
Intentó ocultar a su gatito.
-He tried to hide his kitten.

2213 **desafortunado**
adj
[de.sa.for.tu.'na.ðo]
unlucky
No es verdad que sea desafortunado.
-It is not true that I am unlucky.

2214 **refuerzo**
m
[re.'fwɛr.so]
backing
Cuando entreno a perros, utilizo el refuerzo positivo.
-When I'm training dogs, I use positive reinforcement.

2215 **jabón**
soap

	m	Límpialo cuidadosamente con agua y jabón.
	[xa.'βõn]	-Clean it carefully with soap and water.
2216	**método**	**method**
	m	Este podría ser el método más simple y efectivo.
	['mɛ.to.ðo]	-This may be the most simple and effective method.
2217	**mercancía**	**goods**
	f	Depositamos el dinero y recibimos la mercancía.
	[mɛr.kãn.'si.a]	-We drop off the money and get the merchandise.
2218	**acento**	**accent**
	m	¡Tu acento es lo máximo!
	[a.'sɛ̃n.to!	-Your accent is top notch!
2219	**escala**	**ladder**
	f	Pero nadie sabía la escala que alcanzaría.
	[ɛs.'ka.la]	-But no one knew how big in scale it would become.
2220	**engaño**	**deception**
	m	No participaré más en este engaño.
	[ɛ̃ŋ.'ga.ɲo]	-I will not participate further in this deception.
2221	**tenis**	**tennis**
	m	Jim está a cargo del torneo de tenis de este año.
	['te.nis]	-Jim is in charge of this year's tennis tournament.
2222	**comentario**	**comment**
	m	Quiero empezar con un comentario general.
	[ko.mɛ̃n.'ta.rjo]	-I want to begin with a general comment.
2223	**miseria**	**misery**
	f	La miseria ajena deja un extraño sabor.
	[mi.'sɛ.rja]	-The misery of others leaves a weird taste.
2224	**mafia**	**mafia**
	f	Y la mafia está intentando matarme.
	['ma.fja]	-And the mafia is trying to kill me.
2225	**estructura**	**structure**
	f	El edificio es una estructura enorme.
	[ɛs.truk̚.'tu.ra]	-The building is a huge structure.
2226	**gastar(se)**	**spend, use; wear out**
	vb; vbr	No tenemos demasiada munición que gastar.
	[gas.'tar.se)]	-We don't have a lot of ammo to waste.
2227	**desfile**	**parade**
	m	El desfile comenzará en aproximadamente media hora.
	[dɛs.'fi.le]	-The parade will begin in roughly a half an hour.
2228	**importe**	**amount**
	m	El importe de los billetes no utilizados ha sido devuelto a la empresa.
	[ĩm.'por.te]	-The cost of the unused tickets has been reimbursed to the company.
2229	**lápiz**	**pencil**
	m	Ana recogió un lápiz del suelo.
	['la.pis]	-Ana picked up a pencil off the floor.
2230	**editor**	**editor**
	m	Anteriormente ejerció de abogado y editor jurídico.
	[e.ði.'tor]	-Previously, he worked as an attorney and legal editor.
2231	**fortaleza**	**fortress, strength**

f
[for.ta.ˈle.sa]

Juntos, tenemos la fortaleza para afrontar este reto.
-Together, we have the strength to meet this challenge.

2232 pesa   **weight**

f
[ˈpe.sa]

No quiero saber cuánto pesa su hígado.
-I don't want to know how much her liver weighs.

2233 respiración   **breathing**

f
[rɛs.pi.ra.ˈsjõn]

No puedes matarte conteniendo la respiración.
-You cannot kill yourself by holding your breath.

2234 cuero   **leather**

m
[ˈkwɛ.ro]

Están hechos del mejor cuero italiano.
-They're made of the finest Italian leather.

2235 fuga   **jailbreak, leak**

f
[ˈfu.ɣa]

Quiero decir algo respecto a esta fuga.
-I wish to say something respecting this escape.

2236 inconsciente   **unconscious, thoughtless; subconscious**

adj; m
[ĩŋ.kõns.ˈsjẽn.te]

Fue trasladado inconsciente al hospital de la ciudad.
-He was transferred, unconscious, to the hospital in town.

2237 grabación   **recording**

f
[gra.βa.ˈsjõn]

Te llamaré cuando tenga la grabación.
-I'll call back when I have the recording.

2238 pacífico   **peaceful**

adj
[pa.ˈsi.fi.ko]

Soy pacífico y no me gustan las peleas.
-I'm pacific and I don't like fights.

2239 horario   **schedule; time**

m; adj
[o.ˈra.rjo]

Tengo que organizar mi horario antes de fin de mes.
-I have to organize my schedule before the end of the month.

2240 complejo   **complex; complex**

adj; m
[kõm.ˈple.xo]

Lo dejamos encadenado en el complejo.
-We left him chained up at the compound.

2241 maletín   **briefcase**

m
[ma.lɛ.ˈtĩn]

He dejado tu maletín en recepción.
-I've left your bag at the reception.

2242 materia   **matter**

f
[ma.ˈtɛ.rja]

Detecto grandes cantidades de materia oscura.
-I'm detecting vast quantities of dark matter.

2243 positivo   **positive**

adj
[po.si.ˈti.βo]

Creo que los resultados pueden calificarse como positivos.
-I think that the results can be described as positive.

2244 chófer   **driver**

m/f
[ˈtʃo.fɛr]

Cada oficina cuenta también con un asistente y un chófer.
-Each office also had an assistant and a driver.

2245 eléctrico   **electric**

adj
[e.ˈlek.tri.ko]

Naturalmente, fabricar un coche eléctrico competitivo conlleva un trabajo inmenso.
-Of course, it takes a great deal of work to produce a competitive electric car.

2246 cabra   **goat**

f
[ˈka.βra]

Devolveremos la cabra después del partido.
-We're returning the goat after the game.

2247 enero   **January**

m
[e.'nɛ.ro]

Contó un incidente que había sucedido en enero de 2004.
-He reported an incident that had occurred in January 2004.

2248 comedor

m
[ko.me.'ðor]

dining room

Hay mucha conversación mientras desayunamos en el comedor.
-There is a lot of talking as we eat our breakfast in the dining room.

2249 república

f
[re.'pu.βli.ka]

republic

Austria es una república parlamentaria de Europa central formada por nueve estados federales.
-Austria is a parliamentary republic in central Europe and consists of nine federal states.

2250 sabio

adj; m
['sa.βjo]

wise; sage

Allí vivía el sabio que el muchacho buscaba.
-There lived the sage that the young man was looking for.

2251 apariencia

f
[a.pa.'rjẽn.sja]

appearance

Uno no puede juzgar a la gente solo por su apariencia externa.
-One cannot judge people only by their outward appearances.

2252 agallas

fpl
[a.'ɣa.ʝas]

guts

Tiene más agallas que todos los jugadores.
-You have more guts than all the gamblers.

2253 mezcla

f
['mɛs.kla]

mixture

Es solo una mezcla que hice.
-It's just a mix that I made.

2254 ejecución

f
[e.xe.ku.'sjõn]

execution

No estamos obligados a presenciar esta ejecución.
-We're under no obligation to watch this execution.

2255 licor

m
[li.'kor]

liquor

No creo que sirvan licor aquí.
-I don't think they serve liquor here.

2256 mágico

adj
['ma.xi.ko]

magic

Este anillo es un objeto mágico que otorga un gran poder a su usuario.
-This ring is a magic item that gives great power to its user.

2257 reconocimiento

m
[re.ko.no.si.'mjẽn̪.to]

recognition

Nos gustaría darles las gracias a todos los que han hecho posible este reconocimiento.
-We would like to thank everybody who made this recognition possible.

2258 involucrar(se)

vb
[ĩm.bo.lu.'krar.se)]

involve

Tenemos que involucrar a la policía.
-We have to involve the police.

2259 desesperado

adj; m
[de.sɛs.pɛ.'ra.ðo]

desperate; desperate

Está desesperado por ponerte una trampa.
-He's desperate to set a trap for you.

2260 elefante

m
[e.le.'fãn̪.te]

elephant

Nunca había visto un elefante en la vida real.
-I had never seen an elephant in real life.

2261 desorden

m
[de.'sor.ðẽn]

disturbance, chaos

De acuerdo, limpiemos este desorden.
-All right, let's clean up this mess.

2262 torneo

m
[tor.'ne.o]

tournament

Él ganó el primer premio en el torneo de ajedrez.
-He won the first prize at the chess tournament.

2263	**apetito**	**appetite**
	m	Y no hay apetito como el apetito por la tierra.
	[a.pɛˈti.to]	-And there's no hunger like the hunger for land.

2264	**orilla**	**shore**
	f	Paseamos por la orilla del lago.
	[oˈri.ja]	-We walked along the shore of the lake.

2265	**fenómeno**	**phenomenon**
	m	Puede observarse un fenómeno similar en China.
	[feˈno.me.no]	-A similar phenomenon can also be observed in China.

2266	**alimento**	**food**
	m	Déjenme compartir algo de alimento con ustedes.
	[a.liˈmẽṇ.to]	-Let me share some of the food with you.

2267	**mancha**	**stain**
	f	Esa mancha pudo haber estado allí meses.
	[ˈmãṇ.tʃa]	-That stain could've been there for months.

2268	**giro**	**turn**
	m	Haremos el primer giro en unos pocos minutos.
	[ˈxi.ro]	-We'll be making the first turn in a few minutes.

2269	**submarino**	**underwater; submarine**
	adj; m	Un cable submarino fue puesto en medio de los dos países.
	[suβ.maˈri.no]	-A submarine cable was laid between the two countries.

2270	**sabiduría**	**wisdom**
	f	Confiamos en la sabiduría del hombre.
	[sa.βi.ðu.ˈri.a]	-We trust in the wisdom of the man.

2271	**policial**	**police**
	adj	Todo interrogatorio policial deberá ser recogido bajo acta firmada.
	[po.li.ˈsjal]	-Any interrogation by the police must be included in a signed record.

2272	**campana**	**bell**
	f	El torneo empezará cuando suene este campana.
	[kãm.ˈpa.na]	-The tournament will start at the sound of this bell.

2273	**criado**	**servant**
	m	Tu criado estará esperando allí con los caballos.
	[ˈkrja.ðo]	-Your servant will be waiting there with the horses.

2274	**gesto**	**gesture**
	m	La aerolínea ofreció alojamiento gratuito a los pasajeros atrapados como un gesto de buena voluntad.
	[ˈxɛs.to]	-The airline provided free accommodation to stranded passengers as a goodwill gesture.

2275	**comercio**	**shop**
	m	Ahora quieren arruinar nuestro comercio marítimo.
	[ko.ˈmɛr.sjo]	-Now they want to ruin our maritime trade.

2276	**interrumpir**	**interrupt**
	vb	Su médico decidirá cuando interrumpir el tratamiento.
	[ĩṇ.tɛ.rũm.ˈpir]	-Your doctor will decide when to stop the treatment.

2277	**capullo**	**cocoon, idiot (ES) (coll)**
	m	La mariposa de seda es una mariposa grande cuya oruga teje un capullo usado en la fabricación de seda.
	[ka.ˈpu.jo]	-The silk moth is a large moth whose caterpillar spins a cocoon used for silk production.

| 2278 | **creación** | **creation** |

f

[kre.a.ˈsjõn]

Han estado luchando desde la creación del mundo.
-They've been fighting since the creation of the world.

2279 **camiseta** **shirt**

f

[ka.mi.ˈsɛ.ta]

Una camiseta de manga larga, posiblemente vaqueros.
-A long-sleeved t-shirt, possibly jeans.

2280 **gusano** **worm**

m

[gu.ˈsa.no]

Está buscando algo, quizás un gusano.
-He's digging for something, maybe a worm.

2281 **lógico** **logical**

adj

[ˈlo.xi.ko]

Hablo desde el punto de vista lógico.
-I am talking from the logical point of view.

2282 **excepción** **exception**

f

[ɛk.sɛp.ˈsjõn]

Esta es una excepción a la regla.
-This is an exception to the rule.

2283 **lectura** **reading**

f

[lek.ˈtu.ra]

Me gustaría que preparases una lectura para mañana.
-I'd like you to prepare a reading for tomorrow.

2284 **seda** **silk**

f

[ˈse.ða]

Estaba atrapada entre una dama robusta vestida con seda rosa y una chica alta, de aspecto desdeñoso, con un vestido de encaje blanco.
-She was wedged in between a stout lady in pink silk and a tall, scornful-looking girl in a white lace dress.

2285 **atmósfera** **atmosphere**

f

[atˈmos.fɛ.ra]

No se detectaron explosiones en la atmósfera.
-No explosions were detected in the atmosphere.

2286 **deberes** **homework**

mpl

[de.ˈβɛ.res]

Había terminado mis deberes cuando me llamaste.
-I had finished my homework when you called me.

2287 **resuelto** **solved**

adj

[re.ˈswɛl̪.to]

Esto no significa que hayamos resuelto todos nuestros problemas.
-This does not mean that we have solved all our problems.

2288 **quemar(se)** **burn**

vb

[ke.ˈmar.se)]

Siento que quiero quemar esta cosa.
-I feel like I want to burn this thing.

2289 **tarta** **cake**

f

[ˈtar.ta]

Pensé que estaba comiendo demasiada tarta.
-I thought I was just eating too much pie.

2290 **ganancia** **gain**

f

[ga.ˈnãn.sja]

Como comerciante necesito sentir que logro una ganancia.
-As a businessman, I need to feel like I made a profit.

2291 **timar** **cheat**

vb

[ti.ˈmar]

Yo no quiero timar a nadie.
-I don't want to cheat on anyone.

2292 **cosecha** **harvest**

f

[ko.ˈse.tʃa]

Además, seguirían necesitando asistencia alimentaria hasta la cosecha.
-Moreover, they would continue to require food assistance until the harvest.

2293 **disciplina** **discipline**

f

[dis.sip̚.ˈli.na]

No sabía que esa disciplina existiera.
-I wasn't aware such a discipline existed.

2294 **oficio** **job**

	m	Resulta que es un oficio altamente demandado.
	[o.ˈfi.sjo]	-It turns out it's a highly demanding craft.
2295	**bahía**	**bay**
	f	Tomarán el almuerzo en una bahía tranquila.
	[ba.ˈi.a]	-You will have lunch in a peaceful bay.
2296	**norma**	**rule**
	f	El director no explicó qué norma había violado.
	[ˈnor.ma]	-The warden did not explain which rule had been violated.
2297	**salario**	**wage**
	m	Su elevado salario le permitió vivir cómodamente.
	[sa.ˈla.rjo]	-His high salary enabled him to live in comfort.
2298	**cuerdo**	**sane**
	adj	Hace dos días se despertó totalmente cuerdo.
	[ˈkwɛr.ðo]	-Two days ago, he woke up perfectly sane.
2299	**conversar**	**talk**
	vb	Ojala tuviera tiempo para quedarme y conversar contigo.
	[kõm.bɛr.ˈsar]	-I wish I had the time to stay and talk with you.
2300	**pelotón**	**squad**
	m	Tenemos órdenes de unirnos a tu pelotón.
	[pe.lo.ˈtõn]	-We were given orders to report to your squad.
2301	**pasaje**	**ticket**
	m	Nos han dado un pasaje que no permite cambios.
	[pa.ˈsa.xe]	-We have been given a ticket that does not allow changes.
2302	**fianza**	**bail, deposit**
	f	Le entregamos al tribunal su fianza.
	[ˈfjãn.sa]	-We have supplied the court with his bail.
2303	**misa**	**mass**
	f	Estoy en medio de una misa.
	[ˈmi.sa]	-I'm in the middle of a mass.
2304	**carbón**	**carbon**
	m	Él traerá el carbón y las salchichas.
	[kar.ˈβõn]	-He is bringing the charcoal and the sausages.
2305	**grosero**	**rude**
	adj	Es grosero mirar fijamente a desconocidos.
	[gro.ˈsɛ.ro]	-It is rude to stare at strangers.
2306	**quejarse**	**complain**
	vbr	El camarero era tan simpático que no nos quisimos quejar de la comida.
	[ke.ˈxar.se]	-The waiter was such a nice man we didn't want to complain about the meal.
2307	**cristiano**	**Christian; Christian**
	adj; m	Visitaremos también los barrios judíos y cristianos.
	[kris.ˈtja.no]	-We will also visit the districts Jewish and Christian.
2308	**misterioso**	**mysterious**
	adj	Pensábamos en sus películas como algo serio y ligeramente misterioso.
	[mis.tɛ.ˈrjo.so]	-We thought of his films as something serious and slightly mysterious.
2309	**instinto**	**instinct**
	m	Si estamos asustados, corremos. Es nuestro instinto.
	[ĩns.ˈtĩɲ.to]	-If we're frightened, we run. It's our instinct.
2310	**negociar**	**negotiate**

	vb	No estoy aquí para negociar contigo.
	[ne.ɣo.ˈsjar]	-I'm not here to bargain with you.
2311	**plazo**	**period, deadline**
	m	El plazo acaba el lunes a las 2:30.
	[ˈpla.so]	-The deadline is 2:30 on Monday.
2312	**confusión**	**confusion**
	f	Hubo una confusión en la tintorería.
	[kõɱ.fu.ˈsjõn]	-There was a mix-up at the dry cleaners.
2313	**orquestar**	**orchestrate**
	vb	Sabría cómo orquestar algo como esto.
	[or.kɛs.ˈtar]	-He'd know how to orchestrate something like this.
2314	**afectar**	**affect**
	vb	Sus lágrimas no pueden afectar a una persona sin corazón.
	[a.fek̚.ˈtar]	-Your tears can't affect a heartless person.
2315	**tribu**	**tribe**
	f	La tribu Zulú de Sudáfrica tiene su propia lengua.
	[ˈtri.βu]	-The Zulu tribe in South Africa has its own language.
2316	**horno**	**oven**
	m	Tuvimos un problema con el horno.
	[ˈor.no]	-We did have a problem with the oven.
2317	**rabia**	**rage**
	f	No cometen crímenes de rabia y venganza.
	[ˈra.βja]	-They don't commit crimes of rage and revenge.
2318	**espantoso**	**frightening**
	adj	Quiero sacudirme este espantoso cansancio pero no puedo.
	[ɛs.pãn̪.ˈto.so]	-I want to shake off this awful tiredness and I can't.
2319	**aguardar**	**wait**
	vb	Solo tendrán que aguardar un momento.
	[a.ɣwar.ˈðar]	-You'll just have to wait a minute.
2320	**cocaína**	**cocaine**
	f	Mascar coca no es lo mismo que consumir cocaína.
	[ko.ka.ˈi.na]	-Chewing coca is not the same as consuming cocaine.
2321	**estacionamiento**	**parking**
	m	Casi no había autos en el estacionamiento.
	[ɛs.ta.sjo.na.ˈmjẽn̪.to]	-There were almost no cars in the parking lot.
2322	**aproximado**	**approximate**
	adj	Deberíamos poder determinar el lugar aproximado.
	[a.prok.si.ˈma.ðo]	-We should be able to determine its approximate location.
2323	**alivio**	**relief**
	m	Debe ser un alivio tener algo de seguridad económica.
	[a.ˈli.βjo]	-It must be a relief to have some financial security.
2324	**clan**	**clan**
	m	El clan Sonozaki probablemente ignore todo esto.
	[ˈklãn]	-The Sonozaki clan will probably ignore this whole thing.
2325	**tubo**	**tube**
	m	No encontrarás un tubo aquí abajo.
	[ˈtu.βo]	-You won't find a pipe down here.
2326	**aterrizaje**	**landing**

m
[a.tɛ.ri.ˈsa.xe]
El avión hizo un aterrizaje forzoso.
-The plane made a forced landing.

2327 **revolver** — **stir**
vb
[re.βol.ˈβɛr]
No olvides revolver el estofado.
-Don't forget to stir the stew.

2328 **profundidad** — **depth**
f
[pro.fũn̯.di.ˈðað]
Eso demuestra la profundidad de su amor por su familia.
-That shows the depth of his love for his family.

2329 **araña** — **spider**
f
[a.ˈra.ɲa]
Esta araña gigante salió del drenaje.
-This huge spider came out of the drain.

2330 **contener(se)** — **contain**
vb
[kõn̯.te.ˈnɛr.se)]
Dice que puede contener la respiración durante cuatro minutos.
-He claims he can hold his breath over four minutes.

2331 **certeza** — **certainty**
f
[sɛr.ˈte.sa]
El sector también necesita alguna certeza.
-The sector also needs to be given some certainty.

2332 **afecto** — **affection**
m
[a.ˈfek̚.to]
Toma esto como muestra de afecto.
-Take this as a token of my affection.

2333 **consuelo** — **relief**
m
[kõn.ˈswe.lo]
Es un consuelo saber que no estamos solos.
-It is a consolation to know we are not alone.

2334 **micrófono** — **microphone**
m
[mi.ˈkro.fo.no]
Jim le arrebató el micrófono a Ana.
-Jim took the microphone away from Ana.

2335 **formación** — **training**
f
[for.ma.ˈsjõn]
Los niños analfabetos reciben una formación especial.
-Special training was given to children who were illiterate.

2336 **evidente** — **apparent**
adj
[e.βi.ˈðẽn̯.te]
Me parece evidente que algo está yendo muy mal.
-It is obvious to me that something is going very seriously wrong.

2337 **retrasar(se)** — **delay**
vb
[rɛ.tra.ˈsar.se)]
Solo servirán para retrasar el procedimiento.
-They will only serve to delay the procedure.

2338 **estrategia** — **strategy**
f
[ɛs.tra.ˈte.xja]
No necesitaban diseñar una estrategia colectiva.
-They did not need to design a corporate strategy.

2339 **rango** — **rank**
m
[ˈrãŋ.go]
Tendrás todas las ventajas de tu rango.
-You'll have all the privileges of your rank.

2340 **ajá** — **uh-huh**
int
[a.ˈxa]
Pero, ajá, yo lo sabía.
-But, aha, I knew it.

2341 **procedimiento** — **procedure**
m
[pro.se.ði.ˈmjẽn̯.to]
Expresó su grave preocupación por el procedimiento.
-He expressed his deep concern about the procedure.

2342 **comprobar** — **check**

vb
[kõm.pro.'βar]

Debes desconectar la alimentación antes de comprobar el circuito.
-You must switch off the power before checking the circuit.

2343 **exposición**
f
[ɛks.po.si.'sjõn]

exposure

El médico probablemente te aconsejará limitar la exposición al sol.
-Your doctor will probably advise you to limit your sun exposure.

2344 **espiritual**
adj
[ɛs.pi.ri.'twal]

spiritual

El matrimonio se considera cuestión tanto espiritual como corporal.
-Marriage is considered as a matter of both spirit and body.

2345 **potencial**
adj; m
[po.tẽn.'sjal]

potential; strength

Tiene todavía un gran potencial de desarrollo.
-It still has a lot of potential for development.

2346 **raíz**
f
[ra.'is]

root

La raíz cuadrada de uno es uno.
-The square root of one is one.

2347 **nido**
m
['ni.ðo]

nest

Las aves pusieron un nido en una rama.
-The birds placed a nest on a branch.

2348 **temporal**
adj; m
[tẽm.po.'ral]

temporary; storm

El personal será contratado con carácter temporal.
-The staff shall be recruited on a temporary basis.

2349 **leal**
adj
[le.'al]

loyal

Mi esposa no solo es la mujer más hermosa que he conocido, también es la más leal y trabajadora.
-My wife is not only the most beautiful woman I've ever met, but she's also the most loyal and hardworking.

2350 **asociación**
f
[a.so.sja.'sjõn]

association

Nosotros continuaremos fortaleciendo esta estrecha asociación.
-We will continue to further strengthen this close partnership.

2351 **llenar**
vb
[ʎe.'nar]

fill

Necesitas llenar este formulario una sola vez.
-You will be required to fill out this form only once.

2352 **doña**
f
['do.ɲa]

miss, lady

Todavía me quedan cinco minutos, doña Helen.
-I still have five minutes, Mrs. Helen.

2353 **moderno**
adj
[mo.'ðɛr.no]

modern

El problema fundamental es que en el mundo moderno el tonto está completamente seguro de sí, mientras que el listo está lleno de dudas.
-The fundamental problem is that in the modern world the foolish are completely sure of themselves, while the smart are full of doubts.

2354 **nocturno**
adj
[nok.'tur.no]

night

Soy el conductor del tren nocturno.
-I am the conductor of the night train.

2355 **resistir(se)**
vb
[re.sis.'tir.se)]

resist

Pero es importante resistir ese impulso.
-But it is important to resist this urge.

2356 **regimiento**
m
[re.xi.'mjẽn̪.to]

regiment

Tienes que volver al regimiento.
-You have to go back to the regiment.

2357 **coro**

choir

	m	Cuando entró el rey, el coro comenzó a entonar alabanzas.
	['ko.ɾo]	-When the king came in, the choir began intoning praises.
2358	**muerto**	**dead**
	m	A mí no me parece que esté muerto.
	['mwɛɾ.to]	-He doesn't seem dead to me.
2359	**duelo**	**duel**
	m	Este es el duelo decisivo.
	['dwe.lo]	-This is the decisive duel.
2360	**dificultad**	**difficulty**
	f	Una dificultad fundamental es la gran desconfianza entre las partes.
	[di.fi.kul̪.'tað]	-A crucial difficulty is the basic lack of trust between the parties.
2361	**ausencia**	**absence**
	f	Su ausencia ahora levantaría demasiadas preguntas.
	[au̯.'sẽn.sja]	-Your absence now would raise too many questions.
2362	**eliminar**	**remove**
	vb	Es fundamental eliminar las causas del conflicto armado.
	[e.li.mi.'naɾ]	-It is essential to eliminate the causes of armed conflict.
2363	**graduación**	**graduation**
	f	Jim asistió a la ceremonia de graduación de Ana.
	[gɾa.ðwa.'sjõn]	-Jim attended Ana's graduation ceremony.
2364	**texto**	**text**
	m	Este libro de texto, al ser publicado con prisas, tiene muchas erratas.
	['tɛks.to]	-This textbook, having been printed in haste, has a lot of printing mistakes.
2365	**transmisión**	**transmission**
	f	Acabamos de perder nuestra transmisión de vídeo.
	[trãns̪.mi.'sjõn]	-We just lost our video transmission.
2366	**separar**	**separate**
	vb	Debemos separar nuestras actividades por regiones.
	[se.pa.'ɾaɾ]	-We have to separate our activities by region.
2367	**padrino**	**godfather**
	m	Mi padrino me dio esa camisa roja.
	[pa.'ðɾi.no]	-My godfather gave me that red shirt.
2368	**fraude**	**fraud**
	m	Llamó para decirte que alguien había descubierto tu fraude.
	['fɾau̯.ðe]	-He called to tell you someone had discovered your scam.
2369	**astuto**	**cunning**
	adj	Sé astuto y ganaremos mucho dinero.
	[as.'tu.to]	-Be smart and we'll all make a lot of money.
2370	**solar**	**solar; site**
	adj; m	Tendréis que perderos el eclipse solar.
	[so.'laɾ]	-You'll have to miss the solar eclipse.
2371	**edición**	**edition**
	f	Siempre puede encontrar la última edición aquí.
	[e.ði.'sjõn]	-The latest issue can always be found here.
2372	**suizo**	**Swiss; Swiss**
	adj; m	El teclado suizo no tiene la letra ß.
	['swi.so]	-The Swiss keyboard doesn't have the letter ß.
2373	**rodear(se)**	**go around**

vb
[ro.ðe.ˈar.se)]

Necesito a gente para rodear esta casa ya mismo.
 -I need some people to surround this house right now.

2374 concentración — **concentration**

f
[kõn.sẽn̪.ˈtra.sjõn]

No quiero que pierda la concentración.
 -I don't want her to lose focus.

2375 conspiración — **conspiracy**

f
[kõns.pi.ra.ˈsjõn]

Algunas personas ven una conspiración detrás de casi cualquier cosa.
 -Some people see a conspiracy behind almost everything.

2376 alejar(se) — **move away**

vb
[a.le.ˈxar.se)]

Nada me puede alejar de ti.
 -Nothing can keep me from you.

2377 habitual — **habitual**

adj
[a.βi.ˈtwal]

Esta investigación se ha realizado según el procedimiento habitual.
 -This investigation has been carried out according to the usual procedure.

2378 acompañar — **accompany**

vb
[a.kõm.pa.ˈɲar]

Decidimos acompañar a los fieles a la iglesia.
 -We decided to accompany worshipers to church.

2379 filosofía — **philosophy**

f
[fi.lo.so.ˈfi.a]

La verdadera filosofía es ver las cosas tal y como son.
 -True philosophy is seeing things as they are.

2380 enfrentar — **confront**

vb
[ẽɱ.frẽn̪.ˈtar]

Juntos podemos y debemos enfrentarnos a esos retos.
 -Together, we can and must confront those challenges.

2381 delicado — **delicate**

adj
[de.li.ˈka.ðo]

Este equipo no solo es caro, también es extremadamente delicado.
 -Not only is this equipment expensive, it's also extremely sensitive.

2382 potencia — **power**

f
[po.ˈtẽn.sja]

Europa no quiere ser una potencia militar.
 -Europe does not want to be a military power.

2383 herido — **injured; wounded**

m; adj
[ɛ.ˈri.ðo]

No esperaba que nadie saliera herido.
 -I didn't expect anyone to be hurt.

2384 pervertir(se) — **pervert**

vb
[pɛr.βɛr.ˈtir.se)]

No puedes pervertir el curso de la justicia.
 -You cannot pervert the course of justice.

2385 bendito — **blessed**

adj
[bẽn̪.ˈdi.to]

Está utilizando un farol bendito de la catedral.
 -He is using a blessed lantern from the cathedral.

2386 dosis — **dose**

f
[ˈdo.sis]

Alguien le dio a Jim una dosis letal de esteroides.
 -Somebody gave Jim a lethal dose of steroids.

2387 incapaz — **unable; incompetent**

adj; m/f
[ĩŋ.ˈka.pas]

Él es incapaz de concentrarse en su trabajo escolar.
 -He is unable to concentrate on his academic work.

2388 unido — **united**

adj
[u.ˈni.ðo]

Este es un mundo unido por las nuevas tecnologías de la comunicación.
 -This is a world united by the new technologies of communication.

2389 oración — **prayer, sentence**

f
[o.ra.ˈsjõn]
Podría ilustrar esto con solo una oración.
-I could illustrate this simply with just one sentence.

2390 tímido shy
adj
[ˈti.mi.ðo]
Quería conocerla, pero soy tímido.
-I wanted to meet her, but I'm shy.

2391 danza dance
f
[ˈdãn.sa]
Su hija tiene un recital de danza esta noche.
-Her daughter has a dance recital tonight.

2392 juzgar judge
vb
[xuş.ˈɣar]
Permítame juzgar quién tiene la culpa.
-Permit me to judge who is at fault.

2393 aclarar clarify
vb
[a.kla.ˈrar]
Cabe esperar que las explicaciones facilitadas sirvan para aclarar la situación.
-It is hoped that the explanations provided will serve to clarify the situation.

2394 conclusión conclusion
f
[kõŋ.klu.ˈsjõn]
La lógica es un método sistemático de llegar a la conclusión incorrecta con seguridad.
-Logic is a systematic method of coming to the wrong conclusion with confidence.

2395 secuencia sequence
f
[se.ˈkwẽn.sja]
Normalmente no encontraríamos brechas en la secuencia.
-Normally, we'd find no gaps in the sequence.

2396 brillar shine
vb
[bri.ˈjar]
Ahora sería un momento grandioso para brillar.
-Now it'd be a great time to shine.

2397 mensajero messenger
m
[mẽn.sa.ˈxɛ.ro]
El tipo de la gorra amarilla resultó ser un mensajero.
-The guy with the yellow cap turned out to be a messenger.

2398 vidrio glass
m
[ˈbi.ðrjo]
Quiero que examines el fragmento de vidrio.
-I want you to examine the shard of glass.

2399 acostado lying down
adj
[a.kos.ˈta.ðo]
Ese hombre está acostado ahí.
-That guy is lying down there.

2400 beneficio benefit
m
[be.ne.ˈfi.sjo]
Me sacrificaste por tu beneficio propio.
-You sacrificed me for your own personal gain.

2401 empujar push
vb
[ẽm.pu.ˈxar]
Vas a tener que empujar desde arriba.
-You're going to need to push from the top.

2402 extremado extreme
adj
[ɛks.tre.ˈma.ðo]
¿El clima es ahora más variable o extremado?
-Has the climate become more variable or extreme?

2403 hambriento hungry; hungry person
adj; m
[ãm.ˈbrjẽn̪.to]
Debes estar hambriento para comer tanto arroz.
-You must be hungry to eat so much rice.

2404 tabla board
f
[ˈta.βla]
Esa tabla está llena de información.
-That table is full of information.

2405 maldad wickedness

	f	Hay mucha maldad en el mundo.
	[maḻ.ˈdað]	-There is so much wickedness in the world.
2406	**condicional**	**conditional**
	adj	El carácter condicional de la declaración es incuestionable.
	[kõn.di.sjo.ˈnal]	-The conditional nature of the declaration is indisputable.
2407	**dorado**	**golden**
	adj	Aquí estoy buscando nuestro ticket dorado.
	[do.ˈra.ðo]	-Here I am looking for our golden ticket.
2408	**Cuba**	**Cuba**
	f	Cuba estaba realizando esfuerzos ingentes para integrarse en la economía mundial.
	[ˈku.βa]	-Cuba was making considerable efforts to integrate itself into the global economy.
2409	**dispuesto**	**handy (ES), ready**
	adj	En ese momento dije que estaba dispuesto a hacerlo.
	[dis.ˈpwɛs.to]	-I said at the time that I was willing to do so.
2410	**literal**	**literal**
	adj	Nos referimos a algo un poco más literal.
	[li.tɛ.ˈral]	-We're talking something a little more literal.
2411	**filmar**	**film**
	vb	Dile que es muy difícil filmar niños.
	[fil.ˈmar]	-You tell him that it is very tricky to film children.
2412	**antecedente**	**precedent**
	m	Estás sentando un antecedente peligroso aquí.
	[ãn.te.se.ˈðẽn.te]	-You're setting a dangerous precedent here.
2413	**paro**	**unemployment (ES), strike**
	m	Queremos ayudar a todos aquellos que tienen miedo del paro y la inestabilidad.
	[ˈpa.ro]	-We want to help all those who fear unemployment and instability.
2414	**acusación**	**accusation**
	f	Descubriré si su acusación es cierta.
	[a.ku.sa.ˈsjõn]	-I'll find out if his accusation is true.
2415	**prestar**	**lend**
	vb	Debes prestar más atención si quieres triunfar.
	[prɛs.ˈtar]	-You must pay more attention if you wish to succeed.
2416	**secuestro**	**kidnapping**
	m	Nosotros no hablamos del secuestro.
	[se.ˈkwɛs.tro]	-We didn't talk about the kidnapping.
2417	**vulgar**	**vulgar, common**
	adj	Pensarás que es una observación vulgar.
	[bul.ˈɣar]	-You probably think that's a vulgar remark.
2418	**algodón**	**cotton**
	m	Este algodón es orgánico, estoy bastante seguro.
	[al.ɣo.ˈðõn]	-This cotton is organic, I'm pretty sure.
2419	**colonia**	**colony**
	f	Antiguamente, Nigeria era una colonia británica.
	[ko.ˈlo.nja]	-At one time Nigeria was a British colony.
2420	**disposición**	**aptitude, disposal**
	f	Tengo mucho dinero a mi disposición.
	[dis.po.si.ˈsjõn]	-I have a lot of money at my disposal.
2421	**avisar**	**warn**

vb
[a.βi.ˈsar]
Deberían avisar a la gente de que no hay ascensor.
-You should warn people there's no elevator.

2422 continuo — **continuous**
adj
[kõn̪.ˈti.nwo]
Esperamos que este ejercicio sea un proceso continuo.
-We hope that this exercise will be a continuous process.

2423 liberar(se) — **set free**
vb
[li.βɛ.ˈrar.se]]
Imagina si pudiésemos liberar el cerebro del cuerpo.
-Imagine if we could free the brain from the body.

2424 saludable — **healthy**
adj
[sa.lu.ˈða.βle]
Pienso que es poco saludable comer más de 20 naranjas en un día.
-I think it's unhealthy to eat more than 20 oranges a day.

2425 rodar — **roll**
vb
[ro.ˈðar]
Quiere rodar su vídeo en el Montecito.
-He wants to shoot his video in the Montecito.

2426 pantano — **swamp**
m
[pãn̪.ˈta.no]
No puedes esperar encontrar nada en este pantano.
-You can not expect to find anything in this swamp.

2427 envío — **shipping**
m
[ẽm.ˈbi.o]
Podemos meterlos en su próximo envío.
-We can fold them into their next shipment.

2428 bigote — **mustache**
m
[bi.ˈɣo.te]
Solo tendrás que afeitarte el bigote.
-You will only have to shave off your mustache.

2429 instrumento — **instrument**
m
[ĩns.tru.ˈmẽn̪.to]
¿Es la cítara un instrumento difícil de aprender?
-Is the citar a hard instrument to learn?

2430 distinto — **different**
adj
[dis.ˈtĩn̪.to]
También cabe señalar que cada país es distinto.
-It should also be pointed out that each country is different.

2431 tiburón — **shark**
m
[ti.βu.ˈrõn]
Quiero ayudarte a encontrar a ese tiburón.
-I want to help you find that shark.

2432 graso — **fatty, oily**
adj
[ˈgra.so]
Su sabor es láctico, suave y para nada graso.
-Its flavor is milky, mild, and not at all greasy.

2433 iris — **iris**
m
[ˈi.ris]
La inflamación del iris se denomina iritis.
-Inflammation of the iris is called iritis.

2434 matemático — **mathematical; mathematician**
adj; m
[ma.te.ˈma.ti.ko]
Sabía que resolverías mi problemita matemático.
-I knew you'd figure out my little math problem.

2435 honrado — **honest**
adj
[õn.ˈra.ðo]
Sabía que ese hombre era un criminal honrado.
-I knew that man was an honest criminal.

2436 dieta — **diet**
f
[ˈdjɛ.ta]
Es necesario proporcionarles una dieta nutritiva y equilibrada.
-It is necessary to provide them with a balanced and nutritious diet.

2437 salvación — **salvation**

f
[sal.βa.ˈsjõn]
Puedes buscar la salvación donde quieras.
-You can search everywhere you want for salvation.

2438 shock — **shock**

n
[ˈsokk]
Parecía estar en estado de shock.
-He seemed to be in a state of shock.

2439 munición — **ammunition**

f
[mu.ni.ˈsjõn]
Tienes toda la munición que necesitas.
-You have all the ammunition that you need.

2440 enano — **shorty; very small**

m; adj
[e.ˈna.no]
Bien, enano, conseguimos algunas pruebas.
-Well, shorty, we got ourselves some evidence.

2441 orientar(se) — **guide**

vb
[o.rjẽn̪.ˈtar.se)]
Deberíamos utilizar ese conocimiento para orientar mejor nuestros propios esfuerzos.
-We should use that understanding to better direct our own efforts.

2442 águila — **eagle**

m
[ˈa.ɣi.la]
El águila es la reina de los vientos.
-The eagle is the queen of the winds.

2443 justa — **joust**

f
[ˈxus.ta]
Esperamos que la evaluación sea justa e imparcial.
-We hope that the assessment will be fair and impartial.

2444 clásico — **classic**

adj
[ˈkla.si.ko]
Es un regalo clásico para un joven empresario.
-It's a classic gift for a young businessman.

2445 lámpara — **lamp**

f
[ˈlãm.pa.ra]
La lámpara cuelga del techo.
-The lamp is hanging from the ceiling.

2446 estadio — **stadium**

m
[ɛs.ˈta.ðjo]
Gracias por ayudarnos a construir este estadio.
-Thank you for helping us to build this stadium.

2447 alimentar(se) — **feed**

vb
[a.li.mẽn̪.ˈtar.se)]
Podríamos ser capaces de alimentar a la primera fila.
-We might be able to feed the front row.

2448 torpe — **clumsy**

adj
[ˈtor.pe]
Siempre fuiste un torpe, Jim.
-You always were a clumsy one, Jim.

2449 ordenador — **computer (ES)**

m
[or.ðe.na.ˈðor]
Este ordenador nos ahorra mucho trabajo.
-This computer saves us a lot of work.

2450 agenda — **calendar**

f
[a.ˈxẽn̪.da]
Ajustaré tu agenda, contrataré a un asistente.
-I'll adjust your schedule, hire an assistant.

2451 alianza — **alliance**

f
[a.ˈljãn.sa]
Alemania formó una alianza con Italia.
-Germany made an alliance with Italy.

2452 dedicar(se) — **devote**

vb
[de.ði.ˈkar.se)]
Pretendo dedicar un par de horas al día a estudiar inglés.
-I intend to devote a few hours a day to the study of English.

2453 criar — **raise**

	vb	Helen y yo intentamos criar a seres humanos decentes.
	['krjar]	-Helen and I are trying to raise decent human beings.
2454	**ida**	**going**
	f	Mi padre permitió mi ida al extranjero.
	['i.ða]	-My father consented to my going abroad.
2455	**globo**	**balloon**
	m	Está flotando por ahí como un gran globo.
	['glo.βo]	-She's floating around like a big balloon.
2456	**global**	**global**
	adj	Necesitamos encontrar una solución global lo antes posible.
	[glo.'βal]	-We need to find a global solution as soon as possible.
2457	**manual**	**handmade; manual**
	adj; m	El manual se actualiza cada año.
	[ma.'nwal]	-The manual is updated on an annual basis.
2458	**rebelde**	**rebel; rebel**
	adj; m	Da la alarma si ves cualquier tipo de actividad rebelde.
	[re.'βɛl̪.de]	-Sound the alarm if you see any rebel activity.
2459	**explosivo**	**explosive; explosive**
	adj; m	Tiene que ser un segundo explosivo.
	[ɛks.plo.'si.βo]	-There's got to be a second explosive.
2460	**superar(se)**	**overcome**
	vb	Él me ayudó a superar las dificultades.
	[su.pɛ.'rar.se)]	-He helped me to overcome the difficulties.
2461	**cajón**	**drawer**
	m	Puedes ponerlas en el mismo cajón.
	[ka.'xõn]	-You can put them in that same drawer.
2462	**divino**	**divine**
	adj	Tengo que contarte algo absolutamente divino.
	[di.'βi.no]	-I have to tell you something absolutely divine.
2463	**objeción**	**objection**
	f	No escuché ninguna objeción a ese entendimiento.
	[oβ.xe.'sjõn]	-I didn't hear any objection to that understanding.
2464	**riqueza**	**wealth**
	f	La guerra redujo la riqueza del país.
	[ri.'ke.sa]	-The war diminished the wealth of the country.
2465	**receta**	**recipe**
	f	Mi abuela tenía una receta deliciosa de bacalao.
	[re.'sɛ.ta]	-My grandmother had a delicious recipe of cod.
2466	**granjero**	**farmer**
	m	Además de ingeniero agrónomo, también soy granjero.
	[grãŋ.'xɛ.ro]	-In addition to being an agricultural engineer, I am also a farmer.
2467	**martillo**	**hammer**
	m	Guardo mi martillo en la caja de herramientas.
	[mar.'ti.jo]	-I keep my hammer in the toolbox.
2468	**continuación**	**continuation**
	f	Nos preocupa la posible continuación de esta tendencia.
	[kõn̪.ti.nwa.'sjõn]	-We are concerned about a possible continuation of this trend.
2469	**radar**	**radar**

m
[ra.ˈðar]
Tiene algún tipo de radar mental.
-She's got some kind of mental radar.

2470 pintor — **painter**
m
[pĩn̪.ˈtor]
Jim es un pintor descuidado.
-Jim is a sloppy painter.

2471 elemento — **element**
m
[e.le.ˈmẽn̪.to]
Hay un elemento muy notable en esta etapa.
-There is one very noteworthy element in this stage.

2472 lente — **lens**
f
[ˈlẽn̪.te]
Tiene características de lente de contacto.
-It's got characteristics like a contact lens.

2473 vapor — **steam**
m
[ba.ˈpor]
Nos gustaría revisar su cañería de vapor.
-We'd like to have a look at your steam pipe.

2474 independiente — **independent**
adj
[ĩn̪.de.pẽn̪.ˈdjẽn̪.te]
Ser independiente del sistema no te hace ser libre.
-Becoming independent of the system doesn't make you free.

2475 honorable — **honorable**
adj
[o.no.ˈra.βle]
Lee esto y entenderás nuestra honorable ambición.
-Read this and you'll see our honorable ambition.

2476 ginebra — **gin**
f
[xi.ˈne.βra]
No tolero la ginebra con agua tónica, y lo sabes.
-I cannot abide gin and tonic, and you know it.

2477 arrancar(se) — **pull up, start**
vb
[a.rãŋ.ˈkar.se)]
Olvidaré todo y podremos arrancar de cero.
-I'll forget everything and we can start over.

2478 hígado — **liver**
m
[ˈi.ɣa.ðo]
Puedes donar parte de tu hígado en vida.
-You can donate part of your liver while you're still alive.

2479 barro — **mud**
m
[ˈba.ro]
Ni siquiera le han quitado el barro.
-They didn't even wipe the mud off it.

2480 gentil — **pleasant**
adj
[xẽn̪.ˈtil]
Era severo cuando debí haber sido gentil.
-I was stern when I should have been gentle.

2481 griego — **Greek; Greek**
adj; m
[ˈgrje.ɣo]
El griego es difícil de aprender.
-Greek is difficult to learn.

2482 tejado — **roof**
m
[te.ˈxa.ðo]
El tejado reluce a la luz del sol.
-The roof is glittering in the sunshine.

2483 drama — **drama**
m
[ˈdra.ma]
Aquí tenemos todos los elementos del drama.
-Here we have all the elements of drama.

2484 dentista — **dentist**
m/f
[dẽn̪.ˈtis.ta]
Soy tan cobarde que casi no voy al dentista.
-I'm such a coward that I rarely visit the dentist.

2485 chimenea — **hearth**

	f	Ni siquiera tienes una chimenea.
	[tʃi.me.ˈne.a]	-You don't even have a fireplace.
2486	**calcetín**	**sock**
	m	Tenías cien dólares en el calcetín.
	[kal.sɛ.ˈtĩn]	-You had a hundred dollars in your sock.
2487	**tranquilidad**	**tranquility**
	f	Tendrías paz y tranquilidad para estudiar.
	[trãŋ.ki.li.ˈðað]	-You would have peace and quiet to study.
2488	**galería**	**gallery**
	f	Esta galería contiene algunas fotos de él y de su perro.
	[ga.lɛ.ˈri.a]	-This gallery contains some pictures of him and his dog.
2489	**cocinero**	**cook**
	m	Ella es una cocinera pésima.
	[ko.si.ˈnɛ.ro]	-She is an appalling cook.
2490	**pito**	**whistle**
	m	Tiene que haber un pito por aquí.
	[ˈpi.to]	-There's got to be a horn here somewhere.
2491	**campesino**	**peasant; rural**
	m; adj	Mire los pantalones del campesino español.
	[kãm.pe.ˈsi.no]	-Look at the pants on the Spanish peasant.
2492	**liberación**	**release**
	f	Debemos exigir la liberación de los detenidos.
	[li.βɛ.ra.ˈsjõn]	-We must call for the release of those detained.
2493	**doloroso**	**painful**
	adj	Resulta difícil asimilar este doloroso acontecimiento.
	[do.lo.ˈro.so]	-It is difficult to come to terms with this painful event.
2494	**permanente**	**permanent**
	adj	El proceso no debería tener carácter permanente.
	[pɛr.ma.ˈnẽn̪.te]	-The process should not be of a permanent character.
2495	**lastimar(se)**	**hurt**
	vb	No creo que pudiera lastimar a una mosca.
	[las.ti.ˈmar.se)]	-I can't believe he'd hurt a fly.
2496	**escolar**	**school; schoolchild**
	adj; m/f	Los profesores impartieron voluntariamente clases extraordinarias antes y después del horario escolar.
	[ɛs.ko.ˈlar]	-Extra class periods before and after school hours were provided by the teaching staff on a voluntary basis.
2497	**impedir**	**prevent**
	vb	Realicé este gesto para impedir cualquier malentendido.
	[ĩm.pe.ˈðir]	-I made this gesture in order to prevent any misunderstandings.
2498	**vagabundo**	**vagabond; wandering**
	m; adj	Sería otro vagabundo que intentaba sacarte algo de dinero.
	[ba.ɣa.ˈβũn̪.do]	-It must have been another tramp trying to get some money out of you.
2499	**suite**	**suite**
	f	Jim está intentando conseguirnos una suite.
	[ˈswi.te]	-Jim is trying to find us a suite.
2500	**retirada**	**withdrawal**
	f	La retirada se notificará al depositario.
	[rɛ.ti.ˈra.ða]	-The withdrawal shall be notified to the depositary.
2501	**episodio**	**episode**

m
[e.pi.ˈso.ðjo]

Gracias por este episodio, aunque es relajante.
-Thank you for this episode, although it's relaxing.

2502 **durar**　　　　　　　**last**
vb
[du.ˈrar]

No sé cuánto más podré durar.
-I'm not sure how much longer I can last.

2503 **organizar**　　　　　**organize**
vb
[or.ɣa.ni.ˈsar]

Acabo de organizar mi escritorio.
-I just organized my desk.

2504 **ligero**　　　　　　　**light**
adj
[li.ˈxɛ.ro]

Tengo un ligero dolor de cabeza en estos momentos.
-I have a slight headache now.

2505 **músculo**　　　　　　**muscle**
m
[ˈmus.ku.lo]

¡Ya llegan! No muevas un músculo o arruinarás la sorpresa.
-They're coming! Don't move a muscle or you'll ruin the surprise.

2506 **misil**　　　　　　　**missile**
m
[mi.ˈsil]

La integridad estructural del misil parece estar intacta.
-The structural integrity of the missile appears to be intact.

2507 **obispo**　　　　　　**bishop**
m
[o.ˈβis.po]

He ofrecido mi resignación al obispo.
-I've tendered my resignation with the bishop.

2508 **herencia**　　　　　**heritage**
f[ɛ.ˈrẽn.sja]

Digamos que estoy apostando mi herencia. -You could say I'm gambling my inheritance.

2509 **monje**　　　　　　　**monk**
m
[ˈmõɲ.xe]

Pedimos la liberación del monje.
-We call for the release of the monk.

2510 **atravesar**　　　　　**cross**
vb
[a.tra.βe.ˈsar]

Sin autorización legal, nadie puede atravesar la frontera.
-Without legal permission, no one is allowed to cross the borderline.

2511 **valioso**　　　　　　**valuable**
adj
[ba.ˈljo.so]

Este instrumento es demasiado importante y valioso como para desaprovecharlo.
-This instrument is too important, and too valuable, to squander.

2512 **tiroteo**　　　　　　**gunfire**
m
[ti.ro.ˈte.o]

Vi un tiroteo aquí, en la estación.
-I saw a firefight here on the station.

2513 **cordero**　　　　　　**lamb**
m
[kor.ˈðɛ.ro]

Ana tenía un cordero cuya lana era blanca como la nieve.
-Ana had a little lamb whose fleece was white as snow.

2514 **sellar**　　　　　　　**seal, stamp**
vb
[se.ˈjar]

Tenemos que sellar la entrada.
-We have to seal the entrance.

2515 **aplauso**　　　　　　**applause**
m
[apˈlau̯.so]

Caballeros, un caluroso aplauso para la encantadora Ana.
-Gentlemen, a warm applause for the lovely Ana.

2516 **píldora**　　　　　　**pill**
f
[ˈpil.do.ra]

Le aconsejé que se tomara la píldora.
-I advised her to go on the pill.

2517 **puño**　　　　　　　**fist**

m
['pu.ɲo']
Llevas una hora apretando el puño.
-You've been clenching that fist for the last hour.

2518 **marea** **tide**

f
[ma.'re.a]
Dicen que la marea arrastró los cuerpos.
-They say that the tide washed away the bodies.

2519 **estimar** **estimate, respect**

vb
[ɛs.ti.'mar]
No fue posible estimar los costes de estas actividades.
-It was not possible to estimate the costs for these activities.

2520 **disfraz** **costume**

m
['dis.fras]
Se puso un disfraz de pirata para Halloween.
-He wore a pirate costume for Halloween.

2521 **navaja** **knife**

f
[na.'βa.xa]
Los detectives encontraron una navaja vieja debajo de la casa.
-The detectives found an old knife under the house.

2522 **indicar** **indicate**

vb
[ĩɲ.di.'kar]
Indica a tu pareja dónde quieres que pise.
-Indicate to your partner where you want her to step.

2523 **fracasar** **fail**

vb
[fra.ka.'sar]
Ya no tenemos derecho a fracasar.
-We no longer have the right to fail.

2524 **injusto** **unfair**

adj
[ĩŋ.'xus.to]
Estás siendo muy injusto conmigo.
-You're being very unfair to me.

2525 **tremendo** **tremendous**

adj
[tre.'mẽn̪.do]
El Vicepresidente Kinnock pone un entusiasmo tremendo en todo lo que hace.
-Vice-President Kinnock has tremendous enthusiasm for everything he does.

Adjectives

Rank	Spanish-PoS	Translation(s)
21	**bien**-*adj; adv; m*	well; well; good
23	**ese**-*adj; prn*	that; that one
28	**más**-*adj; adv; m*	more; more; plus
29	**todo**-*adj; adv; m; prn*	every, each; all; whole; everything
32	**este**-*adj; prn; m*	this; this one; east
44	**solo**-*adv; adj*	only, just; alone
49	**bueno**-*adj; adv; int*	good; well, okay; enough, well
53	**señor**-*m; adj*	sir; huge
64	**mucho**-*adj; prn; adv*	a lot of; many, much; a lot, lots
87	**mi**-*adj*	my
88	**pocos**-*adj*	few
89	**otro**-*adj; prn*	other, another; other, another
95	**hecho**-*m; adj*	fact, incident; done, made
97	**mismo**-*adj*	same, just
100	**claro**-*adj; int; m*	clear, light; of course; clearing
102	**después**-*adv; adj*	after; after, later
106	**tal**-*adj; adv*	such, that; just as
111	**seguro**-*adj; m*	safe, reliable; insurance
116	**tu**-*adj*	your
125	**nuevo**-*adj*	ours
128	**nuestro**-*adj*	ours
129	**menos**-*adj; adv; prp*	fewer; less; except
131	**tipo**-*m; adj*	type; like
133	**mal**-*m; adv; adj*	evil; badly; bad
142	**tanto**-*adv; adj; m*	so long; so much, so many; point
143	**cada**-*adj*	each, every
153	**cierto**-*adj; adv*	true, one; certainly
155	**alguno**-*adj; prn*	someone, somebody; one
158	**chico**-*m; adj*	boy; small
159	**real**-*adj*	real, royal
163	**serio**-*adj*	serious
173	**rápido**-*adj; adv*	fast; quickly
174	**viejo**-*adj; m*	old; old man
185	**cualquier**-*adj*	any, whatever
202	**feliz**-*adj*	happy
212	**loco**-*adj; m*	crazy; lunatic
221	**juntos**-*adj*	together
223	**importante**-*adj*	important
230	**grande**-*adj*	big
231	**ninguno**-*adj*	none
234	**bajo**-*adj; prp; m*	low, small; under; bass
239	**único**-*adj*	only, unique
242	**pequeño**-*adj; m*	small, young; youngster
246	**igual**-*adj; adv; m/f*	like; the same; equal
247	**listo**-*adj; int*	ready, smart; done
253	**suficiente**-*adj*	enough
255	**joven**-*adj; m/f*	young; young person
258	**genial**-*adj; adv*	great; wonderful
259	**justo**-*adj; adv*	fair, exact; just
263	**fuerte**-*adj; m*	strong; fort
266	**basto**-*adj*	coarse, rude
267	**bastante**-*adv; adj*	quite a bit; enough
270	**difícil**-*adj*	difficult
272	**final**-*adj; m*	last; end
282	**último**-*adj; m*	last; latest
287	**malo**-*adj; m*	bad; villain
289	**fácil**-*adj*	easy
290	**alto**-*adj; adv; int*	tall; high; stop
291	**posible**-*adj*	possible
292	**maldito**-*adj*	damn, cursed
295	**incluso**-*adv; adj*	including; even
300	**medio**-*m; adj; adv*	middle, means; half; halfway
301	**querido**-*adj; m*	loved, dear; lover
309	**idiota**-*m/f; adj*	idiot; idiotic
319	**vivo**-*adj; m*	alive; alive
326	**general**-*adj; m/f*	common; general
328	**exacto**-*adj; adv*	identical, exact; exactly
331	**par**-*m; adj*	pair, couple; even, paired
351	**demás**-*adj*	the rest
354	**extraño**-*adj; m*	strange; stranger
355	**pobre**-*adj; m/f*	poor; poor
361	**libre**-*adj*	free
363	**especial**-*adj*	special
367	**derecho**-*adj; adv; m*	right; straight; law
368	**negro**-*adj*	black
371	**correcto**-*adj; int*	correct; right
376	**duro**-*adj; adv*	hard; hard
388	**perfecto**-*adj*	perfect
389	**tranquilo**-*adj*	quiet, peaceful
392	**largo**-*adj; int*	long; get out (coll)
396	**bonito**-*adj; m*	pretty; tuna

397	**increíble**-*adj*	incredible
398	**tonto**-*adj; m*	stupid; fool
399	**simple**-*adj*	simple
421	**blanco**-*adj; m*	white; target
425	**secreto**-*adj; m*	secret; secret
432	**hermoso**-*adj*	beautiful
435	**futuro**-*adj; m*	future; future
437	**médico**-*m; adj*	doctor; medical
441	**raro**-*adj*	rare
443	**diferente**-*adj*	different
444	**imposible**-*adj*	impossible
450	**propio**-*adj*	your own, typical
451	**siguiente**-*adj; m/f*	following; next
457	**oficial**-*adj; m/f*	official; officer
464	**estúpido**-*adj; m*	stupid; idiot, jerk
470	**maravilloso**-*adj*	wonderful
472	**divertido**-*adj*	funny
473	**próximo**-*adj*	next
478	**amable**-*adj*	kind
497	**necesario**-*adj*	necessary
499	**terrible**-*adj*	terrible
502	**izquierdo**-*adj*	left
504	**normal**-*adj*	normal
519	**dulce**-*adj; m*	sweet; candy
522	**interesante**-*adj*	interesting
525	**horrible**-*adj*	horrible
527	**gracioso**-*adj; m*	amusing; clown
528	**personal**-*m; adj*	staff; personal
529	**completo**-*adj*	full
532	**lindo**-*adj*	cute (LA)
546	**ambos**-*adj; prn*	both; both
551	**verdadero**-*adj*	true
559	**triste**-*adj*	sad
567	**san(to)**-*adj; m*	saint; saint
589	**temprano**-*adj; adv*	early; early
590	**público**-*adj; m*	public; audience
595	**caliente**-*adj*	hot
600	**enfermo**-*adj; m*	ill; sick person
601	**excelente**-*adj; int*	excellent; great
606	**aquel**-*adj; prn*	that; that one
613	**trasero**-*adj; m*	rear; butt (coll)
616	**imbécil**-*m/f; adj*	imbecile; moron
619	**agradable**-*adj*	pleasant
625	**peligroso**-*adj*	dangerous
640	**rico**-*m; adj*	rich person; wealthy, tasty
642	**capaz**-*adj*	capable
645	**lleno**-*adj*	full
654	**humano**-*adj; m*	humane; human
655	**fantástico**-*adj*	fantastic
659	**bienvenido**-*adj; int*	welcome; welcome
669	**animal**-*adj; m*	animal; animal
675	**azul**-*adj*	blue
679	**inteligente**-*adj*	intelligent
683	**inglés**-*adj; m*	English; Englishman
685	**rojo**-*adj*	red
699	**molesto**-*adj*	annoying
705	**despierto**-*adj*	awake
706	**estupendo**-*adj*	wonderful
753	**doble**-*adj; adv*	double; double
754	**culpable**-*adj; m/f*	guilty; culprit
763	**común**-*adj; m*	common; majority
766	**principal**-*adj*	main
767	**ridículo**-*adj; m*	ridiculous; embarrassment
774	**absoluto**-*adj*	absolute
777	**vuestro**-*adj; prn*	your; yours
789	**interior**-*adj; m*	interior; the inside
790	**bello**-*adj*	beautiful
800	**borracho**-*adj; m*	drunk; drunk
805	**verde**-*adj*	green
820	**nervioso**-*adj*	nervous
827	**brillante**-*adj*	shiny, bright
831	**enorme**-*adj*	huge
833	**inocente**-*adj; m/f*	naive; innocent
838	**precioso**-*adj*	beautiful
848	**contrario**-*adj; m/f*	contrary; foe
850	**sentado**-*adj*	sitting
851	**motivo**-*m; adj*	reason; motive
867	**presente**-*adj; m*	present; current
871	**grave**-*adj*	grave
872	**periódico**-*m; adj*	newspaper; periodical
875	**total**-*adj; m; adv*	complete; whole; in the end (coll)
877	**contento**-*adj; m*	happy; happiness
890	**responsable**-*adj; m/f*	responsible; person responsible
893	**objetivo**-*adj; m*	impartial; objective
894	**dormido**-*adj*	asleep
901	**guapo**-*adj*	good-looking
903	**preocupado**-*adj*	worried
906	**inútil**-*adj; m/f*	useless; good-for-nothing

907	**abierto**-*adj*	open
909	**americano**-*adj; m*	American; American person
910	**primo**-*m; adj*	cousin; prime
911	**nacional**-*adj*	national
914	**diario**-*adj; m*	daily; diary, newspaper
915	**francés**-*adj; m*	French; French person
916	**orgulloso**-*adj*	proud
918	**central**-*adj; f*	central; headquarters
920	**militar**-*adj; m/f*	military; soldier
923	**natural**-*adj*	natural
926	**chino**-*adj; m*	Chinese; Chinese person
928	**cansado**-*adj*	tired
929	**alemán**-*adj; m*	German; German person
932	**quieto**-*adj*	still
936	**entero**-*adj*	entire
942	**inmediato**-*adj*	immediate
943	**paciente**-*adj; m/f*	patient; patient
944	**varios**-*adj*	several
963	**gordo**-*adj*	fat
964	**valiente**-*adj; m/f*	courageous; brave person
967	**oscuro**-*adj*	dark
975	**metido**-*adj; m*	inside, nosy (LA); meddler (LA)
976	**limpio**-*adj*	clean
983	**definitivo**-*adj*	definitive
984	**directo**-*adj*	direct
995	**cerrado**-*adj*	closed
998	**profesional**-*adj; m/f*	professional; professional
1014	**gratis**-*adj; adv*	free; free
1018	**sucio**-*adj*	dirty
1026	**familiar**-*adj*	family, familiar
1040	**parecido**-*adj; m*	similar; resemblance
1048	**desgraciado**-*adj; m*	jerk (coll), miserable; scoundrel (coll)
1050	**local**-*adj; m*	local; store
1053	**frío**-*adj; m*	cold; cold
1060	**grandioso**-*adj*	grand
1061	**débil**-*adj; m/f*	weak; weakling
1068	**asustado**-*adj*	frightened
1069	**invitado**-*adj; m*	invited; guest
1073	**profundo**-*adj*	deep
1076	**privado**-*adj*	private
1083	**corriente**-*adj; f*	common; current, electricity
1084	**desierto**-*adj; m*	desert; desert
1090	**obvio**-*adj; int*	obvious; obviously
1098	**cobarde**-*adj; m/f*	cowardly; coward
1104	**ciego**-*adj*	blind
1106	**sabido**-*adj*	known
1107	**corto**-*adj*	short
1120	**poco**-*adj; adv*	little; quite
1133	**virgen**-*adj; m/f*	virgin; virgin
1141	**salvaje**-*adj; m/f*	wild, violent; savage
1149	**parado**-*adj*	standing (LA)
1151	**casado**-*adj; m*	married; married person
1153	**mentiroso**-*m; adj*	liar; liar
1155	**firme**-*adj; adv*	firm; steady, firmly
1157	**vacío**-*m; adj*	emptiness; empty, superficial
1163	**antiguo**-*adj; m*	ancient; old fashioned
1164	**material**-*adj; m*	material; equipment
1166	**judío**-*adj; m*	Jewish; Jew
1171	**helado**-*m; adj*	ice cream; frozen
1173	**social**-*adj*	social
1176	**superior**-*adj; m*	greater than, upper; boss
1180	**encantador**-*adj*	charming
1182	**motor**-*m; adj*	engine; motor
1187	**sujeto**-*m; adj*	subject; subject to
1193	**puro**-*adj; m*	pure; cigar
1196	**apuesto**-*adj*	handsome
1198	**sospechoso**-*adj; m*	suspicious; suspect
1216	**sexual**-*adj*	sexual
1220	**efectivo**-*m; adj*	cash; effective
1224	**mono**-*m; adj*	monkey; cute
1225	**FALSE**-*adj*	false, fake
1228	**criminal**-*adj; m/f*	criminal; criminal
1234	**sencillo**-*adj*	simple
1237	**indio**-*adj; m*	Native Indian; Indian
1239	**uniforme**-*m; adj*	uniform; uniform
1243	**suave**-*adj*	soft
1247	**aparte**-*adj; adv*	unusual; aside
1249	**original**-*adj*	original
1262	**curioso**-*adj*	curious
1266	**cruel**-*adj*	cruel
1274	**vecino**-*adj; m*	adjacent; neighbor
1278	**harto**-*adj*	full, sick of
1279	**feo**-*adj*	ugly
1296	**legal**-*adj*	legal
1298	**fiscal**-*adj; m/f*	fiscal; district attorney
1300	**honesto**-*adj*	honest

1311	**asqueroso**-*adj*	disgusting
1314	**preciso**-*adj*	precise, essential
1316	**útil**-*adj; m*	useful; tool
1327	**favorito**-*adj; m*	favorite; favorite
1333	**fresco**-*adj; m*	cool, fresh; shameless
1339	**magnífico**-*adj*	magnificent
1351	**complicado**-*adj*	complicated
1358	**suelto**-*adj*	loose
1364	**distinto**-*adj*	different
1375	**interesado**-*adj*	interested, selfish
1381	**caro**-*adj*	expensive
1385	**liso**-*adj*	flat
1390	**impresionante**-*adj*	impressive
1403	**urgente**-*adj*	urgent
1405	**elegante**-*adj*	elegant
1416	**particular**-*adj*	peculiar, private
1418	**poderoso**-*adj*	powerful
1419	**perdido**-*adj*	lost
1421	**noble**-*adj*	noble, kind
1422	**extranjero**-*adj; m*	foreign; foreigner
1426	**popular**-*adj*	popular
1431	**cómodo**-*adj*	comfortable
1433	**ruso**-*adj; m*	Russian; Russian
1459	**anterior**-*adj*	previous
1464	**moral**-*adj; f*	moral; morals
1470	**secundario**-*adj; m*	secondary; side effect
1483	**franco**-*adj*	honest
1493	**alegre**-*adj*	happy
1507	**experto**-*adj; m*	expert; expert
1511	**combustible**-*m; adj*	fuel; combustible
1527	**decente**-*adj*	proper
1533	**probable**-*adj*	likely
1536	**exterior**-*m; adj*	exterior; external
1540	**desagradable**-*adj*	unpleasant
1544	**comercial**-*adj*	commercial
1545	**lento**-*adj; adv*	slow; slowly
1550	**ayudante**-*adj; m*	assistant; assistant
1551	**italiano**-*adj; m*	Italian; Italian
1554	**ilegal**-*adj*	illegal
1557	**civil**-*adj; m/f*	civil; civilian
1563	**emocionante**-*adj*	exciting
1565	**afortunado**-*adj*	lucky
1568	**trabajador**-*m; adj*	worker; hard-working
1569	**federal**-*adj*	federal
1580	**ciudadano**-*m; adj*	citizen; civic
1581	**traidor**-*m; adj*	traitor; treacherous
1594	**aparente**-*adj*	apparent
1597	**absurdo**-*adj; m*	absurd; nonsense
1598	**miserable**-*adj*	miserable
1605	**gigante**-*adj; m*	gigantic; giant
1610	**mental**-*adj*	mental
1613	**celoso**-*adj*	jealous
1621	**sincero**-*adj*	sincere
1628	**barato**-*adj*	cheap
1629	**español**-*adj; m*	Spanish; Spaniard
1633	**asombroso**-*adj*	amazing
1635	**pánico**-*adj; m*	panic; panic
1648	**mortal**-*adj; m/f*	lethal; mortal
1656	**japonés**-*adj; m*	Japanese; Japanese person
1667	**romántico**-*adj*	romantic
1669	**internacional**-*adj*	international
1682	**razonable**-*adj*	reasonable
1692	**capital**-*adj; f; m*	primary; capital; resources
1701	**atractivo**-*adj; m*	attractive; attraction
1706	**delicioso**-*adj*	delicious
1707	**infeliz**-*adj; m/f*	unhappy; poor thing, fool
1710	**peor**-*adj; adv*	worse; worse
1711	**científico**-*adj; m/f*	scientific; scientist
1714	**rosa**-*adj; f*	pink; rose
1715	**pasajero**-*m; adj*	passenger; temporary
1717	**adecuado**-*adj*	suitable
1725	**político**-*adj; m*	political; politician
1730	**solitario**-*adj*	solitary, empty
1732	**ideal**-*adj; m*	likely, theoretical; ideal
1733	**rubio**-*adj*	blond
1737	**fiel**-*adj; m*	faithful; believer
1742	**fabuloso**-*adj*	fabulous
1743	**básico**-*adj*	basic
1754	**desnudo**-*adj; m*	naked; nude
1759	**breve**-*adj*	brief
1761	**práctico**-*adj*	practical
1771	**alternativo**-*adj*	alternative
1773	**gallina**-*f; adj*	hen; coward
1774	**extraordinario**-*adj*	extraordinary
1776	**egoísta**-*adj; m/f*	selfish; selfish person
1786	**sensible**-*adj*	sensitive
1791	**incidente**-*adj; m*	incidental; incident
1792	**actual**-*adj*	present
1794	**significado**-*m; adj*	meaning; important
1798	**terrorista**-*adj; m/f*	terrorist; terrorist

1799	**sagrado**-*adj*	sacred	2104	**sordo**-*adj; m*	deaf; deaf
1800	**físico**-*adj; m/f*	physical; physicist	2114	**furioso**-*adj*	furious
1827	**ajustado**-*adj*	tight	2116	**pesado**-*adj*	heavy
1831	**espacial**-*adj*	spatial	2117	**británico**-*adj; m*	British; Briton
1832	**disponible**-*adj*	available	2140	**extremo**-*adj; m*	extreme; end
1842	**adulto**-*adj; m*	adult; adult	2144	**invisible**-*adj*	invisible
1849	**auténtico**-*adj*	authentic	2151	**infantil**-*adj*	infantile
1851	**estadounidense**-*adj; m*	American; American person	2160	**patético**-*adj*	pathetic
1857	**consciente**-*adj*	aware	2169	**estatal**-*adj*	state
1862	**amarillo**-*adj*	yellow	2170	**repugnante**-*adj*	disgusting
1868	**sorprendente**-*adj*	surprising	2178	**pleno**-*adj; m*	full; plenary session
1879	**musical**-*adj; m*	musical; musical	2183	**canalla**-*m/f; adj*	swine (coll); despicable
1881	**algún**-*adj*	some, any	2189	**digno**-*adj*	worthy
1883	**fatal**-*adj*	fatal	2200	**marinero**-*m; adj*	sailor; naval
1886	**cercano**-*adj*	nearby	2205	**violento**-*adj*	violent
1892	**anciano**-*m; adj*	elder; old	2209	**constante**-*adj*	constant
1897	**sano**-*adj*	healthy	2210	**humilde**-*adj*	humble
1902	**apropiado**-*adj*	appropriate	2213	**desafortunado**-*adj*	unlucky
1904	**móvil**-*adj; m*	mobile; cell phone	2236	**inconsciente**-*adj; m*	unconscious, thoughtless; subconscious
1907	**prestado**-*adj*	borrowed	2238	**pacífico**-*adj*	peaceful
1911	**plano**-*adj; m*	level; plan, map	2239	**horario**-*m; adj*	schedule; time
1915	**semejante**-*adj*	similar	2240	**complejo**-*adj; m*	complex; complex
1918	**productor**-*m; adj*	producer; producer	2243	**positivo**-*adj*	positive
1923	**cumplido**-*m; adj*	compliment; courteous	2245	**eléctrico**-*adj*	electric
1924	**gris**-*adj*	gray	2250	**sabio**-*adj; m*	wise; sage
1928	**seco**-*adj*	dry	2256	**mágico**-*adj*	magic
1931	**negativo**-*adj*	negative	2259	**desesperado**-*adj; m*	desperate; desperate
1934	**macho**-*adj; m*	manly; male	2269	**submarino**-*adj; m*	underwater; submarine
1950	**técnico**-*adj; m/f*	technical; technician	2271	**policial**-*adj*	police
1963	**comunista**-*adj; m/f*	communist; communist	2281	**lógico**-*adj*	logical
1969	**nuclear**-*adj*	nuclear	2287	**resuelto**-*adj*	solved
1988	**guerrero**-*m; adj*	fighter; warlike	2298	**cuerdo**-*adj*	sane
1993	**naranja**-*f; adj*	orange; orange	2305	**grosero**-*adj*	rude
1997	**generoso**-*adj*	generous	2307	**cristiano**-*adj; m*	Christian; Christian
1999	**cretino**-*adj; m*	stupid; idiot	2308	**misterioso**-*adj*	mysterious
2005	**roto**-*adj*	broken	2318	**espantoso**-*adj*	frightening
2010	**soltero**-*adj; m*	single; single man	2322	**aproximado**-*adj*	approximate
2016	**típico**-*adj*	typical	2336	**evidente**-*adj*	apparent
2025	**fascinante**-*adj*	fascinating	2344	**espiritual**-*adj*	spiritual
2034	**eterno**-*adj*	eternal	2345	**potencial**-*adj; m*	potential; strength
2043	**cortado**-*adj; m*	shy; coffee	2348	**temporal**-*adj; m*	temporary; storm
2068	**simpático**-*adj*	likeable	2349	**leal**-*adj*	loyal
2086	**reciente**-*adj*	recent	2353	**moderno**-*adj*	modern
2089	**plástico**-*adj; m*	plastic; plastic	2354	**nocturno**-*adj*	night
2097	**cuyo**-*adj*	whose			

2369	**astuto**-*adj*	cunning
2370	**solar**-*adj; m*	solar; site
2372	**suizo**-*adj; m*	Swiss; Swiss
2377	**habitual**-*adj*	habitual
2381	**delicado**-*adj*	delicate
2383	**herido**-*m; adj*	injured; wounded
2385	**bendito**-*adj*	blessed
2387	**incapaz**-*adj; m/f*	unable; incompetent
2388	**unido**-*adj*	united
2390	**tímido**-*adj*	shy
2399	**acostado**-*adj*	lying down
2402	**extremado**-*adj*	extreme
2403	**hambriento**-*adj; m*	hungry; hungry person
2406	**condicional**-*adj*	conditional
2407	**dorado**-*adj*	golden
2409	**dispuesto**-*adj*	handy (ES), ready
2410	**literal**-*adj*	literal
2417	**vulgar**-*adj*	vulgar, common
2422	**continuo**-*adj*	continuous
2424	**saludable**-*adj*	healthy
2430	**distinto**-*adj*	different
2432	**graso**-*adj*	fatty, oily
2434	**matemático**-*adj; m*	mathematical; mathematician
2435	**honrado**-*adj*	honest
2440	**enano**-*m; adj*	shorty; very small
2444	**clásico**-*adj*	classic
2448	**torpe**-*adj*	clumsy
2456	**global**-*adj*	global
2457	**manual**-*adj; m*	handmade; manual
2458	**rebelde**-*adj; m*	rebel; rebel
2459	**explosivo**-*adj; m*	explosive; explosive
2462	**divino**-*adj*	divine
2474	**independiente**-*adj*	independent
2475	**honorable**-*adj*	honorable
2480	**gentil**-*adj*	pleasant
2481	**griego**-*adj; m*	Greek; Greek
2491	**campesino**-*m; adj*	peasant; rural
2493	**doloroso**-*adj*	painful
2494	**permanente**-*adj*	permanent
2496	**escolar**-*adj; m/f*	school; schoolchild
2498	**vagabundo**-*m; adj*	vagabond; wandering
2504	**ligero**-*adj*	light
2511	**valioso**-*adj*	valuable
2524	**injusto**-*adj*	unfair
2525	**tremendo**-*adj*	tremendous

Adverbs

Rank	Spanish-PoS	Translation(s)
3	**no**-*adv*	not
11	**qué**-*prn; adv*	what, which; this
21	**bien**-*adj; adv; m*	well; well; good
24	**aquí**-*adv*	here
27	**como**-*adv; con; prp*	as, like; since, because; as
28	**más**-*adj; adv; m*	more; more; plus
29	**todo**-*adj; adv; m; prn*	every, each; all; whole; everything
30	**ya**-*adv*	already, now
31	**muy**-*adv*	very
35	**ahora**-*adv*	now
36	**algo**-*adv; prn*	something; some
38	**así**-*adv*	like this, like that
39	**nada**-*adv; f*	nothing at all; nothing, void
41	**cuando**-*adv; con; prp*	when; since, if; when
43	**cómo**-*adv*	how, why
44	**solo**-*adv; adj*	only, just; alone
49	**bueno**-*adj; adv; int*	good; well, okay; enough, well
57	**tan**-*adv*	so, such, as
60	**dónde**-*adv*	where
61	**nunca**-*adv*	never, ever
64	**mucho**-*adj; prn; adv*	a lot of; many, much; a lot, lots
65	**entonces**-*adv*	then, so
69	**también**-*adv*	too, also
73	**siempre**-*adv*	always, every time
75	**hasta**-*prp; adv*	until, up to; even
76	**ahí**-*adv*	there
86	**antes**-*adv*	before, first
101	**mañana**-*f; m; adv*	morning; future; tomorrow
102	**después**-*adv; adj*	after; after, later
106	**tal**-*adj; adv*	such, that; just as
109	**donde**-*adv; prp*	where; with
115	**allí**-*adv*	there
123	**hoy**-*adv*	today, nowadays
126	**luego**-*adv; con*	later, then; therefore
129	**menos**-*adj; adv; prp*	fewer; less; except
133	**mal**-*m; adv; adj*	evil; badly; bad
138	**tarde**-*f; adv*	afternoon; late
141	**aún**-*adv*	yet, still
142	**tanto**-*adv; adj; m*	so long; so much, so many; point
147	**demasiado**-*adv*	too much
153	**cierto**-*adj; adv*	true, one; certainly
162	**quizá(s)**-*adv*	maybe
172	**todavía**-*adv*	yet, still
173	**rápido**-*adj; adv*	fast; quickly
179	**mientras**-*con; adv*	while; while
183	**pronto**-*adv*	early, soon
184	**casi**-*adv*	almost
194	**dentro**-*adv*	inside, within
207	**adelante**-*adv; int*	forward, ahead; come in
211	**allá**-*adv*	there
224	**arriba**-*adv; int*	up, above; come on
235	**cuándo**-*adv*	when
241	**cerca**-*adv; f*	near; fence
246	**igual**-*adj; adv; m/f*	like; the same; equal
257	**abajo**-*adv*	below, down
258	**genial**-*adj; adv*	great; wonderful
259	**justo**-*adj; adv*	fair, exact; just
267	**bastante**-*adv; adj*	quite a bit; enough
269	**atrás**-*adv; int*	behind; get back
290	**alto**-*adj; adv; int*	tall; high; stop
295	**incluso**-*adv; adj*	including; even
299	**lejos**-*adv*	far away
300	**medio**-*m; adj; adv*	middle, means; half; halfway
324	**además**-*adv*	besides
328	**exacto**-*adj; adv*	identical, exact; exactly
335	**afuera**-*adv*	outside
343	**jamás**-*adv*	never
364	**anoche**-*adv*	last night
367	**derecho**-*adj; adv; m*	right; straight; law
369	**acá**-*adv*	here (LA)
373	**detrás**-*adv*	behind
376	**duro**-*adj; adv*	hard; hard
381	**encima**-*adv*	on top of, not only that
383	**cual**-*prn; adv*	whom; as
394	**ayer**-*adv; m*	yesterday; past
445	**enseguida**-*adv*	immediately
486	**adentro**-*adv*	inside
509	**alrededor**-*adv*	around
550	**salvo**-*prp; adv*	except; unless
561	**delante**-*adv*	before, in front
589	**temprano**-*adj; adv*	early; early
634	**acaso**-*adv*	perhaps

697	**debajo**-*adv*	under
736	**a menudo**-*adv*	often
753	**doble**-*adj; adv*	double; double
758	**de repente**-*adv*	suddenly
780	**deprisa**-*adv; int*	quickly; hurry
806	**despacio**-*adv*	slowly
875	**total**-*adj; m; adv*	complete; whole; in the end (coll)
1014	**gratis**-*adj; adv*	free; free
1066	**a bordo**-*adv*	on board
1091	**recién**-*adv*	newly
1120	**poco**-*adj; adv*	little; quite
1148	**extra**-*adv; mpl*	extra; extras
1155	**firme**-*adj; adv*	firm; steady, firmly
1200	**adonde**-*adv; prp*	where; to the house of
1247	**aparte**-*adj; adv*	unusual; aside
1473	**enfrente**-*adv*	opposite
1495	**cuán**-*adv*	how
1545	**lento**-*adj; adv*	slow; slowly
1710	**peor**-*adj; adv*	worse; worse

Conjunctions

Rank	Spanish-PoS	Translation(s)
2	que-*con; prn*	that; that
6	y-*con*	and
18	si-*con*	if
20	pero-*con*	but
27	como-*adv; con; prp*	as, like; since, because; as
41	cuando-*adv; con; prp*	when; since, if; when
45	o-*con*	or, either
56	porque-*con*	because
78	ni-*con*	nor, not even
126	luego-*adv; con*	later, then; therefore
156	pues-*con*	well, since
179	mientras-*con; adv*	while; while
238	aunque-*con*	although
297	tampoco-*con*	neither, either
582	según-*prp; con*	according to; depending on
598	sin embargo-*con*	nevertheless

Prepositions

Rank	Spanish-PoS	Translation(s)
1	**de**-*prp*	of, from
4	**a**-*prp*	to, at
8	**en**-*prp*	in, on, about
10	**por**-*prp*	by, for
15	**con**-*prp*	with
16	**para**-*prp*	for, to
27	**como**-*adv; con; prp*	as, like; since, because; as
41	**cuando**-*adv; con; prp*	when; since, if; when
71	**sin**-*prp*	without
75	**hasta**-*prp; adv*	until, up to; even
79	**sobre**-*prp; m*	on, about; envelope
103	**desde**-*prp*	from, since
109	**donde**-*adv; prp*	where; with
129	**menos**-*adj; adv; prp*	fewer; less; except
150	**entre**-*prp*	between, among
181	**contra**-*prp; m*	against; cons
192	**hacia**-*prp*	towards
199	**durante**-*prp*	during
234	**bajo**-*adj; prp; m*	low, small; under; bass
358	**sino**-*prp; m*	but; fate
428	**tras**-*prp*	after, behind
498	**ante**-*prp*	facing, before
542	**a través de**-*prp*	through
550	**salvo**-*prp; adv*	except; unless
582	**según**-*prp; con*	according to; depending on
711	**excepto**-*prp*	except
841	**a pesar de**-*prp*	despite
1200	**adonde**-*adv; prp*	where; to the house of

Pronouns

Rank	Spanish-PoS	Translation(s)
2	que-*con; prn*	that; that
11	qué-*prn; adv*	what, which; this
12	yo-*prn*	I
13	tú-*prn*	you
19	él-*prn*	he
22	suyo-*prn*	his, yours, theirs, hers, their
23	ese-*adj; prn*	that; that one
29	todo-*adj; adv; m; prn*	every, each; all; whole; everything
32	este-*adj; prn; m*	this; this one; east
36	algo-*adv; prn*	something; some
40	nosotros-*prn*	us, we
42	ella-*prn*	she
52	usted-*prn*	you
54	quién-*prn*	who, whom
64	mucho-*adj; prn; adv*	a lot of; many, much; a lot, lots
85	alguien-*prn*	someone, anyone, somebody, anybody
89	otro-*adj; prn*	other, another; other, another
90	nadie-*prn*	nobody, no one
96	les-*prn*	them, to them
132	conmigo-*prn*	with me
136	mío-*prn*	mine
146	quien-*prn*	who
155	alguno-*adj; prn*	someone, somebody; one
161	ustedes-*prn*	you
187	os-*prn*	you
188	cuánto-*prn*	how many, how long
208	cuál-*prn*	what, which
308	cuanto-*prn*	the more, whatever
383	cual-*prn; adv*	whom; as
413	tuyo-*prn*	yours
491	vosotros-*prn*	you
546	ambos-*adj; prn*	both; both
606	aquel-*adj; prn*	that; that one
608	vos-*prn*	you (LA)
777	vuestro-*adj; prn*	your; yours
1232	consigo-*prn*	with her, with him

Nouns

Rank	Spanish-PoS	Translation(s)
7	ser-*vb; av; m*	be; was, were; being
9	un-*art; num*	a, an; one
21	bien-*adj; adv; m*	well; well; good
28	más-*adj; adv; m*	more; more; plus
29	todo-*adj; adv; m; prn*	every, each; all; whole; everything
32	este-*adj; prn; m*	this; this one; east
39	nada-*adv; f*	nothing at all; nothing, void
47	gracias-*f*	thank you
48	poder(se)-*vb; m*	be able to, might; power
50	vez-*f*	time, turn
53	señor-*m; adj*	sir; huge
55	casa-*f*	house
58	por favor-*m*	please
62	dos-*num*	two
63	verdad-*f*	truth
66	tiempo-*m*	time, weather
67	hombre-*m*	man
68	dios-*m*	god, deity
70	vida-*f*	life
79	sobre-*prp; m*	on, about; envelope
80	año-*m*	year
81	uno-*num*	one
82	día-*m*	day
83	noche-*f*	night
84	cosa-*f*	thing
91	padre-*m*	father
92	gente-*f*	people
93	parecer(se)-*vb; m*	appear, seem; opinion
94	dinero-*m*	money
95	hecho-*m; adj*	fact, incident; done, made
99	trabajo-*m*	work, job
100	claro-*adj; int; m*	clear, light; of course; clearing
101	mañana-*f; m; adv*	morning; future; tomorrow
104	mundo-*m*	world
107	acuerdo-*m*	agreement
108	momento-*m*	moment
110	hijo-*m*	son
111	seguro-*adj; m*	safe, reliable; insurance
112	mujer-*f*	woman
113	amigo-*m*	friend
114	madre-*f*	mother
117	lugar-*m*	place
119	mamá-*f*	mom
120	mierda-*f; int*	garbage (coll), crap (coll); shit
121	papá-*m*	dad
124	estado-*m*	condition, government
127	tres-*num*	three
131	tipo-*m; adj*	type; like
133	mal-*m; adv; adj*	evil; badly; bad
134	nombre-*m*	name
135	amor-*m*	love
138	tarde-*f; adv*	afternoon; late
140	parte-*f; m*	part; report
142	tanto-*adv; adj; m*	so long; so much, so many; point
144	hora-*f*	hour, time
151	adiós-*m; int*	farewell; goodbye
152	problema-*m*	problem
154	razón-*f*	reason
157	idea-*f*	idea
158	chico-*m; adj*	boy; small
160	policía-*m/f; f*	police officer; police
164	cabeza-*f*	head
165	hermano-*m*	brother
168	familia-*f*	family
169	cariño-*m*	affection, darling
171	señora-*f*	lady, madam
174	viejo-*adj; m*	old; old man
175	lado-*m*	side
176	suerte-*f*	luck
177	cuidado-*m; int*	care; watch out
180	miedo-*m*	fear
181	contra-*prp; m*	against; cons
182	puerta-*f*	door
186	agua-*m*	water
189	niño-*m*	kid
190	camino-*m*	way
191	primer(o)-*num*	first
195	ciudad-*f*	city
196	historia-*f*	history
200	forma-*f*	form, way
203	ojo-*m*	eye
204	guerra-*f*	war
205	caso-*m*	case
209	mano-*f*	hand

210	**muerte**-*f*	death
212	**loco**-*adj; m*	crazy; lunatic
215	**minuto**-*m*	minute
217	**corazón**-*m*	heart
218	**semana**-*f*	week
219	**jefe**-*m*	boss
220	**ayuda**-*f*	help
225	**persona**-*f*	person
226	**tierra**-*f*	land, ground
227	**manera**-*f*	way
228	**fin**-*m*	end, purpose
229	**cara**-*f*	face, side
232	**cinco**-*num*	five
234	**bajo**-*adj; prp; m*	low, small; under; bass
237	**tío**-*m*	uncle, buddy (coll)
241	**cerca**-*adv; f*	near; fence
242	**pequeño**-*adj; m*	small, young; youngster
244	**auto**-*m*	car (LA)
245	**cuatro**-*num*	four
246	**igual**-*adj; adv; m/f*	like; the same; equal
249	**capitán**-*m*	captain
250	**clase**-*f*	classroom, kind
252	**doctor**-*m*	doctor
255	**joven**-*adj; m/f*	young; young person
263	**fuerte**-*adj; m*	strong; fort
264	**número**-*m*	number
271	**punto**-*m*	spot, point
272	**final**-*adj; m*	last; end
273	**escuela**-*f*	school
274	**pueblo**-*m*	village, town
275	**sangre**-*f*	blood
276	**mes**-*m*	month
277	**coche**-*m*	car (ES)
278	**juego**-*m*	game
280	**realidad**-*f*	reality
281	**cuerpo**-*m*	body
282	**último**-*adj; m*	last; latest
284	**paz**-*f*	peace
285	**vuelta**-*f*	return, stroll
287	**malo**-*adj; m*	bad; villain
288	**dólar**-*m*	dollar
294	**pregunta**-*f*	question
296	**fiesta**-*f*	party, holiday
298	**cama**-*f*	bed
300	**medio**-*m; adj; adv*	middle, means; half; halfway
301	**querido**-*adj; m*	loved, dear; lover
304	**teléfono**-*m*	phone
306	**equipo**-*m*	team, gear
307	**palabra**-*f*	word
309	**idiota**-*m/f; adj*	idiot; idiotic
310	**luz**-*f*	light
311	**país**-*m*	country
312	**segundo**-*num*	second
313	**diablo**-*m*	devil
314	**oportunidad**-*f*	opportunity
316	**seis**-*num*	six
317	**cuarto**-*num; m*	fourth; room
318	**cielo**-*m*	sky
319	**vivo**-*adj; m*	alive; alive
320	**perdón**-*m; int*	forgiveness; sorry
321	**falta**-*f*	offense, shortage
323	**película**-*f*	movie
325	**perro**-*m*	dog
326	**general**-*adj; m/f*	common; general
327	**calle**-*f*	street
329	**rey**-*m*	king
330	**habitación**-*f*	room
331	**par**-*m; adj*	pair, couple; even, paired
332	**fuego**-*m*	fire
333	**música**-*f*	music
334	**sentido**-*m*	sense, meaning
336	**café**-*m*	coffee, coffee shop
338	**sitio**-*m*	place
339	**libro**-*m*	book
341	**bebé**-*m*	baby
345	**viaje**-*m*	trip
346	**muchacho**-*m*	lad
349	**diez**-*num*	ten
350	**mil**-*num*	thousand
352	**orden**-*m; f*	order; command
353	**cambio**-*m*	change
354	**extraño**-*adj; m*	strange; stranger
355	**pobre**-*adj; m/f*	poor; poor
356	**ropa**-*f*	clothes
357	**oficina**-*f*	office
358	**sino**-*prp; m*	but; fate
359	**modo**-*m*	mode
362	**presidente**-*m*	president
365	**millón**-*num*	million
367	**derecho**-*adj; adv; m*	right; straight; law

370	**caballero**-*m*	gentleman, knight		449	**error**-*m*	mistake
372	**frente**-*f*	front, forehead		451	**siguiente**-*adj; m/f*	following; next
375	**asunto**-*m*	matter		453	**ley**-*f*	law
379	**boca**-*f*	mouth		454	**dolor**-*m*	pain
380	**atención**-*f*	attention		455	**oro**-*m*	gold
382	**demonio**-*m*	demon		456	**maldición**-*f; int*	curse; damn
385	**hospital**-*m*	hospital		457	**oficial**-*adj; m/f*	official; officer
386	**sueño**-*m*	dream		458	**situación**-*f*	situation
387	**resto**-*m*	remainder		459	**daño**-*m*	damage
390	**seguridad**-*f*	certainty, safety		460	**deseo**-*m*	wish
394	**ayer**-*adv; m*	yesterday; past		461	**mente**-*f*	mind
396	**bonito**-*adj; m*	pretty; tuna		462	**ejército**-*m*	army
398	**tonto**-*adj; m*	stupid; fool		464	**estúpido**-*adj; m*	stupid; idiot, jerk
400	**aire**-*m*	air		465	**sonar**-*m; vb*	sonar; sound
401	**fuerza**-*f*	strength		466	**mitad**-*f*	half
402	**carta**-*f*	letter		467	**caballo**-*m*	horse
403	**trato**-*m*	agreement, behavior		468	**asesino**-*m*	murderer
404	**plan**-*m*	plan		469	**permiso**-*m*	permission, license
405	**hambre**-*m*	hunger		471	**mesa**-*f*	table
407	**campo**-*m*	field, countryside		474	**mar**-*m*	sea
409	**barco**-*m*	ship		475	**siete**-*num*	seven
410	**hotel**-*m*	hotel		476	**sexo**-*m*	sex, gender
411	**grupo**-*m*	group		479	**mensaje**-*m*	message
412	**sol**-*m*	sun		480	**información**-*f*	information
414	**voz**-*f*	voice		482	**alma**-*f*	soul
415	**baño**-*m*	bathroom		483	**coronel**-*m/f*	colonel
418	**placer**-*m*	pleasure		484	**cena**-*f*	dinner
419	**profesor**-*m*	teacher		485	**culo**-*m*	butt
421	**blanco**-*adj; m*	white; target		487	**canción**-*f*	song
422	**pie**-*m*	foot		488	**gobierno**-*m*	government
424	**edad**-*f*	age		493	**foto**-*f*	photo
425	**secreto**-*adj; m*	secret; secret		494	**accidente**-*m*	accident
426	**compañía**-*f*	company, firm		496	**centro**-*m*	center
427	**tren**-*m*	train		500	**teniente**-*m/f*	lieutenant
430	**prisa**-*f*	hurry		501	**luna**-*f*	moon
431	**vista**-*f*	view		503	**servicio**-*m*	service
433	**negocio**-*m*	shop, business		505	**tienda**-*f*	shop
435	**futuro**-*adj; m*	future; future		506	**Navidad**-*f*	Christmas
436	**silencio**-*m*	silence		507	**dirección**-*f*	direction, management
437	**médico**-*m; adj*	doctor; medical		508	**abuelo**-*m*	grandfather
438	**maestro**-*m*	teacher, master		510	**libertad**-*f*	freedom
440	**control**-*m*	control		512	**línea**-*f*	line
442	**novio**-*m*	boyfriend, fiancé		514	**honor**-*m*	honor
446	**llamada**-*f*	signal, call		516	**papel**-*m*	paper, role
447	**avión**-*m*	plane		519	**dulce**-*adj; m*	sweet; candy
448	**pelo**-*m*	hair		521	**principio**-*m*	start, principle

523	**caja**-*f*	box
524	**ocho**-*num*	eight
526	**respuesta**-*f*	answer
527	**gracioso**-*adj; m*	amusing; clown
528	**personal**-*m; adj*	staff; personal
530	**cárcel**-*f*	prison
531	**sistema**-*m*	system
533	**salud**-*f*	health
534	**paso**-*m*	step
535	**pase**-*m*	pass
537	**cámara**-*f*	camera, vault
538	**agente**-*m*	agent
539	**infierno**-*m*	hell
540	**regalo**-*m*	present
541	**río**-*m*	river
543	**carne**-*f*	meat
544	**piso**-*m*	apartment (ES), floor, ground (LA)
545	**sargento**-*m/f*	sergeant
548	**calma**-*f*	calm
552	**basura**-*f*	garbage
553	**suelo**-*m*	ground, soil
554	**carrera**-*f*	career, race
555	**cumpleaños**-*m*	birthday
556	**rato**-*m*	a short time
557	**universidad**-*f*	university
560	**iglesia**-*f*	church
562	**nene**-*m*	baby (coll), darling
563	**banco**-*m*	bank, bench
565	**programa**-*m*	program, schedule
567	**san(to)**-*adj; m*	saint; saint
568	**porqué**-*m*	reason
569	**broma**-*f*	joke
571	**partido**-*m*	match
573	**radio**-*f*	radio
576	**disculpa**-*f*	apology
577	**cerveza**-*f*	beer
578	**destino**-*m*	destination, fate
579	**matrimonio**-*m*	marriage
580	**norte**-*m*	north
581	**sala**-*f*	room
583	**ataque**-*m*	attack
585	**ejemplo**-*m*	example
586	**sorpresa**-*f*	surprise
587	**té**-*m*	tea
588	**club**-*m*	club
590	**público**-*adj; m*	public; audience
591	**ventana**-*f*	window
592	**duda**-*f*	doubt
593	**boda**-*f*	wedding
594	**peligro**-*m*	danger
597	**reina**-*f*	queen
599	**sur**-*m*	south
600	**enfermo**-*adj; m*	ill; sick person
602	**escena**-*f*	scene
603	**encuentro**-*m*	meeting, match
604	**asesinato**-*m*	murder
605	**obra**-*f*	work, play
607	**prueba**-*f*	test, evidence
611	**llave**-*f*	key
612	**regreso**-*m*	comeback
613	**trasero**-*adj; m*	rear; butt (coll)
616	**imbécil**-*m/f; adj*	imbecile; moron
617	**opinión**-*f*	opinion
618	**señal**-*f*	signal, mark
620	**cocina**-*f*	kitchen
621	**relación**-*f*	relationship, link
623	**cerebro**-*m*	brain
624	**locura**-*f*	madness
626	**cine**-*m*	cinema
627	**reunión**-*f*	meeting
629	**causa**-*f*	cause
630	**pelea**-*f*	fight
631	**prisión**-*f*	prison
632	**mayoría**-*f*	most
633	**fondo**-*m*	bottom
635	**montón**-*m*	pile, bunch
636	**comandante**-*m/f*	major
637	**misión**-*f*	mission
638	**decisión**-*f*	decision
639	**hogar**-*m*	home
640	**rico**-*m; adj*	rich person; wealthy, tasty
643	**cargo**-*m*	position, charge
646	**bar**-*m*	bar
647	**estrella**-*f*	star
648	**posición**-*f*	position
649	**estación**-*f*	station, season
651	**edificio**-*m*	building
652	**consejo**-*m*	advice, council
653	**pistola**-*f*	gun
654	**humano**-*adj; m*	humane; human

656	**zapato**-*m*	shoe	
657	**flor**-*f*	flower	
660	**zona**-*f*	zone	
661	**contacto**-*m*	contact	
663	**tema**-*m*	topic	
666	**intento**-*m*	attempt	
667	**calor**-*m*	heat	
669	**animal**-*adj; m*	animal; animal	
670	**departamento**-*m*	department, apartment (LA)	
671	**enemigo**-*m*	enemy	
672	**color**-*m*	color	
673	**valor**-*m*	value, courage	
674	**cien(to)**-*num*	hundred	
676	**espacio**-*m*	space	
680	**arte**-*m*	art	
681	**respeto**-*m*	respect	
682	**juez**-*m*	judge	
683	**inglés**-*adj; m*	English; Englishman	
684	**precio**-*m*	price	
686	**verano**-*m*	summer	
687	**pierna**-*f*	leg	
688	**isla**-*f*	island	
689	**dama**-*f*	lady	
690	**guardia**-*m/f; f*	police officer; police department	
691	**espalda**-*f*	back	
693	**banda**-*f*	band	
694	**marcha**-*f*	march	
695	**crimen**-*m*	crime	
696	**diferencia**-*f*	difference	
698	**compañero**-*m*	partner	
702	**juicio**-*m*	judgment, wisdom	
703	**estilo**-*m*	style	
704	**salida**-*f*	exit	
707	**nave**-*f*	ship, plane	
708	**base**-*f*	base	
710	**vuelo**-*m*	flight	
712	**golpe**-*m*	hit	
713	**viento**-*m*	wind	
714	**acción**-*f*	action, share	
715	**tontería**-*f*	nonsense	
716	**respecto**-*m*	regarding	
718	**beso**-*m*	kiss	
719	**cuestión**-*f*	matter	
720	**regla**-*f*	rule	
721	**ruido**-*m*	noise	

723	**mentira**-*f*	lie
724	**brazo**-*m*	arm
726	**experiencia**-*f*	experience
727	**esperanza**-*f*	hope
730	**espíritu**-*m*	spirit
731	**vacaciones**-*fpl*	vacation
732	**copa**-*f*	cup
733	**investigación**-*f*	research
738	**visita**-*f*	visit, guest
739	**nueve**-*num*	nine
740	**bomba**-*f*	bomb, pump
741	**energía**-*f*	energy
742	**bolsa**-*f*	bag
743	**pan**-*m*	bread
744	**piel**-*f*	skin
745	**metro**-*m*	metro
747	**cuello**-*m*	neck
751	**especie**-*f*	species, kind
752	**fe**-*f*	faith
754	**culpable**-*adj; m/f*	guilty; culprit
755	**bosque**-*m*	forest
756	**taxi**-*m*	taxi
760	**planeta**-*m*	planet
761	**leche**-*f*	milk
763	**común**-*adj; m*	common; majority
764	**informe**-*m*	report
765	**máquina**-*f*	machine
767	**ridículo**-*adj; m*	ridiculous; embarrassment
768	**entrada**-*f*	entry
769	**príncipe**-*m*	prince
771	**propósito**-*m*	purpose
772	**cliente**-*m/f*	customer, client
773	**árbol**-*m*	tree
775	**belleza**-*f*	beauty
778	**oeste**-*m*	west
779	**Francia**-*f*	France
781	**tiro**-*m*	shot
782	**cerdo**-*m*	pig
783	**gato**-*m*	cat
784	**vistazo**-*m*	glance
785	**defensa**-*f*	defense
786	**reloj**-*m*	clock
787	**batalla**-*f*	battle
789	**interior**-*adj; m*	interior; the inside
791	**apartamento**-*m*	apartment

792	**teatro**-*m*	theater
794	**hielo**-*m*	ice
795	**detective**-*m*	detective
799	**lucha**-*f*	fight
800	**borracho**-*adj; m*	drunk; drunk
801	**héroe**-*m*	hero
802	**camión**-*m*	truck
803	**cabo**-*m*	ending, corporal
804	**diente**-*m*	tooth
808	**sociedad**-*f*	society
809	**pareja**-*f*	couple
810	**nariz**-*f*	nose
811	**vergüenza**-*f*	shame
814	**pista**-*f*	clue, track
815	**sonido**-*m*	sound
816	**sombrero**-*m*	hat
818	**memoria**-*f*	memory
821	**lástima**-*f*	shame, pity
822	**época**-*f*	era, time
823	**naturaleza**-*f*	nature
825	**política**-*f*	policy, politics
828	**nivel**-*m*	level
830	**justicia**-*f*	justice
833	**inocente**-*adj; m/f*	naive; innocent
834	**pantalón**-*m*	pants
835	**ministro**-*m*	minister
837	**mando**-*m*	authority, control
840	**pesar**-*m*	regret
844	**autobús**-*m*	bus
848	**contrario**-*adj; m/f*	contrary; foe
849	**movimiento**-*m*	movement
851	**motivo**-*m; adj*	reason; motive
852	**puente**-*m*	bridge
854	**huevo**-*m*	egg
855	**botella**-*f*	bottle
857	**confianza**-*f*	confidence, trust
858	**felicidad**-*f*	happiness
859	**espada**-*f*	sword
860	**silla**-*f*	chair
861	**noticia**-*f*	news
862	**televisión**-*f*	television
864	**pared**-*f*	wall
865	**prensa**-*f*	press
866	**trampa**-*f*	trap
867	**presente**-*adj; m*	present; current
868	**jardín**-*m*	garden
869	**cabello**-*m*	hair
870	**espectáculo**-*m*	show
872	**periódico**-*m; adj*	newspaper; periodical
873	**anillo**-*m*	ring
874	**monstruo**-*m*	monster
875	**total**-*adj; m; adv*	complete; whole; in the end (coll)
876	**piedra**-*f*	stone
877	**contento**-*adj; m*	happy; happiness
878	**contrato**-*m*	contract
879	**playa**-*f*	beach
880	**costa**-*f*	coast
881	**asiento**-*m*	seat
882	**tarjeta**-*f*	card
883	**restaurante**-*m*	restaurant
884	**paseo**-*m*	walk
885	**domingo**-*m*	Sunday
886	**velocidad**-*f*	speed
887	**proyecto**-*m*	project
888	**operación**-*f*	operation
889	**imagen**-*f*	image
890	**responsable**-*adj; m/f*	responsible; person responsible
891	**aspecto**-*m*	aspect
892	**sentimiento**-*m*	feeling
893	**objetivo**-*adj; m*	impartial; objective
895	**historial**-*m*	history
897	**turno**-*m*	turn
898	**montaña**-*f*	mountain
899	**enfermedad**-*f*	disease
900	**dedo**-*m*	finger
902	**viernes**-*m*	Friday
904	**rayo**-*m*	ray
905	**Majestad**-*m/f*	Majesty
906	**inútil**-*adj; m/f*	useless; good-for-nothing
908	**oscuridad**-*f*	darkness
909	**americano**-*adj; m*	American; American person
910	**primo**-*m; adj*	cousin; prime
912	**colegio**-*m*	school
913	**cuchillo**-*m*	knife
914	**diario**-*adj; m*	daily; diary, newspaper
915	**francés**-*adj; m*	French; French person
917	**ladrón**-*m*	thief
918	**central**-*adj; f*	central; headquarters
919	**voluntad**-*f*	will

920	**militar**-*adj; m/f*	military; soldier		999	**opción**-*f*	option
922	**lluvia**-*f*	rain		1000	**tribunal**-*m*	tribunal
924	**gusto**-*m*	taste		1001	**lago**-*m*	lake
925	**lengua**-*f*	language, tongue		1002	**unidad**-*f*	unit
926	**chino**-*adj; m*	Chinese; Chinese person		1003	**efecto**-*m*	effect
927	**testigo**-*m/f*	witness		1004	**presión**-*f*	pressure
929	**alemán**-*adj; m*	German; German person		1005	**robo**-*m*	theft
				1006	**alcalde**-*m*	mayor
930	**pago**-*m*	payment		1007	**empleo**-*m*	employment
931	**mirada**-*f*	look		1008	**pollo**-*m*	chicken
934	**mercado**-*m*	market		1009	**wiski**-*m*	whiskey
935	**humor**-*m*	mood, humor		1010	**carretera**-*f*	road
937	**dueño**-*m*	owner		1011	**sábado**-*m*	Saturday
939	**emergencia**-*f*	emergency		1012	**aeropuerto**-*m*	airport
943	**paciente**-*adj; m/f*	patient; patient		1013	**medicina**-*f*	medicine
945	**polvo**-*m*	dust, powder		1015	**fortuna**-*f*	fortune
947	**distancia**-*f*	distance		1016	**nieve**-*f*	snow
949	**Europa**-*f*	Europe		1017	**riesgo**-*m*	risk
950	**recuerdo**-*m*	memory, souvenir		1019	**conversación**-*f*	conversation
951	**toque**-*m*	touch		1020	**comienzo**-*m*	beginning
952	**ángel**-*m*	angel		1021	**elección**-*f*	choice
954	**carga**-*f*	load, burden		1022	**carro**-*m*	car (LA), cart
955	**acto**-*m*	act		1023	**rostro**-*m*	face
957	**desastre**-*m*	disaster		1024	**propiedad**-*f*	property
958	**bote**-*m*	boat, pot		1025	**comedor**-*m*	dining room
962	**gracia**-*f*	grace		1027	**libra**-*f*	pound
964	**valiente**-*adj; m/f*	courageous; brave person		1028	**cola**-*f*	tail
				1029	**marca**-*f*	brand, mark
965	**gloria**-*f*	glory		1030	**líder**-*m/f*	leader
970	**tumba**-*f*	tomb		1031	**socorro**-*m; int*	help; help
973	**director**-*m*	director		1032	**fútbol**-*m*	football
974	**área**-*m*	area		1033	**detalle**-*m*	detail
975	**metido**-*adj; m*	inside, nosy (LA); meddler (LA)		1034	**tesoro**-*m*	treasure
				1035	**camisa**-*f*	shirt
977	**descanso**-*m*	rest		1037	**alegría**-*f*	joy
978	**posibilidad**-*f*	possibility		1039	**interés**-*m*	interest
979	**uso**-*m*	use		1040	**parecido**-*adj; m*	similar; resemblance
980	**talento**-*m*	talent		1043	**desayuno**-*m*	breakfast
982	**código**-*m*	code		1045	**víctima**-*f*	victim
985	**parque**-*m*	park		1046	**barrio**-*m*	neighborhood
986	**cinta**-*f*	ribbon, tape		1047	**oferta**-*f*	offer
990	**empresa**-*f*	company		1048	**desgraciado**-*adj; m*	jerk (coll), miserable; scoundrel (coll)
991	**intención**-*f*	intention				
993	**abrigo**-*m*	coat, shelter		1049	**resultado**-*m*	result
997	**genio**-*m*	genius, temper		1050	**local**-*adj; m*	local; store
998	**profesional**-*adj; m/f*	professional; professional		1051	**responsabilidad**-*f*	responsibility

1052	**combate**-*m*	combat	1112	**piloto**-*m*	pilot
1053	**frío**-*adj; m*	cold; cold	1113	**veinte**-*num*	twenty
1054	**tormenta**-*f*	storm	1114	**almuerzo**-*m*	lunch
1055	**nota**-*f*	note, grade	1116	**correo**-*m*	mail
1056	**olor**-*m*	smell	1117	**condición**-*f*	condition
1057	**cantidad**-*f*	amount	1118	**violencia**-*f*	violence
1058	**bala**-*f*	bullet	1119	**presencia**-*f*	presence
1059	**kilómetro**-*m*	kilometer	1121	**lord**-*m*	lord
1061	**débil**-*adj; m/f*	weak; weakling	1123	**serie**-*f*	series
1062	**laboratorio**-*m*	laboratory	1124	**labio**-*m*	lip
1064	**entrenador**-*m*	coach	1126	**espera**-*f*	wait
1065	**premio**-*m*	prize	1127	**teoría**-*f*	theory
1067	**agujero**-*m*	hole	1128	**actor**-*m*	actor
1069	**invitado**-*adj; m*	invited; guest	1129	**enfermero**-*m*	nurse
1070	**mapa**-*m*	map	1130	**siglo**-*m*	century
1071	**granja**-*f*	farm	1131	**tamaño**-*m*	size
1072	**jurado**-*m*	jury	1132	**chocolate**-*m*	chocolate
1074	**roca**-*f*	rock	1133	**virgen**-*adj; m/f*	virgin; virgin
1075	**pastel**-*m*	cake	1135	**disco**-*m*	disk
1077	**lunes**-*m*	Monday	1136	**milagro**-*m*	miracle
1078	**cuenta**-*f*	bill, account	1137	**pelota**-*f*	ball
1079	**socio**-*m*	associate, member	1138	**vaso**-*m*	glass
1081	**necesidad**-*f*	necessity	1139	**universo**-*m*	universe
1082	**importancia**-*f*	importance	1140	**gira**-*f*	tour
1083	**corriente**-*adj; f*	common; current, electricity	1141	**salvaje**-*adj; m/f*	wild, violent; savage
1084	**desierto**-*adj; m*	desert; desert	1143	**curso**-*m*	course
1085	**modelo**-*m*	model, pattern	1144	**firma**-*f*	signature, firm
1086	**invierno**-*m*	winter	1145	**herida**-*f*	wound
1087	**plata**-*f*	silver, money (LA)	1146	**queso**-*m*	cheese
1088	**apoyo**-*m*	support	1148	**extra**-*adv; mpl*	extra; extras
1089	**tercer(o)**-*num*	third	1150	**magia**-*f*	magic
1092	**techo**-*m*	ceiling	1151	**casado**-*adj; m*	married; married person
1093	**campeón**-*m*	champion	1152	**campamento**-*m*	campsite
1094	**salón**-*m*	lounge	1153	**mentiroso**-*m; adj*	liar; liar
1095	**gas**-*m*	gas	1156	**estómago**-*m*	stomach
1096	**cura**-*m; f*	priest; cure	1157	**vacío**-*m; adj*	emptiness; empty, superficial
1097	**escenario**-*m*	stage, scene			
1098	**cobarde**-*adj; m/f*	cowardly; coward	1159	**torre**-*f*	tower
1101	**pecho**-*m*	chest	1161	**frontera**-*f*	border
1102	**esquina**-*f*	corner	1162	**huella**-*f*	footprint, trace
1103	**sensación**-*f*	sensation	1163	**antiguo**-*adj; m*	ancient; old fashioned
1105	**fábrica**-*f*	factory	1164	**material**-*adj; m*	material; equipment
1108	**artista**-*m/f*	artist	1166	**judío**-*adj; m*	Jewish; Jew
1109	**pescado**-*m*	fish	1167	**cadáver**-*m*	corpse
1111	**reino**-*m*	kingdom	1168	**milla**-*f*	mile
			1169	**emperador**-*m*	emperor

1170	**cigarro**-*m*	cigar	1238	**sonrisa**-*f*	smile
1171	**helado**-*m; adj*	ice cream; frozen	1239	**uniforme**-*m; adj*	uniform; uniform
1172	**miembro**-*m*	member, limb	1240	**solución**-*f*	solution, answer
1174	**paciencia**-*f*	patience	1241	**conciencia**-*f*	conscience
1176	**superior**-*adj; m*	greater than, upper; boss	1242	**bolsillo**-*m*	pocket
1181	**felicitación**-*f*	congratulations	1244	**cero**-*num*	zero
1182	**motor**-*m; adj*	engine; motor	1245	**tropa**-*f*	troop
1184	**lío**-*m*	mess	1246	**protección**-*f*	protection
1185	**primavera**-*f*	spring	1248	**venganza**-*f*	revenge
1186	**proceso**-*m*	process	1250	**comisario**-*m*	commissioner
1187	**sujeto**-*m; adj*	subject; subject to	1251	**saco**-*m*	bad, coat (LA)
1189	**gobernador**-*m*	governor	1252	**ritmo**-*m*	rhythm, pace
1191	**ciencia**-*f*	science	1253	**cruz**-*f*	cross
1192	**conde**-*m*	count	1254	**lobo**-*m*	wolf
1193	**puro**-*adj; m*	pure; cigar	1256	**pintura**-*f*	painting, paint
1195	**alcohol**-*m*	alcohol	1257	**esfuerzo**-*m*	effort
1197	**funeral**-*m*	funeral	1258	**espejo**-*m*	mirror
1198	**sospechoso**-*adj; m*	suspicious; suspect	1259	**bestia**-*f*	beast
1199	**sopa**-*f*	soup	1260	**camarada**-*m/f; m/f*	comrade; pal (coll)
1201	**orgullo**-*m*	pride	1261	**inteligencia**-*f*	intelligence
1202	**discurso**-*m*	speech	1263	**declaración**-*f*	statement
1204	**tarea**-*f*	task, homework (LA)	1265	**artículo**-*m*	article, item
1205	**compra**-*f*	purchase	1267	**criatura**-*f*	creature
1206	**cheque**-*m*	check	1269	**diversión**-*f*	fun
1209	**oído**-*m*	ear	1271	**chaqueta**-*f*	jacket
1210	**desgracia**-*f*	misfortune	1272	**excelencia**-*f*	excellence
1213	**palacio**-*m*	palace	1273	**vídeo**-*m*	video
1214	**amistad**-*f*	friendship	1274	**vecino**-*adj; m*	adjacent; neighbor
1215	**bola**-*f*	ball	1275	**camioneta**-*f*	van
1217	**educación**-*f*	education	1276	**azúcar**-*m*	sugar
1218	**centavo**-*m*	penny	1277	**colega**-*m/f*	colleague, friend
1219	**taza**-*f*	cup	1280	**cadena**-*f*	chain
1220	**efectivo**-*m; adj*	cash; effective	1281	**cuerda**-*f*	rope, cord
1222	**madera**-*f*	wood	1282	**pez**-*m*	fish
1223	**amenaza**-*f*	threat	1283	**pérdida**-*f*	loss
1224	**mono**-*m; adj*	monkey; cute	1284	**guarda**-*m/f*	guard
1227	**ocasión**-*f*	chance, occasion	1286	**promesa**-*f*	promise
1228	**criminal**-*adj; m/f*	criminal; criminal	1287	**amén**-*m*	amen
1229	**bebida**-*f*	drink	1288	**temporada**-*f*	season, time
1230	**fuente**-*f*	source, fountain	1290	**humanidad**-*f*	humanity, mankind
1231	**estudiante**-*m/f*	student	1291	**dato**-*m*	fact
1233	**pájaro**-*m*	bird	1292	**maravilla**-*f*	wonder
1235	**lección**-*f*	lesson	1293	**maleta**-*f*	suitcase
1236	**examen**-*m*	exam	1295	**arena**-*f*	sand, ring
1237	**indio**-*adj; m*	Native Indian; Indian	1297	**doce**-*num*	twelve
			1298	**fiscal**-*adj; m/f*	fiscal; district attorney

1299	**mina**-*f*	mine	1368	**pieza**-*f*	piece
1301	**oso**-*m*	bear	1370	**comité**-*m*	committee
1302	**miel**-*f*	honey	1371	**fila**-*f*	row
1303	**pesadilla**-*f*	nightmare	1372	**medianoche**-*f*	midnight
1304	**hueso**-*m*	bone	1373	**éxito**-*m*	success
1306	**sombra**-*f*	shadow	1374	**parada**-*f*	stop
1307	**muñeca**-*f*	wrist, doll	1376	**sección**-*f*	section, division
1308	**canal**-*m*	channel	1377	**altura**-*f*	height
1309	**planta**-*f*	plant	1378	**documento**-*m*	document
1310	**visión**-*f*	vision, view	1379	**compromiso**-*m*	commitment, dilemma
1313	**personaje**-*m/f*	celebrity, character	1380	**martes**-*m*	Tuesday
1315	**moda**-*f*	fashion	1382	**templo**-*m*	temple
1316	**útil**-*adj; m*	useful; tool	1383	**meta**-*f*	goal
1317	**revolución**-*f*	revolution	1384	**pasta**-*f*	pasta
1318	**impresión**-*f*	impression	1386	**guion**-*m*	script
1320	**habla**-*m*	speech	1387	**pensamiento**-*m*	thought
1321	**paquete**-*m*	package	1388	**treinta**-*num*	thirty
1323	**comunidad**-*f*	community	1389	**hierba**-*f*	grass
1326	**senador**-*m*	senator	1391	**teta**-*f*	tit
1327	**favorito**-*adj; m*	favorite; favorite	1392	**pasión**-*f*	passion
1328	**humo**-*m*	smoke	1393	**actitud**-*f*	attitude
1329	**sótano**-*m*	basement	1394	**prometido**-*m*	fiancé
1330	**julio**-*m*	July	1395	**clave**-*f*	key
1331	**venta**-*f*	sale	1397	**lágrima**-*f*	tear
1333	**fresco**-*adj; m*	cool, fresh; shameless	1398	**suicidio**-*m*	suicide
1334	**bolso**-*m*	purse	1399	**gasolina**-*f*	gasoline
1336	**búsqueda**-*f*	search	1400	**jugador**-*m*	player, gambler
1337	**rodilla**-*f*	knee	1401	**encargo**-*m*	errand
1338	**licencia**-*f*	license	1402	**puerto**-*m*	port
1340	**nación**-*f*	nation	1404	**Rusia**-*f*	Russia
1341	**caza**-*f*	hunt	1406	**copia**-*f*	copy
1342	**plato**-*m*	dish	1407	**aventura**-*f*	adventure, affair
1343	**fecha**-*f*	date	1408	**entrenamiento**-*m*	training
1344	**escalera**-*f*	staircase	1409	**océano**-*m*	ocean
1345	**crédito**-*m*	credit	1410	**ruta**-*f*	route
1349	**ira**-*f*	anger	1412	**paraíso**-*m*	paradise
1350	**brujo**-*m*	wizard	1413	**guía**-*m/f; f*	guide; manual
1352	**casualidad**-*f*	chance	1414	**curiosidad**-*f*	curiosity
1353	**castigo**-*m*	punishment	1417	**fotografía**-*f*	photograph
1354	**amanecer**-*m; vb*	dawn; wake up	1422	**extranjero**-*adj; m*	foreign; foreigner
1356	**computadora**-*f*	computer (LA)	1423	**rata**-*f*	rat
1359	**título**-*m*	title, degree	1424	**instituto**-*m*	high school
1360	**jueves**-*m*	Thursday	1425	**asco**-*m*	disgust
1362	**piano**-*m*	piano	1429	**piscina**-*f*	swimming pool
1363	**despacho**-*m*	office	1432	**aviso**-*m*	warning
1367	**prisionero**-*m*	prisoner	1433	**ruso**-*adj; m*	Russian; Russian

1434	**ambulancia**-*f*	ambulance
1436	**grado**-*m*	degree
1437	**vaca**-*f*	cow
1438	**territorio**-*m*	territory
1439	**conocimiento**-*m*	knowledge
1440	**reputación**-*f*	reputation
1441	**imaginación**-*f*	imagination
1442	**excusa**-*f*	excuse
1443	**campaña**-*f*	campaign
1445	**escritor**-*m*	writer
1446	**página**-*f*	page
1448	**autoridad**-*f*	authority
1450	**paliza**-*f*	beating
1451	**armario**-*m*	closet
1452	**instante**-*m*	instant
1453	**arroz**-*m*	rice
1454	**crisis**-*f*	crisis
1456	**piedad**-*m*	piety
1457	**kilo**-*m*	kilo
1458	**divorcio**-*m*	divorce
1460	**fiebre**-*f*	fever
1461	**registro**-*m*	search, register
1462	**esposa**-*f*	wife
1464	**moral**-*adj; f*	moral; morals
1465	**acceso**-*m*	access
1466	**pasillo**-*m*	hall
1467	**asistente**-*m/f*	assistant
1468	**tráfico**-*m*	traffic
1470	**secundario**-*adj; m*	secondary; side effect
1471	**garganta**-*f*	throat
1474	**museo**-*m*	museum
1475	**valle**-*m*	valley
1476	**misterio**-*m*	mystery
1477	**alarma**-*f*	alarm
1479	**joya**-*f*	jewel
1480	**coma**-*f; m*	comma; coma
1481	**auxilio**-*m; int*	help; help
1482	**zorro**-*m*	fox
1484	**don**-*m*	talent
1485	**entrega**-*f*	delivery
1486	**celda**-*f*	cell
1487	**ganador**-*m*	winner
1489	**serpiente**-*f*	snake
1490	**Biblia**-*f*	Bible
1491	**terreno**-*m*	land
1492	**fantasma**-*m*	ghost

1494	**explosión**-*f*	explosion
1496	**circunstancia**-*f*	circumstance
1497	**cable**-*m*	cable
1499	**celular**-*m*	cell phone (LA)
1500	**puesto**-*m*	post, stand
1501	**ambiente**-*m*	environment
1503	**bota**-*f*	boot
1504	**pene**-*m*	penis
1505	**costumbre**-*f*	custom
1506	**cuadro**-*m*	painting, frame
1507	**experto**-*adj; m*	expert; expert
1508	**veneno**-*m*	venom
1509	**partida**-*f*	departure, game
1510	**bandera**-*f*	flag
1511	**combustible**-*m; adj*	fuel; combustible
1512	**recompensa**-*f*	reward
1513	**organización**-*f*	organization
1514	**cáncer**-*m*	cancer
1515	**deuda**-*f*	debt
1516	**raza**-*f*	race
1517	**juventud**-*f*	youth
1519	**comportamiento**-*m*	behavior
1524	**plaza**-*f*	square
1525	**rumbo**-*m*	in the direction of
1526	**pata**-*f*	leg
1528	**producción**-*f*	production
1529	**nacimiento**-*m*	birth
1530	**aldea**-*f*	village
1531	**letra**-*f*	letter
1532	**biblioteca**-*f*	library
1534	**marco**-*m*	framework, frame
1535	**explicación**-*f*	explanation
1536	**exterior**-*m; adj*	exterior; external
1537	**incendio**-*m*	fire
1539	**unión**-*f*	union
1541	**distrito**-*m*	district
1542	**apellido**-*m*	surname
1543	**patio**-*m*	courtyard
1546	**diamante**-*m*	diamond
1547	**ducha**-*f*	shower
1549	**mayo**-*m*	May
1550	**ayudante**-*adj; m*	assistant; assistant
1551	**italiano**-*adj; m*	Italian; Italian
1552	**saludo**-*m*	greeting
1553	**pantalla**-*f*	screen

1555	**colina**-*f*	hill	1614	**sesión**-*f*	session
1556	**porquería**-*f*	filth	1616	**sofá**-*m*	sofa
1557	**civil**-*adj; m/f*	civil; civilian	1617	**tratamiento**-*m*	treatment
1558	**cementerio**-*m*	cemetery	1618	**despertar(se)**-*m; vb*	awakening; wake up
1559	**ala**-*m*	wing	1619	**conexión**-*f*	connection
1560	**conductor**-*m*	driver	1620	**rumor**-*m*	rumor
1562	**periodista**-*m/f*	journalist	1622	**leyenda**-*f*	legend
1564	**tripulación**-*f*	crew	1624	**lenguaje**-*m*	language
1566	**estupidez**-*f*	stupidity	1626	**clima**-*m*	climate
1567	**circo**-*m*	circus	1629	**español**-*adj; m*	Spanish; Spaniard
1568	**trabajador**-*m; adj*	worker; hard-working	1634	**virus**-*m*	virus
1570	**quince**-*num*	fifteen	1635	**pánico**-*adj; m*	panic; panic
1572	**león**-*m*	lion	1636	**acero**-*m*	steel
1573	**aliento**-*m*	breath	1638	**helicóptero**-*m*	helicopter
1574	**patrón**-*m*	pattern	1639	**pasaporte**-*m*	passport
1575	**ron**-*m*	rum	1640	**sal**-*f*	salt
1577	**equipaje**-*m*	luggage	1641	**bicicleta**-*f*	bicycle
1578	**salsa**-*f*	sauce	1642	**cincuenta**-*num*	fifty
1579	**escritorio**-*m*	desk	1643	**objeto**-*m*	object, goal
1580	**ciudadano**-*m; adj*	citizen; civic	1644	**coraje**-*m*	courage
1581	**traidor**-*m; adj*	traitor; treacherous	1645	**aceite**-*m*	oil
1582	**alquiler**-*m*	rent	1646	**billete**-*m*	ticket, bill
1583	**instrucción**-*f*	instruction	1647	**publicidad**-*f*	advertising
1585	**práctica**-*f*	practice	1648	**mortal**-*adj; m/f*	lethal; mortal
1586	**España**-*f*	Spain	1649	**botón**-*m*	button
1588	**duque**-*m*	duke	1650	**cristal**-*m*	crystal
1589	**límite**-*m*	limit	1651	**pizza**-*f*	pizza
1590	**arresto**-*m*	arrest	1652	**moneda**-*f*	currency, coin
1592	**superficie**-*f*	surface	1654	**metal**-*m*	metal
1593	**tono**-*m*	tone	1656	**japonés**-*adj; m*	Japanese; Japanese person
1595	**condado**-*m*	county	1657	**septiembre**-*m*	September
1596	**religión**-*f*	religion	1658	**petróleo**-*m*	oil
1597	**absurdo**-*adj; m*	absurd; nonsense	1659	**archivo**-*m*	archive, file
1599	**homicidio**-*m*	homicide	1660	**vera**-*f*	edge, side
1600	**cultura**-*f*	culture	1661	**versión**-*f*	version
1601	**ceremonia**-*f*	ceremony	1662	**pozo**-*m*	well
1602	**punta**-*f*	tip	1663	**ventaja**-*f*	advantage
1603	**anuncio**-*m*	advertisement, announcement	1664	**dormitorio**-*m*	bedroom
1604	**nube**-*f*	cloud	1665	**cartera**-*f*	wallet, schoolbag
1605	**gigante**-*adj; m*	gigantic; giant	1666	**mediodía**-*m*	midday
1606	**sacerdote**-*m*	priest	1668	**alcance**-*m*	scope, significance
1607	**estudio**-*m*	studio, survey	1670	**competencia**-*f*	competition, rival
1609	**coincidencia**-*f*	coincidence	1671	**esclavo**-*m*	slave
1611	**Internet**-*m/f*	Internet	1672	**escándalo**-*m*	scandal
1612	**carácter**-*m*	personality	1673	**tecnología**-*f*	technology

1674	**sobrino**-*m*	nephew
1675	**rueda**-*f*	wheel
1676	**división**-*f*	division, split
1678	**ascensor**-*m*	elevator
1679	**crema**-*f*	cream
1680	**hierro**-*m*	iron
1681	**pastor**-*m*	pastor, shepherd
1683	**miércoles**-*m*	Wednesday
1684	**hombro**-*m*	shoulder
1685	**comisión**-*f*	commission
1686	**calidad**-*f*	quality
1687	**identidad**-*f*	identity
1689	**palo**-*m*	stick
1690	**moto**-*f*	motorcycle
1691	**manzana**-*f*	apple
1692	**capital**-*adj; f; m*	primary; capital; resources
1693	**conejo**-*m*	rabbit
1695	**actuación**-*f*	performance
1696	**nervio**-*m*	nerve
1697	**conferencia**-*f*	conference
1698	**junio**-*m*	June
1699	**grano**-*m*	grain, pimple
1700	**espía**-*m/f*	spy
1701	**atractivo**-*adj; m*	attractive; attraction
1702	**recibo**-*m*	invoice, receipt
1703	**resistencia**-*f*	resistance
1704	**transporte**-*m*	transport
1705	**frase**-*f*	phrase
1707	**infeliz**-*adj; m/f*	unhappy; poor thing, fool
1708	**cinturón**-*m*	belt
1709	**dragón**-*m*	dragon
1711	**científico**-*adj; m/f*	scientific; scientist
1712	**cantante**-*m/f*	singer
1713	**esperanza**-*f*	hope
1714	**rosa**-*adj; f*	pink; rose
1715	**pasajero**-*m; adj*	passenger; temporary
1718	**vía**-*f*	street, tract
1719	**cometido**-*m*	mission
1720	**función**-*f*	function
1721	**industria**-*f*	industry
1722	**corona**-*f*	crown
1723	**asalto**-*m*	assault
1724	**flota**-*f*	fleet
1725	**político**-*adj; m*	political; politician
1727	**imperio**-*m*	empire
1728	**llegada**-*f*	arrival
1729	**rifle**-*m*	rifle
1731	**refugio**-*m*	refuge
1732	**ideal**-*adj; m*	likely, theoretical; ideal
1734	**cabaña**-*f*	cabin
1735	**sufrimiento**-*m*	suffering
1736	**expresión**-*f*	expression
1737	**fiel**-*adj; m*	faithful; believer
1738	**secretario**-*m*	secretary
1739	**cuartel**-*m*	headquarters
1741	**ejercicio**-*m*	exercise
1744	**grito**-*m*	shout
1746	**túnel**-*m*	tunnel
1748	**identificación**-*f*	identification
1749	**rastro**-*m*	trail
1750	**invitación**-*f*	invitation
1751	**cañón**-*m*	cannon
1752	**alguacil**-*m/f*	sheriff
1753	**risa**-*f*	laughter
1754	**desnudo**-*adj; m*	naked; nude
1755	**gasto**-*m*	spending
1756	**once**-*num*	eleven
1757	**golf**-*m*	golf
1758	**monte**-*m*	hill
1760	**terror**-*m*	terror
1764	**tanque**-*m*	tank
1765	**vehículo**-*m*	vehicle
1766	**capacidad**-*f*	capacity
1768	**viuda**-*f*	widow
1769	**oreja**-*f*	ear
1770	**concurso**-*m*	contest
1773	**gallina**-*f; adj*	hen; coward
1775	**depósito**-*m*	deposit, warehouse
1776	**egoísta**-*adj; m/f*	selfish; selfish person
1777	**vestido**-*m*	dress
1778	**tragedia**-*f*	tragedy
1779	**círculo**-*m*	circle
1781	**gafas**-*fpl*	glasses
1782	**abril**-*m*	April
1783	**payaso**-*m*	clown
1784	**emoción**-*f*	emotion
1785	**borde**-*m*	edge
1787	**existencia**-*f*	existence
1788	**clínica**-*f*	clinic
1789	**escape**-*m*	escape
1790	**barón**-*m*	baron

1791	**incidente**-*adj; m*	incidental; incident	
1794	**significado**-*m; adj*	meaning; important	
1795	**cima**-*f*	top	
1796	**temperatura**-*m*	temperature	
1798	**terrorista**-*adj; m/f*	terrorist; terrorist	
1800	**físico**-*adj; m/f*	physical; physicist	
1801	**reacción**-*f*	reaction	
1802	**revés**-*m*	setback	
1804	**tigre**-*m*	tiger	
1806	**aprecio**-*m*	appreciation	
1807	**destrucción**-*f*	destruction	
1809	**sabor**-*m*	taste	
1810	**perdedor**-*m*	loser	
1811	**ensayo**-*m*	rehearsal, essay	
1812	**sueldo**-*m*	salary	
1813	**construcción**-*f*	construction	
1814	**delito**-*m*	crime	
1816	**máscara**-*f*	mask	
1817	**guitarra**-*f*	guitar	
1818	**figura**-*f*	figure	
1820	**análisis**-*m*	analysis	
1821	**vendedor**-*m*	seller	
1823	**consecuencia**-*f*	consequence	
1825	**personalidad**-*f*	personality	
1826	**disparo**-*m*	shot	
1828	**traducción**-*f*	translation	
1829	**profesión**-*f*	profession	
1830	**pastilla**-*f*	pill	
1834	**habilidad**-*f*	skill	
1835	**galleta**-*f*	cookie	
1836	**costado**-*m*	side	
1837	**remedio**-*m*	remedy	
1838	**aniversario**-*m*	anniversary	
1839	**generación**-*f*	generation	
1840	**trozo**-*m*	piece	
1841	**caída**-*f*	drop	
1842	**adulto**-*adj; m*	adult; adult	
1844	**caos**-*m*	chaos	
1846	**prostituta**-*f*	prostitute	
1848	**producto**-*m*	product	
1850	**condesa**-*f*	countess	
1851	**estadounidense**-*adj; m*	American; American person	
1852	**octubre**-*m*	October	
1853	**poesía**-*f*	poetry	
1854	**electricidad**-*f*	electricity	

1859	**reverendo**-*m*	reverend	
1860	**sacrificio**-*m*	sacrifice	
1861	**propuesta**-*f*	proposal	
1863	**experimento**-*m*	experiment	
1864	**hoja**-*f*	leaf, sheet	
1865	**comisaría**-*f*	police station	
1867	**barba**-*f*	beard	
1869	**jersey**-*m*	jersey	
1870	**toro**-*m*	bull	
1871	**comunicación**-*f*	communication	
1872	**vigilancia**-*f*	surveillance	
1873	**arreglo**-*m*	arrangement, repair	
1875	**discusión**-*f*	argument, debate	
1877	**lealtad**-*f*	loyalty	
1878	**ánimo**-*m*	spirits, mood	
1879	**musical**-*adj; m*	musical; musical	
1880	**champán**-*m*	champagne	
1884	**salto**-*m*	jump	
1885	**cabina**-*f*	cabin	
1887	**telegrama**-*m*	telegram	
1889	**fracaso**-*m*	failure	
1892	**anciano**-*m; adj*	elder; old	
1894	**corbata**-*f*	tie	
1895	**canto**-*m*	singing	
1896	**poema**-*m*	poem	
1898	**truco**-*m*	trick	
1899	**fantasía**-*f*	fantasy	
1900	**vela**-*f*	candle	
1901	**tradición**-*f*	tradition	
1904	**móvil**-*adj; m*	mobile; cell phone	
1905	**compasión**-*f*	sympathy	
1906	**placa**-*f*	nameplate, badge	
1908	**camarero**-*m*	waiter	
1909	**collar**-*m*	necklace	
1911	**plano**-*adj; m*	level; plan, map	
1912	**lanzamiento**-*m*	launch	
1913	**maquillaje**-*m*	makeup	
1914	**almirante**-*m/f*	admiral	
1916	**huelga**-*f*	strike	
1917	**caridad**-*f*	charity	
1918	**productor**-*m; adj*	producer; producer	
1920	**colección**-*f*	collection	
1921	**fama**-*f*	fame	
1922	**maíz**-*m*	corn	
1923	**cumplido**-*m; adj*	compliment; courteous	
1925	**onda**-*f*	wave	

1926	**molestia**-*f*	annoyance
1929	**congreso**-*m*	congress
1930	**cuarenta**-*num*	forty
1932	**traición**-*f*	treason
1933	**multitud**-*f*	crowd
1934	**macho**-*adj; m*	manly; male
1935	**frecuencia**-*f*	frequency
1936	**mago**-*m*	magician
1937	**pariente**-*m/f*	relative
1938	**limpieza**-*f*	cleaning
1939	**influencia**-*f*	influence
1940	**lista**-*f*	list
1941	**enhorabuena**-*f; int*	congratulations; congratulations
1944	**papa**-*m; f*	pope; potato (LA)
1946	**conducta**-*f*	behavior
1947	**idioma**-*m*	language
1948	**cueva**-*f*	cave
1949	**batería**-*f*	battery, drums
1950	**técnico**-*adj; m/f*	technical; technician
1952	**barra**-*f*	bar
1956	**cuento**-*m*	story
1957	**sentencia**-*f*	sentence
1958	**mueble**-*m*	piece of furniture
1959	**villa**-*f*	villa
1960	**horror**-*m*	horror
1961	**embajador**-*m*	ambassador
1962	**ministerio**-*m*	ministry
1963	**comunista**-*adj; m/f*	communist; communist
1964	**diciembre**-*m*	December
1965	**voto**-*m*	vote
1966	**actividad**-*f*	activity
1971	**trono**-*m*	throne
1972	**pato**-*m*	duck
1973	**jugo**-*m*	juice (LA)
1974	**rutina**-*f*	routine
1975	**patria**-*f*	homeland
1976	**taller**-*m*	workshop
1977	**muestra**-*f*	sample
1980	**casino**-*m*	casino
1981	**gerente**-*m/f*	manager
1983	**alumno**-*m*	student
1984	**diseño**-*m*	design
1986	**reporte**-*m*	report
1987	**masa**-*f*	mass, dough
1988	**guerrero**-*m; adj*	fighter; warlike
1989	**niebla**-*f*	fog
1991	**noviembre**-*m*	November
1992	**logro**-*m*	achievement
1993	**naranja**-*f; adj*	orange; orange
1995	**garaje**-*m*	garage
1996	**ingeniero**-*m*	engineer
1998	**academia**-*f*	academy
1999	**cretino**-*adj; m*	stupid; idiot
2000	**recurso**-*m*	resource
2001	**poeta**-*m*	poet
2002	**dignidad**-*f*	dignity
2003	**testamento**-*m*	will
2004	**infancia**-*f*	childhood
2006	**población**-*f*	population
2007	**almacén**-*m*	storehouse
2008	**soledad**-*f*	loneliness
2009	**medalla**-*f*	medal
2010	**soltero**-*adj; m*	single; single man
2011	**suma**-*f*	sum
2012	**escuadrón**-*m*	squadron
2019	**tristeza**-*f*	sadness
2020	**deporte**-*m*	sport
2021	**recepción**-*f*	reception
2022	**festival**-*m*	festival
2023	**progreso**-*m*	progress
2024	**brindis**-*m*	toast
2026	**región**-*f*	region
2028	**terapia**-*f*	therapy
2029	**hoyo**-*m*	hole
2030	**arco**-*m*	arc
2031	**pesca**-*f*	fishing
2033	**ola**-*f*	wave
2038	**tabaco**-*m*	tobacco
2039	**capítulo**-*m*	chapter
2040	**selva**-*f*	jungle
2041	**columna**-*f*	column
2043	**cortado**-*adj; m*	shy; coffee
2044	**impacto**-*m*	impact
2045	**herramienta**-*f*	tool
2046	**balón**-*m*	ball
2048	**confesión**-*f*	confession
2049	**símbolo**-*m*	symbol
2050	**expediente**-*m*	record
2051	**petición**-*f*	request
2053	**casco**-*m*	helmet
2054	**patata**-*f*	potato

2055	**pandilla-**f	gang	2117	**británico-**adj; m	British; Briton
2056	**preocupación-**f	concern	2118	**economía-**f	economy
2057	**advertencia-**f	warning	2119	**lanzar(se)-**f	launch
2058	**preso-**m	prisoner	2120	**ensalada-**f	salad
2059	**otoño-**m	autumn	2121	**motel-**m	motel
2060	**estatua-**f	statue	2122	**susto-**m	scare
2061	**perrito-**m	puppy	2123	**pluma-**f	pen, feather
2062	**violación-**f	violation	2124	**demanda-**f	demand
2063	**corredor-**m	corridor, runner	2125	**comando-**m	commando
2064	**guante-**m	glove	2126	**embajada-**f	embassy
2065	**vaquero-**m	cowboy, denim	2127	**fruta-**f	fruit
2066	**cita-**f	appointment, date	2128	**vodka-**m	vodka
2069	**jaula-**f	cage	2129	**quinto-**num	fifth
2071	**ratón-**m	mouse	2130	**coca-**f	cocaine
2072	**período-**m	period	2132	**préstamo-**m	loan
2073	**capa-**f	layer	2133	**pañuelo-**m	handkerchief
2074	**gota-**f	drop	2134	**ataúd-**m	coffin
2075	**docena-**f	dozen	2137	**tensión-**f	tension
2076	**traje-**m	suit	2138	**robot-**m	robot
2079	**jugada-**f	play	2139	**aumento-**m	increase
2080	**evento-**m	event	2140	**extremo-**adj; m	extreme; end
2082	**administración-**f	administration	2141	**pulso-**m	pulse
2083	**alfombra-**f	carpet	2142	**pensión-**f	pension, hostel
2084	**vecindario-**m	neighborhood	2143	**juguete-**m	toy
2085	**presentación-**f	presentation	2145	**cirugía-**f	surgery
2087	**retraso-**m	delay	2146	**eternidad-**f	eternity
2089	**plástico-**adj; m	plastic; plastic	2147	**bailarín-**m	dancer
2090	**marzo-**m	March	2148	**chance-**m/f	chance (LA)
2092	**sector-**m	sector	2152	**pavo-**m	turkey
2093	**sindicato-**m	union	2156	**civilización-**f	civilization
2095	**bondad-**f	kindness	2157	**burro-**m	donkey
2096	**temor-**m	fear	2158	**democracia-**f	democracy
2098	**retrato-**m	portrait	2159	**gimnasio-**m	gym
2099	**ópera-**f	opera	2162	**fase-**f	phase
2101	**nieto-**m	grandson	2163	**ilusión-**f	hope, thrill
2102	**campeonato-**m	championship	2164	**debilidad-**f	weakness
2103	**retiro-**m	retirement	2165	**psiquiatra-**m/f	psychiatrist
2104	**sordo-**adj; m	deaf; deaf	2166	**autor-**m	author
2106	**romance-**m	romance	2167	**condena-**f	conviction
2107	**representante-**m/f	representative	2168	**muelle-**m	dock, spring
2108	**boleto-**m	ticket	2174	**dibujo-**m	drawing
2110	**oxígeno-**m	oxygen	2176	**mantequilla-**f	butter
2111	**liga-**f	league	2177	**aparato-**m	device
2112	**ceniza-**f	ash	2178	**pleno-**adj; m	full; plenary session
2113	**ave-**m	bird	2180	**cazador-**m	hunter
2115	**bendición-**f	blessing	2181	**hall-**m	hall

2182	**autopista**-*f*	freeway	
2183	**canalla**-*m/f; adj*	swine (coll); despicable	
2186	**postre**-*m*	dessert	
2187	**concepto**-*m*	concept	
2188	**desarrollo**-*m*	development	
2190	**juramento**-*m*	oath	
2191	**vampiro**-*m*	vampire	
2192	**combinación**-*f*	combination	
2193	**término**-*m*	term	
2194	**cartel**-*m*	poster	
2196	**toalla**-*f*	towel	
2197	**autorización**-*f*	authorization	
2198	**bombero**-*m/f*	firefighter	
2199	**gravedad**-*f*	gravity	
2200	**marinero**-*m; adj*	sailor; naval	
2201	**tortura**-*f*	torture	
2202	**rehén**-*m/f*	hostage	
2203	**chaval**-*m*	kid (ES) (coll)	
2204	**oveja**-*f*	sheep	
2206	**feria**-*f*	fair	
2207	**desafío**-*m*	challenge	
2208	**origen**-*m*	origin	
2211	**patada**-*f*	kick	
2214	**refuerzo**-*m*	backing	
2215	**jabón**-*m*	soap	
2216	**método**-*m*	method	
2217	**mercancía**-*f*	goods	
2218	**acento**-*m*	accent	
2219	**escala**-*f*	ladder	
2220	**engaño**-*m*	deception	
2221	**tenis**-*m*	tennis	
2222	**comentario**-*m*	comment	
2223	**miseria**-*f*	misery	
2224	**mafia**-*f*	mafia	
2225	**estructura**-*f*	structure	
2227	**desfile**-*m*	parade	
2228	**importe**-*m*	amount	
2229	**lápiz**-*m*	pencil	
2230	**editor**-*m*	editor	
2231	**fortaleza**-*f*	fortress, strength	
2232	**pesa**-*f*	weight	
2233	**respiración**-*f*	breathing	
2234	**cuero**-*m*	leather	
2235	**fuga**-*f*	jailbreak, leak	
2236	**inconsciente**-*adj; m*	unconscious, thoughtless; subconscious	

2237	**grabación**-*f*	recording	
2239	**horario**-*m; adj*	schedule; time	
2240	**complejo**-*adj; m*	complex; complex	
2241	**maletín**-*m*	briefcase	
2242	**materia**-*f*	matter	
2244	**chófer**-*m/f*	driver	
2246	**cabra**-*f*	goat	
2247	**enero**-*m*	January	
2248	**comedor**-*m*	dining room	
2249	**república**-*f*	republic	
2250	**sabio**-*adj; m*	wise; sage	
2251	**apariencia**-*f*	appearance	
2252	**agallas**-*fpl*	guts	
2253	**mezcla**-*f*	mixture	
2254	**ejecución**-*f*	execution	
2255	**licor**-*m*	liquor	
2257	**reconocimiento**-*m*	recognition	
2259	**desesperado**-*adj; m*	desperate; desperate	
2260	**elefante**-*m*	elephant	
2261	**desorden**-*m*	disturbance, chaos	
2262	**torneo**-*m*	tournament	
2263	**apetito**-*m*	appetite	
2264	**orilla**-*f*	shore	
2265	**fenómeno**-*m*	phenomenon	
2266	**alimento**-*m*	food	
2267	**mancha**-*f*	stain	
2268	**giro**-*m*	turn	
2269	**submarino**-*adj; m*	underwater; submarine	
2270	**sabiduría**-*f*	wisdom	
2272	**campana**-*f*	bell	
2273	**criado**-*m*	servant	
2274	**gesto**-*m*	gesture	
2275	**comercio**-*m*	shop	
2277	**capullo**-*m*	cocoon, idiot (ES) (coll)	
2278	**creación**-*f*	creation	
2279	**camiseta**-*f*	shirt	
2280	**gusano**-*m*	worm	
2282	**excepción**-*f*	exception	
2283	**lectura**-*f*	reading	
2284	**seda**-*f*	silk	
2285	**atmósfera**-*f*	atmosphere	
2286	**deberes**-*mpl*	homework	
2289	**tarta**-*f*	cake	
2290	**ganancia**-*f*	gain	
2292	**cosecha**-*f*	harvest	

2293	**disciplina**-*f*	discipline	2363	**graduación**-*f*	graduation
2294	**oficio**-*m*	job	2364	**texto**-*m*	text
2295	**bahía**-*f*	bay	2365	**transmisión**-*f*	transmission
2296	**norma**-*f*	rule	2367	**padrino**-*m*	godfather
2297	**salario**-*m*	wage	2368	**fraude**-*m*	fraud
2300	**pelotón**-*m*	squad	2370	**solar**-*adj; m*	solar; site
2301	**pasaje**-*m*	ticket	2371	**edición**-*f*	edition
2302	**fianza**-*f*	bail, deposit	2372	**suizo**-*adj; m*	Swiss; Swiss
2303	**misa**-*f*	mass	2374	**concentración**-*f*	concentration
2304	**carbón**-*m*	carbon	2375	**conspiración**-*f*	conspiracy
2307	**cristiano**-*adj; m*	Christian; Christian	2379	**filosofía**-*f*	philosophy
2309	**instinto**-*m*	instinct	2382	**potencia**-*f*	power
2311	**plazo**-*m*	period, deadline	2383	**herido**-*m; adj*	injured; wounded
2312	**confusión**-*f*	confusion	2386	**dosis**-*f*	dose
2315	**tribu**-*f*	tribe	2387	**incapaz**-*adj; m/f*	unable; incompetent
2316	**horno**-*m*	oven	2389	**oración**-*f*	prayer, sentence
2317	**rabia**-*f*	rage	2391	**danza**-*f*	dance
2320	**cocaína**-*f*	cocaine	2394	**conclusión**-*f*	conclusion
2321	**estacionamiento**-*m*	parking	2395	**secuencia**-*f*	sequence
2323	**alivio**-*m*	relief	2397	**mensajero**-*m*	messenger
2324	**clan**-*m*	clan	2398	**vidrio**-*m*	glass
2325	**tubo**-*m*	tube	2400	**beneficio**-*m*	benefit
2326	**aterrizaje**-*m*	landing	2403	**hambriento**-*adj; m*	hungry; hungry person
2328	**profundidad**-*f*	depth	2404	**tabla**-*f*	board
2329	**araña**-*f*	spider	2405	**maldad**-*f*	wickedness
2331	**certeza**-*f*	certainty	2408	**Cuba**-*f*	Cuba
2332	**afecto**-*m*	affection	2412	**antecedente**-*m*	precedent
2333	**consuelo**-*m*	relief	2413	**paro**-*m*	unemployment (ES), strike
2334	**micrófono**-*m*	microphone			
2335	**formación**-*f*	training	2414	**acusación**-*f*	accusation
2338	**estrategia**-*f*	strategy	2416	**secuestro**-*m*	kidnapping
2339	**rango**-*m*	rank	2418	**algodón**-*m*	cotton
2341	**procedimiento**-*m*	procedure	2419	**colonia**-*f*	colony
2343	**exposición**-*f*	exposure	2420	**disposición**-*f*	aptitude, disposal
2345	**potencial**-*adj; m*	potential; strength	2426	**pantano**-*m*	swamp
2346	**raíz**-*f*	root	2427	**envío**-*m*	shipping
2347	**nido**-*m*	nest	2428	**bigote**-*m*	mustache
2348	**temporal**-*adj; m*	temporary; storm	2429	**instrumento**-*m*	instrument
2350	**asociación**-*f*	association	2431	**tiburón**-*m*	shark
2352	**doña**-*f*	miss, lady	2433	**iris**-*m*	iris
2356	**regimiento**-*m*	regiment	2434	**matemático**-*adj; m*	mathematical; mathematician
2357	**coro**-*m*	choir			
2358	**muerto**-*m*	dead	2436	**dieta**-*f*	diet
2359	**duelo**-*m*	duel	2437	**salvación**-*f*	salvation
2360	**dificultad**-*f*	difficulty	2439	**munición**-*f*	ammunition
2361	**ausencia**-*f*	absence	2440	**enano**-*m; adj*	shorty; very small
			2442	**águila**-*m*	eagle

2443	justa-*f*	joust
2445	lámpara-*f*	lamp
2446	estadio-*m*	stadium
2449	ordenador-*m*	computer (ES)
2450	agenda-*f*	calendar
2451	alianza-*f*	alliance
2454	ida-*f*	going
2455	globo-*m*	balloon
2457	manual-*adj; m*	handmade; manual
2458	rebelde-*adj; m*	rebel; rebel
2459	explosivo-*adj; m*	explosive; explosive
2461	cajón-*m*	drawer
2463	objeción-*f*	objection
2464	riqueza-*f*	wealth
2465	receta-*f*	recipe
2466	granjero-*m*	farmer
2467	martillo-*m*	hammer
2468	continuación-*f*	continuation
2469	radar-*m*	radar
2470	pintor-*m*	painter
2471	elemento-*m*	element
2472	lente-*f*	lens
2473	vapor-*m*	steam
2476	ginebra-*f*	gin
2478	hígado-*m*	liver
2479	barro-*m*	mud
2481	griego-*adj; m*	Greek; Greek
2482	tejado-*m*	roof
2483	drama-*m*	drama
2484	dentista-*m/f*	dentist
2485	chimenea-*f*	hearth
2486	calcetín-*m*	sock
2487	tranquilidad-*f*	tranquility
2488	galería-*f*	gallery
2489	cocinero-*m*	cook
2490	pito-*m*	whistle
2491	campesino-*m; adj*	peasant; rural
2492	liberación-*f*	release
2496	escolar-*adj; m/f*	school; schoolchild
2498	vagabundo-*m; adj*	vagabond; wandering
2499	suite-*f*	suite
2500	retirada-*f*	withdrawal
2501	episodio-*m*	episode
2505	músculo-*m*	muscle
2506	misil-*m*	missile
2507	obispo-*m*	bishop
2508	herencia-*f*	heritage
2509	monje-*m*	monk
2512	tiroteo-*m*	gunfire
2513	cordero-*m*	lamb
2515	aplauso-*m*	applause
2516	píldora-*f*	pill
2517	puño-*m*	fist
2518	marea-*f*	tide
2520	disfraz-*m*	costume
2521	navaja-*f*	knife

Numerals

Rank	Spanish-*PoS*	Translation(s)
9	**un**-*art; num*	a, an; one
62	**dos**-*num*	two
81	**uno**-*num*	one
127	**tres**-*num*	three
191	**primer(o)**-*num*	first
232	**cinco**-*num*	five
245	**cuatro**-*num*	four
312	**segundo**-*num*	second
316	**seis**-*num*	six
317	**cuarto**-*num; m*	fourth; room
349	**diez**-*num*	ten
350	**mil**-*num*	thousand
365	**millón**-*num*	million
475	**siete**-*num*	seven
524	**ocho**-*num*	eight
674	**cien(to)**-*num*	hundred
739	**nueve**-*num*	nine
1089	**tercer(o)**-*num*	third
1113	**veinte**-*num*	twenty
1244	**cero**-*num*	zero
1297	**doce**-*num*	twelve
1388	**treinta**-*num*	thirty
1570	**quince**-*num*	fifteen
1642	**cincuenta**-*num*	fifty
1756	**once**-*num*	eleven
1930	**cuarenta**-*num*	forty
2129	**quinto**-*num*	fifth

Verbs

Rank	Spanish-PoS	Translation(s)
7	ser-*vb; av; m*	be; was, were; being
14	saber(se)-*vb*	know
17	estar(se)-*vb*	be
33	ir(se)-*vb; vbr*	go; leave
34	haber-*av; vb*	have; there is, there are
37	tener-*vb*	have, must
46	querer(se)-*vb*	want, love
48	poder(se)-*vb; m*	be able to, might; power
51	hacer(se)-*vb; vbr*	do, make; move, pretend to be
72	ver(se)-*vb*	see, watch
77	decir(se)-*vb*	say, tell, speak
93	parecer(se)-*vb; m*	appear, seem; opinion
98	mirar(se)-*vb*	look, watch
105	hablar-*vb*	talk, speak
118	gustar(se)-*vb*	like
122	esperar(se)-*vb*	wait
130	deber(se)-*m; vb; vbr*	duty; must; owe
139	importar-*vb*	matter, import
145	necesitar-*vb*	need
148	oír(se)-*vb*	hear
166	pasar(se)-*vb; vbr*	go, pass, happen (coll); go over, forget
167	salir(se)-*vb*	leave
170	valer(se)-*vb*	cost, be good for
178	dar(se)-*vb*	give
193	pensar-*vb*	think
197	venir(se)-*vb*	come
198	dejar(se)-*vb*	leave, allow
201	volver(se)-*vb*	come back
206	esposar(se)-*vb*	handcuff
214	tomar(se)-*vb; vbr*	take; drink
216	entender-*vb*	understand
222	suponer-*vb*	suppose, assume
233	llamar(se)-*vb; vbr*	call; name
236	escuchar(se)-*vb*	listen
243	seguir-*vb*	follow
248	significar-*vb*	mean
251	llegar-*vb*	arrive, reach
254	vivir-*vb*	live
256	trabajar-*vb*	work
260	comer(se)-*vb*	eat
261	conocer(se)-*vb*	know, meet
262	entrar-*vb*	get in
265	morir(se)-*vb*	die
268	amar(se)-*vb*	love
279	encontrar(se)-*vb*	find
283	quedar(se)-*vb; vbr*	be left; stay
286	culpar(se)-*vb*	blame
293	dormir(se)-*vb*	sleep
302	preocupar(se)-*vb*	worry
305	tratar-*vb*	treat, address
315	matar-*vb*	kill
322	creer(se)-*vb*	believe, think
337	llevar(se)-*vb*	take, wear
340	buscar-*vb*	search for
342	callar(se)-*vb*	hush
344	armar(se)-*vb*	assemble, supply with arms
347	perder(se)-*vb*	lose
348	jugar-*vb*	play
360	ocurrir-*vb*	happen
366	acercar(se)-*vb*	move closer
374	poner(se)-*vb; vbr*	put; put on
377	suceder-*vb*	happen, follow
378	disculpar(se)-*vb; vbr*	forgive; apologize
384	odiar-*vb*	hate
391	ayudar-*vb*	help
395	probar(se)-*vb; vbr*	try, prove; try on
406	empezar-*vb*	begin
408	acabar-*vb*	finish
416	usar-*vb*	use
417	conseguir-*vb*	get, achieve
420	lamentar(se)-*vb; vbr*	regret; feel sorry for yourself
423	andar(se)-*vb; vbr*	walk; behave
429	sentar(se)-*vb*	sit
434	pagar-*vb*	pay
439	cambiar(se)-*vb*	swap, change
452	ganar-*vb*	win
463	comprar(se)-*vb*	buy
465	sonar-*m; vb*	sonar; sound
477	encantar-*vb*	love, bewitch
481	traer(se)-*vb*	bring
489	temer(se)-*vb*	fear
490	abrir-*vb*	open
492	freír-*vb*	fry
495	funcionar-*vb*	work, operate
511	salar-*vb*	salt

513	**abogar**-*vb*	plead	
515	**regresar**-*vb*	return	
517	**terminar**-*vb*	finish	
518	**jurar**-*vb*	swear, pledge	
520	**sentir**-*vb*	feel	
536	**citar**-*vb*	quote, make an appointment	
547	**beber(se)**-*vb*	drink	
549	**vestir(se)**-*vb*	dress	
558	**bailar**-*vb*	dance	
564	**existir**-*vb*	exist	
566	**alegrar(se)**-*vb*	cheer up, be happy	
570	**prometer**-*vb*	promise	
572	**preguntar**-*vb*	ask	
574	**cenar**-*vb*	have dinner	
575	**correr**-*vb*	run	
584	**parir**-*vb*	give birth	
596	**escribir**-*vb*	write	
609	**crear**-*vb*	create	
610	**apenar(se)**-*vb*	sadden	
615	**leer**-*vb*	read	
622	**cortar(se)**-*vb*	cut	
628	**tocar**-*vb*	touch	
641	**tragar(se)**-*vb*	swallow	
644	**unir**-*vb*	join, unite	
650	**interesar(se)**-*vb*	interest	
658	**ocupar(se)**-*vb; vbr*	occupy; take responsibility for	
662	**sacar**-*vb*	take out	
664	**pedir**-*vb*	request	
665	**cerrar**-*vb*	close	
668	**equivocar(se)**-*vb; vbr*	confuse; be mistaken	
677	**mantener(se)**-*vb*	keep	
678	**aprender(se)**-*vb*	learn	
692	**parar**-*vb*	stop	
700	**contar**-*vb*	count, tell	
701	**cansar(se)**-*vb*	tire, bother	
709	**subir**-*vb*	go up	
717	**desear**-*vb*	wish	
722	**olvidar(se)**-*vb*	forget	
725	**calmar(se)**-*vb*	calm	
728	**casar**-*vb*	marry	
729	**drogar(se)**-*vb*	drug	
734	**preferir**-*vb*	prefer	
735	**soler**-*vb*	used to	
737	**partir(se)**-*vb; vbr*	depart; break	
746	**perdonar**-*vb*	forgive	
748	**escapar(se)**-*vb*	escape	
749	**salvar(se)**-*vb*	save	
750	**servir**-*vb*	serve	
757	**volar**-*vb*	fly	
759	**bromear**-*vb*	joke	
762	**depender**-*vb*	depend	
770	**preparar(se)**-*vb*	prepare	
776	**intentar**-*vb*	try	
788	**caminar**-*vb*	walk	
793	**confiar**-*vb*	trust	
796	**cantar**-*vb*	sing	
797	**bajar(se)**-*vb*	lower	
798	**pelear(se)**-*vb*	fight	
807	**decidir(se)**-*vb*	decide	
812	**caer(se)**-*vb*	fall	
813	**herir(se)**-*vb*	hurt	
817	**evitar**-*vb*	avoid	
819	**llorar**-*vb*	cry	
824	**vender**-*vb*	sell	
826	**levantar(se)**-*vb; vbr*	lift; wake up	
829	**permitir(se)**-*vb; vbr*	allow; afford	
832	**charlar**-*vb*	chat	
836	**referir(se)**-*vb*	refer	
839	**pesar(se)**-*vb*	weigh	
842	**extrañar(se)**-*vb*	surprise, miss	
843	**enamorar(se)**-*vb*	make someone fall in love	
845	**recordar**-*vb*	remember	
846	**luchar**-*vb*	fight	
847	**datar**-*vb*	date back to	
853	**comprender**-*vb*	understand	
856	**costar**-*vb*	cost	
863	**acordar(se)**-*vb; vbr*	agree to; remember	
896	**arreglar(se)**-*vb; vbr*	repair; get ready	
921	**agradecer**-*vb*	thank	
933	**descansar**-*vb*	rest	
938	**echar(se)**-*vb; vbr*	kick, pour; lie down	
940	**romper(se)**-*vb*	break	
941	**actuar**-*vb*	act	
946	**coger**-*vb*	take, f*ck (LA)	
953	**amamantar**-*vb*	breastfeed	
956	**robar**-*vb*	rob	
959	**oler(se)**-*vb*	smell	
960	**embarazar**-*vb*	get pregnant	
961	**mostrar(se)**-*vb*	show	

966	**aceptar(se)**-*vb*	accept	1212	**averiguar**-*vb*	find out
968	**cuidar(se)**-*vb*	look after	1221	**construir**-*vb*	build
969	**rogar**-*vb*	beg	1226	**detener(se)**-*vb*	stop
971	**resultar**-*vb*	result	1255	**mentir**-*vb*	lie
972	**comenzar**-*vb*	start	1264	**aburrir(se)**-*vb; vbr*	bore; be bored
981	**continuar**-*vb*	continue	1268	**gritar**-*vb*	scream
987	**mover(se)**-*vb*	move	1270	**aparecer(se)**-*vb*	appear
988	**disparar(se)**-*vb*	shoot	1285	**recuperar(se)**-*vb; vbr*	recover; get well
992	**recibir**-*vb*	receive			
994	**dar**-*vb*	give	1289	**convertir(se)**-*vb*	change, transform
996	**imaginar(se)**-*vb*	imagine	1294	**descubrir**-*vb*	discover
1036	**conducir**-*vb*	drive, lead	1305	**enojar(se)**-*vb*	anger
1038	**enviar**-*vb*	send	1312	**cumplir(se)**-*vb; vbr*	accomplish; expire
1041	**pertenecer**-*vb*	belong	1319	**compartir**-*vb*	share
1042	**presentar(se)**-*vb; vbr*	introduce; appear	1322	**resolver**-*vb*	solve
			1324	**nacer**-*vb*	be born
1044	**merecer**-*vb*	deserve	1325	**nadar**-*vb*	swim
1063	**fumar**-*vb*	smoke	1332	**sorprender(se)**-*vb*	surprise
1080	**explicar(se)**-*vb*	explain	1335	**meter(se)**-*vb*	put, get into
1099	**asegurar(se)**-*vb; vbr*	secure; check	1346	**aguantar(se)**-*vb*	put up with, tolerate
			1347	**responder**-*vb*	answer
1100	**obtener**-*vb*	obtain, acquire	1348	**soportar**-*vb*	support, bear
1110	**desaparecer**-*vb*	disappear	1354	**amanecer**-*m; vb*	dawn; wake up
1115	**discutir**-*vb*	argue	1355	**mandar**-*vb*	send, be in charge
1122	**quitar(se)**-*vb; vbr*	remove; get out of the way	1357	**controlar(se)**-*vb*	control
1134	**manejar(se)**-*vb; vbr*	manage, drive (LA); handle yourself	1361	**entrevistar**-*vb*	interview
			1365	**saltar(se)**-*vb; vbr*	jump; skip, break
1142	**elegir**-*vb*	choose	1366	**concertar**-*vb*	arrange
1147	**limpiar(se)**-*vb*	clean, tidy	1369	**visitar**-*vb*	visit
1154	**disponer(se)**-*vb; vbr*	arrange, have; get ready	1396	**acusar**-*vb*	accuse
			1411	**abandonar**-*vb*	abandon
1158	**tirar**-*vb*	throw, waste, pull	1415	**apetecer**-*vb*	crave
1160	**destruir**-*vb*	destroy	1420	**alertar**-*vb*	alert
1165	**relajar(se)**-*vb*	relax	1427	**adorar**-*vb*	worship
1175	**apurar(se)**-*vb*	hurry	1428	**imponer(se)**-*vb; vbr*	impose; prevail
1177	**dudar**-*vb*	doubt			
1178	**invitar**-*vb*	invite	1430	**sufrir**-*vb*	suffer
1179	**estudiar**-*vb*	study	1435	**bendecir**-*vb*	bless
1183	**sobrevivir**-*vb*	survive	1444	**enseñar**-*vb*	teach, show
1188	**respirar**-*vb*	breathe	1447	**atrapar**-*vb*	catch
1190	**proteger(se)**-*vb*	protect	1449	**firmar**-*vb*	sign
1194	**viajar**-*vb*	travel	1455	**cruzar**-*vb*	cross
1203	**pecar**-*vb*	sin	1469	**faltar**-*vb*	lack, miss
1207	**huir**-*vb*	run away	1472	**asustar(se)**-*vb*	scare
1208	**recoger**-*vb*	pick up, collect	1478	**contestar**-*vb*	answer
1211	**asesinar**-*vb*	murder	1488	**cubrir(se)**-*vb*	cover

1498	**prohibir**-*vb*	prohibit
1502	**lograr**-*vb*	achieve
1518	**crecer**-*vb*	grow
1520	**reír**-*vb*	laugh
1521	**rescatar**-*vb*	rescue
1522	**repetir**-*vb*	repeat
1523	**montar**-*vb*	mount
1538	**atacar**-*vb*	attack
1548	**fijar(se)**-*vb; vbr*	set; pay attention to
1561	**guardar(se)**-*vb; vbr*	keep, retain; take precautions against
1571	**demostrar**-*vb*	prove, show
1576	**adivinar**-*vb*	guess
1584	**atreverse**-*vbr*	dare
1587	**celebrar**-*vb*	celebrate
1591	**permanecer**-*vb*	stay, remain
1608	**dirigir**-*vb*	lead, address
1615	**medir(se)**-*vb*	measure
1618	**despertar(se)**-*m; vb*	awakening; wake up
1623	**sugerir**-*vb*	suggest
1625	**despedir(se)**-*vb; vbr*	dismiss, lay off; say goodbye
1627	**enfadar(se)**-*vb*	irritate
1630	**esconder(se)**-*vb*	hide
1631	**condenar**-*vb*	condemn
1632	**reservar(se)**-*vb*	save, book
1637	**cocinar**-*vb*	cook
1653	**apestar**-*vb*	stink
1655	**opinar**-*vb*	believe, give your opinion
1677	**desconocer**-*vb*	not know, not recognize
1688	**apagar**-*vb*	turn off
1694	**agarrar(se)**-*vb*	grab
1716	**almorzar**-*vb*	have lunch
1726	**revisar**-*vb*	inspect, examine
1740	**soñar**-*vb*	dream
1745	**picar**-*vb*	sting
1747	**arrestar**-*vb*	arrest
1762	**hallar(se)**-*vb; vbr*	find; be
1763	**disfrutar**-*vb*	enjoy
1767	**alcanzar**-*vb*	reach
1772	**planear**-*vb*	plan
1780	**golpear(se)**-*vb*	hit
1793	**mejorar**-*vb*	improve
1797	**lucir(se)**-*vb*	flaunt
1803	**emplear(se)**-*vb*	use
1805	**entregar**-*vb*	deliver
1808	**patrullar**-*vb*	patrol
1815	**ofrecer**-*vb*	offer
1819	**tranquilizar(se)**-*vb*	calm down
1822	**admitir**-*vb*	admit
1824	**cazar**-*vb*	hunt
1833	**votar**-*vb*	vote
1843	**encerrar(se)**-*vb*	lock somebody up
1845	**apostar**-*vb*	bet
1847	**pescar**-*vb*	fish
1855	**sonreír**-*vb*	smile
1856	**molestar(se)**-*vb; vbr*	disturb; be offended
1858	**pasear**-*vb*	walk
1866	**reconocer**-*vb*	recognize
1874	**renunciar**-*vb*	give up
1876	**encargar(se)**-*vb; vbr*	order, request; take charge of
1882	**convencer**-*vb*	convince
1888	**requerir**-*vb*	require
1891	**fallar**-*vb*	fail
1893	**agradar**-*vb*	please
1903	**rezar**-*vb*	pray
1910	**defender(se)**-*vb*	defend
1919	**investigar**-*vb*	investigate
1927	**advertir**-*vb*	warn
1942	**satisfacer**-*vb*	satisfy
1943	**representar**-*vb*	represent
1945	**besar**-*vb*	kiss
1951	**explotar**-*vb*	explode, exploit
1953	**engañar**-*vb*	deceive
1954	**marchar(se)**-*vb; vbr*	march; leave
1955	**cargar**-*vb*	load
1967	**fotografiar**-*vb*	photograph
1968	**lavar(se)**-*vb*	wash
1970	**notar**-*vb*	notice
1978	**devolver**-*vb*	return
1979	**desayunar**-*vb*	have breakfast
1982	**practicar**-*vb*	practice
1985	**vigilar**-*vb*	guard
1990	**rondar**-*vb*	wander around
1994	**considerar(se)**-*vb*	consider
2013	**abrazar**-*vb*	hug
2014	**enterarse**-*vbr*	realize, find out
2015	**colgar(se)**-*vb*	hang, hang up
2017	**confundir(se)**-*vb; vbr*	confuse; make a mistake

2018	**utilizar**-*vb*	use
2027	**arruinar(se)**-*vb*	ruin
2032	**acostumbrar(se)**-*vb*	get used to
2035	**obligar(se)**-*vb*	force
2036	**formar**-*vb*	form, train
2037	**ordenar**-*vb*	order, arrange
2042	**enterrar(se)**-*vb*	bury
2047	**fingir**-*vb*	pretend
2052	**participar**-*vb*	participate
2067	**pegar**-*vb*	hit, glue
2070	**incluir**-*vb*	include
2077	**vomitar**-*vb*	vomit
2078	**testimoniar**-*vb*	testify
2081	**suplicar**-*vb*	supplicate
2088	**pintar**-*vb*	paint
2091	**escoger**-*vb*	choose
2094	**cometer**-*vb*	commit
2100	**mencionar**-*vb*	mention
2105	**convenir**-*vb*	be advisable
2109	**negar(se)**-*vb; vbr*	deny; refuse
2131	**atender**-*vb*	deal with, pay attention
2135	**saludar**-*vb*	greet
2136	**sobrar**-*vb*	be left over
2149	**cobrar**-*vb*	collect, charge
2150	**realizar**-*vb*	perform
2153	**custodiar**-*vb*	flank
2154	**ultimar**-*vb*	finalize
2155	**encender**-*vb*	turn on
2161	**observar**-*vb*	observe
2171	**aterrizar**-*vb*	land
2172	**vencer**-*vb*	overcome
2173	**copiar**-*vb*	copy
2175	**causar**-*vb*	cause
2179	**sospechar**-*vb*	suspect
2184	**informar(se)**-*vb; vbr*	inform; find out
2185	**despejar(se)**-*vb; vbr*	clear; clear your mind
2195	**sangrar**-*vb*	bleed
2212	**ocultar(se)**-*vb*	hide
2226	**gastar(se)**-*vb; vbr*	spend, use; wear out
2258	**involucrar(se)**-*vb*	involve
2276	**interrumpir**-*vb*	interrupt
2288	**quemar(se)**-*vb*	burn
2291	**timar**-*vb*	cheat
2299	**conversar**-*vb*	talk

2306	**quejarse**-*vbr*	complain
2310	**negociar**-*vb*	negotiate
2313	**orquestar**-*vb*	orchestrate
2314	**afectar**-*vb*	affect
2319	**aguardar**-*vb*	wait
2327	**revolver**-*vb*	stir
2330	**contener(se)**-*vb*	contain
2337	**retrasar(se)**-*vb*	delay
2342	**comprobar**-*vb*	check
2351	**llenar**-*vb*	fill
2355	**resistir(se)**-*vb*	resist
2362	**eliminar**-*vb*	remove
2366	**separar**-*vb*	separate
2373	**rodear(se)**-*vb*	go around
2376	**alejar(se)**-*vb*	move away
2378	**acompañar**-*vb*	accompany
2380	**enfrentar**-*vb*	confront
2384	**pervertir(se)**-*vb*	pervert
2392	**juzgar**-*vb*	judge
2393	**aclarar**-*vb*	clarify
2396	**brillar**-*vb*	shine
2401	**empujar**-*vb*	push
2411	**filmar**-*vb*	film
2415	**prestar**-*vb*	lend
2421	**avisar**-*vb*	warn
2423	**liberar(se)**-*vb*	set free
2425	**rodar**-*vb*	roll
2441	**orientar(se)**-*vb*	guide
2447	**alimentar(se)**-*vb*	feed
2452	**dedicar(se)**-*vb*	devote
2453	**criar**-*vb*	raise
2460	**superar(se)**-*vb*	overcome
2477	**arrancar(se)**-*vb*	pull up, start
2495	**lastimar(se)**-*vb*	hurt
2497	**impedir**-*vb*	prevent
2502	**durar**-*vb*	last
2503	**organizar**-*vb*	organize
2510	**atravesar**-*vb*	cross
2514	**sellar**-*vb*	seal, stamp
2519	**estimar**-*vb*	estimate, respect
2522	**indicar**-*vb*	indicate
2523	**fracasar**-*vb*	fail

Alphabetical order

Rank	Spanish-PoS	Translation(s)
	A	
257	**abajo**-adv	below, down
1411	**abandonar**-vb	abandon
907	**abierto**-adj	open
513	**abogar**-vb	plead
2013	**abrazar**-vb	hug
993	**abrigo**-m	coat, shelter
1782	**abril**-m	April
490	**abrir**-vb	open
774	**absoluto**-adj	absolute
1597	**absurdo**-adj; m	absurd; nonsense
508	**abuelo**-m	grandfather
1264	**aburrir(se)**-vb; vbr	bore; be bored
369	**acá**-adv	here (LA)
408	**acabar**-vb	finish
1998	**academia**-f	academy
634	**acaso**-adv	perhaps
1465	**acceso**-m	access
494	**accidente**-m	accident
714	**acción**-f	action, share
1645	**aceite**-m	oil
2218	**acento**-m	accent
966	**aceptar(se)**-vb	accept
366	**acercar(se)**-vb	move closer
1636	**acero**-m	steel
2393	**aclarar**-vb	clarify
2378	**acompañar**-vb	accompany
863	**acordar(se)**-vb; vbr	agree to; remember
2399	**acostado**-adj	lying down
2032	**acostumbrar(se)**-vb	get used to
1393	**actitud**-f	attitude
1966	**actividad**-f	activity
955	**acto**-m	act
1128	**actor**-m	actor
1695	**actuación**-f	performance
1792	**actual**-adj	present
941	**actuar**-vb	act
107	**acuerdo**-m	agreement
2414	**acusación**-f	accusation
1396	**acusar**-vb	accuse
1717	**adecuado**-adj	suitable
207	**adelante**-adv; int	forward, ahead; come in
324	**además**-adv	besides
486	**adentro**-adv	inside
151	**adiós**-m; int	farewell; goodbye
1576	**adivinar**-vb	guess
2082	**administración**-f	administration
1822	**admitir**-vb	admit
1200	**adonde**-adv; prp	where; to the house of worship
1427	**adorar**-vb	
1842	**adulto**-adj; m	adult; adult
2057	**advertencia**-f	warning
1927	**advertir**-vb	warn
1012	**aeropuerto**-m	airport
2314	**afectar**-vb	affect
2332	**afecto**-m	affection
1565	**afortunado**-adj	lucky
335	**afuera**-adv	outside
2252	**agallas**-fpl	guts
1694	**agarrar(se)**-vb	grab
2450	**agenda**-f	calendar
538	**agente**-m	agent
619	**agradable**-adj	pleasant
1893	**agradar**-vb	please
921	**agradecer**-vb	thank
186	**agua**-m	water
1346	**aguantar(se)**-vb	put up with, tolerate
2319	**aguardar**-vb	wait
2442	**águila**-m	eagle
1067	**agujero**-m	hole
76	**ahí**-adv	there
149	**ah**-int	ah
35	**ahora**-adv	now
400	**aire**-m	air
2340	**ajá**-int	uh-huh
1827	**ajustado**-adj	tight
1559	**ala**-m	wing
1477	**alarma**-f	alarm
1006	**alcalde**-m	mayor
1668	**alcance**-m	scope, significance
1767	**alcanzar**-vb	reach

1195	**alcohol**-*m*	alcohol	
26	**al**-*contr*	to the, at the (a+el)	
1530	**aldea**-*f*	village	
566	**alegrar(se)**-*vb*	cheer up, be happy	
1493	**alegre**-*adj*	happy	
1037	**alegría**-*f*	joy	
2376	**alejar(se)**-*vb*	move away	
929	**alemán**-*adj; m*	German; German person	
1420	**alertar**-*vb*	alert	
2083	**alfombra**-*f*	carpet	
36	**algo**-*adv; prn*	something; some	
2418	**algodón**-*m*	cotton	
1752	**alguacil**-*m/f*	sheriff	
85	**alguien**-*prn*	someone, anyone, somebody, anybody	
1881	**algún**-*adj*	some, any	
155	**alguno**-*adj; prn*	someone, somebody; one	
2451	**alianza**-*f*	alliance	
1573	**aliento**-*m*	breath	
2447	**alimentar(se)**-*vb*	feed	
2266	**alimento**-*m*	food	
2323	**alivio**-*m*	relief	
211	**allá**-*adv*	there	
115	**allí**-*adv*	there	
2007	**almacén**-*m*	storehouse	
482	**alma**-*f*	soul	
1914	**almirante**-*m/f*	admiral	
1716	**almorzar**-*vb*	have lunch	
1114	**almuerzo**-*m*	lunch	
1582	**alquiler**-*m*	rent	
509	**alrededor**-*adv*	around	
1771	**alternativo**-*adj*	alternative	
290	**alto**-*adj; adv; int*	tall; high; stop	
1377	**altura**-*f*	height	
1983	**alumno**-*m*	student	
478	**amable**-*adj*	kind	
953	**amamantar**-*vb*	breastfeed	
1354	**amanecer**-*m; vb*	dawn; wake up	
268	**amar(se)**-*vb*	love	
1862	**amarillo**-*adj*	yellow	
1501	**ambiente**-*m*	environment	

546	**ambos**-*adj; prn*	both; both	
1434	**ambulancia**-*f*	ambulance	
1223	**amenaza**-*f*	threat	
1287	**amén**-*m*	amen	
909	**americano**-*adj; m*	American; American person	
113	**amigo**-*m*	friend	
1214	**amistad**-*f*	friendship	
135	**amor**-*m*	love	
1820	**análisis**-*m*	analysis	
1892	**anciano**-*m; adj*	elder; old	
423	**andar(se)**-*vb; vbr*	walk; behave	
952	**ángel**-*m*	angel	
873	**anillo**-*m*	ring	
669	**animal**-*adj; m*	animal; animal	
1878	**ánimo**-*m*	spirits, mood	
1838	**aniversario**-*m*	anniversary	
364	**anoche**-*adv*	last night	
80	**año**-*m*	year	
2412	**antecedente**-*m*	precedent	
498	**ante**-*prp*	facing, before	
1459	**anterior**-*adj*	previous	
86	**antes**-*adv*	before, first	
1163	**antiguo**-*adj; m*	ancient; old fashioned	
1603	**anuncio**-*m*	advertisement, announcement	
1688	**apagar**-*vb*	turn off	
2177	**aparato**-*m*	device	
1270	**aparecer(se)**-*vb*	appear	
1594	**aparente**-*adj*	apparent	
2251	**apariencia**-*f*	appearance	
791	**apartamento**-*m*	apartment	
1247	**aparte**-*adj; adv*	unusual; aside	
1542	**apellido**-*m*	surname	
610	**apenar(se)**-*vb*	sadden	
1653	**apestar**-*vb*	stink	
1415	**apetecer**-*vb*	crave	
2263	**apetito**-*m*	appetite	
2515	**aplauso**-*m*	applause	
1845	**apostar**-*vb*	bet	
1088	**apoyo**-*m*	support	
1806	**aprecio**-*m*	appreciation	
678	**aprender(se)**-*vb*	learn	
1902	**apropiado**-*adj*	appropriate	
2322	**aproximado**-*adj*	approximate	

4	**a**-*prp*	to, at	
1196	**apuesto**-*adj*	handsome	
1175	**apurar(se)**-*vb*	hurry	
606	**aquel**-*adj; prn*	that; that one	
24	**aquí**-*adv*	here	
2329	**araña**-*f*	spider	
773	**árbol**-*m*	tree	
1659	**archivo**-*m*	archive, file	
2030	**arco**-*m*	arc	
974	**área**-*m*	area	
1295	**arena**-*f*	sand, ring	
344	**armar(se)**-*vb*	assemble, supply with arms	
1451	**armario**-*m*	closet	
2477	**arrancar(se)**-*vb*	pull up, start	
896	**arreglar(se)**-*vb; vbr*	repair; get ready	
1873	**arreglo**-*m*	arrangement, repair	
1747	**arrestar**-*vb*	arrest	
1590	**arresto**-*m*	arrest	
224	**arriba**-*adv; int*	up, above; come on	
1453	**arroz**-*m*	rice	
2027	**arruinar(se)**-*vb*	ruin	
680	**arte**-*m*	art	
1265	**artículo**-*m*	article, item	
1108	**artista**-*m/f*	artist	
1723	**asalto**-*m*	assault	
1678	**ascensor**-*m*	elevator	
1425	**asco**-*m*	disgust	
1099	**asegurar(se)**-*vb; vbr*	secure; check	
1211	**asesinar**-*vb*	murder	
604	**asesinato**-*m*	murder	
468	**asesino**-*m*	murderer	
38	**así**-*adv*	like this, like that	
881	**asiento**-*m*	seat	
1467	**asistente**-*m/f*	assistant	
2350	**asociación**-*f*	association	
1633	**asombroso**-*adj*	amazing	
891	**aspecto**-*m*	aspect	
1311	**asqueroso**-*adj*	disgusting	
2369	**astuto**-*adj*	cunning	
375	**asunto**-*m*	matter	
1068	**asustado**-*adj*	frightened	

1472	**asustar(se)**-*vb*	scare	
1538	**atacar**-*vb*	attack	
583	**ataque**-*m*	attack	
2134	**ataúd**-*m*	coffin	
380	**atención**-*f*	attention	
2131	**atender**-*vb*	deal with, pay attention	
2326	**aterrizaje**-*m*	landing	
2171	**aterrizar**-*vb*	land	
2285	**atmósfera**-*f*	atmosphere	
1701	**atractivo**-*adj; m*	attractive; attraction	
1447	**atrapar**-*vb*	catch	
269	**atrás**-*adv; int*	behind; get back	
2510	**atravesar**-*vb*	cross	
1584	**atreverse**-*vbr*	dare	
2139	**aumento**-*m*	increase	
141	**aún**-*adv*	yet, still	
238	**aunque**-*con*	although	
2361	**ausencia**-*f*	absence	
1849	**auténtico**-*adj*	authentic	
844	**autobús**-*m*	bus	
244	**auto**-*m*	car (LA)	
2182	**autopista**-*f*	freeway	
1448	**autoridad**-*f*	authority	
2197	**autorización**-*f*	authorization	
2166	**autor**-*m*	author	
1481	**auxilio**-*m; int*	help; help	
2113	**ave**-*m*	bird	
1407	**aventura**-*f*	adventure, affair	
1212	**averiguar**-*vb*	find out	
447	**avión**-*m*	plane	
2421	**avisar**-*vb*	warn	
1432	**aviso**-*m*	warning	
394	**ayer**-*adv; m*	yesterday; past	
303	**ay**-*int*	ouch, oh dear	
220	**ayuda**-*f*	help	
1550	**ayudante**-*adj; m*	assistant; assistant	
391	**ayudar**-*vb*	help	
1276	**azúcar**-*m*	sugar	
675	**azul**-*adj*	blue	

B

2295	**bahía**-*f*	bay	

2147	**bailarín**-*m*	dancer
558	**bailar**-*vb*	dance
797	**bajar(se)**-*vb*	lower
234	**bajo**-*adj; prp; m*	low, small; under; bass
1058	**bala**-*f*	bullet
2046	**balón**-*m*	ball
563	**banco**-*m*	bank, bench
693	**banda**-*f*	band
1510	**bandera**-*f*	flag
415	**baño**-*m*	bathroom
1628	**barato**-*adj*	cheap
1867	**barba**-*f*	beard
409	**barco**-*m*	ship
646	**bar**-*m*	bar
1790	**barón**-*m*	baron
1952	**barra**-*f*	bar
1046	**barrio**-*m*	neighborhood
2479	**barro**-*m*	mud
708	**base**-*f*	base
1743	**básico**-*adj*	basic
267	**bastante**-*adv; adj*	quite a bit; enough
266	**basto**-*adj*	coarse, rude
552	**basura**-*f*	garbage
787	**batalla**-*f*	battle
1949	**batería**-*f*	battery, drums
341	**bebé**-*m*	baby
547	**beber(se)**-*vb*	drink
1229	**bebida**-*f*	drink
775	**belleza**-*f*	beauty
790	**bello**-*adj*	beautiful
1435	**bendecir**-*vb*	bless
2115	**bendición**-*f*	blessing
2385	**bendito**-*adj*	blessed
2400	**beneficio**-*m*	benefit
1945	**besar**-*vb*	kiss
718	**beso**-*m*	kiss
1259	**bestia**-*f*	beast
1490	**Biblia**-*f*	Bible
1532	**biblioteca**-*f*	library
1641	**bicicleta**-*f*	bicycle
21	**bien**-*adj; adv; m*	well; well; good
659	**bienvenido**-*adj; int*	welcome; welcome
2428	**bigote**-*m*	mustache
1646	**billete**-*m*	ticket, bill
421	**blanco**-*adj; m*	white; target
379	**boca**-*f*	mouth
593	**boda**-*f*	wedding
1215	**bola**-*f*	ball
2108	**boleto**-*m*	ticket
742	**bolsa**-*f*	bag
1242	**bolsillo**-*m*	pocket
1334	**bolso**-*m*	purse
740	**bomba**-*f*	bomb, pump
2198	**bombero**-*m/f*	firefighter
2095	**bondad**-*f*	kindness
396	**bonito**-*adj; m*	pretty; tuna
1785	**borde**-*m*	edge
1066	**a bordo**-*adv*	on board
800	**borracho**-*adj; m*	drunk; drunk
755	**bosque**-*m*	forest
1503	**bota**-*f*	boot
855	**botella**-*f*	bottle
958	**bote**-*m*	boat, pot
1649	**botón**-*m*	button
948	**bravo**-*int*	bravo
724	**brazo**-*m*	arm
1759	**breve**-*adj*	brief
827	**brillante**-*adj*	shiny, bright
2396	**brillar**-*vb*	shine
2024	**brindis**-*m*	toast
2117	**británico**-*adj; m*	British; Briton
569	**broma**-*f*	joke
759	**bromear**-*vb*	joke
1350	**brujo**-*m*	wizard
49	**bueno**-*adj; adv; int*	good; well, okay; enough, well
2157	**burro**-*m*	donkey
340	**buscar**-*vb*	search for
1336	**búsqueda**-*f*	search

C

370	**caballero**-*m*	gentleman, knight
467	**caballo**-*m*	horse
1734	**cabaña**-*f*	cabin
869	**cabello**-*m*	hair
164	**cabeza**-*f*	head
1885	**cabina**-*f*	cabin
1497	**cable**-*m*	cable

803	**cabo**-*m*	ending, corporal	
2246	**cabra**-*f*	goat	
143	**cada**-*adj*	each, every	
1167	**cadáver**-*m*	corpse	
1280	**cadena**-*f*	chain	
812	**caer(se)**-*vb*	fall	
336	**café**-*m*	coffee, coffee shop	
1841	**caída**-*f*	drop	
523	**caja**-*f*	box	
2461	**cajón**-*m*	drawer	
2486	**calcetín**-*m*	sock	
1686	**calidad**-*f*	quality	
595	**caliente**-*adj*	hot	
342	**callar(se)**-*vb*	hush	
327	**calle**-*f*	street	
548	**calma**-*f*	calm	
725	**calmar(se)**-*vb*	calm	
667	**calor**-*m*	heat	
298	**cama**-*f*	bed	
1260	**camarada**-*m/f; m/f*	comrade; pal (coll)	
537	**cámara**-*f*	camera, vault	
1908	**camarero**-*m*	waiter	
439	**cambiar(se)**-*vb*	swap, change	
353	**cambio**-*m*	change	
788	**caminar**-*vb*	walk	
190	**camino**-*m*	way	
1275	**camioneta**-*f*	van	
802	**camión**-*m*	truck	
1035	**camisa**-*f*	shirt	
2279	**camiseta**-*f*	shirt	
1152	**campamento**-*m*	campsite	
2272	**campana**-*f*	bell	
1443	**campaña**-*f*	campaign	
2102	**campeonato**-*m*	championship	
1093	**campeón**-*m*	champion	
2491	**campesino**-*m; adj*	peasant; rural	
407	**campo**-*m*	field, countryside	
2183	**canalla**-*m/f; adj*	swine (coll); despicable	
1308	**canal**-*m*	channel	
1514	**cáncer**-*m*	cancer	
487	**canción**-*f*	song	
1751	**cañón**-*m*	cannon	

928	**cansado**-*adj*	tired	
701	**cansar(se)**-*vb*	tire, bother	
1712	**cantante**-*m/f*	singer	
796	**cantar**-*vb*	sing	
1057	**cantidad**-*f*	amount	
1895	**canto**-*m*	singing	
1844	**caos**-*m*	chaos	
1766	**capacidad**-*f*	capacity	
2073	**capa**-*f*	layer	
642	**capaz**-*adj*	capable	
1692	**capital**-*adj; f; m*	primary; capital; resources	
249	**capitán**-*m*	captain	
2039	**capítulo**-*m*	chapter	
2277	**capullo**-*m*	cocoon, idiot (ES) (coll)	
1612	**carácter**-*m*	personality	
229	**cara**-*f*	face, side	
1463	**caramba**-*int*	good grief, damn	
1125	**caray**-*int*	damn it, heck	
2304	**carbón**-*m*	carbon	
530	**cárcel**-*f*	prison	
954	**carga**-*f*	load, burden	
1955	**cargar**-*vb*	load	
643	**cargo**-*m*	position, charge	
1917	**caridad**-*f*	charity	
169	**cariño**-*m*	affection, darling	
543	**carne**-*f*	meat	
1381	**caro**-*adj*	expensive	
554	**carrera**-*f*	career, race	
1010	**carretera**-*f*	road	
1022	**carro**-*m*	car (LA), cart	
402	**carta**-*f*	letter	
2194	**cartel**-*m*	poster	
1665	**cartera**-*f*	wallet, schoolbag	
1151	**casado**-*adj; m*	married; married person	
55	**casa**-*f*	house	
728	**casar**-*vb*	marry	
2053	**casco**-*m*	helmet	
184	**casi**-*adv*	almost	
1980	**casino**-*m*	casino	
205	**caso**-*m*	case	
1353	**castigo**-*m*	punishment	

1352	casualidad-*f*	chance	
629	causa-*f*	cause	
2175	causar-*vb*	cause	
2180	cazador-*m*	hunter	
1341	caza-*f*	hunt	
1824	cazar-*vb*	hunt	
1486	celda-*f*	cell	
1587	celebrar-*vb*	celebrate	
1613	celoso-*adj*	jealous	
1499	celular-*m*	cell phone (LA)	
1558	cementerio-*m*	cemetery	
484	cena-*f*	dinner	
574	cenar-*vb*	have dinner	
2112	ceniza-*f*	ash	
1218	centavo-*m*	penny	
918	central-*adj; f*	central; headquarters	
496	centro-*m*	center	
241	cerca-*adv; f*	near; fence	
1886	cercano-*adj*	nearby	
782	cerdo-*m*	pig	
623	cerebro-*m*	brain	
1601	ceremonia-*f*	ceremony	
1244	cero-*num*	zero	
995	cerrado-*adj*	closed	
665	cerrar-*vb*	close	
2331	certeza-*f*	certainty	
577	cerveza-*f*	beer	
1880	champán-*m*	champagne	
2148	chance-*m/f*	chance (LA)	
1271	chaqueta-*f*	jacket	
832	charlar-*vb*	chat	
2203	chaval-*m*	kid (ES) (coll)	
1206	cheque-*m*	check	
158	chico-*m; adj*	boy; small	
2485	chimenea-*f*	hearth	
926	chino-*adj; m*	Chinese; Chinese person	
1132	chocolate-*m*	chocolate	
2244	chófer-*m/f*	driver	
1104	ciego-*adj*	blind	
318	cielo-*m*	sky	
674	cien(to)-*num*	hundred	
1191	ciencia-*f*	science	
1711	científico-*adj; m/f*	scientific; scientist	

153	cierto-*adj; adv*	true, one; certainly	
1170	cigarro-*m*	cigar	
1795	cima-*f*	top	
232	cinco-*num*	five	
1642	cincuenta-*num*	fifty	
626	cine-*m*	cinema	
986	cinta-*f*	ribbon, tape	
1708	cinturón-*m*	belt	
1567	circo-*m*	circus	
1779	círculo-*m*	circle	
1496	circunstancia-*f*	circumstance	
2145	cirugía-*f*	surgery	
2066	cita-*f*	appointment, date	
536	citar-*vb*	quote, make an appointment	
1580	ciudadano-*m; adj*	citizen; civic	
195	ciudad-*f*	city	
1557	civil-*adj; m/f*	civil; civilian	
2156	civilización-*f*	civilization	
2324	clan-*m*	clan	
100	claro-*adj; int; m*	clear, light; of course; clearing	
250	clase-*f*	classroom, kind	
2444	clásico-*adj*	classic	
1395	clave-*f*	key	
772	cliente-*m/f*	customer, client	
1626	clima-*m*	climate	
1788	clínica-*f*	clinic	
588	club-*m*	club	
1098	cobarde-*adj; m/f*	cowardly; coward	
2149	cobrar-*vb*	collect, charge	
2130	coca-*f*	cocaine	
2320	cocaína-*f*	cocaine	
277	coche-*m*	car (ES)	
620	cocina-*f*	kitchen	
1637	cocinar-*vb*	cook	
2489	cocinero-*m*	cook	
982	código-*m*	code	
946	coger-*vb*	take, f*ck (LA)	
1609	coincidencia-*f*	coincidence	
1028	cola-*f*	tail	
1920	colección-*f*	collection	
1277	colega-*m/f*	colleague, friend	
912	colegio-*m*	school	

2015	**colgar(se)**-*vb*	hang, hang up
1555	**colina**-*f*	hill
1909	**collar**-*m*	necklace
2419	**colonia**-*f*	colony
672	**color**-*m*	color
2041	**columna**-*f*	column
1480	**coma**-*f; m*	comma; coma
636	**comandante**-*m/f*	major
2125	**comando**-*m*	commando
1052	**combate**-*m*	combat
2192	**combinación**-*f*	combination
1511	**combustible**-*m; adj*	fuel; combustible
1025	**comedor**-*m*	dining room
2248	**comedor**-*m*	dining room
2222	**comentario**-*m*	comment
972	**comenzar**-*vb*	start
260	**comer(se)**-*vb*	eat
1544	**comercial**-*adj*	commercial
2275	**comercio**-*m*	shop
2094	**cometer**-*vb*	commit
1719	**cometido**-*m*	mission
1020	**comienzo**-*m*	beginning
1865	**comisaría**-*f*	police station
1250	**comisario**-*m*	commissioner
1685	**comisión**-*f*	commission
1370	**comité**-*m*	committee
43	**cómo**-*adv*	how, why
27	**como**-*adv; con; prp*	as, like; since, because; as
1431	**cómodo**-*adj*	comfortable
698	**compañero**-*m*	partner
426	**compañía**-*f*	company, firm
1319	**compartir**-*vb*	share
1905	**compasión**-*f*	sympathy
1670	**competencia**-*f*	competition, rival
2240	**complejo**-*adj; m*	complex; complex
529	**completo**-*adj*	full
1351	**complicado**-*adj*	complicated
1519	**comportamiento**-*m*	behavior
1205	**compra**-*f*	purchase
463	**comprar(se)**-*vb*	buy
853	**comprender**-*vb*	understand
2342	**comprobar**-*vb*	check

1379	**compromiso**-*m*	commitment, dilemma
1356	**computadora**-*f*	computer (LA)
763	**común**-*adj; m*	common; majority
1871	**comunicación**-*f*	communication
1323	**comunidad**-*f*	community
1963	**comunista**-*adj; m/f*	communist; communist
2374	**concentración**-*f*	concentration
2187	**concepto**-*m*	concept
1366	**concertar**-*vb*	arrange
1241	**conciencia**-*f*	conscience
2394	**conclusión**-*f*	conclusion
1770	**concurso**-*m*	contest
1595	**condado**-*m*	county
1192	**conde**-*m*	count
2167	**condena**-*f*	conviction
1631	**condenar**-*vb*	condemn
1850	**condesa**-*f*	countess
2406	**condicional**-*adj*	conditional
1117	**condición**-*f*	condition
1036	**conducir**-*vb*	drive, lead
1946	**conducta**-*f*	behavior
1560	**conductor**-*m*	driver
1693	**conejo**-*m*	rabbit
1619	**conexión**-*f*	connection
1697	**conferencia**-*f*	conference
2048	**confesión**-*f*	confession
857	**confianza**-*f*	confidence, trust
793	**confiar**-*vb*	trust
2017	**confundir(se)**-*vb; vbr*	confuse; make a mistake
2312	**confusión**-*f*	confusion
1929	**congreso**-*m*	congress
132	**conmigo**-*prn*	with me
261	**conocer(se)**-*vb*	know, meet
1439	**conocimiento**-*m*	knowledge
15	**con**-*prp*	with
1857	**consciente**-*adj*	aware
1823	**consecuencia**-*f*	consequence
417	**conseguir**-*vb*	get, achieve
652	**consejo**-*m*	advice, council
1994	**considerar(se)**-*vb*	consider
1232	**consigo**-*prn*	with her, with him
2375	**conspiración**-*f*	conspiracy

2209	**constante**-*adj*	constant
1813	**construcción**-*f*	construction
1221	**construir**-*vb*	build
2333	**consuelo**-*m*	relief
661	**contacto**-*m*	contact
700	**contar**-*vb*	count, tell
2330	**contener(se)**-*vb*	contain
877	**contento**-*adj; m*	happy; happiness
1478	**contestar**-*vb*	answer
2468	**continuación**-*f*	continuation
981	**continuar**-*vb*	continue
2422	**continuo**-*adj*	continuous
181	**contra**-*prp; m*	against; cons
848	**contrario**-*adj; m/f*	contrary; foe
878	**contrato**-*m*	contract
1357	**controlar(se)**-*vb*	control
440	**control**-*m*	control
1882	**convencer**-*vb*	convince
2105	**convenir**-*vb*	be advisable
1019	**conversación**-*f*	conversation
2299	**conversar**-*vb*	talk
1289	**convertir(se)**-*vb*	change, transform
732	**copa**-*f*	cup
1406	**copia**-*f*	copy
2173	**copiar**-*vb*	copy
1644	**coraje**-*m*	courage
217	**corazón**-*m*	heart
1894	**corbata**-*f*	tie
2513	**cordero**-*m*	lamb
2357	**coro**-*m*	choir
1722	**corona**-*f*	crown
483	**coronel**-*m/f*	colonel
371	**correcto**-*adj; int*	correct; right
2063	**corredor**-*m*	corridor, runner
1116	**correo**-*m*	mail
575	**correr**-*vb*	run
1083	**corriente**-*adj; f*	common; current, electricity
2043	**cortado**-*adj; m*	shy; coffee
622	**cortar(se)**-*vb*	cut
1107	**corto**-*adj*	short
84	**cosa**-*f*	thing
2292	**cosecha**-*f*	harvest
1836	**costado**-*m*	side
880	**costa**-*f*	coast
856	**costar**-*vb*	cost
1505	**costumbre**-*f*	custom
2278	**creación**-*f*	creation
609	**crear**-*vb*	create
1518	**crecer**-*vb*	grow
1345	**crédito**-*m*	credit
322	**creer(se)**-*vb*	believe, think
1679	**crema**-*f*	cream
1999	**cretino**-*adj; m*	stupid; idiot
2273	**criado**-*m*	servant
2453	**criar**-*vb*	raise
1267	**criatura**-*f*	creature
695	**crimen**-*m*	crime
1228	**criminal**-*adj; m/f*	criminal; criminal
1454	**crisis**-*f*	crisis
1650	**cristal**-*m*	crystal
2307	**cristiano**-*adj; m*	Christian; Christian
1266	**cruel**-*adj*	cruel
1455	**cruzar**-*vb*	cross
1253	**cruz**-*f*	cross
1506	**cuadro**-*m*	painting, frame
208	**cuál**-*prn*	what, which
383	**cual**-*prn; adv*	whom; as
185	**cualquier**-*adj*	any, whatever
1495	**cuán**-*adv*	how
235	**cuándo**-*adv*	when
41	**cuando**-*adv; con; prp*	when; since, if; when
308	**cuanto**-*prn*	the more, whatever
188	**cuánto**-*prn*	how many, how long
1930	**cuarenta**-*num*	forty
1739	**cuartel**-*m*	headquarters
317	**cuarto**-*num; m*	fourth; room
245	**cuatro**-*num*	four
2408	**Cuba**-*f*	Cuba
1488	**cubrir(se)**-*vb*	cover
913	**cuchillo**-*m*	knife
747	**cuello**-*m*	neck
1078	**cuenta**-*f*	bill, account
1956	**cuento**-*m*	story
1281	**cuerda**-*f*	rope, cord
2298	**cuerdo**-*adj*	sane

2234	cuero-*m*	leather	
281	cuerpo-*m*	body	
719	cuestión-*f*	matter	
1948	cueva-*f*	cave	
177	cuidado-*m; int*	care; watch out	
968	cuidar(se)-*vb*	look after	
485	culo-*m*	butt	
754	culpable-*adj; m/f*	guilty; culprit	
286	culpar(se)-*vb*	blame	
1600	cultura-*f*	culture	
555	cumpleaños-*m*	birthday	
1923	cumplido-*m; adj*	compliment; courteous	
1312	cumplir(se)-*vb; vbr*	accomplish; expire	
1096	cura-*m; f*	priest; cure	
1414	curiosidad-*f*	curiosity	
1262	curioso-*adj*	curious	
1143	curso-*m*	course	
2153	custodiar-*vb*	flank	
2097	cuyo-*adj*	whose	

D

689	dama-*f*	lady	
459	daño-*m*	damage	
2391	danza-*f*	dance	
393	dar(se) pena-*phr*	feel sorry	
178	dar(se)-*vb*	give	
994	dar-*vb*	give	
847	datar-*vb*	date back to	
1291	dato-*m*	fact	
758	de repente-*adv*	suddenly	
697	debajo-*adv*	under	
130	deber(se)-*m; vb; vbr*	duty; must; owe	
2286	deberes-*mpl*	homework	
1061	débil-*adj; m/f*	weak; weakling	
2164	debilidad-*f*	weakness	
1527	decente-*adj*	proper	
807	decidir(se)-*vb*	decide	
77	decir(se)-*vb*	say, tell, speak	
638	decisión-*f*	decision	
1263	declaración-*f*	statement	
2452	dedicar(se)-*vb*	devote	
900	dedo-*m*	finger	
1910	defender(se)-*vb*	defend	

785	defensa-*f*	defense	
983	definitivo-*adj*	definitive	
198	dejar(se)-*vb*	leave, allow	
561	delante-*adv*	before, in front	
25	del-*contr*	of the, for the (de+el)	
2381	delicado-*adj*	delicate	
1706	delicioso-*adj*	delicious	
1814	delito-*m*	crime	
2124	demanda-*f*	demand	
351	demás-*adj*	the rest	
147	demasiado-*adv*	too much	
2158	democracia-*f*	democracy	
382	demonio-*m*	demon	
1571	demostrar-*vb*	prove, show	
2484	dentista-*m/f*	dentist	
194	dentro-*adv*	inside, within	
670	departamento-*m*	department, apartment (LA)	
762	depender-*vb*	depend	
2020	deporte-*m*	sport	
1775	depósito-*m*	deposit, warehouse	
780	deprisa-*adv; int*	quickly; hurry	
1	de-*prp*	of, from	
367	derecho-*adj; adv; m*	right; straight; law	
2207	desafío-*m*	challenge	
2213	desafortunado-*adj*	unlucky	
1540	desagradable-*adj*	unpleasant	
1110	desaparecer-*vb*	disappear	
2188	desarrollo-*m*	development	
957	desastre-*m*	disaster	
1979	desayunar-*vb*	have breakfast	
1043	desayuno-*m*	breakfast	
933	descansar-*vb*	rest	
977	descanso-*m*	rest	
1677	desconocer-*vb*	not know, not recognize	
1294	descubrir-*vb*	discover	
103	desde-*prp*	from, since	
717	desear-*vb*	wish	
460	deseo-*m*	wish	
2259	desesperado-*adj; m*	desperate; desperate	
2227	desfile-*m*	parade	

1048	**desgraciado**-*adj; m*	jerk (coll), miserable; scoundrel (coll)	973	**director**-*m*	director

1048	**desgraciado**-*adj; m*	jerk (coll), miserable; scoundrel (coll)	973	**director**-*m*	director
1210	**desgracia**-*f*	misfortune	1608	**dirigir**-*vb*	lead, address
1084	**desierto**-*adj; m*	desert; desert	2293	**disciplina**-*f*	discipline
1754	**desnudo**-*adj; m*	naked; nude	1135	**disco**-*m*	disk
2261	**desorden**-*m*	disturbance, chaos	576	**disculpa**-*f*	apology
1363	**despacho**-*m*	office	378	**disculpar(se)**-*vb; vbr*	forgive; apologize
806	**despacio**-*adv*	slowly	1202	**discurso**-*m*	speech
1625	**despedir(se)**-*vb; vbr*	dismiss, lay off; say goodbye	1875	**discusión**-*f*	argument, debate
2185	**despejar(se)**-*vb; vbr*	clear; clear your mind	1115	**discutir**-*vb*	argue
1618	**despertar(se)**-*m; vb*	awakening; wake up	1984	**diseño**-*m*	design
705	**despierto**-*adj*	awake	2520	**disfraz**-*m*	costume
102	**después**-*adv; adj*	after; after, later	1763	**disfrutar**-*vb*	enjoy
578	**destino**-*m*	destination, fate	988	**disparar(se)**-*vb*	shoot
1807	**destrucción**-*f*	destruction	1826	**disparo**-*m*	shot
1160	**destruir**-*vb*	destroy	1154	**disponer(se)**-*vb; vbr*	arrange, have; get ready
1033	**detalle**-*m*	detail	1832	**disponible**-*adj*	available
795	**detective**-*m*	detective	2420	**disposición**-*f*	aptitude, disposal
1226	**detener(se)**-*vb*	stop	2409	**dispuesto**-*adj*	handy (ES), ready
373	**detrás**-*adv*	behind	947	**distancia**-*f*	distance
1515	**deuda**-*f*	debt	1364	**distinto**-*adj*	different
1978	**devolver**-*vb*	return	2430	**distinto**-*adj*	different
313	**diablo**-*m*	devil	1541	**distrito**-*m*	district
82	**día**-*m*	day	1269	**diversión**-*f*	fun
1546	**diamante**-*m*	diamond	472	**divertido**-*adj*	funny
914	**diario**-*adj; m*	daily; diary, newspaper	2462	**divino**-*adj*	divine
2174	**dibujo**-*m*	drawing	1676	**división**-*f*	division, split
1964	**diciembre**-*m*	December	1458	**divorcio**-*m*	divorce
804	**diente**-*m*	tooth	753	**doble**-*adj; adv*	double; double
2436	**dieta**-*f*	diet	2075	**docena**-*f*	dozen
349	**diez**-*num*	ten	1297	**doce**-*num*	twelve
696	**diferencia**-*f*	difference	252	**doctor**-*m*	doctor
443	**diferente**-*adj*	different	1378	**documento**-*m*	document
270	**difícil**-*adj*	difficult	288	**dólar**-*m*	dollar
2360	**dificultad**-*f*	difficulty	454	**dolor**-*m*	pain
2002	**dignidad**-*f*	dignity	2493	**doloroso**-*adj*	painful
2189	**digno**-*adj*	worthy	885	**domingo**-*m*	Sunday
94	**dinero**-*m*	money	2352	**doña**-*f*	miss, lady
68	**dios**-*m*	god, deity	60	**dónde**-*adv*	where
507	**dirección**-*f*	direction, management	109	**donde**-*adv; prp*	where; with
984	**directo**-*adj*	direct	1484	**don**-*m*	talent
			2407	**dorado**-*adj*	golden
			894	**dormido**-*adj*	asleep
			293	**dormir(se)**-*vb*	sleep

1664	**dormitorio**-*m*	bedroom	
2386	**dosis**-*f*	dose	
62	**dos**-*num*	two	
1709	**dragón**-*m*	dragon	
2483	**drama**-*m*	drama	
729	**drogar(se)**-*vb*	drug	
1547	**ducha**-*f*	shower	
592	**duda**-*f*	doubt	
1177	**dudar**-*vb*	doubt	
2359	**duelo**-*m*	duel	
937	**dueño**-*m*	owner	
519	**dulce**-*adj; m*	sweet; candy	
1588	**duque**-*m*	duke	
199	**durante**-*prp*	during	
2502	**durar**-*vb*	last	
376	**duro**-*adj; adv*	hard; hard	

E

938	**echar(se)**-*vb; vbr*	kick, pour; lie down
2118	**economía**-*f*	economy
424	**edad**-*f*	age
2371	**edición**-*f*	edition
651	**edificio**-*m*	building
2230	**editor**-*m*	editor
1217	**educación**-*f*	education
1220	**efectivo**-*m; adj*	cash; effective
1003	**efecto**-*m*	effect
1776	**egoísta**-*adj; m/f*	selfish; selfish person
137	**eh**-*int*	hey
2254	**ejecución**-*f*	execution
585	**ejemplo**-*m*	example
1741	**ejercicio**-*m*	exercise
462	**ejército**-*m*	army
5	**el**-*art*	the
1021	**elección**-*f*	choice
1854	**electricidad**-*f*	electricity
2245	**eléctrico**-*adj*	electric
2260	**elefante**-*m*	elephant
1405	**elegante**-*adj*	elegant
1142	**elegir**-*vb*	choose
2471	**elemento**-*m*	element
2362	**eliminar**-*vb*	remove
42	**ella**-*prn*	she
19	**él**-*prn*	he

2126	**embajada**-*f*	embassy
1961	**embajador**-*m*	ambassador
960	**embarazar**-*vb*	get pregnant
939	**emergencia**-*f*	emergency
1563	**emocionante**-*adj*	exciting
1784	**emoción**-*f*	emotion
1169	**emperador**-*m*	emperor
406	**empezar**-*vb*	begin
1803	**emplear(se)**-*vb*	use
1007	**empleo**-*m*	employment
990	**empresa**-*f*	company
2401	**empujar**-*vb*	push
843	**enamorar(se)**-*vb*	make someone fall in love
2440	**enano**-*m; adj*	shorty; very small
1180	**encantador**-*adj*	charming
477	**encantar**-*vb*	love, bewitch
1876	**encargar(se)**-*vb; vbr*	order, request; take charge of
1401	**encargo**-*m*	errand
2155	**encender**-*vb*	turn on
1843	**encerrar(se)**-*vb*	lock somebody up
381	**encima**-*adv*	on top of, not only that
279	**encontrar(se)**-*vb*	find
603	**encuentro**-*m*	meeting, match
671	**enemigo**-*m*	enemy
741	**energía**-*f*	energy
2247	**enero**-*m*	January
1627	**enfadar(se)**-*vb*	irritate
899	**enfermedad**-*f*	disease
1129	**enfermero**-*m*	nurse
600	**enfermo**-*adj; m*	ill; sick person
2380	**enfrentar**-*vb*	confront
1473	**enfrente**-*adv*	opposite
1953	**engañar**-*vb*	deceive
2220	**engaño**-*m*	deception
1941	**enhorabuena**-*f; int*	congratulations; congratulations
1305	**enojar(se)**-*vb*	anger
831	**enorme**-*adj*	huge
8	**en**-*prp*	in, on, about
2120	**ensalada**-*f*	salad
1811	**ensayo**-*m*	rehearsal, essay
445	**enseguida**-*adv*	immediately
1444	**enseñar**-*vb*	teach, show

216	**entender**-*vb*	understand	
2014	**enterarse**-*vbr*	realize, find out	
936	**entero**-*adj*	entire	
2042	**enterrar(se)**-*vb*	bury	
65	**entonces**-*adv*	then, so	
768	**entrada**-*f*	entry	
262	**entrar**-*vb*	get in	
1485	**entrega**-*f*	delivery	
1805	**entregar**-*vb*	deliver	
1064	**entrenador**-*m*	coach	
1408	**entrenamiento**-*m*	training	
150	**entre**-*prp*	between, among	
1361	**entrevistar**-*vb*	interview	
1038	**enviar**-*vb*	send	
2427	**envío**-*m*	shipping	
2501	**episodio**-*m*	episode	
822	**época**-*f*	era, time	
1577	**equipaje**-*m*	luggage	
306	**equipo**-*m*	team, gear	
668	**equivocar(se)**-*vb; vbr*	confuse; be mistaken	
449	**error**-*m*	mistake	
2219	**escala**-*f*	ladder	
1344	**escalera**-*f*	staircase	
1672	**escándalo**-*m*	scandal	
748	**escapar(se)**-*vb*	escape	
1789	**escape**-*m*	escape	
602	**escena**-*f*	scene	
1097	**escenario**-*m*	stage, scene	
1671	**esclavo**-*m*	slave	
2091	**escoger**-*vb*	choose	
2496	**escolar**-*adj; m/f*	school; schoolchild	
1630	**esconder(se)**-*vb*	hide	
596	**escribir**-*vb*	write	
1579	**escritorio**-*m*	desk	
1445	**escritor**-*m*	writer	
2012	**escuadrón**-*m*	squadron	
236	**escuchar(se)**-*vb*	listen	
273	**escuela**-*f*	school	
23	**ese**-*adj; prn*	that; that one	
1257	**esfuerzo**-*m*	effort	
1831	**espacial**-*adj*	spatial	
676	**espacio**-*m*	space	
859	**espada**-*f*	sword	
691	**espalda**-*f*	back	
1586	**España**-*f*	Spain	
1629	**español**-*adj; m*	Spanish; Spaniard	
2318	**espantoso**-*adj*	frightening	
363	**especial**-*adj*	special	
751	**especie**-*f*	species, kind	
870	**espectáculo**-*m*	show	
1258	**espejo**-*m*	mirror	
1126	**espera**-*f*	wait	
727	**esperanza**-*f*	hope	
1713	**esperanza**-*f*	hope	
122	**esperar(se)**-*vb*	wait	
1700	**espía**-*m/f*	spy	
2344	**espiritual**-*adj*	spiritual	
730	**espíritu**-*m*	spirit	
1462	**esposa**-*f*	wife	
206	**esposar(se)**-*vb*	handcuff	
1102	**esquina**-*f*	corner	
2321	**estacionamiento**-*m*	parking	
649	**estación**-*f*	station, season	
2446	**estadio**-*m*	stadium	
124	**estado**-*m*	condition, government	
1851	**estadounidense**-*adj; m*	American; American person	
17	**estar(se)**-*vb*	be	
2169	**estatal**-*adj*	state	
2060	**estatua**-*f*	statue	
32	**este**-*adj; prn; m*	this; this one; east	
703	**estilo**-*m*	style	
2519	**estimar**-*vb*	estimate, respect	
1156	**estómago**-*m*	stomach	
2338	**estrategia**-*f*	strategy	
647	**estrella**-*f*	star	
2225	**estructura**-*f*	structure	
1231	**estudiante**-*m/f*	student	
1179	**estudiar**-*vb*	study	
1607	**estudio**-*m*	studio, survey	
706	**estupendo**-*adj*	wonderful	
1566	**estupidez**-*f*	stupidity	
464	**estúpido**-*adj; m*	stupid; idiot, jerk	
2146	**eternidad**-*f*	eternity	
2034	**eterno**-*adj*	eternal	

949	**Europa**-*f*	Europe
2080	**evento**-*m*	event
2336	**evidente**-*adj*	apparent
817	**evitar**-*vb*	avoid
328	**exacto**-*adj; adv*	identical, exact; exactly
1236	**examen**-*m*	exam
1272	**excelencia**-*f*	excellence
601	**excelente**-*adj; int*	excellent; great
2282	**excepción**-*f*	exception
711	**excepto**-*prp*	except
1442	**excusa**-*f*	excuse
1787	**existencia**-*f*	existence
564	**existir**-*vb*	exist
1373	**éxito**-*m*	success
2050	**expediente**-*m*	record
726	**experiencia**-*f*	experience
1863	**experimento**-*m*	experiment
1507	**experto**-*adj; m*	expert; expert
1535	**explicación**-*f*	explanation
1080	**explicar(se)**-*vb*	explain
1494	**explosión**-*f*	explosion
2459	**explosivo**-*adj; m*	explosive; explosive
1951	**explotar**-*vb*	explode, exploit
2343	**exposición**-*f*	exposure
1736	**expresión**-*f*	expression
1536	**exterior**-*m; adj*	exterior; external
1148	**extra**-*adv; mpl*	extra; extras
842	**extrañar(se)**-*vb*	surprise, miss
1422	**extranjero**-*adj; m*	foreign; foreigner
354	**extraño**-*adj; m*	strange; stranger
1774	**extraordinario**-*adj*	extraordinary
2402	**extremado**-*adj*	extreme
2140	**extremo**-*adj; m*	extreme; end

F

1105	**fábrica**-*f*	factory
1742	**fabuloso**-*adj*	fabulous
289	**fácil**-*adj*	easy
1891	**fallar**-*vb*	fail
1225	**false**-*adj*	false, fake

321	**falta**-*f*	offense, shortage
1469	**faltar**-*vb*	lack, miss
1921	**fama**-*f*	fame
168	**familia**-*f*	family
1026	**familiar**-*adj*	family, familiar
1899	**fantasía**-*f*	fantasy
1492	**fantasma**-*m*	ghost
655	**fantástico**-*adj*	fantastic
2025	**fascinante**-*adj*	fascinating
2162	**fase**-*f*	phase
1883	**fatal**-*adj*	fatal
1327	**favorito**-*adj; m*	favorite; favorite
1343	**fecha**-*f*	date
1569	**federal**-*adj*	federal
752	**fe**-*f*	faith
858	**felicidad**-*f*	happiness
1181	**felicitación**-*f*	congratulations
202	**feliz**-*adj*	happy
2265	**fenómeno**-*m*	phenomenon
1279	**feo**-*adj*	ugly
2206	**feria**-*f*	fair
2022	**festival**-*m*	festival
2302	**fianza**-*f*	bail, deposit
1460	**fiebre**-*f*	fever
1737	**fiel**-*adj; m*	faithful; believer
296	**fiesta**-*f*	party, holiday
1818	**figura**-*f*	figure
1548	**fijar(se)**-*vb; vbr*	set; pay attention to
1371	**fila**-*f*	row
2411	**filmar**-*vb*	film
2379	**filosofía**-*f*	philosophy
272	**final**-*adj; m*	last; end
2047	**fingir**-*vb*	pretend
228	**fin**-*m*	end, purpose
1144	**firma**-*f*	signature, firm
1449	**firmar**-*vb*	sign
1155	**firme**-*adj; adv*	firm; steady, firmly
1298	**fiscal**-*adj; m/f*	fiscal; district attorney
1800	**físico**-*adj; m/f*	physical; physicist
657	**flor**-*f*	flower
1724	**flota**-*f*	fleet

633	**fondo**-*m*	bottom	
2335	**formación**-*f*	training	
200	**forma**-*f*	form, way	
2036	**formar**-*vb*	form, train	
2231	**fortaleza**-*f*	fortress, strength	
1015	**fortuna**-*f*	fortune	
493	**foto**-*f*	photo	
1417	**fotografía**-*f*	photograph	
1967	**fotografiar**-*vb*	photograph	
2523	**fracasar**-*vb*	fail	
1889	**fracaso**-*m*	failure	
915	**francés**-*adj; m*	French; French person	
779	**Francia**-*f*	France	
1483	**franco**-*adj*	honest	
1705	**frase**-*f*	phrase	
2368	**fraude**-*m*	fraud	
1935	**frecuencia**-*f*	frequency	
492	**freír**-*vb*	fry	
372	**frente**-*f*	front, forehead	
1333	**fresco**-*adj; m*	cool, fresh; shameless	
1053	**frío**-*adj; m*	cold; cold	
1161	**frontera**-*f*	border	
2127	**fruta**-*f*	fruit	
332	**fuego**-*m*	fire	
1230	**fuente**-*f*	source, fountain	
263	**fuerte**-*adj; m*	strong; fort	
401	**fuerza**-*f*	strength	
2235	**fuga**-*f*	jailbreak, leak	
1063	**fumar**-*vb*	smoke	
495	**funcionar**-*vb*	work, operate	
1720	**función**-*f*	function	
1197	**funeral**-*m*	funeral	
2114	**furioso**-*adj*	furious	
1032	**fútbol**-*m*	football	
435	**futuro**-*adj; m*	future; future	

G

1781	**gafas**-*fpl*	glasses	
2488	**galería**-*f*	gallery	
1835	**galleta**-*f*	cookie	
1773	**gallina**-*f; adj*	hen; coward	
1487	**ganador**-*m*	winner	
2290	**ganancia**-*f*	gain	
452	**ganar**-*vb*	win	
1995	**garaje**-*m*	garage	
1471	**garganta**-*f*	throat	
1095	**gas**-*m*	gas	
1399	**gasolina**-*f*	gasoline	
2226	**gastar(se)**-*vb; vbr*	spend, use; wear out	
1755	**gasto**-*m*	spending	
783	**gato**-*m*	cat	
1839	**generación**-*f*	generation	
326	**general**-*adj; m/f*	common; general	
1997	**generoso**-*adj*	generous	
258	**genial**-*adj; adv*	great; wonderful	
997	**genio**-*m*	genius, temper	
92	**gente**-*f*	people	
2480	**gentil**-*adj*	pleasant	
1981	**gerente**-*m/f*	manager	
2274	**gesto**-*m*	gesture	
1605	**gigante**-*adj; m*	gigantic; giant	
2159	**gimnasio**-*m*	gym	
2476	**ginebra**-*f*	gin	
1140	**gira**-*f*	tour	
2268	**giro**-*m*	turn	
2456	**global**-*adj*	global	
2455	**globo**-*m*	balloon	
965	**gloria**-*f*	glory	
1189	**gobernador**-*m*	governor	
488	**gobierno**-*m*	government	
1757	**golf**-*m*	golf	
1780	**golpear(se)**-*vb*	hit	
712	**golpe**-*m*	hit	
963	**gordo**-*adj*	fat	
2074	**gota**-*f*	drop	
2237	**grabación**-*f*	recording	
962	**gracia**-*f*	grace	
47	**gracias**-*f*	thank you	
527	**gracioso**-*adj; m*	amusing; clown	
1436	**grado**-*m*	degree	
2363	**graduación**-*f*	graduation	
230	**grande**-*adj*	big	
1060	**grandioso**-*adj*	grand	
1071	**granja**-*f*	farm	
2466	**granjero**-*m*	farmer	
1699	**grano**-*m*	grain, pimple	

2432	graso-*adj*	fatty, oily	
1014	gratis-*adj; adv*	free; free	
871	grave-*adj*	grave	
2199	gravedad-*f*	gravity	
2481	griego-*adj; m*	Greek; Greek	
1924	gris-*adj*	gray	
1268	gritar-*vb*	scream	
1744	grito-*m*	shout	
2305	grosero-*adj*	rude	
411	grupo-*m*	group	
2064	guante-*m*	glove	
901	guapo-*adj*	good-looking	
1284	guarda-*m/f*	guard	
1561	guardar(se)-*vb; vbr*	keep, retain; take precautions against	
690	guardia-*m/f; f*	police officer; police department	
1890	guau-*int*	wow	
204	guerra-*f*	war	
1988	guerrero-*m; adj*	fighter; warlike	
1413	guía-*m/f; f*	guide; manual	
1386	guion-*m*	script	
1817	guitarra-*f*	guitar	
2280	gusano-*m*	worm	
118	gustar(se)-*vb*	like	
924	gusto-*m*	taste	

H

34	haber-*av; vb*	have; there is, there are	
1834	habilidad-*f*	skill	
330	habitación-*f*	room	
2377	habitual-*adj*	habitual	
1320	habla-*m*	speech	
105	hablar-*vb*	talk, speak	
51	hacer(se)-*vb; vbr*	do, make; move, pretend to be	
192	hacia-*prp*	towards	
1762	hallar(se)-*vb; vbr*	find; be	
2181	hall-*m*	hall	
405	hambre-*m*	hunger	
2403	hambriento-*adj; m*	hungry; hungry person	

1278	harto-*adj*	full, sick of	
75	hasta-*prp; adv*	until, up to; even	
95	hecho-*m; adj*	fact, incident; done, made	
1171	helado-*m; adj*	ice cream; frozen	
1638	helicóptero-*m*	helicopter	
2508	herencia-*f*	heritage	
1145	herida-*f*	wound	
2383	herido-*m; adj*	injured; wounded	
813	herir(se)-*vb*	hurt	
165	hermano-*m*	brother	
432	hermoso-*adj*	beautiful	
801	héroe-*m*	hero	
2045	herramienta-*f*	tool	
794	hielo-*m*	ice	
1389	hierba-*f*	grass	
1680	hierro-*m*	iron	
2478	hígado-*m*	liver	
110	hijo-*m*	son	
196	historia-*f*	history	
895	historial-*m*	history	
639	hogar-*m*	home	
1864	hoja-*f*	leaf, sheet	
59	hola-*int*	hello	
67	hombre-*m*	man	
1684	hombro-*m*	shoulder	
1599	homicidio-*m*	homicide	
1300	honesto-*adj*	honest	
2475	honorable-*adj*	honorable	
514	honor-*m*	honor	
2435	honrado-*adj*	honest	
144	hora-*f*	hour, time	
2239	horario-*m; adj*	schedule; time	
2316	horno-*m*	oven	
525	horrible-*adj*	horrible	
1960	horror-*m*	horror	
385	hospital-*m*	hospital	
410	hotel-*m*	hotel	
123	hoy-*adv*	today, nowadays	
2029	hoyo-*m*	hole	
1916	huelga-*f*	strike	
1162	huella-*f*	footprint, trace	
1304	hueso-*m*	bone	
854	huevo-*m*	egg	

1207	huir-*vb*	run away
1290	humanidad-*f*	humanity, mankind
654	humano-*adj; m*	humane; human
2210	humilde-*adj*	humble
1328	humo-*m*	smoke
935	humor-*m*	mood, humor

I

2454	ida-*f*	going
157	idea-*f*	idea
1732	ideal-*adj; m*	likely, theoretical; ideal
1687	identidad-*f*	identity
1748	identificación-*f*	identification
1947	idioma-*m*	language
309	idiota-*m/f; adj*	idiot; idiotic
560	iglesia-*f*	church
246	igual-*adj; adv; m/f*	like; the same; equal
1554	ilegal-*adj*	illegal
2163	ilusión-*f*	hope, thrill
889	imagen-*f*	image
1441	imaginación-*f*	imagination
996	imaginar(se)-*vb*	imagine
616	imbécil-*m/f; adj*	imbecile; moron
2044	impacto-*m*	impact
2497	impedir-*vb*	prevent
1727	imperio-*m*	empire
1428	imponer(se)-*vb; vbr*	impose; prevail
1082	importancia-*f*	importance
223	importante-*adj*	important
139	importar-*vb*	matter, import
2228	importe-*m*	amount
444	imposible-*adj*	impossible
1390	impresionante-*adj*	impressive
1318	impresión-*f*	impression
2387	incapaz-*adj; m/f*	unable; incompetent
1537	incendio-*m*	fire
1791	incidente-*adj; m*	incidental; incident
2070	incluir-*vb*	include

295	incluso-*adv; adj*	including; even
2236	inconsciente-*adj; m*	unconscious, thoughtless; subconscious
397	increíble-*adj*	incredible
2474	independiente-*adj*	independent
2522	indicar-*vb*	indicate
1237	indio-*adj; m*	Native Indian; Indian
1721	industria-*f*	industry
2004	infancia-*f*	childhood
2151	infantil-*adj*	infantile
1707	infeliz-*adj; m/f*	unhappy; poor thing, fool
539	infierno-*m*	hell
1939	influencia-*f*	influence
480	información-*f*	information
2184	informar(se)-*vb; vbr*	inform; find out
764	informe-*m*	report
1996	ingeniero-*m*	engineer
683	inglés-*adj; m*	English; Englishman
2524	injusto-*adj*	unfair
942	inmediato-*adj*	immediate
833	inocente-*adj; m/f*	naive; innocent
1452	instante-*m*	instant
2309	instinto-*m*	instinct
1424	instituto-*m*	high school
1583	instrucción-*f*	instruction
2429	instrumento-*m*	instrument
1261	inteligencia-*f*	intelligence
679	inteligente-*adj*	intelligent
991	intención-*f*	intention
776	intentar-*vb*	try
666	intento-*m*	attempt
1375	interesado-*adj*	interested, selfish
522	interesante-*adj*	interesting
650	interesar(se)-*vb*	interest
1039	interés-*m*	interest
789	interior-*adj; m*	interior; the inside
1669	internacional-*adj*	international
1611	Internet-*m/f*	Internet
2276	interrumpir-*vb*	interrupt
906	inútil-*adj; m/f*	useless; good-for-nothing

#	Word	Meaning
733	**investigación**-*f*	research
1919	**investigar**-*vb*	investigate
1086	**invierno**-*m*	winter
2144	**invisible**-*adj*	invisible
1750	**invitación**-*f*	invitation
1069	**invitado**-*adj; m*	invited; guest
1178	**invitar**-*vb*	invite
2258	**involucrar(se)**-*vb*	involve
33	**ir(se)**-*vb; vbr*	go; leave
1349	**ira**-*f*	anger
2433	**iris**-*m*	iris
688	**isla**-*f*	island
1551	**italiano**-*adj; m*	Italian; Italian
502	**izquierdo**-*adj*	left

J

#	Word	Meaning
2215	**jabón**-*m*	soap
989	**ja**-*int*	ha
343	**jamás**-*adv*	never
1656	**japonés**-*adj; m*	Japanese; Japanese person
868	**jardín**-*m*	garden
2069	**jaula**-*f*	cage
219	**jefe**-*m*	boss
1869	**jersey**-*m*	jersey
255	**joven**-*adj; m/f*	young; young person
1479	**joya**-*f*	jewel
1166	**judío**-*adj; m*	Jewish; Jew
278	**juego**-*m*	game
1360	**jueves**-*m*	Thursday
682	**juez**-*m*	judge
2079	**jugada**-*f*	play
1400	**jugador**-*m*	player, gambler
348	**jugar**-*vb*	play
1973	**jugo**-*m*	juice (LA)
2143	**juguete**-*m*	toy
702	**juicio**-*m*	judgment, wisdom
1330	**julio**-*m*	July
1698	**junio**-*m*	June
221	**juntos**-*adj*	together
1072	**jurado**-*m*	jury
2190	**juramento**-*m*	oath
518	**jurar**-*vb*	swear, pledge
2443	**justa**-*f*	joust
830	**justicia**-*f*	justice
259	**justo**-*adj; adv*	fair, exact; just
1517	**juventud**-*f*	youth
2392	**juzgar**-*vb*	judge

K

#	Word	Meaning
1457	**kilo**-*m*	kilo
1059	**kilómetro**-*m*	kilometer

L

#	Word	Meaning
1124	**labio**-*m*	lip
1062	**laboratorio**-*m*	laboratory
175	**lado**-*m*	side
917	**ladrón**-*m*	thief
1001	**lago**-*m*	lake
1397	**lágrima**-*f*	tear
420	**lamentar(se)**-*vb; vbr*	regret; feel sorry for yourself
2445	**lámpara**-*f*	lamp
1912	**lanzamiento**-*m*	launch
2119	**lanzar(se)**-*f*	launch
2229	**lápiz**-*m*	pencil
392	**largo**-*adj; int*	long; get out (coll)
821	**lástima**-*f*	shame, pity
2495	**lastimar(se)**-*vb*	hurt
1968	**lavar(se)**-*vb*	wash
2349	**leal**-*adj*	loyal
1877	**lealtad**-*f*	loyalty
1235	**lección**-*f*	lesson
761	**leche**-*f*	milk
2283	**lectura**-*f*	reading
615	**leer**-*vb*	read
1296	**legal**-*adj*	legal
299	**lejos**-*adv*	far away
925	**lengua**-*f*	language, tongue
1624	**lenguaje**-*m*	language
2472	**lente**-*f*	lens
1545	**lento**-*adj; adv*	slow; slowly
1572	**león**-*m*	lion
96	**les**-*prn*	them, to them
1531	**letra**-*f*	letter

826	**levantar(se)**-*vb; vbr*	lift; wake up
1622	**leyenda**-*f*	legend
453	**ley**-*f*	law
2492	**liberación**-*f*	release
2423	**liberar(se)**-*vb*	set free
510	**libertad**-*f*	freedom
1027	**libra**-*f*	pound
361	**libre**-*adj*	free
339	**libro**-*m*	book
1338	**licencia**-*f*	license
2255	**licor**-*m*	liquor
1030	**líder**-*m/f*	leader
2111	**liga**-*f*	league
2504	**ligero**-*adj*	light
1589	**límite**-*m*	limit
1147	**limpiar(se)**-*vb*	clean, tidy
1938	**limpieza**-*f*	cleaning
976	**limpio**-*adj*	clean
532	**lindo**-*adj*	cute (LA)
512	**línea**-*f*	line
1184	**lío**-*m*	mess
1385	**liso**-*adj*	flat
1940	**lista**-*f*	list
247	**listo**-*adj; int*	ready, smart; done
2410	**literal**-*adj*	literal
446	**llamada**-*f*	signal, call
233	**llamar(se)**-*vb; vbr*	call; name
611	**llave**-*f*	key
1728	**llegada**-*f*	arrival
251	**llegar**-*vb*	arrive, reach
2351	**llenar**-*vb*	fill
645	**lleno**-*adj*	full
337	**llevar(se)**-*vb*	take, wear
819	**llorar**-*vb*	cry
922	**lluvia**-*f*	rain
1254	**lobo**-*m*	wolf
1050	**local**-*adj; m*	local; store
212	**loco**-*adj; m*	crazy; lunatic
624	**locura**-*f*	madness
2281	**lógico**-*adj*	logical
1502	**lograr**-*vb*	achieve
1992	**logro**-*m*	achievement
1121	**lord**-*m*	lord
799	**lucha**-*f*	fight
846	**luchar**-*vb*	fight
1797	**lucir(se)**-*vb*	flaunt
126	**luego**-*adv; con*	later, then; therefore
117	**lugar**-*m*	place
501	**luna**-*f*	moon
1077	**lunes**-*m*	Monday
310	**luz**-*f*	light

M

1934	**macho**-*adj; m*	manly; male
1222	**madera**-*f*	wood
114	**madre**-*f*	mother
438	**maestro**-*m*	teacher, master
2224	**mafia**-*f*	mafia
1150	**magia**-*f*	magic
2256	**mágico**-*adj*	magic
1339	**magnífico**-*adj*	magnificent
1936	**mago**-*m*	magician
1922	**maíz**-*m*	corn
905	**Majestad**-*m/f*	Majesty
2405	**maldad**-*f*	wickedness
456	**maldición**-*f; int*	curse; damn
292	**maldito**-*adj*	damn, cursed
1293	**maleta**-*f*	suitcase
2241	**maletín**-*m*	briefcase
133	**mal**-*m; adv; adj*	evil; badly; bad
287	**malo**-*adj; m*	bad; villain
119	**mamá**-*f*	mom
101	**mañana**-*f; m; adv*	morning; future; tomorrow
2267	**mancha**-*f*	stain
1355	**mandar**-*vb*	send, be in charge
837	**mando**-*m*	authority, control
1134	**manejar(se)**-*vb; vbr*	manage, drive (LA); handle yourself
227	**manera**-*f*	way
209	**mano**-*f*	hand
677	**mantener(se)**-*vb*	keep
2176	**mantequilla**-*f*	butter
2457	**manual**-*adj; m*	handmade; manual
1691	**manzana**-*f*	apple
1070	**mapa**-*m*	map

1913	**maquillaje**-*m*	makeup
765	**máquina**-*f*	machine
1292	**maravilla**-*f*	wonder
470	**maravilloso**-*adj*	wonderful
1029	**marca**-*f*	brand, mark
694	**marcha**-*f*	march
1954	**marchar(se)**-*vb; vbr*	march; leave
1534	**marco**-*m*	framework, frame
2518	**marea**-*f*	tide
2200	**marinero**-*m; adj*	sailor; naval
474	**mar**-*m*	sea
1380	**martes**-*m*	Tuesday
2467	**martillo**-*m*	hammer
2090	**marzo**-*m*	March
28	**más**-*adj; adv; m*	more; more; plus
1987	**masa**-*f*	mass, dough
1816	**máscara**-*f*	mask
315	**matar**-*vb*	kill
2434	**matemático**-*adj; m*	mathematical; mathematician
2242	**materia**-*f*	matter
1164	**material**-*adj; m*	material; equipment
579	**matrimonio**-*m*	marriage
1549	**mayo**-*m*	May
632	**mayoría**-*f*	most
2009	**medalla**-*f*	medal
1372	**medianoche**-*f*	midnight
1013	**medicina**-*f*	medicine
437	**médico**-*m; adj*	doctor; medical
1666	**mediodía**-*m*	midday
300	**medio**-*m; adj; adv*	middle, means; half; halfway
1615	**medir(se)**-*vb*	measure
1793	**mejorar**-*vb*	improve
818	**memoria**-*f*	memory
2100	**mencionar**-*vb*	mention
129	**menos**-*adj; adv; prp*	fewer; less; except
479	**mensaje**-*m*	message
2397	**mensajero**-*m*	messenger
1610	**mental**-*adj*	mental
461	**mente**-*f*	mind
723	**mentira**-*f*	lie
1153	**mentiroso**-*m; adj*	liar; liar

1255	**mentir**-*vb*	lie
736	**a menudo**-*adv*	often
934	**mercado**-*m*	market
2217	**mercancía**-*f*	goods
1044	**merecer**-*vb*	deserve
471	**mesa**-*f*	table
276	**mes**-*m*	month
1383	**meta**-*f*	goal
1654	**metal**-*m*	metal
1335	**meter(se)**-*vb*	put, get into
975	**metido**-*adj; m*	inside, nosy (LA); meddler (LA)
2216	**método**-*m*	method
745	**metro**-*m*	metro
2253	**mezcla**-*f*	mixture
87	**mi**-*adj*	my
2334	**micrófono**-*m*	microphone
180	**miedo**-*m*	fear
1302	**miel**-*f*	honey
1172	**miembro**-*m*	member, limb
179	**mientras**-*con; adv*	while; while
1683	**miércoles**-*m*	Wednesday
120	**mierda**-*f; int*	garbage (coll), crap (coll); shit
1136	**milagro**-*m*	miracle
920	**militar**-*adj; m/f*	military; soldier
1168	**milla**-*f*	mile
365	**millón**-*num*	million
350	**mil**-*num*	thousand
1299	**mina**-*f*	mine
1962	**ministerio**-*m*	ministry
835	**ministro**-*m*	minister
215	**minuto**-*m*	minute
136	**mío**-*prn*	mine
931	**mirada**-*f*	look
98	**mirar(se)**-*vb*	look, watch
2303	**misa**-*f*	mass
1598	**miserable**-*adj*	miserable
2223	**miseria**-*f*	misery
2506	**misil**-*m*	missile
637	**misión**-*f*	mission
97	**mismo**-*adj*	same, just
1476	**misterio**-*m*	mystery
2308	**misterioso**-*adj*	mysterious
466	**mitad**-*f*	half

1315	**moda**-*f*	fashion
1085	**modelo**-*m*	model, pattern
2353	**moderno**-*adj*	modern
359	**modo**-*m*	mode
1856	**molestar(se)**-*vb; vbr*	disturb; be offended
1926	**molestia**-*f*	annoyance
699	**molesto**-*adj*	annoying
108	**momento**-*m*	moment
1652	**moneda**-*f*	currency, coin
2509	**monje**-*m*	monk
1224	**mono**-*m; adj*	monkey; cute
874	**monstruo**-*m*	monster
898	**montaña**-*f*	mountain
1523	**montar**-*vb*	mount
1758	**monte**-*m*	hill
635	**montón**-*m*	pile, bunch
1464	**moral**-*adj; f*	moral; morals
265	**morir(se)**-*vb*	die
1648	**mortal**-*adj; m/f*	lethal; mortal
961	**mostrar(se)**-*vb*	show
2121	**motel**-*m*	motel
851	**motivo**-*m; adj*	reason; motive
1690	**moto**-*f*	motorcycle
1182	**motor**-*m; adj*	engine; motor
987	**mover(se)**-*vb*	move
1904	**móvil**-*adj; m*	mobile; cell phone
849	**movimiento**-*m*	movement
346	**muchacho**-*m*	lad
64	**mucho**-*adj; prn; adv*	a lot of; many, much; a lot, lots
1958	**mueble**-*m*	piece of furniture
2168	**muelle**-*m*	dock, spring
210	**muerte**-*f*	death
2358	**muerto**-*m*	dead
1977	**muestra**-*f*	sample
112	**mujer**-*f*	woman
1933	**multitud**-*f*	crowd
104	**mundo**-*m*	world
1307	**muñeca**-*f*	wrist, doll
2439	**munición**-*f*	ammunition
2505	**músculo**-*m*	muscle
1474	**museo**-*m*	museum
333	**música**-*f*	music

1879	**musical**-*adj; m*	musical; musical
31	**muy**-*adv*	very

N

1324	**nacer**-*vb*	be born
1529	**nacimiento**-*m*	birth
911	**nacional**-*adj*	national
1340	**nación**-*f*	nation
39	**nada**-*adv; f*	nothing at all; nothing, void
1325	**nadar**-*vb*	swim
90	**nadie**-*prn*	nobody, no one
1993	**naranja**-*f; adj*	orange; orange
810	**nariz**-*f*	nose
923	**natural**-*adj*	natural
823	**naturaleza**-*f*	nature
2521	**navaja**-*f*	knife
707	**nave**-*f*	ship, plane
506	**Navidad**-*f*	Christmas
497	**necesario**-*adj*	necessary
1081	**necesidad**-*f*	necessity
145	**necesitar**-*vb*	need
2109	**negar(se)**-*vb; vbr*	deny; refuse
1931	**negativo**-*adj*	negative
2310	**negociar**-*vb*	negotiate
433	**negocio**-*m*	shop, business
368	**negro**-*adj*	black
562	**nene**-*m*	baby (coll), darling
1696	**nervio**-*m*	nerve
820	**nervioso**-*adj*	nervous
240	**ni siquiera**-*phr*	not even
78	**ni**-*con*	nor, not even
2347	**nido**-*m*	nest
1989	**niebla**-*f*	fog
2101	**nieto**-*m*	grandson
1016	**nieve**-*f*	snow
231	**ninguno**-*adj*	none
189	**niño**-*m*	kid
828	**nivel**-*m*	level
3	**no**-*adv*	not
1421	**noble**-*adj*	noble, kind
83	**noche**-*f*	night
2354	**nocturno**-*adj*	night
134	**nombre**-*m*	name

2296	norma-*f*	rule
504	normal-*adj*	normal
580	norte-*m*	north
40	nosotros-*prn*	us, we
1055	nota-*f*	note, grade
1970	notar-*vb*	notice
861	noticia-*f*	news
1991	noviembre-*m*	November
442	novio-*m*	boyfriend, fiancé
1604	nube-*f*	cloud
1969	nuclear-*adj*	nuclear
128	nuestro-*adj*	ours
739	nueve-*num*	nine
125	nuevo-*adj*	ours
264	número-*m*	number
61	nunca-*adv*	never, ever

O

2507	obispo-*m*	bishop
2463	objeción-*f*	objection
893	objetivo-*adj; m*	impartial; objective
1643	objeto-*m*	object, goal
2035	obligar(se)-*vb*	force
605	obra-*f*	work, play
2161	observar-*vb*	observe
1100	obtener-*vb*	obtain, acquire
1090	obvio-*adj; int*	obvious; obviously
1227	ocasión-*f*	chance, occasion
1409	océano-*m*	ocean
524	ocho-*num*	eight
45	o-*con*	or, either
1852	octubre-*m*	October
2212	ocultar(se)-*vb*	hide
658	ocupar(se)-*vb; vbr*	occupy; take responsibility for
360	ocurrir-*vb*	happen
384	odiar-*vb*	hate
778	oeste-*m*	west
1047	oferta-*f*	offer
457	oficial-*adj; m/f*	official; officer
357	oficina-*f*	office
2294	oficio-*m*	job

1815	ofrecer-*vb*	offer
74	oh-*int*	oh
1209	oído-*m*	ear
148	oír(se)-*vb*	hear
614	ojalá-*int*	hopefully
203	ojo-*m*	eye
2033	ola-*f*	wave
959	oler(se)-*vb*	smell
1056	olor-*m*	smell
722	olvidar(se)-*vb*	forget
1756	once-*num*	eleven
1925	onda-*f*	wave
999	opción-*f*	option
888	operación-*f*	operation
2099	ópera-*f*	opera
1655	opinar-*vb*	believe, give your opinion
617	opinión-*f*	opinion
314	oportunidad-*f*	opportunity
2389	oración-*f*	prayer, sentence
2449	ordenador-*m*	computer (ES)
2037	ordenar-*vb*	order, arrange
352	orden-*m; f*	order; command
1769	oreja-*f*	ear
1513	organización-*f*	organization
2503	organizar-*vb*	organize
1201	orgullo-*m*	pride
916	orgulloso-*adj*	proud
2441	orientar(se)-*vb*	guide
2208	origen-*m*	origin
1249	original-*adj*	original
2264	orilla-*f*	shore
455	oro-*m*	gold
2313	orquestar-*vb*	orchestrate
908	oscuridad-*f*	darkness
967	oscuro-*adj*	dark
1301	oso-*m*	bear
187	os-*prn*	you
2059	otoño-*m*	autumn
89	otro-*adj; prn*	other, another; other, another
2204	oveja-*f*	sheep
2110	oxígeno-*m*	oxygen

P

1174	**paciencia**-*f*	patience
943	**paciente**-*adj; m/f*	patient; patient
2238	**pacífico**-*adj*	peaceful
91	**padre**-*m*	father
2367	**padrino**-*m*	godfather
434	**pagar**-*vb*	pay
1446	**página**-*f*	page
930	**pago**-*m*	payment
311	**país**-*m*	country
1233	**pájaro**-*m*	bird
307	**palabra**-*f*	word
1213	**palacio**-*m*	palace
1450	**paliza**-*f*	beating
1689	**palo**-*m*	stick
2055	**pandilla**-*f*	gang
1635	**pánico**-*adj; m*	panic; panic
743	**pan**-*m*	bread
1553	**pantalla**-*f*	screen
834	**pantalón**-*m*	pants
2426	**pantano**-*m*	swamp
2133	**pañuelo**-*m*	handkerchief
121	**papá**-*m*	dad
1944	**papa**-*m; f*	pope; potato (LA)
516	**papel**-*m*	paper, role
1321	**paquete**-*m*	package
1374	**parada**-*f*	stop
1149	**parado**-*adj*	standing (LA)
1412	**paraíso**-*m*	paradise
16	**para**-*prp*	for, to
692	**parar**-*vb*	stop
93	**parecer(se)**-*vb; m*	appear, seem; opinion
1040	**parecido**-*adj; m*	similar; resemblance
864	**pared**-*f*	wall
809	**pareja**-*f*	couple
1937	**pariente**-*m/f*	relative
584	**parir**-*vb*	give birth
331	**par**-*m; adj*	pair, couple; even, paired
2413	**paro**-*m*	unemployment (ES), strike
985	**parque**-*m*	park
140	**parte**-*f; m*	part; report
2052	**participar**-*vb*	participate
1416	**particular**-*adj*	peculiar, private
1509	**partida**-*f*	departure, game
571	**partido**-*m*	match
737	**partir(se)**-*vb; vbr*	depart; break
2301	**pasaje**-*m*	ticket
1715	**pasajero**-*m; adj*	passenger; temporary
1639	**pasaporte**-*m*	passport
166	**pasar(se)**-*vb; vbr*	go, pass, happen (coll); go over, forget
1858	**pasear**-*vb*	walk
535	**pase**-*m*	pass
884	**paseo**-*m*	walk
1466	**pasillo**-*m*	hall
1392	**pasión**-*f*	passion
534	**paso**-*m*	step
1384	**pasta**-*f*	pasta
1075	**pastel**-*m*	cake
1830	**pastilla**-*f*	pill
1681	**pastor**-*m*	pastor, shepherd
2211	**patada**-*f*	kick
1526	**pata**-*f*	leg
2054	**patata**-*f*	potato
2160	**patético**-*adj*	pathetic
1543	**patio**-*m*	courtyard
1972	**pato**-*m*	duck
1975	**patria**-*f*	homeland
1574	**patrón**-*m*	pattern
1808	**patrullar**-*vb*	patrol
2152	**pavo**-*m*	turkey
1783	**payaso**-*m*	clown
284	**paz**-*f*	peace
1203	**pecar**-*vb*	sin
1101	**pecho**-*m*	chest
664	**pedir**-*vb*	request
2067	**pegar**-*vb*	hit, glue
630	**pelea**-*f*	fight
798	**pelear(se)**-*vb*	fight
323	**película**-*f*	movie
594	**peligro**-*m*	danger
625	**peligroso**-*adj*	dangerous
448	**pelo**-*m*	hair
1137	**pelota**-*f*	ball
2300	**pelotón**-*m*	squad
1504	**pene**-*m*	penis
1387	**pensamiento**-*m*	thought

193	pensar-*vb*	think	876	piedra-*f*	stone
2142	pensión-*f*	pension, hostel	744	piel-*f*	skin
1710	peor-*adj; adv*	worse; worse	422	pie-*m*	foot
242	pequeño-*adj; m*	small, young; youngster	687	pierna-*f*	leg
			1368	pieza-*f*	piece
1810	perdedor-*m*	loser	2516	píldora-*f*	pill
347	perder(se)-*vb*	lose	1112	piloto-*m*	pilot
1283	pérdida-*f*	loss	2088	pintar-*vb*	paint
1419	perdido-*adj*	lost	2470	pintor-*m*	painter
746	perdonar-*vb*	forgive	1256	pintura-*f*	painting, paint
320	perdón-*m; int*	forgiveness; sorry	1429	piscina-*f*	swimming pool
388	perfecto-*adj*	perfect	544	piso-*m*	apartment (ES), floor, ground (LA)
872	periódico-*m; adj*	newspaper; periodical	814	pista-*f*	clue, track
1562	periodista-*m/f*	journalist	653	pistola-*f*	gun
2072	período-*m*	period	2490	pito-*m*	whistle
1591	permanecer-*vb*	stay, remain	1651	pizza-*f*	pizza
2494	permanente-*adj*	permanent	1906	placa-*f*	nameplate, badge
469	permiso-*m*	permission, license	418	placer-*m*	pleasure
829	permitir(se)-*vb; vbr*	allow; afford	1772	planear-*vb*	plan
20	pero-*con*	but	760	planeta-*m*	planet
2061	perrito-*m*	puppy	404	plan-*m*	plan
325	perro-*m*	dog	1911	plano-*adj; m*	level; plan, map
225	persona-*f*	person	1309	planta-*f*	plant
1313	personaje-*m/f*	celebrity, character	2089	plástico-*adj; m*	plastic; plastic
1825	personalidad-*f*	personality	1087	plata-*f*	silver, money (LA)
528	personal-*m; adj*	staff; personal	1342	plato-*m*	dish
1041	pertenecer-*vb*	belong	879	playa-*f*	beach
2384	pervertir(se)-*vb*	pervert	1524	plaza-*f*	square
1303	pesadilla-*f*	nightmare	2311	plazo-*m*	period, deadline
2116	pesado-*adj*	heavy	2178	pleno-*adj; m*	full; plenary session
2232	pesa-*f*	weight	2123	pluma-*f*	pen, feather
841	a pesar de-*prp*	despite	2006	población-*f*	population
839	pesar(se)-*vb*	weigh	355	pobre-*adj; m/f*	poor; poor
840	pesar-*m*	regret	1120	poco-*adj; adv*	little; quite
1109	pescado-*m*	fish	88	pocos-*adj*	few
2031	pesca-*f*	fishing	48	poder(se)-*vb; m*	be able to, might; power
1847	pescar-*vb*	fish			
2051	petición-*f*	request	1418	poderoso-*adj*	powerful
1658	petróleo-*m*	oil	1896	poema-*m*	poem
1282	pez-*m*	fish	1853	poesía-*f*	poetry
1362	piano-*m*	piano	2001	poeta-*m*	poet
1745	picar-*vb*	sting	2271	policial-*adj*	police
1456	piedad-*m*	piety			

160	**policía**-*m/f; f*	police officer; police	
825	**política**-*f*	policy, politics	
1725	**político**-*adj; m*	political; politician	
1008	**pollo**-*m*	chicken	
945	**polvo**-*m*	dust, powder	
374	**poner(se)**-*vb; vbr*	put; put on	
1426	**popular**-*adj*	popular	
58	**por favor**-*m*	please	
213	**por supuesto**-*phr*	of course	
10	**por**-*prp*	by, for	
56	**porque**-*con*	because	
568	**porqué**-*m*	reason	
1556	**porquería**-*f*	filth	
978	**posibilidad**-*f*	possibility	
291	**posible**-*adj*	possible	
648	**posición**-*f*	position	
2243	**positivo**-*adj*	positive	
2186	**postre**-*m*	dessert	
2382	**potencia**-*f*	power	
2345	**potencial**-*adj; m*	potential; strength	
1662	**pozo**-*m*	well	
1585	**práctica**-*f*	practice	
1982	**practicar**-*vb*	practice	
1761	**práctico**-*adj*	practical	
684	**precio**-*m*	price	
838	**precioso**-*adj*	beautiful	
1314	**preciso**-*adj*	precise, essential	
734	**preferir**-*vb*	prefer	
294	**pregunta**-*f*	question	
572	**preguntar**-*vb*	ask	
1065	**premio**-*m*	prize	
865	**prensa**-*f*	press	
2056	**preocupación**-*f*	concern	
903	**preocupado**-*adj*	worried	
302	**preocupar(se)**-*vb*	worry	
770	**preparar(se)**-*vb*	prepare	
1119	**presencia**-*f*	presence	
2085	**presentación**-*f*	presentation	
1042	**presentar(se)**-*vb; vbr*	introduce; appear	
867	**presente**-*adj; m*	present; current	
362	**presidente**-*m*	president	
1004	**presión**-*f*	pressure	
2058	**preso**-*m*	prisoner	

1907	**prestado**-*adj*	borrowed
2132	**préstamo**-*m*	loan
2415	**prestar**-*vb*	lend
1185	**primavera**-*f*	spring
191	**primer(o)**-*num*	first
910	**primo**-*m; adj*	cousin; prime
766	**principal**-*adj*	main
769	**príncipe**-*m*	prince
521	**principio**-*m*	start, principle
430	**prisa**-*f*	hurry
1367	**prisionero**-*m*	prisoner
631	**prisión**-*f*	prison
1076	**privado**-*adj*	private
1533	**probable**-*adj*	likely
395	**probar(se)**-*vb; vbr*	try, prove; try on
152	**problema**-*m*	problem
2341	**procedimiento**-*m*	procedure
1186	**proceso**-*m*	process
1528	**producción**-*f*	production
1848	**producto**-*m*	product
1918	**productor**-*m; adj*	producer; producer
998	**profesional**-*adj; m/f*	professional; professional
1829	**profesión**-*f*	profession
419	**profesor**-*m*	teacher
2328	**profundidad**-*f*	depth
1073	**profundo**-*adj*	deep
565	**programa**-*m*	program, schedule
2023	**progreso**-*m*	progress
1498	**prohibir**-*vb*	prohibit
1286	**promesa**-*f*	promise
570	**prometer**-*vb*	promise
1394	**prometido**-*m*	fiancé
183	**pronto**-*adv*	early, soon
1024	**propiedad**-*f*	property
450	**propio**-*adj*	your own, typical
771	**propósito**-*m*	purpose
1861	**propuesta**-*f*	proposal
1846	**prostituta**-*f*	prostitute
1246	**protección**-*f*	protection
1190	**proteger(se)**-*vb*	protect
473	**próximo**-*adj*	next
887	**proyecto**-*m*	project
607	**prueba**-*f*	test, evidence

2165	**psiquiatra**-*m/f*	psychiatrist	
1647	**publicidad**-*f*	advertising	
590	**público**-*adj; m*	public; audience	
274	**pueblo**-*m*	village, town	
852	**puente**-*m*	bridge	
182	**puerta**-*f*	door	
1402	**puerto**-*m*	port	
156	**pues**-*con*	well, since	
1500	**puesto**-*m*	post, stand	
2141	**pulso**-*m*	pulse	
2517	**puño**-*m*	fist	
1602	**punta**-*f*	tip	
271	**punto**-*m*	spot, point	
1193	**puro**-*adj; m*	pure; cigar	

Q

2	**que**-*con; prn*	that; that
283	**quedar(se)**-*vb; vbr*	be left; stay
2306	**quejarse**-*vbr*	complain
2288	**quemar(se)**-*vb*	burn
11	**qué**-*prn; adv*	what, which; this
46	**querer(se)**-*vb*	want, love
301	**querido**-*adj; m*	loved, dear; lover
1146	**queso**-*m*	cheese
146	**quien**-*prn*	who
54	**quién**-*prn*	who, whom
932	**quieto**-*adj*	still
1570	**quince**-*num*	fifteen
2129	**quinto**-*num*	fifth
1122	**quitar(se)**-*vb; vbr*	remove; get out of the way
162	**quizá(s)**-*adv*	maybe

R

2317	**rabia**-*f*	rage
2469	**radar**-*m*	radar
573	**radio**-*f*	radio
2346	**raíz**-*f*	root
2339	**rango**-*m*	rank
173	**rápido**-*adj; adv*	fast; quickly
441	**raro**-*adj*	rare
1749	**rastro**-*m*	trail

1423	**rata**-*f*	rat
556	**rato**-*m*	a short time
2071	**ratón**-*m*	mouse
904	**rayo**-*m*	ray
1516	**raza**-*f*	race
1682	**razonable**-*adj*	reasonable
154	**razón**-*f*	reason
1801	**reacción**-*f*	reaction
159	**real**-*adj*	real, royal
280	**realidad**-*f*	reality
2150	**realizar**-*vb*	perform
2458	**rebelde**-*adj; m*	rebel; rebel
2021	**recepción**-*f*	reception
2465	**receta**-*f*	recipe
992	**recibir**-*vb*	receive
1702	**recibo**-*m*	invoice, receipt
1091	**recién**-*adv*	newly
2086	**reciente**-*adj*	recent
1208	**recoger**-*vb*	pick up, collect
1512	**recompensa**-*f*	reward
1866	**reconocer**-*vb*	recognize
2257	**reconocimiento**-*m*	recognition
845	**recordar**-*vb*	remember
950	**recuerdo**-*m*	memory, souvenir
1285	**recuperar(se)**-*vb; vbr*	recover; get well
2000	**recurso**-*m*	resource
836	**referir(se)**-*vb*	refer
2214	**refuerzo**-*m*	backing
1731	**refugio**-*m*	refuge
540	**regalo**-*m*	present
2356	**regimiento**-*m*	regiment
2026	**región**-*f*	region
1461	**registro**-*m*	search, register
720	**regla**-*f*	rule
515	**regresar**-*vb*	return
612	**regreso**-*m*	comeback
2202	**rehén**-*m/f*	hostage
597	**reina**-*f*	queen
1111	**reino**-*m*	kingdom
1520	**reír**-*vb*	laugh
621	**relación**-*f*	relationship, link
1165	**relajar(se)**-*vb*	relax
1596	**religión**-*f*	religion

786	**reloj**-*m*	clock
1837	**remedio**-*m*	remedy
1874	**renunciar**-*vb*	give up
1522	**repetir**-*vb*	repeat
1986	**reporte**-*m*	report
2107	**representante**-*m/f*	representative
1943	**representar**-*vb*	represent
2249	**república**-*f*	republic
2170	**repugnante**-*adj*	disgusting
1440	**reputación**-*f*	reputation
1888	**requerir**-*vb*	require
1521	**rescatar**-*vb*	rescue
1632	**reservar(se)**-*vb*	save, book
1703	**resistencia**-*f*	resistance
2355	**resistir(se)**-*vb*	resist
1322	**resolver**-*vb*	solve
716	**respecto**-*m*	regarding
681	**respeto**-*m*	respect
2233	**respiración**-*f*	breathing
1188	**respirar**-*vb*	breathe
1347	**responder**-*vb*	answer
1051	**responsabilidad**-*f*	responsibility
890	**responsable**-*adj; m/f*	responsible; person responsible
526	**respuesta**-*f*	answer
883	**restaurante**-*m*	restaurant
387	**resto**-*m*	remainder
2287	**resuelto**-*adj*	solved
1049	**resultado**-*m*	result
971	**resultar**-*vb*	result
2500	**retirada**-*f*	withdrawal
2103	**retiro**-*m*	retirement
2337	**retrasar(se)**-*vb*	delay
2087	**retraso**-*m*	delay
2098	**retrato**-*m*	portrait
627	**reunión**-*f*	meeting
1859	**reverendo**-*m*	reverend
1802	**revés**-*m*	setback
1726	**revisar**-*vb*	inspect, examine
1317	**revolución**-*f*	revolution
2327	**revolver**-*vb*	stir
329	**rey**-*m*	king
1903	**rezar**-*vb*	pray

640	**rico**-*m; adj*	rich person; wealthy, tasty
767	**ridículo**-*adj; m*	ridiculous; embarrassment
1017	**riesgo**-*m*	risk
1729	**rifle**-*m*	rifle
541	**río**-*m*	river
2464	**riqueza**-*f*	wealth
1753	**risa**-*f*	laughter
1252	**ritmo**-*m*	rhythm, pace
956	**robar**-*vb*	rob
1005	**robo**-*m*	theft
2138	**robot**-*m*	robot
1074	**roca**-*f*	rock
2425	**rodar**-*vb*	roll
2373	**rodear(se)**-*vb*	go around
1337	**rodilla**-*f*	knee
969	**rogar**-*vb*	beg
685	**rojo**-*adj*	red
2106	**romance**-*m*	romance
1667	**romántico**-*adj*	romantic
940	**romper(se)**-*vb*	break
1990	**rondar**-*vb*	wander around
1575	**ron**-*m*	rum
356	**ropa**-*f*	clothes
1714	**rosa**-*adj; f*	pink; rose
1023	**rostro**-*m*	face
2005	**roto**-*adj*	broken
1733	**rubio**-*adj*	blond
1675	**rueda**-*f*	wheel
721	**ruido**-*m*	noise
1525	**rumbo**-*m*	in the direction of
1620	**rumor**-*m*	rumor
1404	**Rusia**-*f*	Russia
1433	**ruso**-*adj; m*	Russian; Russian
1410	**ruta**-*f*	route
1974	**rutina**-*f*	routine

S

1011	**sábado**-*m*	Saturday
14	**saber(se)**-*vb*	know
1106	**sabido**-*adj*	known
2270	**sabiduría**-*f*	wisdom
2250	**sabio**-*adj; m*	wise; sage

1809	**sabor**-*m*	taste	
662	**sacar**-*vb*	take out	
1606	**sacerdote**-*m*	priest	
1251	**saco**-*m*	bad, coat (LA)	
1860	**sacrificio**-*m*	sacrifice	
1799	**sagrado**-*adj*	sacred	
581	**sala**-*f*	room	
2297	**salario**-*m*	wage	
511	**salar**-*vb*	salt	
1640	**sal**-*f*	salt	
704	**salida**-*f*	exit	
167	**salir(se)**-*vb*	leave	
1094	**salón**-*m*	lounge	
1578	**salsa**-*f*	sauce	
1365	**saltar(se)**-*vb; vbr*	jump; skip, break	
1884	**salto**-*m*	jump	
2424	**saludable**-*adj*	healthy	
2135	**saludar**-*vb*	greet	
533	**salud**-*f*	health	
1552	**saludo**-*m*	greeting	
2437	**salvación**-*f*	salvation	
1141	**salvaje**-*adj; m/f*	wild, violent; savage	
749	**salvar(se)**-*vb*	save	
550	**salvo**-*prp; adv*	except; unless	
567	**san(to)**-*adj; m*	saint; saint	
2195	**sangrar**-*vb*	bleed	
275	**sangre**-*f*	blood	
1897	**sano**-*adj*	healthy	
545	**sargento**-*m/f*	sergeant	
1942	**satisfacer**-*vb*	satisfy	
1376	**sección**-*f*	section, division	
1928	**seco**-*adj*	dry	
1738	**secretario**-*m*	secretary	
425	**secreto**-*adj; m*	secret; secret	
2092	**sector**-*m*	sector	
2395	**secuencia**-*f*	sequence	
2416	**secuestro**-*m*	kidnapping	
1470	**secundario**-*adj; m*	secondary; side effect	
2284	**seda**-*f*	silk	
243	**seguir**-*vb*	follow	
312	**segundo**-*num*	second	
582	**según**-*prp; con*	according to; depending on	
390	**seguridad**-*f*	certainty, safety	

111	**seguro**-*adj; m*	safe, reliable; insurance	
316	**seis**-*num*	six	
2514	**sellar**-*vb*	seal, stamp	
2040	**selva**-*f*	jungle	
218	**semana**-*f*	week	
1915	**semejante**-*adj*	similar	
1326	**senador**-*m*	senator	
618	**señal**-*f*	signal, mark	
1234	**sencillo**-*adj*	simple	
171	**señora**-*f*	lady, madam	
53	**señor**-*m; adj*	sir; huge	
1103	**sensación**-*f*	sensation	
1786	**sensible**-*adj*	sensitive	
850	**sentado**-*adj*	sitting	
429	**sentar(se)**-*vb*	sit	
1957	**sentencia**-*f*	sentence	
334	**sentido**-*m*	sense, meaning	
892	**sentimiento**-*m*	feeling	
520	**sentir**-*vb*	feel	
2366	**separar**-*vb*	separate	
1657	**septiembre**-*m*	September	
1123	**serie**-*f*	series	
163	**serio**-*adj*	serious	
1489	**serpiente**-*f*	snake	
7	**ser**-*vb; av; m*	be; was, were; being	
503	**servicio**-*m*	service	
750	**servir**-*vb*	serve	
1614	**sesión**-*f*	session	
476	**sexo**-*m*	sex, gender	
1216	**sexual**-*adj*	sexual	
2438	**shock**-*n*	shock	
18	**si**-*con*	if	
73	**siempre**-*adv*	always, every time	
475	**siete**-*num*	seven	
1130	**siglo**-*m*	century	
1794	**significado**-*m; adj*	meaning; important	
248	**significar**-*vb*	mean	
451	**siguiente**-*adj; m/f*	following; next	
436	**silencio**-*m*	silence	
860	**silla**-*f*	chair	
2049	**símbolo**-*m*	symbol	
2068	**simpático**-*adj*	likeable	
399	**simple**-*adj*	simple	

598	sin embargo-con	nevertheless
1621	sincero-adj	sincere
2093	sindicato-m	union
358	sino-prp; m	but; fate
71	sin-prp	without
531	sistema-m	system
338	sitio-m	place
458	situación-f	situation
2136	sobrar-vb	be left over
79	sobre-prp; m	on, about; envelope
1183	sobrevivir-vb	survive
1674	sobrino-m	nephew
1173	social-adj	social
808	sociedad-f	society
1079	socio-m	associate, member
1031	socorro-m; int	help; help
1616	sofá-m	sofa
2370	solar-adj; m	solar; site
2008	soledad-f	loneliness
735	soler-vb	used to
1730	solitario-adj	solitary, empty
412	sol-m	sun
44	solo-adv; adj	only, just; alone
2010	soltero-adj; m	single; single man
1240	solución-f	solution, answer
1306	sombra-f	shadow
816	sombrero-m	hat
465	sonar-m; vb	sonar; sound
1740	soñar-vb	dream
815	sonido-m	sound
1855	sonreír-vb	smile
1238	sonrisa-f	smile
1199	sopa-f	soup
1348	soportar-vb	support, bear
2104	sordo-adj; m	deaf; deaf
1868	sorprendente-adj	surprising
1332	sorprender(se)-vb	surprise
586	sorpresa-f	surprise
2179	sospechar-vb	suspect
1198	sospechoso-adj; m	suspicious; suspect
1329	sótano-m	basement
1243	suave-adj	soft

709	subir-vb	go up
2269	submarino-adj; m	underwater; submarine
377	suceder-vb	happen, follow
1018	sucio-adj	dirty
1812	sueldo-m	salary
553	suelo-m	ground, soil
1358	suelto-adj	loose
386	sueño-m	dream
176	suerte-f	luck
253	suficiente-adj	enough
1735	sufrimiento-m	suffering
1430	sufrir-vb	suffer
1623	sugerir-vb	suggest
1398	suicidio-m	suicide
2499	suite-f	suite
2372	suizo-adj; m	Swiss; Swiss
1187	sujeto-m; adj	subject; subject to
2011	suma-f	sum
2460	superar(se)-vb	overcome
1592	superficie-f	surface
1176	superior-adj; m	greater than, upper; boss
2081	suplicar-vb	supplicate
222	suponer-vb	suppose, assume
599	sur-m	south
2122	susto-m	scare
22	suyo-prn	his, yours, theirs, hers, their

T

2038	tabaco-m	tobacco
2404	tabla-f	board
106	tal-adj; adv	such, that; just as
980	talento-m	talent
1976	taller-m	workshop
1131	tamaño-m	size
69	también-adv	too, also
297	tampoco-con	neither, either
57	tan-adv	so, such, as
1764	tanque-m	tank
142	tanto-adv; adj; m	so long; so much, so many; point

138	**tarde**-*f; adv*	afternoon; late	
1204	**tarea**-*f*	task, homework (LA)	
882	**tarjeta**-*f*	card	
2289	**tarta**-*f*	cake	
756	**taxi**-*m*	taxi	
1219	**taza**-*f*	cup	
792	**teatro**-*m*	theater	
1092	**techo**-*m*	ceiling	
1950	**técnico**-*adj; m/f*	technical; technician	
1673	**tecnología**-*f*	technology	
2482	**tejado**-*m*	roof	
304	**teléfono**-*m*	phone	
1887	**telegrama**-*m*	telegram	
862	**televisión**-*f*	television	
587	**té**-*m*	tea	
663	**tema**-*m*	topic	
489	**temer(se)**-*vb*	fear	
2096	**temor**-*m*	fear	
1796	**temperatura**-*m*	temperature	
1382	**templo**-*m*	temple	
1288	**temporada**-*f*	season, time	
2348	**temporal**-*adj; m*	temporary; storm	
589	**temprano**-*adj; adv*	early; early	
37	**tener**-*vb*	have, must	
500	**teniente**-*m/f*	lieutenant	
2221	**tenis**-*m*	tennis	
2137	**tensión**-*f*	tension	
1127	**teoría**-*f*	theory	
2028	**terapia**-*f*	therapy	
1089	**tercer(o)**-*num*	third	
517	**terminar**-*vb*	finish	
2193	**término**-*m*	term	
1491	**terreno**-*m*	land	
499	**terrible**-*adj*	terrible	
1438	**territorio**-*m*	territory	
1798	**terrorista**-*adj; m/f*	terrorist; terrorist	
1760	**terror**-*m*	terror	
1034	**tesoro**-*m*	treasure	
2003	**testamento**-*m*	will	
927	**testigo**-*m/f*	witness	
2078	**testimoniar**-*vb*	testify	
1391	**teta**-*f*	tit	
2364	**texto**-*m*	text	
2431	**tiburón**-*m*	shark	
66	**tiempo**-*m*	time, weather	
505	**tienda**-*f*	shop	
226	**tierra**-*f*	land, ground	
1804	**tigre**-*m*	tiger	
2291	**timar**-*vb*	cheat	
2390	**tímido**-*adj*	shy	
237	**tío**-*m*	uncle, buddy (coll)	
2016	**típico**-*adj*	typical	
131	**tipo**-*m; adj*	type; like	
1158	**tirar**-*vb*	throw, waste, pull	
781	**tiro**-*m*	shot	
2512	**tiroteo**-*m*	gunfire	
1359	**título**-*m*	title, degree	
2196	**toalla**-*f*	towel	
628	**tocar**-*vb*	touch	
172	**todavía**-*adv*	yet, still	
29	**todo**-*adj; adv; m; prn*	every, each; all; whole; everything	
214	**tomar(se)**-*vb; vbr*	take; drink	
1593	**tono**-*m*	tone	
715	**tontería**-*f*	nonsense	
398	**tonto**-*adj; m*	stupid; fool	
951	**toque**-*m*	touch	
1054	**tormenta**-*f*	storm	
2262	**torneo**-*m*	tournament	
1870	**toro**-*m*	bull	
2448	**torpe**-*adj*	clumsy	
1159	**torre**-*f*	tower	
2201	**tortura**-*f*	torture	
875	**total**-*adj; m; adv*	complete; whole; in the end (coll)	
1568	**trabajador**-*m; adj*	worker; hard-working	
256	**trabajar**-*vb*	work	
99	**trabajo**-*m*	work, job	
1901	**tradición**-*f*	tradition	
1828	**traducción**-*f*	translation	
481	**traer(se)**-*vb*	bring	
1468	**tráfico**-*m*	traffic	
641	**tragar(se)**-*vb*	swallow	
1778	**tragedia**-*f*	tragedy	
1932	**traición**-*f*	treason	

1581	**traidor**-*m; adj*	traitor; treacherous
2076	**traje**-*m*	suit
866	**trampa**-*f*	trap
2487	**tranquilidad**-*f*	tranquility
1819	**tranquilizar(se)**-*vb*	calm down
389	**tranquilo**-*adj*	quiet, peaceful
2365	**transmisión**-*f*	transmission
1704	**transporte**-*m*	transport
613	**trasero**-*adj; m*	rear; butt (coll)
428	**tras**-*prp*	after, behind
1617	**tratamiento**-*m*	treatment
305	**tratar**-*vb*	treat, address
403	**trato**-*m*	agreement, behavior
542	**a través de**-*prp*	through
1388	**treinta**-*num*	thirty
2525	**tremendo**-*adj*	tremendous
427	**tren**-*m*	train
127	**tres**-*num*	three
2315	**tribu**-*f*	tribe
1000	**tribunal**-*m*	tribunal
1564	**tripulación**-*f*	crew
559	**triste**-*adj*	sad
2019	**tristeza**-*f*	sadness
1971	**trono**-*m*	throne
1245	**tropa**-*f*	troop
1840	**trozo**-*m*	piece
1898	**truco**-*m*	trick
116	**tu**-*adj*	your
2325	**tubo**-*m*	tube
970	**tumba**-*f*	tomb
1746	**túnel**-*m*	tunnel
13	**tú**-*prn*	you
897	**turno**-*m*	turn
413	**tuyo**-*prn*	yours

U

2154	**ultimar**-*vb*	finalize
282	**último**-*adj; m*	last; latest
9	**un**-*art; num*	a, an; one
239	**único**-*adj*	only, unique
1002	**unidad**-*f*	unit
2388	**unido**-*adj*	united

1239	**uniforme**-*m; adj*	uniform; uniform
1539	**unión**-*f*	union
644	**unir**-*vb*	join, unite
557	**universidad**-*f*	university
1139	**universo**-*m*	universe
81	**uno**-*num*	one
1403	**urgente**-*adj*	urgent
416	**usar**-*vb*	use
979	**uso**-*m*	use
161	**ustedes**-*prn*	you
52	**usted**-*prn*	you
1316	**útil**-*adj; m*	useful; tool
2018	**utilizar**-*vb*	use

V

731	**vacaciones**-*fpl*	vacation
1437	**vaca**-*f*	cow
1157	**vacío**-*m; adj*	emptiness; empty, superficial
2498	**vagabundo**-*m; adj*	vagabond; wandering
170	**valer(se)**-*vb*	cost, be good for
964	**valiente**-*adj; m/f*	courageous; brave person
2511	**valioso**-*adj*	valuable
1475	**valle**-*m*	valley
673	**valor**-*m*	value, courage
2191	**vampiro**-*m*	vampire
2473	**vapor**-*m*	steam
2065	**vaquero**-*m*	cowboy, denim
944	**varios**-*adj*	several
1138	**vaso**-*m*	glass
2084	**vecindario**-*m*	neighborhood
1274	**vecino**-*adj; m*	adjacent; neighbor
1765	**vehículo**-*m*	vehicle
1113	**veinte**-*num*	twenty
1900	**vela**-*f*	candle
886	**velocidad**-*f*	speed
2172	**vencer**-*vb*	overcome
1821	**vendedor**-*m*	seller
824	**vender**-*vb*	sell
1508	**veneno**-*m*	venom
1248	**venganza**-*f*	revenge

197	**venir(se)**-*vb*	come
1331	**venta**-*f*	sale
1663	**ventaja**-*f*	advantage
591	**ventana**-*f*	window
72	**ver(se)**-*vb*	see, watch
1660	**vera**-*f*	edge, side
686	**verano**-*m*	summer
551	**verdadero**-*adj*	true
63	**verdad**-*f*	truth
805	**verde**-*adj*	green
811	**vergüenza**-*f*	shame
1661	**versión**-*f*	version
1777	**vestido**-*m*	dress
549	**vestir(se)**-*vb*	dress
50	**vez**-*f*	time, turn
1718	**vía**-*f*	street, tract
1194	**viajar**-*vb*	travel
345	**viaje**-*m*	trip
1045	**víctima**-*f*	victim
70	**vida**-*f*	life
1273	**vídeo**-*m*	video
2398	**vidrio**-*m*	glass
174	**viejo**-*adj; m*	old; old man
713	**viento**-*m*	wind
902	**viernes**-*m*	Friday
1872	**vigilancia**-*f*	surveillance
1985	**vigilar**-*vb*	guard
1959	**villa**-*f*	villa
2062	**violación**-*f*	violation
1118	**violencia**-*f*	violence
2205	**violento**-*adj*	violent
1133	**virgen**-*adj; m/f*	virgin; virgin
1634	**virus**-*m*	virus
1310	**visión**-*f*	vision, view
738	**visita**-*f*	visit, guest
1369	**visitar**-*vb*	visit
431	**vista**-*f*	view
784	**vistazo**-*m*	glance
1768	**viuda**-*f*	widow
254	**vivir**-*vb*	live
319	**vivo**-*adj; m*	alive; alive
2128	**vodka**-*m*	vodka
757	**volar**-*vb*	fly
919	**voluntad**-*f*	will
201	**volver(se)**-*vb*	come back
2077	**vomitar**-*vb*	vomit
491	**vosotros**-*prn*	you
608	**vos**-*prn*	you (LA)
1833	**votar**-*vb*	vote
1965	**voto**-*m*	vote
414	**voz**-*f*	voice
710	**vuelo**-*m*	flight
285	**vuelta**-*f*	return, stroll
777	**vuestro**-*adj; prn*	your; yours
2417	**vulgar**-*adj*	vulgar, common

W

1009	**wiski**-*m*	whiskey

Y

30	**ya**-*adv*	already, now
6	**y**-*con*	and
12	**yo**-*prn*	I

Z

656	**zapato**-*m*	shoe
660	**zona**-*f*	zone
1482	**zorro**-*m*	fox

Contact, Further Reading and Resources

For more tools, tips & tricks visit our site www.mostusedwords.com. We publish various language learning resources. If you have a great idea you want to pitch us, please send an e-mail to info@mostusedwords.com.

Frequency Dictionaries

In this series:

Spanish Frequency Dictionary 1 – Essential Vocabulary – 2500 Most Common Spanish Words
Spanish Frequency Dictionary 2 - Intermediate Vocabulary – 2501-5000 Most Common Spanish Words
Spanish Frequency Dictionary 3 - Advanced Vocabulary – 5001-7500 Most Common Spanish Words
Spanish Frequency Dictionary 4 - Master Vocabulary – 7501-10000 Most Common Spanish Words

Our mission is to provide language learners worldwide with frequency dictionaries for every major and minor language. We are working hard to accomplish this goal. You can view our selection on https://store.mostusedwords.com/frequency-dictionaries

Bilingual books

We're creating a selection of parallel texts. We decided to rework timeless classics, such as Alice in Wonderland, Sherlock Holmes, Dracula, The Picture of Dorian Gray, etc.

Our books are paragraph aligned: on one side of the page you will find the English version of the story, and on the right side is the Spanish version..

To help you in your language learning journey, all our bilingual books come with a dictionary included, created for that particular book.

Current bilingual books available are English, Spanish, Portuguese, Italian, German, and Spanish.

For more information, check https://store.mostusedwords.com/bilingual-books . Check back regularly for new books and languages.

Other language learning methods

You'll find reviews of other 3rd party language learning applications, software, audio courses, and apps. There are so many available, and some are (much) better than others.

Check out our reviews at www.mostusedwords.com/reviews.

Contact

If you have any questions, you can contact us through e-mail info@mostusedwords.com.

Made in United States
Troutdale, OR
01/09/2024

16812182R00133